Hands-on Scala Programming

Author	Li Haoyi
Published	1 June 2020
Website	www.handsonscala.com
ISBN	978-981-14-5693-0

Reviewers

Thanks to all the reviewers who helped review portions of this book and provide the feedback that helped refine this book and make it what it is today.

In alphabetical order:

Alex Allain, Alwyn Tan, Bryan Jadot, Chan Ying Hao, Choo Yang, Dean Wampler, Dimitar Simeonov, Eric Marion, Grace Tang, Guido Van Rossum, Jez Ng, Karan Malik, Liang Yuan Ruo, Mao Ting, Martin MacKerel, Martin Odersky, Michael Wu, Olafur Pall Geirsson, Ong Ming Yang, Pathikrit Bhowmick

Table of Contents

Foreword   9

I Introduction to Scala   13
1 Hands-on Scala   15
2 Setting Up   25
3 Basic Scala   39
4 Scala Collections   59
5 Notable Scala Features   81

II Local Development   105
6 Implementing Algorithms in Scala   107
7 Files and Subprocesses   127
8 JSON and Binary Data Serialization   147
9 Self-Contained Scala Scripts   163
10 Static Build Pipelines   179

III Web Services   203
11 Scraping Websites   205
12 Working with HTTP APIs   221
13 Fork-Join Parallelism with Futures   239
14 Simple Web and API Servers   261
15 Querying SQL Databases   287

IV Program Design   307
16 Message-based Parallelism with Actors   309
17 Multi-Process Applications   329
18 Building a Real-time File Synchronizer   347
19 Parsing Structured Text   365
20 Implementing a Programming Language   387

Conclusion   413

Part I Introduction to Scala

1 Hands-on Scala   15

1.1 Why Scala?   16

1.2 Why This Book?   17

1.3 How This Book Is Organized   18

1.4 Code Snippet and Examples   20

1.5 Online Materials   22

2 Setting Up   25

2.1 Windows Setup (Optional)   26

2.2 Installing Java   27

2.3 Installing Ammonite   28

2.4 Installing Mill   31

2.5 IDE Support   33

3 Basic Scala   39

3.1 Values   40

3.2 Loops, Conditionals, Comprehensions   47

3.3 Methods and Functions   51

3.4 Classes and Traits   55

4 Scala Collections   59

4.1 Operations   60

4.2 Immutable Collections   67

4.3 Mutable Collections   72

4.4 Common Interfaces   77

5 Notable Scala Features   81

5.1 Case Classes and Sealed Traits   82

5.2 Pattern Matching   85

5.3 By-Name Parameters   90

5.4 Implicit Parameters   93

5.5 Typeclass Inference   96

Part II Local Development

6 Implementing Algorithms in Scala   107

6.1 Merge Sort   108

6.2 Prefix Tries   112

6.3 Breadth First Search   118

6.4 Shortest Paths   121

7 Files and Subprocesses   127

7.1 Paths   128

7.2 Filesystem Operations   130

7.3 Folder Syncing   135

7.4 Simple Subprocess Invocations   139

7.5 Interactive and Streaming Subprocesses   142

8 JSON and Binary Data Serialization   147

8.1 Manipulating JSON   148

8.2 JSON Serialization of Scala Data Types   152

8.3 Writing your own Generic Serialization Methods   156

8.4 Binary Serialization   158

9 Self-Contained Scala Scripts   163

9.1 Reading Files Off Disk   164

9.2 Rendering HTML with Scalatags   165

9.3 Rendering Markdown with Commonmark-Java   167

9.4 Links and Bootstrap   172

9.5 Optionally Deploying the Static Site   175

10 Static Build Pipelines   179

10.1 Mill Build Pipelines   180

10.2 Mill Modules   185

10.3 Revisiting our Static Site Script   189

10.4 Conversion to a Mill Build Pipeline   190

10.5 Extending our Static Site Pipeline   194

Part III Web Services

11 Scraping Websites   205

11.1 Scraping Wikipedia   206

11.2 MDN Web Documentation   210

11.3 Scraping MDN   212

11.4 Putting it Together   217

12 Working with HTTP APIs   221

12.1 The Task: Github Issue Migrator   222

12.2 Creating Issues and Comments   224

12.3 Fetching Issues and Comments   226

12.4 Migrating Issues and Comments   232

13 Fork-Join Parallelism with Futures   239

13.1 Parallel Computation using Futures   240

13.2 N-Ways Parallelism   243

13.3 Parallel Web Crawling   246

13.4 Asynchronous Futures   252

13.5 Asynchronous Web Crawling   255

14 Simple Web and API Servers   261

14.1 A Minimal Webserver   262

14.2 Serving HTML   266

14.3 Forms and Dynamic Data   268

14.4 Dynamic Page Updates via API Requests   275

14.5 Real-time Updates with Websockets   280

15 Querying SQL Databases   287

15.1 Setting up Quill and PostgreSQL   288

15.2 Mapping Tables to Case Classes   290

15.3 Querying and Updating Data   293

15.4 Transactions   299

15.5 A Database-Backed Chat Website   300

Part IV Program Design

16 Message-based Parallelism with Actors   309

16.1 Castor Actors   310

16.2 Actor-based Background Uploads   311

16.3 Concurrent Logging Pipelines   317

16.4 Debugging Actors   324

17 Multi-Process Applications   329

17.1 Two-Process Build Setup   330

17.2 Remote Procedure Calls   333

17.3 The Agent Process   336

17.4 The Sync Process   337

17.5 Pipelined Syncing   341

18 Building a Real-time File Synchronizer   347

18.1 Watching for Changes   348

18.2 Real-time Syncing with Actors   349

18.3 Testing the Syncer   357

18.4 Pipelined Real-time Syncing   358

18.5 Testing the Pipelined Syncer   361

19 Parsing Structured Text   365

19.1 Simple Parsers   366

19.2 Parsing Structured Values   371

19.3 Implementing a Calculator   376

19.4 Parser Debugging and Error Reporting   381

20 Implementing a Programming Language   387

20.1 Interpreting Jsonnet   388

20.2 Jsonnet Language Features   389

20.3 Parsing Jsonnet   390

20.4 Evaluating the Syntax Tree   399

20.5 Serializing to JSON   406

Foreword

Scala as a language delegates much to libraries. Instead of many primitive concepts and types it offers a few powerful abstractions that let libraries define flexible interfaces that are natural to use.

Haoyi's Scala libraries are a beautiful example of what can be built on top of these foundations. There's a whole universe he covers in this book: libraries for interacting with the operating system, testing, serialization, parsing, web-services to a full-featured REPL and build tool. A common thread of all these libraries is that they are simple and user-friendly.

Hands-On Scala is a great resource for learning how to use Scala. It covers a lot of ground with over a hundred mini-applications using Haoyi's Scala libraries in a straightforward way. Its code-first philosophy gets to the point quickly with minimal fuss, with code that is simple and easy to understand.

Making things simple is not easy. It requires restraint, thought, and expertise. Haoyi has laid out his approach in an illuminating blog post titled *Strategic Scala Style: The Principle of Least Power*, arguing that less power means more predictable code, faster understanding and easier maintenance for developers. I see *Hands-On Scala* as the *Principle of Least Power* in action: it shows that one can build powerful applications without needing complex frameworks.

The *Principle of Least Power* is what makes Haoyi's Scala code so easy to understand and his libraries so easy to use. *Hands-On Scala* is the best way to learn about writing Scala in this simple and straightforward manner, and a great resource for getting things done using the Scala ecosystem.

- Martin Odersky, creator of the Scala Language

Author's Note

I first used Scala in 2012. Back then, the language was young and it was a rough experience: weak tooling, confusing libraries, and a community focused more on fun experiments rather than serious workloads. But something caught my interest. Here was a programming language that had the convenience of scripting, the performance and scalability of a compiled language, and a strong focus on safety and correctness. Normally convenience, performance, and safety were things you had to trade off against each other, but with Scala for the first time it seemed I could have them all.

Since then, I've worked in a wide range of languages: websites in PHP and Javascript, software in Java or C# or F#, and massive codebases in Python and Coffeescript. Problems around convenience, performance, and safety were ever-present, no matter which language I was working in. It was clear to me that Scala has already solved many of these eternal problems without compromise, but it was difficult to reap these benefits unless the ecosystem of tools, libraries and community could catch up.

Today, the Scala ecosystem has caught up. Tooling has matured, simpler libraries have emerged, and the community is increasingly using Scala in serious production deployments. I myself have played a part in this, building tools and libraries to help push Scala into the mainstream. The Scala experience today is better in every way than my experience in 2012.

This book aims to introduce the Scala programming experience of today. You will learn how to use Scala in real-world applications like building websites, concurrent data pipelines, or programming language interpreters. Through these projects, you will see how Scala is the easiest way to tackle complex and difficult problems in an elegant and straightforward manner.

- **Li Haoyi, author of *Hands-on Scala Programming***

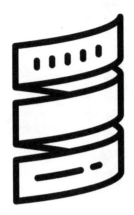

Part I: Introduction to Scala

1 Hands-on Scala   15

2 Setting Up   25

3 Basic Scala   39

4 Scala Collections   59

5 Notable Scala Features   81

The first part of this book is a self-contained introduction to the Scala language. We assume that you have some background programming before, and aim to help translate your existing knowledge and apply it to Scala. You will come out of this familiar with the Scala language itself, ready to begin using it in a wide variety of interesting use cases.

1

Hands-on Scala

1.1 Why Scala?   16

1.2 Why This Book?   17

1.3 How This Book Is Organized   18

1.4 Code Snippet and Examples   20

1.5 Online Materials   22

```scala
package app
object MinimalApplication extends cask.MainRoutes {
  @cask.get("/")
  def hello() = {
    "Hello World!"
  }


  initialize()
}                                                    </> 1.1.scala
```

Snippet 1.1: a tiny Scala web app, one of many example programs we will encounter in this book

Hands-on Scala teaches you how to use the Scala programming language in a practical, project-based fashion. Rather than trying to develop expertise in the deep details of the Scala language itself, *Hands-on Scala* aims to develop expertise using Scala in a broad range of practical applications. This book takes you from "hello world" to building interactive websites, parallel web crawlers, and distributed applications in Scala.

The book covers the concrete skills necessary for anyone using Scala professionally: handling files, data serializing, querying databases, concurrency, and so on. *Hands-on Scala* will guide you through completing several non-trivial projects which reflect the applications you may end up building as part of a software engineering job. This will let you quickly hit the ground running using Scala professionally.

Hands-on Scala assumes you are a software developer who already has experience working in another programming language, and want to quickly become productive working with Scala. If you fall into any of the following categories, this book is for you.

- Doing big data processing using software like Apache Spark which is written in Scala

- Joining one of the many companies using Scala, and need to quickly get up to speed

- Hitting performance limits in Ruby or Python, and looking for a faster compiled language

- Working with Java or Go, and looking for a language that allows more rapid development

- Already experienced working with Scala, but want to take your skills to the next level

- Founding a tech startup, looking for a language that can scale with your company as it grows

Note that this book is not targeted at complete newcomers to programming. We expect you to be familiar with basic programming concepts: variables, integers, conditionals, loops, functions, classes, and so on. We will touch on any cases where these concepts behave differently in Scala, but expect that you already have a basic understanding of how they work.

1.1 Why Scala?

Scala combines object-oriented and functional programming in one concise, high-level language. Scala's static types help avoid bugs in complex applications, and its JVM (Java Virtual Machine) runtime lets you build high-performance systems with easy access to a huge ecosystem of tools and libraries.

Scala is a general-purpose programming language, and has been applied to a wide variety of problems and domains:

- The Twitter social network has most of its backend systems written in Scala
- The Apache Spark big data engine is implemented using in Scala
- The Chisel hardware design language is built on top of Scala

While Scala has never been as mainstream as languages like Python, Java, or C++, it remains heavily used in a wide range of companies and open source projects.

1.1.1 A Compiled Language that feels Dynamic

Scala is a language that scales well from one-line snippets to million-line production codebases, with the convenience of a scripting language and the performance and scalability of a compiled language. Scala's conciseness makes rapid prototyping a joy, while its optimizing compiler and fast JVM runtime provide great performance to support your heaviest production workloads. Rather than being forced to learn a different language for each use case, Scala lets you re-use your existing skills so you can focus your attention on the actual task at hand.

1.1.2 Easy Safety and Correctness

Scala's functional programming style and type-checking compiler helps rule out entire classes of bugs and defects, saving you time and effort you can instead spend developing features for your users. Rather than fighting `TypeErrors` and `NullPointerExceptions` in production, Scala surfaces mistakes and issues early on during compilation so you can resolve them before they impact your bottom line. Deploy your code with the confidence that you won't get woken up by outages caused by silly bugs or trivial mistakes.

1.1.3 A Broad and Deep Ecosystem

As a language running on the Java Virtual Machine, Scala has access to the large Java ecosystem of standard libraries and tools that you will inevitably need to build production applications. Whether you are looking for a Protobuf parser, a machine learning toolkit, a database access library, a profiler to find bottlenecks, or monitoring tools for your production deployment, Scala has everything you need to bring your code to production.

1.2 Why This Book?

The goal of *Hands-on Scala* is to make a software engineer productive using the Scala programming language as quickly as possible.

1.2.1 Beyond the Scala Language

Most existing Scala books focus on teaching you the language. However, knowing the minutiae of language details is neither necessary nor sufficient when the time comes to set up a website, integrate with a third-party API, or structure non-trivial applications. *Hands-on Scala* aims to bridge that gap.

This book goes beyond the Scala language itself, to also cover the various tools and libraries you need to use Scala for typical real-world work. *Hands-on Scala* will ensure you have the supporting skills necessary to use the Scala language to the fullest.

1.2.2 Focused on Real Projects

The chapters in *Hands-on Scala* are project-based: every chapter builds up to a small project in Scala to accomplish something immediately useful in real-world workplaces. These are followed up with exercises (*1.5.3*) to consolidate your knowledge and test your intuition for the topic at hand.

In the course of *Hands-on Scala*, you will work through projects such as:

- An incremental static website generator
- A project migration tool using the Github API
- A parallel web crawler
- An interactive database-backed chat website
- A real-time networked file synchronizer
- A programming language interpreter

These projects serve dual purposes: to motivate the tools and techniques you will learn about in each chapter, and also to build up your engineering toolbox. The API clients, web scrapers, file synchronizers, static site generators, web apps, and other projects you will build are all based on real-world projects implemented in Scala. By the end of this book, you will have concrete experience in the specifics tasks common when doing professional work using Scala.

1.2.3 Code First

Hands-on Scala starts and ends with working code. The concepts you learn in this book are backed up by over 140 executable code examples that demonstrate the concepts in action, and every chapter ends with a set of exercises with complete executable solutions. More than just a source of knowledge, *Hands-on Scala* can also serve as a cookbook you can use to kickstart any project you work on in future.

Hands-on Scala acknowledges that as a reader, your time is valuable. Every chapter, section and paragraph has been carefully crafted to teach the important concepts needed and get you to a working application. You can then take your working code and evolve it into your next project, tool, or product.

1.3 How This Book Is Organized

This book is organized into four parts:

Part I Introduction to Scala is a self-contained introduction to the Scala language. We assume that you have some background programming before, and aim to help translate your existing knowledge and apply it to Scala. You will come out of this familiar with the Scala language itself, ready to begin using it in a wide variety of interesting use cases.

Part II Local Development explores the core tools and techniques necessary for writing Scala applications that run on a single computer. We will cover algorithms, files and subprocess management, data serialization, scripts and build pipelines. This chapter builds towards a capstone project where we write an efficient incremental static site generator using the Scala language.

Part III Web Services covers using Scala in a world of servers and clients, systems and services. We will explore using Scala both as a client and as a server, exchanging HTML and JSON over HTTP or Websockets. This part builds towards two capstone projects: a parallel web crawler and an interactive database-backed chat website, each representing common use cases you are likely to encounter using Scala in a networked, distributed environment.

Part IV Program Design explores different ways of structuring your Scala application to tackle real-world problems. This chapter builds towards another two capstone projects: building a real-time file synchronizer and building a programming-language interpreter. These projects will give you a glimpse of the very different ways the Scala language can be used to implement challenging applications in an elegant and intuitive manner.

Each part is broken down into five chapters, each of which has its own small projects and exercises. Each chapter contains both small code snippets as well as entire programs, which can be accessed via links (*1.5*) for copy-pasting into your editor or command-line.

The libraries and tools used in this book have their own comprehensive online documentation. *Hands-on Scala* does not aim to be a comprehensive reference to every possible topic, but instead will link you to the online documentation if you wish to learn more. Each chapter will also make note of alternate sets of libraries or tools that you may encounter using Scala in the wild.

1.3.1 Chapter Dependency Graph

While *Hands-on Scala* is intended to be read cover-to-cover, you can also pick and choose which specific topics you want to read about. The following diagram shows the dependencies between chapters, so you can chart your own path through the book focusing on the things you are most interested in learning.

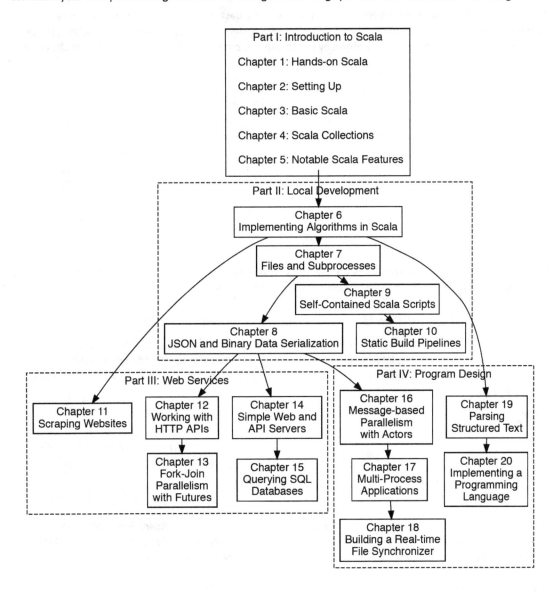

1.4 Code Snippet and Examples

In this book, we will be going through a lot of code. As a reader, we expect you to follow along with the code throughout the chapter: that means working with your terminal and your editor open, entering and executing the code examples given. Make sure you execute the code and see it working, to give yourself a feel for how the code behaves. This section will walk through what you can expect from the code snippets and examples.

1.4.1 Command-Line Snippets

Our command-line code snippets will assume you are using `bash` or a compatible shell like `sh` or `zsh`. On Windows, the shell can be accessed through Windows Subsystem for Linux. All these shells behave similarly, and we will be using code snippets prefixed by a $ to indicate commands being entered into the Unix shell:

```
$ ls
build.sc
foo
mill

$ find . -type f
.
./build.sc
./foo/src/Example.scala
./mill                                                          </> 1.2.bash
```

In each case, the command entered is on the line prefixed by $, followed by the expected output of the command, and separated from the next command by an empty line.

1.4.2 Scala REPL Snippets

Within Scala, the simplest way to write code is in the Scala REPL (Read-Eval-Print-Loop). This is an interactive command-line that lets you enter lines of Scala code to run and immediately see their output. In this book, we will be using the Ammonite Scala REPL, and code snippets to be entered into the REPL are prefixed by @:

```
@ 1 + 1
res0: Int = 2

@ println("Hello World")
Hello World                                                     </> 1.3.scala
```

In each case, the command entered is on the line prefixed by @, with the following lines being the expected output of the command. The value of the entered expression may be implicitly printed to the terminal, as is the case for the `1 + 1` snippet above, or it may be explicitly printed via `println`.

The Ammonite Scala REPL also supports multi-line input, by enclosing the lines in a curly brace {} block:

```
@ {
  println("Hello" + (" " * 5) + "World")
  println("Hello" + (" " * 10) + "World")
  println("Hello" + (" " * 15) + "World")
  }
Hello     World
Hello          World
Hello               World
```
`</> 1.4.scala`

This is useful when we want to ensure the code is run as a single unit, rather than in multiple steps with a delay between them while the user is typing. Installation of Ammonite will be covered in **Chapter 2: Setting Up**.

1.4.3 Source Files

Many examples in this book require source files on disk: these may be run as scripts, or compiled and run as part of a larger project. All such snippets contain the name of the file in the top-right corner:

`build.sc`

```
import mill._, scalalib._

object foo extends ScalaModule {
  def scalaVersion = "2.13.2"
}
```
`</> 1.5.scala`

`foo/src/Example.scala`

```
package foo
object Example {
  def main(args: Array[String]): Unit = {
    println("Hello World")
  }
}
```
`</> 1.6.scala`

1.4.4 Diffs

We will illustrate changes to the a file via *diffs*. A diff is a snippet of code with + and - indicating the lines that were added and removed:

```
    def hello() = {
-       "Hello World!"
+       doctype("html")(
+         html(
+           head(),
+           body(
+             h1("Hello!"),
+             p("World")
+           )
+         )
+       )
    }
                                                                              </> 1.7.scala
```

The above diff represents the removal of one line - "Hello World!" - and the addition of 9 lines of code in its place. This helps focus your attention on the changes we are making to a program. After we have finished walking through a set of changes, we will show the full code for the files we were modifying, for easy reference.

1.5 Online Materials

The following Github repository acts as an online hub for all *Hands-on Scala* notes, errata, discussion, materials, and code examples:

- https://github.com/handsonscala/handsonscala

1.5.1 Code Snippets

Every code snippet in this book is available in the `snippets/` folder of the *Hands-on Scala* online repository:

- https://github.com/handsonscala/handsonscala/blob/v1/snippets

For example the code snippet with the following tag:

- </> 1.1.scala

Is available at the following URL:

- https://github.com/handsonscala/handsonscala/blob/v1/snippets/1.1.scala

This lets you copy-paste code where convenient, rather than tediously typing out the code snippets by hand. Note that these snippets may include diffs and fragments that are not executable on their own. For executable examples, this book also provides complete Executable Code Examples (*1.5.2*).

1.5.2 Executable Code Examples

The code presented in this book is executable, and by following the instructions and code snippets in each chapter you should be able to run and reproduce all examples shown. *Hands-on Scala* also provides a set of complete executable examples online at:

- https://github.com/handsonscala/handsonscala/blob/v1/examples

Each of the examples in the `handsonscala/handsonscala` repository contains a `readme.md` file containing the command necessary to run that example. Throughout the book, we will refer to the online examples via callouts such as:

> **See example 6.1 - MergeSort**

As we progress through each chapter, we will often start from an initial piece of code and modify it via Diffs (*1.4.4*) or Code Snippets (*1.5.1*) to produce the final program. The intermediate programs would be too verbose to show in full at every step in the process, but these executable code examples give you a chance to see the complete working code at each stage of modification.

Each example is fully self-contained: following the setup in **Chapter 2: Setting Up**, you can run the command in each folder's `readme.md` and see the code execute in a self-contained fashion. You can use the working code as a basis for experimentation, or build upon it to create your own programs and applications. All code snippets and examples in this book are MIT licensed.

1.5.3 Exercises

Starting from chapter 5, every chapter come with some exercises at the end:

> **Exercise:** Tries can come in both mutable and immutable variants. Define an `ImmutableTrie` class that has the same methods as the `Trie` class we discussed in this chapter, but instead of a `def add` method it should take a sequence of strings during construction and construct the data structure without any use of `var`s or mutable collections.
>
> **See example 6.7 - ImmutableTrie**

The goal of these exercises is to synthesize what you learned in the chapter into useful skills. Some exercises ask you to make use of what you learned to write new code, others ask you to modify the code presented in the chapter, while others ask you to combine techniques from multiple chapters to achieve some outcome. These will help you consolidate what you learned and build a solid foundation that you can apply to future tasks and challenges.

The solutions to these exercises are also available online as executable code examples.

1.5.4 Resources

The last set of files in the `handsonscala/handsonscala` Github respository are the *resources*: sample data files that are used to exercise the code in a chapter. These are available at:

- https://github.com/handsonscala/handsonscala/blob/v1/resources

For the chapters that make use of these resource files, you can download them by going to the linked file on Github, clicking the `Raw` button to view the raw contents of the file in the browser, and then `Cmd-S/Ctrl-S` to save the file to your disk for your code to access.

1.5.5 Online Discussion

For further help or discussion about this book, feel free to visit our online chat room below. There you may be able to find other readers to compare notes with or discuss the topics presented in this book:

- http://www.handsonscala.com/chat

There are also chapter-specific discussion threads, which will be linked to at the end of each chapter. You can use these threads to discuss topics specific to each chapter, without it getting mixed up in other discussion. A full listing of these chapter-specific discussion threads can be found at the following URLs:

- http://www.handsonscala.com/discuss (listing of all chapter discussions)
- http://www.handsonscala.com/discuss/2 (chapter 2 discussion)

1.6 Conclusion

This first chapter should have given you an idea of what this book is about, and what you can expect working your way through it. Now that we have covered how this book works, we will proceed to set up your Scala development environment that you will be using for the rest of this book.

Discuss Chapter 1 online at https://www.handsonscala.com/discuss/1

2

Setting Up

2.1 Windows Setup (Optional)   26

2.2 Installing Java   27

2.3 Installing Ammonite   28

2.4 Installing Mill   31

2.5 IDE Support   33

```
$ amm
Loading...
Welcome to the Ammonite Repl 2.2.0 (Scala 2.13.2 Java 11.0.7)
@ 1 + 1
res0: Int = 2


@ println("hello world" + "!" * 10)
hello world!!!!!!!!!!                                           </> 2.1.scala
```

Snippet 2.1: getting started with the Ammonite Scala REPL

In this chapter, we will set up a simple Scala programming environment, giving you the ability to write, run, and test your Scala code. We will use this setup throughout the rest of the book. It will be a simple setup, but enough so you can get productive immediately with the Scala language.

Setting up your development environment is a crucial step in learning a new programming language. Make sure you get the setup in this chapter working. If you have issues, come to the online chat room https://www.handsonscala.com/chat to get help resolving them so you can proceed with the rest of the book in peace without tooling-related distractions.

We will be installing following tools for writing and running Scala code:

- Java, the underlying runtime which Scala runs on
- Ammonite, a lightweight REPL and script runner
- Mill, a build tool for larger Scala projects
- Intellij IDEA, an integrated development environment that supports Scala
- VSCode, a lightweight text editor with support for Scala

These tools will be all you need from your first line of Scala code to building and deploying production systems in Scala.

2.1 Windows Setup (Optional)

If you are on Windows, the easiest way to get started using Scala is to use the *Windows Subsystem for Linux 2* (WSL2) to provide a unix-like environment to run your code in. This can be done by following the documentation on the Microsoft website:

- https://docs.microsoft.com/en-us/windows/wsl/wsl2-install

WSL2 allows you to choose which Linux environment to host on your Windows computer. For this book, we will be using Ubuntu 18.04 LTS.

Completing the setup, you should have a Ubuntu terminal open with a standard linux filesystem and your Windows filesystem available under the /mnt/c/ folder:

```
$ cd /mnt/c

$ ls
'Documents and Settings'    PerfLogs        'Program Files (x86)'    Recovery
'Program Files'             ProgramData     Recovery.txt             Users
...
                                                                     </> 2.2.bash
```

The files in /mnt/c/ are shared between your Windows environment and your Linux environment:

- You can edit your code on Windows, and run it through the terminal on Linux.

- You can generate files on disk on Linux, and view them in the Windows Explorer

Many of the chapters in this book assume you are running your code in WSL2's Ubuntu/Linux environment, while graphical editors like IntelliJ or VSCode will need to be running on your Windows environment, and WSL2 allows you to swap between Linux and Windows seamlessly. While the Scala language can also be developed directly on Windows, using WSL2 will allow you to avoid compatibility issues and other distractions as you work through this book.

2.2 Installing Java

Scala is a language that runs on the Java Virtual Machine (JVM), and needs Java pre-installed in order to run. To check if you have Java installed, open up your command line (The `Terminal` app on Mac OS-X, WSL2/Ubuntu on Windows) and type in the `java -version` command. If you see the following output (or something similar) it means you already have Java installed:

```
$ java -version
openjdk version "11.0.7" 2020-04-14
OpenJDK Runtime Environment AdoptOpenJDK (build 11.0.7+9)
OpenJDK 64-Bit Server VM AdoptOpenJDK (build 11.0.7+9, mixed mode)
```
</> *2.3.bash*

If you already have Java, you can skip forward to Installing Ammonite (*2.3*). On the other hand, if you see something like the following, it means you do not have Java installed yet:

```
$ java -version
-bash: java: command not found
```
</> *2.4.bash*

You can download and install a version of the JVM (we will be using version 11 in our examples) via one of the following websites:

- https://adoptopenjdk.net/?variant=openjdk11&jvmVariant=hotspot
- https://docs.aws.amazon.com/corretto/latest/corretto-11-ug/downloads-list.html

The installation instructions vary per operating system, but there are instructions provided for Windows, Mac OS-X, and different flavors of Linux (`.deb` and `.rpm` bundles). Once you have downloaded and installed Java, go back to your command line and make sure that running the `java -version` command correctly produces the above output.

If you are installing Java through the terminal, e.g. on a WSL Ubuntu distribution or on a headless server, you can do so through your standard package manager. e.g. on Ubuntu 18.04 that would mean the following commands:

```
$ sudo apt update

$ sudo apt install default-jdk

$ java -version
openjdk version "11.0.6" 2020-01-14
OpenJDK Runtime Environment (build 11.0.6+10-post-Ubuntu1ubuntu118.04.1)
OpenJDK 64-Bit Server VM (build 11.0.6+10-post-Ubuntu-1ubuntu118.04.1, ...)
```
</> *2.5.bash*

Java versions have a high degree of compatibility, so as long as you have some version of Java installed that should be enough to make the examples in this book work regardless of which specific version it is.

2.3 Installing Ammonite

On Mac OS-X, Linux, and Windows WSL2, we can install Ammonite via the following command line commands:

```bash
$ sudo curl -L https://github.com/lihaoyi/Ammonite/releases/download/2.2.0/2.13-2.2.0 \
  -o /usr/local/bin/amm

$ sudo chmod +x /usr/local/bin/amm

$ amm
```
</> 2.6.bash

This should open up the following Ammonite Scala REPL:

```scala
Loading...
Welcome to the Ammonite Repl 2.2.0 (Scala 2.13.2 Java 11.0.7)
@
```
</> 2.7.scala

Once you see this output, it means you are ready to go. You can exit Ammonite using `Ctrl-D`.

On Max OS-X, Ammonite is also available through the Homebrew package manager via `brew install ammonite-repl`

2.3.1 The Scala REPL

The Ammonite REPL is an interactive Scala command-line in which you can enter code expressions and have their result printed:

```scala
@ 1 + 1
res0: Int = 2

@ "i am cow".substring(2, 4)
res1: String = "am"
```
</> 2.8.scala

Invalid code prints an error:

```scala
@ "i am cow".substing(2, 3)
cmd0.sc:1: value substing is not a member of String
did you mean substring?
val res0 = "i am cow".substing(2, 3)
                      ^
Compilation Failed
```
</> 2.9.scala

You can use tab-completion after a `.` to display the available methods on a particular object, a partial method name to filter that listing, or a complete method name to display the method signatures:

```
@ "i am cow".<tab>
...

exists              maxOption           stripSuffix              //
filter              min                 stripTrailing
filterNot           minBy               subSequence
find                minByOption         substring

@ "i am cow".sub<tab>
subSequence    substring

@ "i am cow".substring<tab>
def substring(x$1: Int): String
def substring(x$1: Int, x$2: Int): String                   </> 2.10.scala
```

If a REPL command is taking too long to run, you can kill it via `Ctrl-C`:

```
@ while (true) { Thread.sleep(1000); println(1 + 1) } // loop forever
2
2
2
2
2
<Ctrl-C>
Interrupted! (`repl.LastException.printStackTrace` for details)

@                                                            </> 2.11.scala
```

2.3.2 Scala Scripts

In addition to providing a REPL, Ammonite can run Scala Script files. A Scala Script is any file containing Scala code, ending in `.sc`. Scala Scripts are a lightweight way of running Scala code that is more convenient, though less configurable, than using a fully-featured build tool like Mill.

For example, we can create the following file `myScript.sc`, using any text editor of your choice (Vim, Sublime Text, VSCode, etc.):

```
println(1 + 1) // 2                                          myScript.sc


println("hello" + " " + "world") // hello world


println(List("I", "am", "cow")) // List(I,am,cow)           </> 2.12.scala
```

Note that in scripts, you need to `println` each expression since scripts do not echo out their values. After that, you can then run the script via `amm myScript.sc`:

```
$ amm myScript.sc
Compiling /Users/lihaoyi/myScript.sc
2
hello world
List(I, am, cow)
```
`</> 2.13.bash`

The first time you run the script file, it will take a moment to compile the script to an executable. Subsequent runs will be faster since the script is already compiled.

2.3.2.1 Watching Scripts

If you are working on a single script, you can use the amm -w or amm --watch command to watch a script and re-run it when things change:

```
$ amm -w myScript.sc
2
hello world
am
Watching for changes to 2 files... (Ctrl-C to exit)
```
`</> 2.14.bash`

Now whenever you make changes to the script file, it will automatically get re-compiled and re-run. This is much faster than running it over and over manually, and is convenient when you are actively working on a single script to try and get it right.

You can edit your Scala scripts with whatever editor you feel comfortable with: IntelliJ (*2.5.1*), VSCode (*2.5.3*), or any other text editor.

2.3.3 Using Scripts from the REPL

You can open up a REPL with access to the functions in a Scala Script by running amm with the --predef flag. For example, given the following script:

```
def hello(n: Int) = {
  "hello world" + "!" * n
}
```
`myScript.sc`
`</> 2.15.scala`

You can then open a REPL with access to it as follows:

```
$ amm --predef myScript.sc
Loading...
Welcome to the Ammonite Repl 2.2.0 (Scala 2.13.2 Java 11.0.7)
@ hello(12)
res0: String = "hello world!!!!!!!!!!!!"
```
`</> 2.16.bash`

This is convenient when your code snippet is large enough that you want to save it to a file and edit it in a proper editor, but you still want to use the Scala REPL to interactively test its behavior.

Note that if you make changes to the script file, you need to exit the REPL using `Ctrl-D` and re-open it to make use of the modified script. You can also combine `--predef` with `--watch/-w`, in which case when you exit with `Ctrl-D` it will automatically restart the REPL if the script file has changed.

2.4 Installing Mill

Mill is a build tool for Scala projects, designed for working with larger Scala projects. While the Ammonite REPL and scripts are great for small pieces of code, they lack support for things like running unit tests, packaging your code, deployment, and other such tasks. For larger projects that require such things, you need to use a build tool like Mill.

2.4.1 Mill Projects

The easiest way to get started with Mill is to download the example project:

```bash
$ curl -L https://github.com/lihaoyi/mill/releases/download/0.8.0/0.8.0-example-3.zip \
  -o example-3.zip


$ unzip example-3.zip


$ cd example-3


$ find . -type f
./build.sc
./mill
./foo/test/src/ExampleTests.scala
./foo/src/Example.scala
```
</> 2.17.bash

You can see that the example project has 4 files. A `build.sc` file that contains the project definition, defining a module `foo` with a test module `test` inside:

```scala
import mill._, scalalib._

object foo extends ScalaModule {
  def scalaVersion = "2.13.2"
  object test extends Tests {
    def ivyDeps = Agg(ivy"com.lihaoyi::utest:0.7.4")
    def testFrameworks = Seq("utest.runner.Framework")
  }
}
```
</> 2.18.scala

The `test` module definition above comes with a dependency on one third party library: `ivy"com.lihaoyi::utest:0.7.4"`. We will see other libraries as we progress through the book and how to use them in our Mill projects.

The Scala code for the foo module lives inside the foo/src/ folder:

```scala
package foo                                              foo/src/Example.scala
object Example {
  def main(args: Array[String]): Unit = {
    println(hello())
  }
  def hello(): String = "Hello World"
}
```
</> 2.19.scala

While the Scala code for the foo.test test module lives inside the foo/test/src/ folder:

```scala
package foo                                      foo/test/src/ExampleTests.scala
import utest._
object ExampleTests extends TestSuite {
  def tests = Tests {
    test("hello") {
      val result = Example.hello()
      assert(result == "Hello World")
      result
    }
  }
}
```
</> 2.20.scala

Lastly, the example project contains a mill file. You can use the mill file to compile and run the project, via ./mill ...:

```bash
$ ./mill foo.compile
Compiling /Users/lihaoyi/test2/example-1/build.sc
...
7 warnings found
[info] Compiling 1 Scala source to /Users/lihaoyi/test2/example-1/out/foo/compile/dest...
[info] Done compiling.

$ ./mill foo.run
Hello World
```
</> 2.21.bash

Note that the first time you run ./mill, it will take a few seconds to download the correct version of Mill for you to use. While above we run both ./mill foo.compile and ./mill foo.run, if you want to run your code you can always just run ./mill foo.run. Mill will automatically re-compile your code if necessary before running it.

To use Mill in any other project, or to start a brand-new project using Mill, it is enough to copy over the mill script file to that project's root directory. You can also download the startup script via:

```
$ curl -L https://github.com/lihaoyi/mill/releases/download/0.8.0/0.8.0 -o mill

$ chmod +x mill                                                      </> 2.22.bash
```

2.4.2 Running Unit Tests

To get started with testing in Mill, you can run `./mill foo.test`:

```
$ ./mill foo.test
------------------------------ Running Tests ------------------------------
+ foo.ExampleTests.hello 10ms   Hello World                         </> 2.23.bash
```

This shows the successful result of the one test that comes built in to the example repository.

2.4.3 Creating a Stand-Alone Executable

So far, we have only been running code within the Mill build tool. But what if we want to prepare our code to run without Mill, e.g. to deploy it to production systems? To do so, you can run `./mill foo.assembly`:

```
$ ./mill foo.assembly
```

This creates an `out.jar` file that can be distributed, deployed and run without the Mill build tool in place. By default, Mill creates the output for the `foo.assembly` task in `out/foo/assembly/dest`, but you can use `./mill show` to print out the full path:

```
$ ./mill show foo.assembly
"ref:18e58778:/Users/lihaoyi/test/example-3/out/foo/assembly/dest/out.jar" </> 2.24.scala
```

You can run the executable assembly to verify that it does what you expect:

```
$ out/foo/assembly/dest/out.jar
Hello World                                                          </> 2.25.bash
```

Now your code is ready to be deployed!

In general, running Scala code in a Mill project requires a bit more setup than running it interactively in the Ammonite Scala REPL or Scala Scripts, but the ability to easily test and package your code is crucial for any production software.

2.5 IDE Support

The most common editors used for working with Scala programs is IntelliJ or VSCode. This section will walk you through installing both of them, but you only really need to install whichever one you prefer to make your way through this book.

2.5.1 Installing IntelliJ for Scala

You can install IntelliJ from the following website. The free Community edition will be enough.

- https://www.jetbrains.com/idea/download

Next, we need to install the IntelliJ Scala plugin, either via the loading screen:

or via the menu bar

From there, go to the Plugins page:

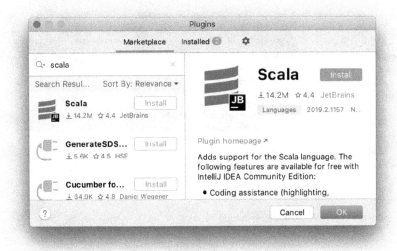

Search for `Scala` and click `Install`. You will then need to re-start the editor.

2.5.2 Integrating IntelliJ with Mill

Once you have IntelliJ installed on your machine, you can load your Mill project via the following terminal command:

```
$ ./mill mill.scalalib.GenIdea/idea
```

Next, use IntelliJ's `File` / `Open` menu item and select the folder your `build.sc` file is in. That will open up the Mill project, with IntelliJ providing code assistance when editing all the code:

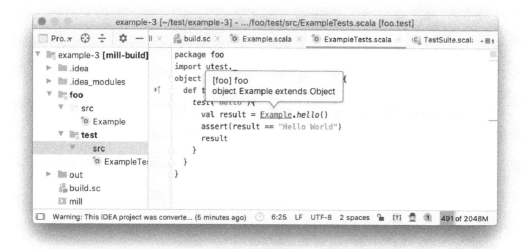

You may see a `Project JDK is not defined: Setup JDK` prompt: in that case, click the `Setup JDK` link and select the version of Java that you installed earlier (*2.2*). Note that every time you make changes to add dependencies or add new modules to your `build.sc`, you need to re-run the `./mill mill.scalalib.GenIdea/idea` command, and restart IntelliJ to have it pick up the changes.

2.5.3 Visual Studio Code Support

Scala also comes with support for the Visual Studio Code text editor, via the Metals plugin:

- https://code.visualstudio.com/

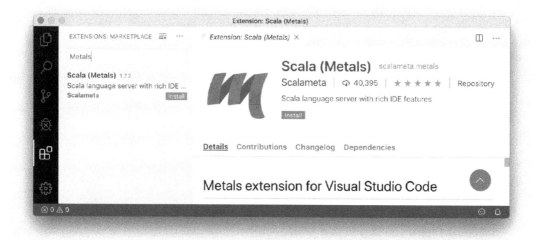

To use VSCode within a Mill build, we need to specify the Mill version in a `.mill-version` file. Then you can open the folder that your Mill build is in and select `Import build`:

```
$ echo "0.8.0" > .mill-version
```

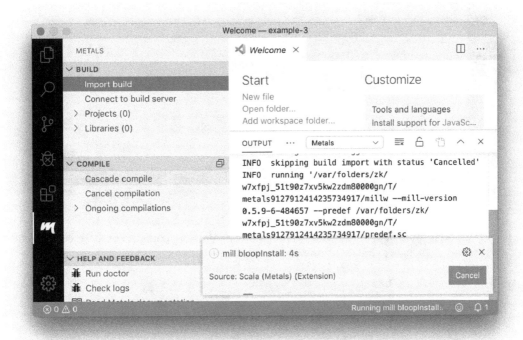

Sometimes the import may time out if your computer is slow or under load, and may need to be retried. If you have trouble getting the import to work even after retrying, you can try using a more recent version of the Metals plugin. Use `F1`, search for `Open Settings (UI)`, and update `Extensions > Metals > Server Version` e.g. to the latest SNAPSHOT version on the Metals/VSCode website:

- https://scalameta.org/metals/docs/editors/vscode.html#using-latest-metals-snapshot

You can also try enabling VSCode Remote Development, by using `F1` and searching for `Remote-WSL: Reopen in WSL`. This will run the VSCode code analysis logic inside the Ubuntu virtual machine, which may be more reliable than doing so directly on the Windows host environment:

- https://code.visualstudio.com/docs/remote/wsl

Once complete, you should be able to show method signature by mousing over them with `Cmd` or `Ctrl`.

Metals also supports other editors such as Vim, Sublime Text, Atom, and others. For more details, refer to their documentation for how to install the relevant editor plugin:

- https://scalameta.org/metals/docs/editors/overview.html

2.6 Conclusion

By now, you should have three main things set up:

- Your Ammonite Scala REPL and Script Runner, that you can run via `amm` or `amm myScript.sc`
- A Mill example project, which you can run via `./mill foo.run` or test via `./mill foo.test`
- Either IntelliJ or VSCode support for your Mill example projects

We will be using Mill as the primary build tool throughout this book, as it is the easiest to get started with. You may also encounter alternate build tools in the wild:

- **SBT:** https://www.scala-sbt.org/
- **Gradle:** https://docs.gradle.org/current/userguide/scala_plugin.html
- **Maven:** https://docs.scala-lang.org/tutorials/scala-with-maven.html

Before you move on to the following chapters, take some time to experiment with these tools: write some code in the Ammonite REPL, create some more scripts, add code and tests to the Mill example projects and run them. These are the main tools that we will use throughout this book.

> **Discuss Chapter 2 online at** https://www.handsonscala.com/discuss/2

3

Basic Scala

3.1 Values   40

3.2 Loops, Conditionals, Comprehensions   47

3.3 Methods and Functions   51

3.4 Classes and Traits   55

```scala
for (i <- Range.inclusive(1, 100)) {
  println(
    if (i % 3 == 0 && i % 5 == 0) "FizzBuzz"
    else if (i % 3 == 0) "Fizz"
    else if (i % 5 == 0) "Buzz"
    else i
  )
}
```
</> 3.1.scala

Snippet 3.1: the popular "FizzBuzz" programming challenge, implemented in Scala

This chapter is a quick tour of the Scala language. For now we will focus on the basics of Scala that are similar to what you might find in any mainstream programming language.

The goal of this chapter is to get familiar you enough that you can take the same sort of code you are used to writing in some other language and write it in Scala without difficulty. This chapter will not cover more Scala-specific programming styles or language features: those will be left for **Chapter 5: Notable Scala Features**.

For this chapter, we will write our code in the Ammonite Scala REPL:

```bash
$ amm
Loading...
Welcome to the Ammonite Repl 2.2.0 (Scala 2.13.2 Java 11.0.7)
@
```
</> 3.2.bash

3.1 Values

3.1.1 Primitives

Scala has the following sets of primitive types:

Type	Values	Type	Values
Byte	-128 to 127	Boolean	true, false
Short	-32,768 to 32,767	Char	'a', '0', 'Z', '包', ...
Int	-2,147,483,648 to 2,147,483,647	Float	32-bit Floating point
Long	-9,223,372,036,854,775,808 to 9,223,372,036,854,775,807	Double	64-bit Floating point

These types are identical to the primitive types in Java, and would be similar to those in C#, C++, or any other statically typed programming language. Each type supports the typical operations, e.g. booleans support boolean logic || &&, numbers support arithmetic + - * / and bitwise operations | &, and so on. All values support == to check for equality and != to check for inequality.

Numbers default to 32-bit Ints. Precedence for arithmetic operations follows other programming languages: * and / have higher precedence than + or -, and parentheses can be used for grouping.

```scala
@ 1 + 2 * 3
res0: Int = 7

@ (1 + 2) * 3
res1: Int = 9
```
</> 3.3.scala

Ints are signed and wrap-around on overflow, while 64-bit Longs suffixed with L have a bigger range and do not overflow as easily:

```
@ 2147483647
res2: Int = 2147483647
```

```
@ 2147483647L
res4: Long = 2147483647L
```

```
@ 2147483647 + 1
res3: Int = -2147483648                              </> 3.4.scala
```

```
@ 2147483647L + 1L
res5: Long = 2147483648L                             </> 3.5.scala
```

Apart from the basic operators, there are a lot of useful methods on java.lang.Integer and java.lang.Long:

```
@ java.lang.Integer.<tab>
BYTES                   decode                  numberOfTrailingZeros
signum                  MAX_VALUE               divideUnsigned
getInteger              parseUnsignedInt        toBinaryString
...

@ java.lang.Integer.toBinaryString(123)
res6: String = "1111011"

@ java.lang.Integer.numberOfTrailingZeros(24)
res7: Int = 3                                                        </> 3.6.scala
```

64-bit Doubles are specified using the 1.0 syntax, and have a similar set of arithmetic operations. You can also use the 1.0F syntax to ask for 32-bit Floats:

```
@ 1.0 / 3.0
res8: Double = 0.3333333333333333

@ 1.0F / 3.0F
res9: Float = 0.33333334F                                           </> 3.7.scala
```

32-bit Floats take up half as much memory as 64-bit Doubles, but are more prone to rounding errors during arithmetic operations. java.lang.Float and java.lang.Double have a similar set of useful operations you can perform on Floats and Doubles.

3.1.2 Strings

Strings in Scala are arrays of 16-bit Chars:

```
@ "hello world"
res10: String = "hello world"                                       </> 3.8.scala
```

Strings can be sliced with .substring, constructed via concatenation using +, or via string interpolation by prefixing the literal with s"..." and interpolating the values with $ or ${...}:

```
@ "hello world".substring(0, 5)
res11: String = "hello"


@ "hello world".substring(5, 10)
res12: String = " worl"
```
```
@ "hello" + 1 + " " + "world" + 2
res13: String = "hello1 world2"


@ val x = 1; val y = 2


@ s"Hello $x World $y"
res15: String = "Hello 1 World 2"


@ s"Hello ${x + y} World ${x - y}"
res16: String = "Hello 3 World -1"
```
</> 3.9.scala   </> 3.10.scala

3.1.3 Local Values and Variables

You can name local values with the val keyword:

```
@ val x = 1


@ x + 2
res18: Int = 3
```
</> 3.11.scala

Note that vals are immutable: you cannot re-assign the val x to a different value after the fact. If you want a local variable that can be re-assigned, you must use the var keyword.

```
@ x = 3
cmd41.sc:1: reassignment to val
val res26 = x = 3

          ^

Compilation Failed
```
```
@ var y = 1


@ y + 2
res20: Int = 3


@ y = 3


@ y + 2
res22: Int = 5
```
</> 3.12.scala </> 3.13.scala

In general, you should try to use val where possible: most named values in your program likely do not need to be re-assigned, and using val helps prevent mistakes where you re-assign something accidentally. Use var only if you are sure you will need to re-assign something later.

Both vals and vars can be annotated with explicit types. These can serve as documentation for people reading your code, as well as a way to catch errors if you accidentally assign the wrong type of value to a variable

```
@ val x: Int = 1

@ var s: String = "Hello"
s: String = "Hello"

@ s = "World"
                                    </> 3.14.scala
```

```
@ val z: Int = "Hello"
cmd33.sc:1: type mismatch;
 found    : String("Hello")
 required: Int
val z: Int = "Hello"
              ^
Compilation Failed              </> 3.15.scala
```

3.1.4 Tuples

Tuples are fixed-length collections of values, which may be of different types:

```
@ val t = (1, true, "hello")
t: (Int, Boolean, String) = (1, true, "hello")

@ t._1
res27: Int = 1

@ t._2
res28: Boolean = true

@ t._3
res29: String = "hello"                           </> 3.16.scala
```

Above, we are storing a tuple into the local value t using the (a, b, c) syntax, and then using ._1, ._2 and ._3 to extract the values out of it. The fields in a tuple are immutable.

The type of the local value t can be annotated as a tuple type:

```
@ val t: (Int, Boolean, String) = (1, true, "hello")
```

You can also use the val (a, b, c) = t syntax to extract all the values at once, and assign them to meaningful names:

```
@ val (a, b, c) = t
a: Int = 1
b: Boolean = true
c: String = "hello"

                                    </> 3.17.scala
```

```
@ a
res31: Int = 1

@ b
res32: Boolean = true

@ c
res33: String = "hello"         </> 3.18.scala
```

Tuples come in any size from 1 to 22 items long:

```scala
@ val t = (1, true, "hello", 'c', 0.2, 0.5f, 12345678912345L)
t: (Int, Boolean, String, Char, Double, Float, Long) = (
  1,
  true,
  "hello",
  'c',
  0.2,
  0.5F,
  12345678912345L
)
```
</> 3.19.scala

Most tuples should be relatively small. Large tuples can easily get confusing: while working with ._1 ._2 and ._3 is probably fine, when you end up working with ._11 ._13 it becomes easy to mix up the different fields. If you find yourself working with large tuples, consider defining a Class (*3.4*) or Case Class that we will see in **Chapter 5: Notable Scala Features**.

3.1.5 Arrays

Arrays are instantiated using the Array[T](a, b, c) syntax, and entries within each array are retrieved using a(n):

```scala
@ val a = Array[Int](1, 2, 3, 4)

@ a(0) // first entry, array indices start from 0
res36: Int = 1

@ a(3) // last entry
res37: Int = 4

@ val a2 = Array[String]("one", "two", "three", "four")
a2: Array[String] = Array("one", "two", "three", "four")

@ a2(1) // second entry
res39: String = "two"
```
</> 3.20.scala

The type parameter inside the square brackets [Int] or [String] determines the type of the array, while the parameters inside the parenthesis (1, 2, 3, 4) determine its initial contents. Note that looking up an Array by index is done via parentheses a(3) rather than square brackets a[3] as is common in many other programming languages.

You can omit the explicit type parameter and let the compiler infer the Array's type, or create an empty array of a specified type using new Array[T](length), and assign values to each index later:

```
@ val a = Array(1, 2, 3, 4)
a: Array[Int] = Array(1, 2, 3, 4)


@ val a2 = Array(
    "one", "two",
    "three", "four"
  )
a2: Array[String] = Array(
  "one", "two",
  "three", "four"
)
```
</> 3.21.scala

```
@ val a = new Array[Int](4)
a: Array[Int] = Array(0, 0, 0, 0)


@ a(0) = 1


@ a(2) = 100


@ a
res45: Array[Int] = Array(1, 0, 100, 0)
```
</> 3.22.scala

For `Arrays` created using `new Array`, all entries start off with the value `0` for numeric arrays, `false` for `Boolean` arrays, and `null` for `Strings` and other types. `Arrays` are mutable but fixed-length: you can change the value of each entry but cannot change the number of entries by adding or removing values. We will see how to create variable-length collections later in **Chapter 4: Scala Collections**.

Multi-dimensional arrays, or arrays-of-arrays, are also supported:

```
@ val multi = Array(Array(1, 2), Array(3, 4))
multi: Array[Array[Int]] = Array(Array(1, 2), Array(3, 4))


@ multi(0)(0)
res47: Int = 1


@ multi(0)(1)
res48: Int = 2


@ multi(1)(0)
res49: Int = 3


@ multi(1)(1)
res50: Int = 4
```
</> 3.23.scala

Multi-dimensional arrays can be useful to represent grids, matrices, and similar values.

3.1.6 Options

Scala's Option[T] type allows you to represent a value that may or may not exist. An Option[T] can either be Some(v: T) indicating that a value is present, or None indicating that it is absent:

```scala
@ def hello(title: String, firstName: String, lastNameOpt: Option[String]) = {
    lastNameOpt match {
      case Some(lastName) => println(s"Hello $title. $lastName")
      case None => println(s"Hello $firstName")
    }
  }


@ hello("Mr", "Haoyi", None)
Hello Haoyi


@ hello("Mr", "Haoyi", Some("Li"))
Hello Mr. Li
```
</> 3.24.scala

The above example shows you how to construct Options using Some and None, as well as matching on them in the same way. Many APIs in Scala rely on Options rather than nulls for values that may or may not exist. In general, Options force you to handle both cases of present/absent, whereas when using nulls it is easy to forget whether or not a value is null-able, resulting in confusing NullPointerExceptions at runtime. We will go deeper into pattern matching in *Chapter 5: Notable Scala Features*.

Options contain some helper methods that make it easy to work with the optional value, such as getOrElse, which substitutes an alternate value if the Option is None:

```scala
@ Some("Li").getOrElse("<unknown>")
res54: String = "Li"


@ None.getOrElse("<unknown>")
res55: String = "<unknown>"
```
</> 3.25.scala

Options are very similar to a collection whose size is 0 or 1. You can loop over them like normal collections, or transform them with standard collection operations like .map.

```
@ def hello2(name: Option[String]) = {
    for (s <- name) println(s"Hello $s")
}

@ hello2(None) // does nothing

@ hello2(Some("Haoyi"))
Hello Haoyi
```
</> 3.26.scala

```
@ def nameLength(name: Option[String]) = {
    name.map(_.length).getOrElse(-1)
}

@ nameLength(Some("Haoyi"))
res60: Int = 5

@ nameLength(None)
res61: Int = -1
```
</> 3.27.scala

Above, we combine `.map` and `.getOrElse` to print out the length of the name if present, and otherwise print `-1`. We will learn more about collection operations in **Chapter 4: Scala Collections**.

> See example 3.1 - Values

3.2 Loops, Conditionals, Comprehensions

3.2.1 For-Loops

For-loops in Scala are similar to "foreach" loops in other languages: they directly loop over the elements in a collection, without needing to explicitly maintain and increment an index. If you want to loop over a range of indices, you can loop over a `Range` such as `Range(0, 5)`:

```
@ var total = 0

@ val items = Array(1, 10, 100, 1000)

@ for (item <- items) total += item

@ total
res65: Int = 1111
```
</> 3.28.scala

```
@ var total = 0

@ for (i <- Range(0, 5)) {
    println("Looping " + i)
    total = total + 1
}
Looping 0
Looping 1
Looping 2
Looping 3
Looping 4

@ total
res68: Int = 10
```
</> 3.29.scala

You can loop over nested `Array`s by placing multiple `<-`s in the header of the loop:

```
@ val multi = Array(Array(1, 2, 3), Array(4, 5, 6))

@ for (arr <- multi; i <- arr) println(i)
1
2
3
4
5
6
```
</> 3.30.scala

Loops can have guards using an `if` syntax:

```
@ for (arr <- multi; i <- arr; if i % 2 == 0) println(i)
2
4
6
```
</> 3.31.scala

3.2.2 If-Else

`if-else` conditionals are similar to those in any other programming language. One thing to note is that in Scala `if-else` can also be used as an expression, similar to the `a ? b : c` ternary expressions in other languages. Scala does not have a separate ternary expression syntax, and so the `if-else` can be directly used as the right-hand-side of the `total +=` below.

```
@ var total = 0

@ for (i <- Range(0, 10)) {
    if (i % 2 == 0) total += i
    else total += 2
  }

@ total
res74: Int = 30
```
</> 3.32.scala

```
@ var total = 0

@ for (i <- Range(0, 10)) {
    total += (if (i % 2 == 0) i else 2)
  }

@ total
res77: Int = 30
```
</> 3.33.scala

3.2.3 Fizzbuzz

Now that we know the basics of Scala syntax, let's consider the common "Fizzbuzz" programming challenge:

Write a short program that prints each number from 1 to 100 on a new line.

For each multiple of 3, print "Fizz" instead of the number.

For each multiple of 5, print "Buzz" instead of the number.

For numbers which are multiples of both 3 and 5, print "FizzBuzz" instead of the number.

We can accomplish this as follows:

```scala
@ for (i <- Range.inclusive(1, 100)) {
    if (i % 3 == 0 && i % 5 == 0) println("FizzBuzz")
    else if (i % 3 == 0) println("Fizz")
    else if (i % 5 == 0) println("Buzz")
    else println(i)
  }
1
2
Fizz
4
Buzz
Fizz
7
8
Fizz
Buzz
11
Fizz
13
14
FizzBuzz
...
```
</> 3.34.scala

Since if-else is an expression, we can also write it as:

```scala
@ for (i <- Range.inclusive(1, 100)) {
    println(
    if (i % 3 == 0 && i % 5 == 0) "FizzBuzz"
    else if (i % 3 == 0) "Fizz"
    else if (i % 5 == 0) "Buzz"
    else i
  )
  }
```
</> 3.35.scala

3.2.4 Comprehensions

Apart from using for to define loops that perform some action, you can also use for together with yield to transform a collection into a new collection:

```
@ val a = Array(1, 2, 3, 4)
```

```
@ val a2 = for (i <- a) yield i * i
a2: Array[Int] = Array(1, 4, 9, 16)
```

```
@ val a3 = for (i <- a) yield "hello " + i
a3: Array[String] = Array("hello 1", "hello 2", "hello 3", "hello 4")        </> 3.36.scala
```

Similar to loops, you can filter which items end up in the final collection using an if guard inside the parentheses:

```
@ val a4 = for (i <- a if i % 2 == 0) yield "hello " + i
a4: Array[String] = Array("hello 2", "hello 4")                              </> 3.37.scala
```

Comprehensions can also take multiple input arrays, a and b below. This flattens them out into one final output Array, similar to using a nested for-loop:

```
@ val a = Array(1, 2); val b = Array("hello", "world")
```

```
@ val flattened = for (i <- a; s <- b) yield s + i
flattened: Array[String] = Array("hello1", "world1", "hello2", "world2")   </> 3.38.scala
```

You can also replace the parentheses () with curly brackets {} if you wish to spread out the nested loops over multiple lines, for easier reading. Note that the order of <-s within the nested comprehension matters, just like how the order of nested loops affects the order in which the loop actions will take place:

```
@ val flattened = for{
    i <- a
    s <- b
  } yield s + i
flattened: Array[String] = Array("hello1", "world1", "hello2", "world2")
```

```
@ val flattened2 = for{
    s <- b
    i <- a
  } yield s + i
flattened2: Array[String] = Array("hello1", "hello2", "world1", "world2")  </> 3.39.scala
```

We can use comprehensions to write a version of FizzBuzz that doesn't print its results immediately to the console, but returns them as a Seq (short for "sequence"):

```scala
@ val fizzbuzz = for (i <- Range.inclusive(1, 100)) yield {
    if (i % 3 == 0 && i % 5 == 0) "FizzBuzz"
    else if (i % 3 == 0) "Fizz"
    else if (i % 5 == 0) "Buzz"
    else i.toString
  }
fizzbuzz: IndexedSeq[String] = Vector(
  "1",
  "2",
  "Fizz",
  "4",
  "Buzz",
...
```
</> 3.40.scala

We can then use the `fizzbuzz` collection however we like: storing it in a variable, passing it into methods, or processing it in other ways. We will cover what you can do with these collections later, in **Chapter 4: Scala Collections**.

See example 3.2 - LoopsConditionals

3.3 Methods and Functions

3.3.1 Methods

You can define methods using the `def` keyword:

```scala
@ def printHello(times: Int) = {
    println("hello " + times)
  }


@ printHello(1)
hello 1


@ printHello(times = 2) // argument name provided explicitly
hello 2
```
</> 3.41.scala

Passing in the wrong type of argument, or missing required arguments, is a compiler error. However, if the argument has a default value, then passing it is optional.

```
@ printHello("1") // wrong type of argument
cmd128.sc:1: type mismatch;
 found    : String("1")
 required: Int
val res128 = printHello("1")
                        ^
Compilation Failed
```

</> 3.42.scala

```
@ def printHello2(times: Int = 0) = {
    println("hello " + times)
  }

@ printHello2(1)
hello 1

@ printHello2()
hello 0
```

</> 3.43.scala

3.3.1.1 Returning Values from Methods

Apart from performing actions like printing, methods can also return values. The last expression within the curly brace {} block is treated as the return value of a Scala method.

```
@ def hello(i: Int = 0) = {
    "hello " + i
  }

@ hello(1)
res96: String = "hello 1"
```

</> 3.44.scala

You can call the method and print out or perform other computation on the returned value:

```
@ println(hello())
hello 0

@ val helloHello = hello(123) + " " + hello(456)
helloHello: String = "hello 123 hello 456"

@ helloHello.reverse
res99: String = "654 olleh 321 olleh"
```

</> 3.45.scala

3.3.2 Function Values

You can define function values using the `=>` syntax. Functions values are similar to methods, in that you call them with arguments and they can perform some action or return some value. Unlike methods, functions themselves are values: you can pass them around, store them in variables, and call them later.

```
@ var g: Int => Int = i => i + 1

@ g(10)
res101: Int = 11

@ g = i => i * 2

@ g(10)
res103: Int = 20                                                    </> 3.46.scala
```

Note that unlike methods, function values cannot have optional arguments (i.e. with default values) and cannot take type parameters via the `[T]` syntax. When a method is converted into a function value, any optional arguments must be explicitly included, and type parameters fixed to concrete types. Function values are also anonymous, which makes stack traces involving them less convenient to read than those using methods.

In general, you should prefer using methods unless you really need the flexibility to pass as parameters or store them in variables. But if you need that flexibility, function values are a great tool to have.

3.3.2.1 Methods taking Functions

One common use case of function values is to pass them into methods that take function parameters. Such methods are often called "higher order methods". Below, we have a class `Box` with a method `printMsg` that prints its contents (an `Int`), and a separate method `update` that takes a function of type `Int => Int` that can be used to update `x`. You can then pass a function literal into `update` in order to change the value of `x`:

```
@ class Box(var x: Int) {
    def update(f: Int => Int) = x = f(x)
    def printMsg(msg: String) = {
      println(msg + x)
    }
}
                              </> 3.47.scala
```

```
@ val b = new Box(1)

@ b.printMsg("Hello")
Hello1

@ b.update(i => i + 5)

@ b.printMsg("Hello")
Hello6                        </> 3.48.scala
```

Simple functions literals like `i => i + 5` can also be written via the shorthand `_ + 5`, with the underscore `_` standing in for the function parameter.

```
@ b.update(_ + 5)
```

```
@ b.printMsg("Hello")
Hello11                                                        </> 3.49.scala
```

This placeholder syntax for function literals also works for multi-argument functions, e.g. (x, y) => x + y can be written as _ + _.

Any method that takes a function as an argument can also be given a method reference, as long as the method's signature matches that of the function type, here Int => Int:

```
@ def increment(i: Int) = i + 1
```

```
@ val b = new Box(123)
```

```
@ b.update(increment) // Providing a method reference
```

```
@ b.update(x => increment(x)) // Explicitly writing out the function literal
```

```
@ b.update{x => increment(x)} // Methods taking a single function can be called with {}s
```

```
@ b.update(increment(_)) // You can also use the `_` placeholder syntax
```

```
@ b.printMsg("result: ")
result: 127                                                    </> 3.50.scala
```

3.3.2.2 Multiple Parameter Lists

Methods can be defined to take multiple parameter lists. This is useful for writing higher-order methods that can be used like control structures, such as the myLoop method below:

```
@ def myLoop(start: Int, end: Int)          @ myLoop(start = 5, end = 10) { i =>
        (callback: Int => Unit) = {            println(s"i has value ${i}")
  for (i <- Range(start, end)) {             }
    callback(i)                            i has value 5
  }                                        i has value 6
}                                          i has value 7
                                           i has value 8
                   </> 3.51.scala         i has value 9        </> 3.52.scala
```

The ability to pass function literals to methods is used to great effect in the standard library, to concisely perform transformations on collections. We will see more of that in **Chapter 4: Scala Collections**.

3.4 Classes and Traits

You can define classes using the `class` keyword, and instantiate them using `new`. By default, all arguments passed into the class constructor are available in all of the class' methods: the `(x: Int)` above defines both the private fields as well as the class' constructor. `x` is thus accessible in the `printMsg` function, but cannot be accessed outside the class:

```scala
@ class Foo(x: Int) {
    def printMsg(msg: String) = {
      println(msg + x)
    }
  }
```
</> 3.53.scala

```scala
@ val f = new Foo(1)

@ f.printMsg("hello")
hello1

@ f.x
cmd120.sc:1: value x is not a member of Foo
Compilation Failed
```
</> 3.54.scala

To make x publicly accessible you can make it a `val`, and to make it mutable you can make it a `var`:

```scala
@ class Bar(val x: Int) {
    def printMsg(msg: String) = {
      println(msg + x)
    }
  }
```
</> 3.55.scala

```scala
@ val b = new Bar(1)

@ b.x
res122: Int = 1
```
</> 3.56.scala

```scala
@ class Qux(var x: Int) {
    def printMsg(msg: String) = {
      x += 1
      println(msg + x)
    }
  }
```
</> 3.57.scala

```scala
@ val q = new Qux(1)

@ q.printMsg("hello")
hello2

@ q.printMsg("hello")
hello3
```
</> 3.58.scala

You can also use `val`s or `var`s in the body of a class to store data. These get computed once when the class is instantiated:

```
@ class Baz(x: Int) {                          @ val z = new Baz(3)
    val bangs = "!" * x
    def printMsg(msg: String) = {              @ z.printMsg("hello")
      println(msg + bangs)                     hello!!!
    }
  }
}                                </> 3.59.scala                              </> 3.60.scala
```

3.4.1 Traits

traits are similar to interfaces in traditional object-oriented languages: a set of methods that multiple classes can inherit. Instances of these classes can then be used interchangeably.

```
@ trait Point{ def hypotenuse: Double }

@ class Point2D(x: Double, y: Double) extends Point{
    def hypotenuse = math.sqrt(x * x + y * y)
  }

@ class Point3D(x: Double, y: Double, z: Double) extends Point{
    def hypotenuse = math.sqrt(x * x + y * y + z * z)
  }

@ val points: Array[Point] = Array(new Point2D(1, 2), new Point3D(4, 5, 6))

@ for (p <- points) println(p.hypotenuse)
2.23606797749979
8.774964387392123                                                        </> 3.61.scala
```

Above, we have defined a Point trait with a single method def hypotenuse: Double. The subclasses Point2D and Point3D both have different sets of parameters, but they both implement def hypotenuse. Thus we can put both Point2Ds and Point3Ds into our points: Array[Point] and treat them all uniformly as objects with a def hypotenuse method, regardless of what their actual class is.

See example 3.4 - ClassesTraits

3.5 Conclusion

In this chapter, we have gone through a lightning tour of the core Scala language. While the exact syntax may be new to you, the concepts should be mostly familiar: primitives, arrays, loops, conditionals, methods, and classes are part of almost every programming language. Next we will look at the core of the Scala standard library: the Scala Collections.

Exercise: Define a `def flexibleFizzBuzz` method that takes a `String => Unit` callback function as its argument, and allows the caller to decide what they want to do with the output. The caller can choose to ignore the output, `println` the output directly, or store the output in a previously-allocated array they already have handy.

```
@ flexibleFizzBuzz(s => {} /* do nothing
*/)


@ flexibleFizzBuzz(s => println(s))
1
2
Fizz
4
Buzz
...
```

```
@ var i = 0

@ val output = new Array[String](100)

@ flexibleFizzBuzz{s =>
    output(i) = s
    i += 1
}

@ output
res125: Array[String] = Array(
  "1",
  "2",
  "Fizz",
  "4",
  "Buzz",
```

</> 3.62.scala ...   </> 3.63.scala

See example 3.5 - FlexibleFizzBuzz

Exercise: Write a recursive method `printMessages` that can receive an array of `Msg` class instances, each with an optional `parent` ID, and use it to print out a threaded fashion. That means that child messages are print out indented underneath their parents, and the nesting can be arbitrarily deep.

```scala
class Msg(val id: Int, val parent: Option[Int], val txt: String)
def printMessages(messages: Array[Msg]): Unit = ...                    </> 3.64.scala
```

```
printMessages(Array(  TestPrintMessages.sc
  new Msg(0, None, "Hello"),
  new Msg(1, Some(0), "World"),
  new Msg(2, None, "I am Cow"),
  new Msg(3, Some(2), "Hear me moo"),
  new Msg(4, Some(2), "Here I stand"),
  new Msg(5, Some(2), "I am Cow"),
  new Msg(6, Some(5), "Here me moo, moo")
))
                              </> 3.65.scala
```

```
                    expected.txt
#0 Hello
    #1 World
#2 I am Cow
    #3 Hear me moo
    #4 Here I stand
    #5 I am Cow
        #6 Here me moo, moo

                    </> 3.66.output
```

See example 3.6 - PrintMessages

Exercise: Define a pair of methods `withFileWriter` and `withFileReader` that can be called as shown below. Each method should take the name of a file, and a function value that is called with a `java.io.BufferedReader` or `java.io.BufferedWriter` that it can use to read or write data. Opening and closing of the reader/writer should be automatic, such that a caller cannot forget to close the file. This is similar to Python "context managers" or Java "try-with-resource" syntax.

```scala
withFileWriter("File.txt") { writer =>          TestContextManagers.sc
  writer.write("Hello\n"); writer.write("World!")
}
val result = withFileReader("File.txt") { reader =>
  reader.readLine() + "\n" + reader.readLine()
}
assert(result == "Hello\nWorld!")
                              </> 3.67.scala
```

You can use the Java standard library APIs `java.nio.file.Files.newBufferedWriter` and `newBufferedReader` for working with file readers and writers. We will get more familiar with working with files and the filesystem in *Chapter 7: Files and Subprocesses*.

See example 3.7 - ContextManagers

Discuss Chapter 3 online at https://www.handsonscala.com/discuss/3

4

Scala Collections

4.1 Operations   60

4.2 Immutable Collections   67

4.3 Mutable Collections   72

4.4 Common Interfaces   77

```scala
@ def stdDev(a: Array[Double]): Double = {
    val mean = a.sum / a.length
    val squareErrors = a.map(x => x - mean).map(x => x * x)
    math.sqrt(squareErrors.sum / a.length)
}
```
</> 4.1.scala

Snippet 4.1: calculating the standard deviation of an array using Scala Collection operations

The core of the Scala standard library is its *collections*: a common set of containers and data structures that are shared by all Scala programs. Scala's collections make it easy for you to manipulate arrays, linked lists, sets, maps and other data structures in convenient ways, providing built-in many of the data structures needed for implementing a typical application.

This chapter will walk through the common operations that apply to all collection types, before discussing the individual data structures and when you might use each of them in practice.

4.1 Operations

Scala collections provide many common operations for constructing them, querying them, or transforming them. These operations are present on the Arrays we saw in **Chapter 3: Basic Scala**, but they also apply to all the collections we will cover in this chapter: Vectors (*4.2.1*), Sets (*4.2.3*), Maps (*4.2.4*), etc.

4.1.1 Builders

```
@ val b = Array.newBuilder[Int]
b: mutable.ArrayBuilder[Int] = ArrayBuilder.ofInt

@ b += 1

@ b += 2

@ b.result()
res3: Array[Int] = Array(1, 2)                                    </> 4.2.scala
```

Builders let you efficiently construct a collection of unknown length, "freezing" it into the collection you want at the end. This is most useful for constructing Arrays or immutable collections where you cannot add or remove elements once the collection has been constructed.

4.1.2 Factory Methods

```
@ Array.fill(5)("hello") // Array with "hello" repeated 5 times
res4: Array[String] = Array("hello", "hello", "hello", "hello", "hello")

@ Array.tabulate(5)(n => s"hello $n") // Array with 5 items, each computed from its index
res5: Array[String] = Array("hello 0", "hello 1", "hello 2", "hello 3", "hello 4")

@ Array(1, 2, 3) ++ Array(4, 5, 6) // Concatenating two Arrays into a larger one
res6: Array[Int] = Array(1, 2, 3, 4, 5, 6)                        </> 4.3.scala
```

Factory methods provide another way to instantiate collections: with every element the same, with each element constructed depending on the index, or from multiple smaller collections. This can be more convenient than using Builders (*4.1.1*) in many common use cases.

See example 4.1 - BuildersFactories

4.1.3 Transforms

```
@ Array(1, 2, 3, 4, 5).map(i => i * 2) // Multiply every element by 2
res7: Array[Int] = Array(2, 4, 6, 8, 10)


@ Array(1, 2, 3, 4, 5).filter(i => i % 2 == 1) // Keep only elements not divisible by 2
res8: Array[Int] = Array(1, 3, 5)


@ Array(1, 2, 3, 4, 5).take(2) // Keep first two elements
res9: Array[Int] = Array(1, 2)


@ Array(1, 2, 3, 4, 5).drop(2) // Discard first two elements
res10: Array[Int] = Array(3, 4, 5)


@ Array(1, 2, 3, 4, 5).slice(1, 4) // Keep elements from index 1-4
res11: Array[Int] = Array(2, 3, 4)


@ Array(1, 2, 3, 4, 5, 4, 3, 2, 1, 2, 3, 4, 5, 6, 7, 8).distinct // Removes all duplicates
res12: Array[Int] = Array(1, 2, 3, 4, 5, 6, 7, 8)                          </> 4.4.scala
```

Transforms take an existing collection and create a new collection modified in some way. Note that these transformations create copies of the collection, and leave the original unchanged. That means if you are still using the original array, its contents will not be modified by the transform:

```
@ val a = Array(1, 2, 3, 4, 5)
a: Array[Int] = Array(1, 2, 3, 4, 5)


@ val a2 = a.map(x => x + 10)
a2: Array[Int] = Array(11, 12, 13, 14, 15)


@ a(0) // Note that `a` is unchanged!
res15: Int = 1


@ a2(0)
res16: Int = 11                                                           </> 4.5.scala
```

The copying involved in these collection transformations does have some overhead, but in most cases that should not cause issues. If a piece of code does turn out to be a bottleneck that is slowing down your program, you can always convert your .map/.filter/etc. transformation code into mutating operations over raw Arrays or In-Place Operations (*4.3.4*) over Mutable Collections (*4.3*) to optimize for performance.

See example 4.2 - Transforms

4.1.4 Queries

```
@ Array(1, 2, 3, 4, 5, 6, 7).find(i => i % 2 == 0 && i > 4)
res17: Option[Int] = Some(6)


@ Array(1, 2, 3, 4, 5, 6, 7).find(i => i % 2 == 0 && i > 10)
res18: Option[Int] = None


@ Array(1, 2, 3, 4, 5, 6, 7).exists(x => x > 1) // are any elements greater than 1?
res19: Boolean = true


@ Array(1, 2, 3, 4, 5, 6, 7).exists(_ < 0) // same as a.exists(x => x < 0)
res20: Boolean = false                                            </> 4.6.scala
```

Queries let you search for elements without your collection, returning either a `Boolean` indicating if a matching element exists, or an `Option` containing the element that was found. This can make it convenient to find things inside your collections without the verbosity of writing for-loops to inspect the elements one by one.

4.1.5 Aggregations

4.1.5.1 mkString

Stringifies the elements in a collection and combines them into one long string, with the given separator. Optionally can take a start and end delimiter:

```
@ Array(1, 2, 3, 4, 5, 6, 7).mkString(",")
res21: String = "1,2,3,4,5,6,7"


@ Array(1, 2, 3, 4, 5, 6, 7).mkString("[", ",", "]")
res22: String = "[1,2,3,4,5,6,7]"                                 </> 4.7.scala
```

4.1.5.2 foldLeft

Takes a starting value and a function that it uses to combine each element of your collection with the starting value, to produce a final result:

```
@ Array(1, 2, 3, 4, 5, 6, 7).foldLeft(0)((x, y) => x + y) // sum of all elements
res23: Int = 28


@ Array(1, 2, 3, 4, 5, 6, 7).foldLeft(1)((x, y) => x * y) // product of all elements
res24: Int = 5040


@ Array(1, 2, 3, 4, 5, 6, 7).foldLeft(1)(_ * _) // same as above, shorthand syntax
res25: Int = 5040                                                 </> 4.8.scala
```

In general, `foldLeft` is similar to a `for`-loop and accumulator `var`, and the above sum-of-all-elements `foldLeft` call can equivalently be written as:

```
@ {
  var total = 0
  for (i <- Array(1, 2, 3, 4, 5, 6, 7)) total += i
  total
  }
total: Int = 28
```
</> 4.9.scala

4.1.5.3 groupBy

Groups your collection into a `Map` of smaller collections depending on a key:

```
@ val grouped = Array(1, 2, 3, 4, 5, 6, 7).groupBy(_ % 2)
grouped: Map[Int, Array[Int]] = Map(0 -> Array(2, 4, 6), 1 -> Array(1, 3, 5, 7))


@ grouped(0)
res26: Array[Int] = Array(2, 4, 6)


@ grouped(1)
res27: Array[Int] = Array(1, 3, 5, 7)
```
</> 4.10.scala

See example 4.3 - QueriesAggregations

4.1.6 Combining Operations

It is common to chain more than one operation together to achieve what you want. For example, here is a function that computes the standard deviation of an array of numbers:

```
@ def stdDev(a: Array[Double]): Double = {
    val mean = a.foldLeft(0.0)(_ + _) / a.length
    val squareErrors = a.map(_ - mean).map(x => x * x)
    math.sqrt(squareErrors.foldLeft(0.0)(_ + _) / a.length)
  }

@ stdDev(Array(1, 2, 3, 4, 5))
res29: Double = 1.4142135623730951


@ stdDev(Array(3, 3, 3))
res30: Double = 0.0
```
</> 4.11.scala

Scala collections provide a convenient helper method `.sum` that is equivalent to `.foldLeft(0.0)(_ + _)`, so the above code can be simplified to:

```scala
@ def stdDev(a: Array[Double]): Double = {
    val mean = a.sum / a.length
    val squareErrors = a.map(_ - mean).map(x => x * x)
    math.sqrt(squareErrors.sum / a.length)
}
```
</> 4.12.scala

As another example, here is a function that uses `.exists`, `.map` and `.distinct` to check if an incoming grid of numbers is a valid Sudoku grid:

```scala
@ def isValidSudoku(grid: Array[Array[Int]]): Boolean = {
    !Range(0, 9).exists{i =>
      val row = Range(0, 9).map(grid(i)(_))
      val col = Range(0, 9).map(grid(_)(i))
      val square = Range(0, 9).map(j => grid((i % 3) * 3 + j % 3)((i / 3) * 3 + j / 3))
      row.distinct.length != row.length ||
      col.distinct.length != col.length ||
      square.distinct.length != square.length
    }
}
```
</> 4.13.scala

This implementation receives a Sudoku grid, represented as a 2-dimensional `Array[Array[Int]]`. For each i from 0 to 9, we pick out a single row, column, and 3x3 square. It then checks that each such row/column/square has 9 unique numbers by calling `.distinct` to remove any duplicates, and then checking if the `.length` has changed as a result of that removal.

We can test this on some example grids to verify that it works:

```
@ isValidSudoku(Array(
    Array(5, 3, 4,   6, 7, 8,   9, 1, 2),
    Array(6, 7, 2,   1, 9, 5,   3, 4, 8),
    Array(1, 9, 8,   3, 4, 2,   5, 6, 7),

    Array(8, 5, 9,   7, 6, 1,   4, 2, 3),
    Array(4, 2, 6,   8, 5, 3,   7, 9, 1),
    Array(7, 1, 3,   9, 2, 4,   8, 5, 6),

    Array(9, 6, 1,   5, 3, 7,   2, 8, 4),
    Array(2, 8, 7,   4, 1, 9,   6, 3, 5),
    Array(3, 4, 5,   2, 8, 6,   1, 7, 9)
))
res33: Boolean = true          </> 4.14.scala
```

```
@ isValidSudoku(Array(
    Array(5, 3, 4,   6, 7, 8,   9, 1, 2),
    Array(6, 7, 2,   1, 9, 5,   3, 4, 8),
    Array(1, 9, 8,   3, 4, 2,   5, 6, 7),

    Array(8, 5, 9,   7, 6, 1,   4, 2, 3),
    Array(4, 2, 6,   8, 5, 3,   7, 9, 1),
    Array(7, 1, 3,   9, 2, 4,   8, 5, 6),

    Array(9, 6, 1,   5, 3, 7,   2, 8, 4),
    Array(2, 8, 7,   4, 1, 9,   6, 3, 5),
    Array(3, 4, 5,   2, 8, 6,   1, 7, 8)
)) // bottom right cell should be 9
res34: Boolean = false          </> 4.15.scala
```

Chaining collection transformations in this manner will always have some overhead, but for most use cases the overhead is worth the convenience and simplicity that these transforms give you. If collection transforms do become a bottleneck, you can optimize the code using Views (*4.1.8*), In-Place Operations (*4.3.4*), or finally by looping over the raw Arrays yourself.

See example 4.4 - Combining

4.1.7 Converters

You can convert among Arrays and other collections like Vector (*4.2.1*)s and Set (*4.2.3*) using the .to method:

```
@ Array(1, 2, 3).to(Vector)
res35: Vector[Int] = Vector(1, 2, 3)


@ Vector(1, 2, 3).to(Array)
res36: Array[Int] = Array(1, 2, 3)


@ Array(1, 1, 2, 2, 3, 4).to(Set)
res37: Set[Int] = Set(1, 2, 3, 4)                          </> 4.16.scala
```

4.1.8 Views

When you chain multiple transformations on a collection, we are creating many intermediate collections that are immediately thrown away. For example, in the following snippet:

```
@ val myArray = Array(1, 2, 3, 4, 5, 6, 7, 8, 9)
```

```
@ val myNewArray = myArray.map(x => x + 1).filter(x => x % 2 == 0).slice(1, 3)
myNewArray: Array[Int] = Array(4, 6)                                      </> 4.17.scala
```

The chain of .map .filter .slice operations ends up traversing the collection three times, creating three new collections, but only the last collection ends up being stored in myNewArray and the others are discarded.

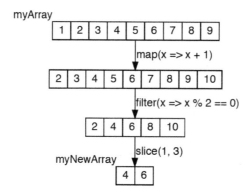

This creation and traversal of intermediate collections is wasteful. In cases where you have long chains of collection transformations that are becoming a performance bottleneck, you can use the .view method together with .to to "fuse" the operations together:

```
@ val myNewArray = myArray.view.map(_ + 1).filter(_ % 2 == 0).slice(1, 3).to(Array)
myNewArray: Array[Int] = Array(4, 6)                                      </> 4.18.scala
```

Using .view before the map/filter/slice transformation operations defers the actual traversal and creation of a new collection until later, when we call .to to convert it back into a concrete collection type:

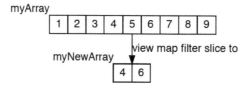

This allows us to perform this chain of map/filter/slice transformations with only a single traversal, and only creating a single output collection. This reduces the amount of unnecessary processing and memory allocations.

4.2 Immutable Collections

While `Arrays` are the low-level primitive, most Scala applications are built upon its mutable and immutable collections: `Vectors`, `Lists`, `Sets`, and `Maps`. Of these, immutable collections are by far the most common.

Immutable collections rule out an entire class of bugs due to unexpected modifications, and are especially useful in multi-threaded scenarios where you can safely pass immutable collections between threads without worrying about thread-safety issues. Most immutable collections use Structural Sharing (4.2.2) to make creating updated copies cheap, allowing you to use them in all but the most performance critical code.

4.2.1 Immutable Vectors

`Vectors` are fixed-size, immutable linear sequences. They are a good general-purpose sequence data structure, and provide efficient $O(log\ n)$ performance for most operations.

```
@ val v = Vector(1, 2, 3, 4, 5)
v: Vector[Int] = Vector(1, 2, 3, 4, 5)


@ v(0)
res42: Int = 1


@ val v2 = v.updated(2, 10)
v2: Vector[Int] = Vector(1, 2, 10, 4, 5)


@ v2
res44: Vector[Int] = Vector(1, 2, 10, 4, 5)


@ v // note that `v` did not change!
res45: Vector[Int] = Vector(1, 2, 3, 4, 5)
                                          </> 4.19.scala
```

```
@ val v = Vector[Int]()
v: Vector[Int] = Vector()


@ val v1 = v :+ 1
v1: Vector[Int] = Vector(1)


@ val v2 = 4 +: v1
v2: Vector[Int] = Vector(4, 1)


@ val v3 = v2.tail
v3: Vector[Int] = Vector(1)




                             </> 4.20.scala
```

Unlike `Arrays` where `a(...) = ...` mutates it in place, a `Vector`'s `.updated` method returns a new `Vector` with the modification while leaving the old `Vector` unchanged. Due to Structural Sharing (4.2.2), this is a reasonably-efficient $O(log\ n)$ operation. Similarly, using `:+` and `+:` to create a new `Vector` with additional elements on either side, or using `.tail` to create a new `Vector` with one element removed, are all $O(log\ n)$ as well:

`Vectors` support the same set of Operations (4.1) that `Arrays` and other collections do: builders (4.1.1), factory methods (4.1.2), transforms (4.1.3), etc.

In general, using Vectors is handy when you have a sequence you know will not change, but need flexibility in how you work with it. Their tree structure makes most operations reasonably efficient, although they will never be quite as fast as Arrays for in-place updates or Immutable Lists (4.2.5) for adding and removing elements at the front.

4.2.2 Structural Sharing

Vectors implement their $O(log\ n)$ copy-and-update operations by re-using portions of their tree structure. This avoids copying the whole tree, resulting in a "new" Vector that shares much of the old tree structure with only minor modifications.

Consider a large Vector, v1:

```
@ val v1 = Vector(1, 2, 0, 9,  7, 2, 9, 6,   ...,  3, 2, 5, 5,  4, 8, 4, 6)
```

This is represented in-memory as a tree structure, whose breadth and depth depend on the size of the Vector:

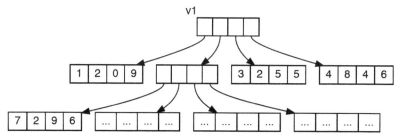

This example is somewhat simplified - a Vector in Scala has 32 elements per tree node rather than the 4 shown above - but it will serve us well enough to illustrate how the Vector data structure works.

Let us consider what happens if we want to perform an update, e.g. replacing the fifth value 7 in the above Vector with the value 8:

```
@ val v2 = v1.updated(4, 8)


@ v2
res50: Vector[Int] = Vector(1, 2, 0, 9, 8, 2, 9, 6, ..., 3, 2, 5, 5, 4, 8, 4, 6)
```
</> 4.21.scala

This is done by making updated copies of the nodes in the tree that are in the direct path down to the value we wish to update, but re-using all other nodes unchanged:

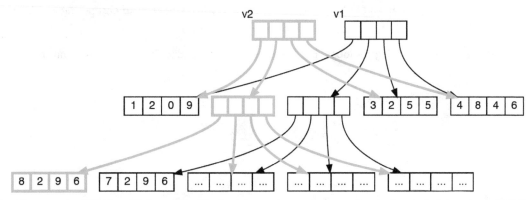

In this example Vector with 9 nodes, only 3 of the nodes end up needing to be copied. In a large Vector, the number of nodes that need to be copied is proportional to the height of the tree, while other nodes can be re-used: this structural sharing is what allows updated copies of the Vector to be created in only $O(log\ n)$ time. This is much less than the $O(n)$ time it takes to make a full copy of a mutable Array or other data structure.

Nevertheless, updating a Vector does always involve a certain amount of copying, and will never be as fast as updating mutable data structures in-place. In some cases where performance is important and you are updating a collection very frequently, you might consider using a mutable ArrayDeque (4.3.1) which has faster $O(1)$ update/append/prepend operations, or raw Arrays if you know the size of your collection in advance.

A similar tree-shaped data structure is also used to implement Immutable Sets (4.2.3) and Immutable Maps (4.2.4).

See example 4.6 - ImmutableVectors

4.2.3 Immutable Sets

Scala's immutable Sets are unordered collections of elements without duplicates, and provide an efficient $O(log\ n)$ .contains method. Sets can be constructed via + and elements removed by -, or combined via ++. Note that duplicates elements are discarded:

```
@ val s = Set(1, 2, 3)
s: Set[Int] = Set(1, 2, 3)


@ s.contains(2)
res51: Boolean = true


@ s.contains(4)
res52: Boolean = false
                              </> 4.22.scala
```

```
@ Set(1, 2, 3) + 4 + 5
res53: Set[Int] = HashSet(5, 1, 2, 3, 4)


@ Set(1, 2, 3) - 2
res54: Set[Int] = Set(1, 3)


@ Set(1, 2, 3) ++ Set(2, 3, 4)
res55: Set[Int] = Set(1, 2, 3, 4)
                              </> 4.23.scala
```

The uniqueness of items within a `Set` is also sometimes useful when you want to ensure that a collection does not contain any duplicates.

You can iterate over `Set`s using for-loops, but the order of items is undefined and should not be relied upon:

```
@ for (i <- Set(1, 2, 3, 4, 5)) println(i)
5
1
2
3
4
```
</> 4.24.scala

Most immutable `Set` operations take time $O(log\ n)$ in the size of the `Set`. This is fast enough for most purposes, but in cases where it isn't you can always fall back to Mutable Sets (*4.3.2*) for better performance. `Set`s also support the standard set of operations common to all collections.

See example 4.7 - ImmutableSets

4.2.4 Immutable Maps

Immutable maps are unordered collections of keys and values, allowing efficient lookup by key:

```
@ val m = Map("one" -> 1, "two" -> 2, "three" -> 3)
m: Map[String, Int] = Map("one" -> 1, "two" -> 2, "three" -> 3)

@ m.contains("two")
res58: Boolean = true

@ m("two")
res59: Int = 2
```
</> 4.25.scala

You can also use `.get` if you're not sure whether a map contains a key or not. This returns `Some(v)` if the key is present, `None` if not:

```
@ m.get("one")
res60: Option[Int] = Some(1)

@ m.get("four")
res61: Option[Int] = None
```
</> 4.26.scala

While `Map`s support the same set of operations as other collections, they are treated as collections of tuples representing each key-value pair. Conversions via `.to` requires a collection of tuples to convert from, `+` adds tuples to the `Map` as key-value pairs, and `for` loops iterate over tuples:

```
@ Vector(("one", 1), ("two", 2), ("three", 3)).to(Map)
res62: Map[String, Int] = Map("one" -> 1, "two" -> 2, "three" -> 3)


@ Map[String, Int]() + ("one" -> 1) + ("three" -> 3)
res63: Map[String, Int] = Map("one" -> 1, "three" -> 3)


@ for ((k, v) <- m) println(k + " " + v)
one 1
two 2
three 3                                                            </> 4.27.scala
```

Like Sets, the order of items when iterating over a Map is undefined and should not be relied upon, and most immutable Map operations take time $O(log\ n)$ in the size of the Map.

See example 4.8 - ImmutableMaps

4.2.5 Immutable Lists

```
@ val myList = List(1, 2, 3, 4, 5)
myList: List[Int] = List(1, 2, 3, 4, 5)


@ myList.head
res66: Int = 1


@ val myTail = myList.tail
myTail: List[Int] = List(2, 3, 4, 5)


@ val myOtherList = 0 :: myList
myOtherList: List[Int] = List(0, 1, 2, 3, 4, 5)


@ val myThirdList = -1 :: myList
myThirdList: List[Int] = List(-1, 1, 2, 3, 4, 5)                   </> 4.28.scala
```

Scala's immutable Lists are a singly-linked list data structure. Each node in the list has a value and pointer to the next node, terminating in a Nil node. Lists have a fast $O(1)$ .head method to look up the first item in the list, a fast $O(1)$ .tail method to create a list without the first element, and a fast $O(1)$ :: operator to create a new List with one more element in front.

.tail and :: are efficient because they can share much of the existing List: .tail returns a reference to the next node in the singly linked structure, while :: adds a new node in front. The fact that multiple lists can share nodes means that in the above example, myList, myTail, myOtherList and myThirdList are actually mostly the same data structure:

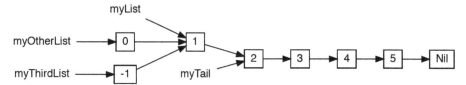

This can result in significant memory savings if you have a large number of collections that have identical elements on one side, e.g. paths on a filesystem which all share the same prefix. Rather than creating an updated copy of an `Array` in $O(n)$ time, or an updated copy of a `Vector` in $O(log\ n)$ time, pre-pending an item to a `List` is a fast $O(1)$ operation.

The downside of `Lists` is that indexed lookup via `myList(i)` is a slow $O(n)$ operation, since you need to traverse the list starting from the left to find the element you want. Appending/removing elements on the right hand side of the list is also a slow $O(n)$, since it needs to make a copy of the entire list. For use cases where you want fast indexed lookup or fast appends/removes on the right, you should consider using Vectors (*4.2.1*) or mutable ArrayDeques (*4.3.1*) instead.

See example 4.9 - ImmutableLists

4.3 Mutable Collections

Mutable collections are in general faster than their immutable counterparts when used for in-place operations. However, mutability comes at a cost: you need to be much more careful sharing them between different parts of your program. It is easy to create bugs where a shared mutable collection is updated unexpectedly, forcing you to hunt down which line in a large codebase is performing the unwanted update.

A common approach is to use mutable collections locally within a function or private to a class where there is a performance bottleneck, but to use immutable collections elsewhere where speed is less of a concern. That gives you the high performance of mutable collections where it matters most, while not sacrificing the safety that immutable collections give you throughout the bulk of your application logic.

4.3.1 Mutable ArrayDeques

ArrayDeques are general-purpose mutable, linear collections that provide efficient $O(1)$ indexed lookups, $O(1)$ indexed updates, and $O(1)$ insertion and removal at both left and right ends:

```scala
@ val myArrayDeque = collection.mutable.ArrayDeque(1, 2, 3, 4, 5)
myArrayDeque: collection.mutable.ArrayDeque[Int] = ArrayDeque(1, 2, 3, 4, 5)

@ myArrayDeque.removeHead()
res71: Int = 1

@ myArrayDeque.append(6)
res72: collection.mutable.ArrayDeque[Int] = ArrayDeque(2, 3, 4, 5, 6)

@ myArrayDeque.removeHead()
res73: Int = 2

@ myArrayDeque
res74: collection.mutable.ArrayDeque[Int] = ArrayDeque(3, 4, 5, 6)          </> 4.29.scala
```

ArrayDeques are implemented as a circular buffer, with pointers to the logical start and end of the collection within the buffer. The operations above can be visualized as follows, from left to right:

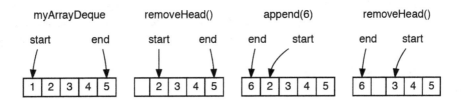

An ArrayDeque tries to re-use the same underlying Array as much as possible, only moving the start and end pointers around as elements get added or removed from either end. Only if the total number of elements grows beyond the current capacity does the underlying Array get re-allocated, and the size is increased by a fix multiple to keep the amortized cost of this re-allocation small.

As a result, operations on an ArrayDeque are much faster than the equivalent operations on an immutable Vector, which has to allocate $O(\log n)$ new tree nodes for every operation you perform.

ArrayDeques have the standard suite of Operations (4.1). They can serve many roles:

- An Array that can grow: an Array.newBuilder does not allow indexed lookup or modification while the array is being built, and an Array does not allow adding more elements. An ArrayDeque allows both

- A faster, mutable alternative to immutable `Vectors`, if you find adding/removing items from either end using `:+`/`+:` or `.tail`/`.init` is a bottleneck in your code. Appending and prepending to `ArrayDeques` is much faster than the equivalent `Vector` operations

- A first-in-first-out Queue, by inserting items to the right via `.append`, and removing items via `.removeHead`

- A first-in-last-out Stack, by inserting items to the right via `.append`, and removing items via `.removeLast`

If you want to "freeze" a mutable `ArrayDeque` into an immutable `Vector`, you can use `.to(Vector)`:

```
@ myArrayDeque.to(Vector)
res75: Vector[Int] = Vector(3, 4, 5, 6)                                    </> 4.30.scala
```

Note that this makes a copy of the entire collection.

`ArrayDeques` implement the abstract `collection.mutable.Buffer` interface, and can also be constructed via the `collection.mutable.Buffer(...)` syntax.

See example 4.10 - MutableArrayDeques

4.3.2 Mutable Sets

The Scala standard library provides mutable `Sets` as a counterpart to the immutable `Sets` we saw earlier. Mutable sets also provide efficient `.contains` checks ($O(1)$), but instead of constructing new copies of the Set via `+` and `-`, you instead add and remove elements from the Set via `.add` and `.remove`:

```
@ val s = collection.mutable.Set(1, 2, 3)        @ s.add(4)
s: mutable.Set[Int] = HashSet(1, 2, 3)

                                                 @ s.remove(1)

@ s.contains(2)
res77: Boolean = true                            @ s
                                                 res81: mutable.Set[Int] = HashSet(2, 3, 4)

@ s.contains(4)
res78: Boolean = false       </> 4.31.scala                            </> 4.32.scala
```

You can "freeze" a mutable `Set` into an immutable `Set` by using `.to(Set)`, which makes a copy you cannot mutate using `.add` or `.remove`, and convert it back to a mutable `Set` the same way. Note that each such conversion makes a copy of the entire set.

See example 4.11 - MutableSets

4.3.3 Mutable Maps

Mutable `Maps` are again just like immutable `Maps`, but allow you to mutate the `Map` by adding or removing key-value pairs:

```scala
@ val m = collection.mutable.Map("one" -> 1, "two" -> 2, "three" -> 3)
m: mutable.Map[String, Int] = HashMap("two" -> 2, "three" -> 3, "one" -> 1)

@ m.remove("two")
res83: Option[Int] = Some(2)

@ m("five") = 5

@ m
res85: mutable.Map[String, Int] = HashMap("five" -> 5, "three" -> 3, "one" -> 1)
```
</> 4.33.scala

Mutable `Maps` have a convenient `getOrElseUpdate` function, that allows you to look up a value by key, and compute/store the value if there isn't one already present:

```scala
@ val m = collection.mutable.Map("one" -> 1, "two" -> 2, "three" -> 3)

@ m.getOrElseUpdate("three", -1) // already present, returns existing value
res87: Int = 3

@ m // `m` is unchanged
res88: mutable.Map[String, Int] = HashMap("two" -> 2, "three" -> 3, "one" -> 1)

@ m.getOrElseUpdate("four", -1) // not present, stores new value in map and returns it
res89: Int = -1

@ m // `m` now contains "four" -> -1
res90: mutable.Map[String, Int] = HashMap(
  "two" -> 2,
  "three" -> 3,
  "four" -> -1,
  "one" -> 1
)
```
</> 4.34.scala

`.getOrElseUpdate` makes it convenient to use a mutable `Map` as a cache: the second parameter to `.getOrElseUpdate` is a lazy "by-name" parameter, and is only evaluated when the key is not found in the `Map`. This provides the common "check if key present, if so return value, otherwise insert new value and return that" workflow built in. We will go into more detail how by-name parameters work in **Chapter 5: Notable Scala Features**.

Chapter 4 Scala Collections

Mutable `Maps` are implemented as hash-tables, with `m(...)` lookups and `m(...) = ...` updates being efficient $O(1)$ operations.

See example 4.12 - MutableMaps

4.3.4 In-Place Operations

All mutable collections, including `Arrays`, have in-place versions of many common collection operations. These allow you to perform the operation on the mutable collection without having to make a transformed copy:

```
@ val a = collection.mutable.ArrayDeque(1, 2, 3, 4)
a: mutable.ArrayDeque[Int] = ArrayDeque(1, 2, 3, 4)


@ a.mapInPlace(_ + 1)
res92: mutable.ArrayDeque[Int] = ArrayDeque(2, 3, 4, 5)


@ a.filterInPlace(_ % 2 == 0)
res93: mutable.ArrayDeque[Int] = ArrayDeque(2, 4)


@ a // `a` was modified in place
res94: mutable.ArrayDeque[Int] = ArrayDeque(2, 4)                    </> 4.35.scala
```

Apart from those shown above, there is also `dropInPlace`, `sliceInPlace`, `sortInPlace`, etc. Using in-place operations rather than normal transformations avoids the cost of allocating new transformed collections, and can help in performance-critical scenarios.

See example 4.13 - InPlaceOperations

4.4 Common Interfaces

In many cases, a piece of code does not care exactly what collection it is working on. For example, code that just needs something that can be iterated over in order can take a `Seq[T]`:

```
@ def iterateOverSomething[T](items: Seq[T]) = {
    for (i <- items) println(i)
  }

@ iterateOverSomething(Vector(1, 2, 3))
1
2
3

@ iterateOverSomething(List(("one", 1), ("two", 2), ("three", 3)))
(one,1)
(two,2)
(three,3)
```
</> 4.36.scala

Code that needs something which provides efficient indexed lookup doesn't care if it's an `Array` or `Vector`, but cannot work with a `List`. In that case, your code can take an `IndexedSeq[T]`:

```
@ def getIndexTwoAndFour[T](items: IndexedSeq[T]) = (items(2), items(4))

@ getIndexTwoAndFour(Vector(1, 2, 3, 4, 5))
res99: (Int, Int) = (3, 5)

@ getIndexTwoAndFour(Array(2, 4, 6, 8, 10))
res100: (Int, Int) = (6, 10)
```
</> 4.37.scala

The hierarchy of data types we have seen so far is as follows:

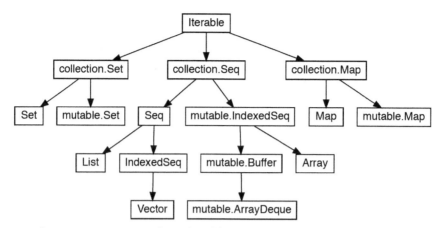

Depending on what you want your code to be able to accept, you can pick the relevant type in the hierarchy: Iterable, IndexedSeq, Seq, collection.Seq, etc. In general, most code defaults to using immutable Seqs, Sets and Maps. Mutable collections under the collection.mutable package are only used where necessary, and it is best to keep them local within a function or private to a class. collection. {Seq,Set,Map} serve as common interfaces to both mutable and immutable collections.

See example 4.14 - **CommonInterfaces**

4.5 Conclusion

In this chapter, we have gone through the basic collections that underlie the Scala standard library: Array, immutable Vector/Set/Map/List, and mutable ArrayDeque/Set/Map. We have seen how to construct collections, query them, convert one to another, and write functions that work with multiple possible collection types.

This chapter should have given you a foundation for competently working with Scala's collections library, which is widely used throughout every Scala program. We will now go through some of the more unique features of the Scala language, to round off your introduction to Scala.

Exercise: Modify the `def isValidSudoku` method we defined in this chapter to allow testing the validity of partially-filled Sudoku grids, with un-filled cells marked by the value 0.

```
@ isValidSudoku(Array(
    Array(3, 1, 6,   5, 7, 8,   4, 9, 2),
    Array(5, 2, 9,   1, 3, 4,   7, 6, 8),
    Array(4, 8, 7,   6, 2, 9,   5, 3, 1),

    Array(2, 6, 3,   0, 1, 0,   0, 8, 0),
    Array(9, 7, 4,   8, 6, 3,   0, 0, 5),
    Array(8, 5, 1,   0, 9, 0,   6, 0, 0),

    Array(1, 3, 0,   0, 0, 0,   2, 5, 0),
    Array(0, 0, 0,   0, 0, 0,   0, 7, 4),
    Array(0, 0, 5,   2, 0, 6,   3, 0, 0)
  ))
```

res101: Boolean = true   `</> 4.38.scala`

```
@ isValidSudoku(Array(
    Array(3, 1, 6,   5, 7, 8,   4, 9, 3),
    Array(5, 2, 9,   1, 3, 4,   7, 6, 8),
    Array(4, 8, 7,   6, 2, 9,   5, 3, 1),

    Array(2, 6, 3,   0, 1, 0,   0, 8, 0),
    Array(9, 7, 4,   8, 6, 3,   0, 0, 5),
    Array(8, 5, 1,   0, 9, 0,   6, 0, 0),

    Array(1, 3, 0,   0, 0, 0,   2, 5, 0),
    Array(0, 0, 0,   0, 0, 0,   0, 7, 4),
    Array(0, 0, 5,   2, 0, 6,   3, 0, 0)
  )) // top right cell should be 2
```

res102: Boolean = false   `</> 4.39.scala`

See example 4.15 - PartialValidSudoku

Exercise: Write a `def` renderSudoku method that can be used to pretty-print a Sudoku grid as shown below: with the zeroes representing unfilled cells left out, and each 3x3 square surrounded by horizontal and vertical lines.

```
@ renderSudoku(Array(              res103: String = """
    Array(3, 1, 6,    5, 7, 8,     4, 9, 2),     +-------+-------+-------+
    Array(5, 2, 9,    1, 3, 4,     7, 6, 8),     | 3 1 6 | 5 7 8 | 4 9 2 |
    Array(4, 8, 7,    6, 2, 9,     5, 3, 1),     | 5 2 9 | 1 3 4 | 7 6 8 |
                                                 | 4 8 7 | 6 2 9 | 5 3 1 |
    Array(2, 6, 3,    0, 1, 0,     0, 8, 0),     +-------+-------+-------+
    Array(9, 7, 4,    8, 6, 3,     0, 0, 5),     | 2 6 3 |   1   |   8   |
    Array(8, 5, 1,    0, 9, 0,     6, 0, 0),     | 9 7 4 | 8 6 3 |     5 |
                                                 | 8 5 1 |   9   | 6     |
    Array(1, 3, 0,    0, 0, 0,     2, 5, 0),     +-------+-------+-------+
    Array(0, 0, 0,    0, 0, 0,     0, 7, 4),     | 1 3   |       | 2 5   |
    Array(0, 0, 5,    2, 0, 6,     3, 0, 0)      |       |       |   7 4 |
))                                               |     5 | 2   6 | 3     |
                                                 +-------+-------+-------+
                    </> 4.40.scala      """
                                                        </> 4.41.output-scala
```

You might find the `Array.grouped` operator useful for this, though you can also do without it:

```
@ Array(3, 1, 6,    5, 7, 8,    4, 9, 2).grouped(3).toArray
res104: Array[Array[Int]] = Array(Array(3, 1, 6), Array(5, 7, 8), Array(4, 9, 2))
                                                                   </> 4.42.scala
```

See example 4.16 - RenderSudoku

Discuss Chapter 4 online at https://www.handsonscala.com/discuss/4

5

Notable Scala Features

5.1 Case Classes and Sealed Traits   82

5.2 Pattern Matching   85

5.3 By-Name Parameters   90

5.4 Implicit Parameters   93

5.5 Typeclass Inference   96

```scala
@ def getDayMonthYear(s: String) = s match {
    case s"$day-$month-$year" => println(s"found day: $day, month: $month, year: $year")
    case _ => println("not a date")
  }

@ getDayMonthYear("9-8-1965")
found day: 9, month: 8, year: 1965

@ getDayMonthYear("9-8")
not a date                                                    </> 5.1.scala
```

Snippet 5.1: using Scala's pattern matching feature to parse simple string patterns

This chapter will cover some of the more interesting and unusual features of Scala. For each such feature, we will cover both what the feature does as well as some common use cases to give you an intuition for what it is useful for.

Not every feature in this chapter will be something you use day-to-day. Nevertheless, even these less-commonly-used features are used often enough that it is valuable to have a high-level understanding for when you eventually encounter them in the wild.

5.1 Case Classes and Sealed Traits

5.1.1 Case Classes

case classes are like normal classes, but meant to represent classes which are "just data": where all the data is immutable and public, without any mutable state or encapsulation. Their use case is similar to "structs" in C/C++, "POJOs" in Java or "Data Classes" in Python or Kotlin. Their name comes from the fact that they support pattern matching (5.2) via the case keyword.

Case classes are defined with the case keyword, and can be instantiated without new. All of their constructor parameters are public fields by default.

```scala
@ case class Point(x: Int, y: Int)

@ val p = Point(1, 2)
p: Point = Point(1, 2)
```
</> 5.2.scala

```scala
@ p.x
res2: Int = 1

@ p.y
res3: Int = 2
```
</> 5.3.scala

case class s give you a few things for free:

- A .toString implemented to show you the constructor parameter values

- A == implemented to check if the constructor parameter values are equal

- A .copy method to conveniently create modified copies of the case class instance

```scala
@ p.toString
res4: String = "Point(1,2)"

@ val p2 = Point(1, 2)

@ p == p2
res6: Boolean = true
```
</> 5.4.scala

```scala
@ val p = Point(1, 2)

@ val p3 = p.copy(y = 10)
p3: Point = Point(1, 10)

@ val p4 = p3.copy(x = 20)
p4: Point = Point(20, 10)
```
</> 5.5.scala

Like normal classes, you can define instance methods or properties in the body of the case class:

```scala
@ case class Point(x: Int, y: Int) {
    def z = x + y
}
```
</> 5.6.scala

```scala
@ val p = Point(1, 2)

@ p.z
res12: Int = 3
```
</> 5.7.scala

case classes are a good replacement for large tuples, since instead of extracting their values via ._1 ._2 ._7 you can extract the values via their names like .x and .y. That is much easier than trying to remember exactly what field ._7 in a large tuple represents!

5.1.2 Sealed Traits

traits can also be defined sealed, and only extended by a fixed set of case classes. In the following example, we define a sealed trait Point extended by two case classes: Point2D and Point3D:

```
@ {
  sealed trait Point
  case class Point2D(x: Double, y: Double) extends Point
  case class Point3D(x: Double, y: Double, z: Double) extends Point
  }

@ def hypotenuse(p: Point) = p match {
    case Point2D(x, y) => math.sqrt(x * x + y * y)
    case Point3D(x, y, z) => math.sqrt(x * x + y * y + z * z)
  }

@ val points: Array[Point] = Array(Point2D(1, 2), Point3D(4, 5, 6))

@ for (p <- points) println(hypotenuse(p))
2.23606797749979
8.774964387392123                                                    </> 5.8.scala
```

The core difference between normal traits and sealed traits can be summarized as follows:

- Normal traits are *open*, so any number of classes can inherit from the trait as long as they provide all the required methods, and instances of those classes can be used interchangeably via the trait's required methods.

- sealed traits are *closed*: they only allow a fixed set of classes to inherit from them, and all inheriting classes must be defined together with the trait itself in the same file or REPL command (hence the curlies {} surrounding the Point/Point2D/Point3D definitions above).

Because there are only a fixed number of classes inheriting from sealed trait Point, we can use pattern matching in the def hypotenuse function above to define how each kind of Point should be handled.

5.1.3 Use Cases for Normal v.s. Sealed Traits

Both normal traits and sealed traits are common in Scala applications: normal traits for interfaces which may have any number of subclasses, and sealed traits where the number of subclasses is fixed.

Normal traits and sealed traits make different things easy:

- A normal `trait` hierarchy makes it easy to add additional sub-classes: just define your class and implement the necessary methods. However, it makes it difficult to add new methods: a new method needs to be added to all existing subclasses, of which there may be many.

- A `sealed trait` hierarchy is the opposite: it is easy to add new methods, since a new method can simply pattern match on each sub-class and decide what it wants to do for each. However, adding new sub-classes is difficult, as you need to go to all existing pattern matches and add the `case` to handle your new sub-class

In general, `sealed trait`s are good for modelling hierarchies where you expect the number of sub-classes to change very little or not-at-all. A good example of something that can be modeled using `sealed trait` is JSON:

```scala
@ {
  sealed trait Json
  case class Null() extends Json
  case class Bool(value: Boolean) extends Json
  case class Str(value: String) extends Json
  case class Num(value: Double) extends Json
  case class Arr(value: Seq[Json]) extends Json
  case class Dict(value: Map[String, Json]) extends Json
}
```
</> 5.9.scala

- A JSON value can only be JSON null, boolean, number, string, array, or dictionary.

- JSON has not changed in 20 years, so it is unlikely that anyone will need to extend our JSON `trait` with additional subclasses.

- While the set of sub-classes is fixed, the range of operations we may want to do on a JSON blob is unbounded: parse it, serialize it, pretty-print it, minify it, sanitize it, etc.

Thus it makes sense to model a JSON data structure as a closed `sealed trait` hierarchy rather than a normal open `trait` hierarchy.

See example 5.2 - SealedTrait

5.2 Pattern Matching

5.2.1 Match

Scala allows pattern matching on values using the `match` keyword. This is similar to the `switch` statement found in other programming languages, but more flexible: apart from `match`ing on primitive integers and strings, you can also use `match` to extract values from ("destructure") composite data types like tuples and `case class`es. Note that in many examples below, there is a `case _ =>` clause which defines the default case if none of the earlier cases matched.

5.2.1.1 Matching on `Int`s

```scala
@ def dayOfWeek(x: Int) = x match {
    case 1 => "Mon"; case 2 => "Tue"
    case 3 => "Wed"; case 4 => "Thu"
    case 5 => "Fri"; case 6 => "Sat"
    case 7 => "Sun"; case _ => "Unknown"
  }


@ dayOfWeek(5)
res19: String = "Fri"


@ dayOfWeek(-1)
res20: String = "Unknown"          </> 5.10.scala
```

5.2.1.2 Matching on `string`s

```scala
@ def indexOfDay(d: String) = d match {
    case "Mon" => 1; case "Tue" => 2
    case "Wed" => 3; case "Thu" => 4
    case "Fri" => 5; case "Sat" => 6
    case "Sun" => 7; case _ => -1
  }


@ indexOfDay("Fri")
res22: Int = 5


@ indexOfDay("???")
res23: Int = -1          </> 5.11.scala
```

5.2.1.3 Matching on tuple `(Int, Int)`

```scala
@ for (i <- Range.inclusive(1, 100)) {
    val s = (i % 3, i % 5) match {
      case (0, 0) => "FizzBuzz"
      case (0, _) => "Fizz"
      case (_, 0) => "Buzz"
      case _ => i
    }
    println(s)
  }
1
2
Fizz
4
Buzz
...                  </> 5.12.scala
```

5.2.1.4 Matching on tuple `(Boolean, Boolean)`

```scala
@ for (i <- Range.inclusive(1, 100)) {
    val s = (i % 3 == 0, i % 5 == 0) match {
      case (true, true) => "FizzBuzz"
      case (true, false) => "Fizz"
      case (false, true) => "Buzz"
      case (false, false) => i
    }
    println(s)
  }
1
2
Fizz
4
Buzz
...                  </> 5.13.scala
```

5.2.1.5 Matching on Case Classes:

```
@ case class Point(x: Int, y: Int)

@ def direction(p: Point) = p match {
    case Point(0, 0) => "origin"
    case Point(_, 0) => "horizontal"
    case Point(0, _) => "vertical"
    case _ => "diagonal"
  }

@ direction(Point(0, 0))
res28: String = "origin"

@ direction(Point(1, 1))
res29: String = "diagonal"

@ direction(Point(10, 0))
res30: String = "horizontal"
```
</> 5.14.scala

5.2.1.6 Matching on String Patterns:

```
@ def splitDate(s: String) = s match {
    case s"$day-$month-$year" =>
      s"day: $day, mon: $month, yr: $year"
    case _ => "not a date"
  }

@ splitDate("9-8-1965")
res32: String = "day: 9, mon: 8, yr: 1965"

@ splitDate("9-8")
res33: String = "not a date"
```
</> 5.15.scala

(Note that pattern matching on string patterns only supports simple glob-like patterns, and doesn't support richer patterns like Regular Expressions. For those, you can use the functionality of the scala.util.matching.Regex class)

5.2.2 Nested Matches

Patterns can also be nested, e.g. this example matches a string pattern within a case class pattern:

```
@ case class Person(name: String, title: String)

@ def greet(p: Person) = p match {
    case Person(s"$firstName $lastName", title) => println(s"Hello $title $lastName")
    case Person(name, title) => println(s"Hello $title $name")
  }

@ greet(Person("Haoyi Li", "Mr"))
Hello Mr Li

@ greet(Person("Who?", "Dr"))
Hello Dr Who?
```
</> 5.16.scala

Patterns can be nested arbitrarily deeply. The following example matches string patterns, inside a case class, inside a tuple:

```
@ def greet2(husband: Person, wife: Person) = (husband, wife) match {
    case (Person(s"$first1 $last1", _), Person(s"$first2 $last2", _)) if last1 == last2 =>
      println(s"Hello Mr and Ms $last1")

    case (Person(name1, _), Person(name2, _)) => println(s"Hello $name1 and $name2")
  }

@ greet2(Person("James Bond", "Mr"), Person("Jane Bond", "Ms"))
Hello Mr and Ms Bond

@ greet2(Person("James Bond", "Mr"), Person("Jane", "Ms"))
Hello James Bond and Jane                                          </> 5.17.scala
```

5.2.3 Loops and Vals

The last two places you an use pattern matching are inside `for`-loops and `val` definitions. Pattern matching in `for`-loops is useful when you need to iterate over collections of tuples:

```
@ val a = Array[(Int, String)]((1, "one"), (2, "two"), (3, "three"))

@ for ((i, s) <- a) println(s + i)
one1
two2
three3                                                             </> 5.18.scala
```

Pattern matching in `val` statements is useful when you are sure the value will match the given pattern, and all you want to do is extract the parts you want. If the value doesn't match, this fails with an exception:

```
@ case class Point(x: Int, y: Int)

@ val p = Point(123, 456)

@ val Point(x, y) = p
x: Int = 123
y: Int = 456
```
</> 5.19.scala

```
@ val s"$first $second" = "Hello World"
first: String = "Hello"
second: String = "World"

@ val flipped = s"$second $first"
flipped: String = "World Hello"

@ val s"$first $second" = "Hello"
scala.MatchError: Hello
```
</> 5.20.scala

5.2.4 Pattern Matching on Sealed Traits and Case Classes

Pattern matching lets you elegantly work with structured data comprising case classes and sealed traits. For example, let's consider a simple sealed trait that represents arithmetic expressions:

```
@ {
  sealed trait Expr
  case class BinOp(left: Expr, op: String, right: Expr) extends Expr
  case class Literal(value: Int) extends Expr
  case class Variable(name: String) extends Expr
}
                                                                    </> 5.21.scala
```

Where BinOp stands for "Binary Operation". This can represent the arithmetic expressions, such as the following

x + 1	BinOp(Variable("x"), "+", Literal(1))

x * (y - 1)	BinOp(
	  Variable("x"),
	  "*",
	  BinOp(Variable("y"), "-", Literal(1))
	) </> 5.22.scala

(x + 1) * (y - 1)	BinOp(
	  BinOp(Variable("x"), "+", Literal(1)),
	  "*",
	  BinOp(Variable("y"), "-", Literal(1))
	) </> 5.23.scala

For now, we will ignore the parsing process that turns the string on the left into the structured case class structure on the right: we will cover that in **Chapter 19: Parsing Structured Text**. Let us instead consider two things you may want to do once you have parsed such an arithmetic expression to the case classes we see above: we may want to print it to a human-friendly string, or we may want to evaluate it given some variable values.

5.2.4.1 Stringifying Our Expressions

Converting the expressions to a string can be done using the following approach:

- If an Expr is a Literal, the string is the value of the literal
- If an Expr is a Variable, the string is the name of the variable
- If an Expr is a BinOp, the string is the stringified left expression, followed by the operation, followed by the stringified right expression

Converted to pattern matching code, this can be written as follows:

```
@ def stringify(expr: Expr): String = expr match {
    case BinOp(left, op, right) => s"(${stringify(left)} $op ${stringify(right)})"
    case Literal(value) => value.toString
    case Variable(name) => name
  }
```
</> 5.24.scala

We can construct some of `Exprs` we saw earlier and feed them into our `stringify` function to see the output:

```
@ val smallExpr = BinOp(
    Variable("x"),
    "+",
    Literal(1)
  )
```

```
@ stringify(smallExpr)
res52: String = "(x + 1)"
```
</> 5.25.scala

```
@ val largeExpr = BinOp(
    BinOp(Variable("x"), "+", Literal(1)),
    "*",
    BinOp(Variable("y"), "-", Literal(1))
  )
```

```
@ stringify(largeExpr)
res54: String = "((x + 1) * (y - 1))"
```
</> 5.26.scala

5.2.4.2 Evaluating Our Expressions

Evaluation is a bit more complex than stringifying the expressions, but only slightly. We need to pass in a `values` map that holds the numeric value of every variable, and we need to treat +, -, and * operations differently:

```
@ def evaluate(expr: Expr, values: Map[String, Int]): Int = expr match {
    case BinOp(left, "+", right) => evaluate(left, values) + evaluate(right, values)
    case BinOp(left, "-", right) => evaluate(left, values) - evaluate(right, values)
    case BinOp(left, "*", right) => evaluate(left, values) * evaluate(right, values)
    case Literal(value) => value
    case Variable(name) => values(name)
  }

@ evaluate(smallExpr, Map("x" -> 10))
res56: Int = 11

@ evaluate(largeExpr, Map("x" -> 10, "y" -> 20))
res57: Int = 209
```
</> 5.27.scala

Overall, this looks relatively similar to the `stringify` function we wrote earlier: a recursive function that pattern matches on the `expr: Expr` parameter to handle each case class that implements `Expr`. The cases handling child-free `Literal` and `Variable` are trivial, while in the `BinOp` case we recurse on both left and right children before combining the result. This is a common way of working with recursive data structures in any language, and Scala's sealed traits, case classes and pattern matching make it concise and easy.

This `Expr` structure and the printer and evaluator we have written are intentionally simplistic, just to give us a chance to see how pattern matching can be used to easily work with structured data modeled as `case` `class`es and `sealed traits`. We will be exploring these techniques much more deeply in **Chapter 20: Implementing a Programming Language**.

See example 5.3 - PatternMatching

5.3 By-Name Parameters

```
@ def func(arg: => String) = ...
```

Scala also supports "by-name" method parameters using a `: => T` syntax, which are evaluated each time they are referenced in the method body. This has three primary use cases:

1. Avoiding evaluation if the argument does not end up being used
2. Wrapping evaluation to run setup and teardown code before and after the argument evaluates
3. Repeating evaluation of the argument more than once

5.3.1 Avoiding Evaluation

The following `log` method uses a by-name parameter to avoid evaluating the `msg: => String` unless it is actually going to get printed. This can help avoid spending CPU time constructing log messages (here via `"Hello " + 123 + " World"`) even when logging is disabled:

```
@ var logLevel = 1

@ def log(level: Int, msg: => String) = {
    if (level > logLevel) println(msg)
  }
                              </> 5.28.scala
```

```
@ log(2, "Hello " + 123 + " World")
Hello 123 World

@ logLevel = 3

@ log(2, "Hello " + 123 + " World")
<no output>
                              </> 5.29.scala
```

Often a method does not end up using all of its arguments all the time. In the above example, by not computing log messages when they are not needed, we can save a significant amount of CPU time and object allocations which may make a difference in performance-sensitive applications.

The `getOrElse` and `getOrElseUpdate` methods we saw in **Chapter 4: Scala Collections** are similar: these methods do not use the argument representing the default value if the value we are looking for is already present. By making the default value a by-name parameter, we do not have to evaluate it in the case where it does not get used.

5.3.2 Wrapping Evaluation

Using by-name parameters to "wrap" the evaluation of your method in some setup/teardown code is another common pattern. The following measureTime function defers evaluation of f: => Unit, allowing us to run System.currentTimeMillis() before and after the argument is evaluated and thus print out the time taken:

```scala
@ def measureTime(f: => Unit) = {
    val start = System.currentTimeMillis()
    f
    val end = System.currentTimeMillis()
    println("Evaluation took " + (end - start) + " milliseconds")
}

@ measureTime(new Array[String](10 * 1000 * 1000).hashCode())
Evaluation took 24 milliseconds

@ measureTime { // methods taking a single arg can also be called with curly brackets
    new Array[String](100 * 1000 * 1000).hashCode()
}
Evaluation took 287 milliseconds
```

</> 5.30.scala

There are many other use cases for such wrapping:

- Setting some thread-local context while the argument is being evaluated
- Evaluating the argument inside a try-catch block so we can handle exceptions
- Evaluating the argument in a Future so the logic runs asynchronously on another thread

These are all cases where using by-name parameter can help.

5.3.3 Repeating Evaluation

The last use case we will cover for by-name parameters is repeating evaluation of the method argument. The following snippet defines a generic `retry` method: this method takes in an argument, evaluates it within a `try-catch` block, and re-executes it on failure with a maximum number of attempts. We test this by using it to wrap a call which may fail, and seeing the `retrying` messages get printed to the console.

```scala
@ def retry[T](max: Int)(f: => T): T = {
    var tries = 0
    var result: Option[T] = None
    while (result == None) {
      try { result = Some(f) }
      catch {case e: Throwable =>
        tries += 1
        if (tries > max) throw e
        else {
          println(s"failed, retry #$tries")
        }
      }
    }
    result.get
  }
                                    </> 5.31.scala
```

```scala
@ val httpbin = "https://httpbin.org"

@ retry(max = 5) {
    // Only succeeds with a 200 response
    // code 1/3 of the time
    requests.get(
      s"$httpbin/status/200,400,500"
    )
  }
call failed, retry #1
call failed, retry #2
res68: requests.Response = Response(
  "https://httpbin.org/status/200,400,500",
  200,
...                                 </> 5.32.scala
```

Above we define `retry` as a generic function taking a type parameter `[T]`, taking a by-name parameter that computes a value of type `T`, and returning a `T` once the code block is successful. We can then use `retry` to wrap a code block of any type, and it will retry that block and return the first `T` it successfully computes.

Making `retry` take a by-name parameter is what allows it to repeat evaluation of the `requests.get` block where necessary. Other use cases for repetition include running performance benchmarks or performing load tests. In general, by-name parameters aren't something you use very often, but when necessary they let you write code that manipulates the evaluation of a method argument in a variety of useful ways: instrumenting it, retrying it, eliding it, etc.

We will learn more about the `requests` library that we used in the above snippet in **Chapter 12: Working with HTTP APIs**.

See example 5.4 - ByName

5.4 Implicit Parameters

An *implicit parameter* is a parameter that is automatically filled in for you when calling a function. For example, consider the following class `Foo` and the function `bar` that takes an `implicit foo: Foo` parameter:

```
@ class Foo(val value: Int)


@ def bar(implicit foo: Foo) = foo.value + 10                          </> 5.33.scala
```

If you try to call `bar` without an implicit `Foo` in scope, you get a compilation error. To call `bar`, you need to define an implicit value of the type `Foo`, such that the call to `bar` can automatically resolve it from the enclosing scope:

```
@ bar
cmd4.sc:1: could not find implicit
         value for parameter foo: Foo
val res4 = bar
         ^
Compilation Failed

                          </> 5.34.scala
```

```
@ implicit val foo: Foo = new Foo(1)
foo: Foo = ammonite.$sess.cmd1$Foo@451882b2


@ bar // `foo` is resolved implicitly
res72: Int = 11


@ bar(foo) // passing in `foo` explicitly
res73: Int = 11               </> 5.35.scala
```

Implicit parameters are similar to the *default values* we saw in **Chapter 3: Basic Scala**. Both of them allow you to pass in a value explicitly or fall back to some default. The main difference is that while default values are "hard coded" at the definition site of the method, implicit parameters take their default value from whatever `implicit` is in scope at the call-site.

We'll now look into a more concrete example where using implicit parameters can help keep your code clean and readable, before going into a more advanced use case of the feature for Typeclass Inference (*5.5*).

5.4.1 Passing ExecutionContext to Futures

As an example, code using `Future` needs an `ExecutionContext` value in order to work. As a result, we end up passing this `ExecutionContext` everywhere, which is tedious and verbose:

```scala
def getEmployee(ec: ExecutionContext, id: Int): Future[Employee] = ...
def getRole(ec: ExecutionContext, employee: Employee): Future[Role] = ...


val executionContext: ExecutionContext = ...

val bigEmployee: Future[EmployeeWithRole] = {
  getEmployee(executionContext, 100).flatMap(
    executionContext,
    e =>
      getRole(executionContext, e)
        .map(executionContext, r => EmployeeWithRole(e, r))
  )
}
```
</> 5.36.scala

`getEmployee` and `getRole` perform asynchronous actions, which we then `map` and `flatMap` to do further work. Exactly how the `Future`s work is beyond the scope of this section: for now, what is notable is how every operation needs to be passed the `executionContext` to do their work. We will will revisit these APIs in **Chapter 13: Fork-Join Parallelism with Futures**.

Without implicit parameters, we have the following options:

- Passing `executionContext` explicitly is verbose and can make your code harder to read: the logic we care about is drowned in a sea of boilerplate `executionContext` passing

- Making `executionContext` global would be concise, but would lose the flexibility of passing different values in different parts of your program

- Putting `executionContext` into a thread-local variable would maintain flexibility and conciseness, but it is error-prone and easy to forget to set the thread-local before running code that needs it

All of these options have tradeoffs, forcing us to either sacrifice conciseness, flexibility, or safety. Scala's implicit parameters provide a fourth option: passing `executionContext` implicitly, which gives us the conciseness, flexibility, and safety that the above options are unable to give us.

5.4.2 Dependency Injection via Implicits

To resolve these issues, we can make all these functions take the `executionContext` as an implicit parameter. This is already the case for standard library operations like `flatMap` and `map` on `Futures`, and we can modify our `getEmployee` and `getRole` functions to follow suit. By defining `executionContext` as an `implicit`, it will automatically get picked up by all the method calls below.

```scala
def getEmployee(id: Int)(implicit ec: ExecutionContext): Future[Employee] = ...
def getRole(employee: Employee)(implicit ec: ExecutionContext): Future[Role] = ...

implicit val executionContext: ExecutionContext = ...

val bigEmployee: Future[EmployeeWithRole] = {
  getEmployee(100).flatMap(e =>
    getRole(e).map(r =>
      EmployeeWithRole(e, r)
    )
  )
}
```
</> 5.37.scala

Using implicit parameters can help clean up code where we pass the same shared context or configuration object throughout your entire application:

- By making the "uninteresting" parameter passing implicit, it can focus the reader's attention on the core logic of your application.

- Since implicit parameters can be passed explicitly, they preserve the flexibility for the developer in case they want to manually specify or override the implicit parameter being passed.

- The fact that missing implicits are a compile time error makes their usage much less error-prone than thread-locals. A missing implicit will be caught early on before code is compiled and deployed to production.

See example 5.5 - ImplicitParameters

5.5 Typeclass Inference

A second way that implicit parameters are useful is by using them to associate values to types. This is often called a *typeclass*, the term originating from the Haskell programming language, although it has nothing to do with types and classes in Scala. While typeclasses are a technique built on the same implicit language feature described earlier, they are an interesting and important enough technique to deserve their own section in this chapter.

5.5.1 Problem Statement: Parsing Command Line Arguments

Let us consider the task of parsing command-line arguments, given as Strings, into Scala values of various types: Ints, Booleans, Doubles, etc. This is a common task that almost every program has to deal with, either directly or by using a library.

A first sketch may be writing a generic method to parse the values. The signature might look something like this:

```scala
def parseFromString[T](s: String): T = ...

val args = Seq("123", "true", "7.5")
val myInt = parseFromString[Int](args(0))
val myBoolean = parseFromString[Boolean](args(1))
val myDouble = parseFromString[Double](args(2))
```
</> 5.38.scala

On the surface this seems impossible to implement:

- How does the parseCliArgument know how to convert the given String into an arbitrary T?

- How does it know what types T a command-line argument can be parsed into, and which it cannot? For example, we should not be able to parse a java.net.DatagramSocket from an input string.

5.5.2 Separate Parser Objects

A second sketch at a solution may be to define separate parser objects, one for each type we need to be able to parse. For example:

```scala
trait StrParser[T]{ def parse(s: String): T }
object ParseInt extends StrParser[Int]{ def parse(s: String) = s.toInt }
object ParseBoolean extends StrParser[Boolean]{ def parse(s: String) = s.toBoolean }
object ParseDouble extends StrParser[Double]{ def parse(s: String) = s.toDouble }
```
</> 5.39.scala

We can then call these as follows:

```scala
val args = Seq("123", "true", "7.5")
val myInt = ParseInt.parse(args(0))
val myBoolean = ParseBoolean.parse(args(1))
val myDouble = ParseDouble.parse(args(2))                          </> 5.40.scala
```

This works. However, it then leads to another problem: if we wanted to write a method that didn't parse a string directly, but parsed a value from the console, how would we do that? We have two options.

5.5.2.1 Re-Using Our StrParsers

The first option is writing a whole new set of `object`s dedicated to parsing from the console:

```scala
trait ConsoleParser[T]{ def parse(): T }
object ConsoleParseInt extends ConsoleParser[Int]{
  def parse() = scala.Console.in.readLine().toInt
}
object ConsoleParseBoolean extends ConsoleParser[Boolean]{
  def parse() = scala.Console.in.readLine().toBoolean
}
object ConsoleParseDouble extends ConsoleParser[Double]{
  def parse() = scala.Console.in.readLine().toDouble
}

val myInt = ConsoleParseInt.parse()
val myBoolean = ConsoleParseBoolean.parse()
val myDouble = ConsoleParseDouble.parse()                         </> 5.41.scala
```

The second option is defining a helper method that receives a `StrParser[T]` as an argument, which we would need to pass in to tell it how to parse the type `T`

```scala
def parseFromConsole[T](parser: StrParser[T]) = parser.parse(scala.Console.in.readLine())

val myInt = parseFromConsole[Int](ParseInt)
val myBoolean = parseFromConsole[Boolean](ParseBoolean)
val myDouble = parseFromConsole[Double](ParseDouble)              </> 5.42.scala
```

Both of these solutions are clunky:

1. The first because we need to duplicate all the `Int`/`Boolean`/`Double`/etc. parsers. What if we need to parse input from the network? From files? We would need to duplicate every parser for each case.

2. The second because we need to pass these `ParseFoo` objects everywhere. Often there is only a single `StrParser[Int]` we can pass to `parseFromConsole[Int]`. Why can't the compiler infer it for us?

5.5.3 Solution: Implicit StrParser

The solution to the problems above is to make the instances of StrParser `implicit`:

```scala
trait StrParser[T]{ def parse(s: String): T }
object StrParser{
  implicit object ParseInt extends StrParser[Int]{
    def parse(s: String) = s.toInt
  }
  implicit object ParseBoolean extends StrParser[Boolean]{
    def parse(s: String) = s.toBoolean
  }
  implicit object ParseDouble extends StrParser[Double]{
    def parse(s: String) = s.toDouble
  }
}
```
</> 5.43.scala

We put the `implicit object` ParseInt, ParseBoolean, etc. in an `object` StrParser with the same name as the `trait` StrParser next to it. An `object` with the same name as a `class` that it is defined next to is called a *companion object*. Companion objects are often used to group together implicits, static methods, factory methods, and other functionality that is related to a `trait` or `class` but does not belong to any specific instance. Implicits in the companion object are also treated specially, and do not need to be imported into scope in order to be used as an implicit parameter.

Note that if you are entering this into the Ammonite Scala REPL, you need to surround both declarations with an extra pair of curly brackets `{...}` so that both the `trait` and `object` are defined in the same REPL command.

Now, while we can still explicitly call `ParseInt.parse(args(0))` to parse literal strings as before, we can now write a generic function that automatically uses the correct instance of StrParser depending on what type we asked it to parse:

```scala
def parseFromString[T](s: String)(implicit parser: StrParser[T]) = {
  parser.parse(s)
}

val args = Seq("123", "true", "7.5")
val myInt = parseFromString[Int](args(0))
val myBoolean = parseFromString[Boolean](args(1))
val myDouble = parseFromString[Double](args(2))
```
</> 5.44.scala

This looks similar to our initial sketch, except by taking an `(implicit parser: StrParser[T])` parameter the function can now automatically infer the correct StrParser for each type it is trying to parse.

5.5.3.1 Re-Using Our Implicit StrParsers

Making our `StrParser[T]`s implicit means we can re-use them without duplicating our parsers or passing them around manually. For example, we can write a function that parses strings from the console:

```scala
def parseFromConsole[T](implicit parser: StrParser[T]) = {
  parser.parse(scala.Console.in.readLine())
}


val myInt = parseFromConsole[Int]
```
</> 5.45.scala

The call to `parseFromConsole[Int]` automatically infers the `StrParser.ParseInt` implicit in the `StrParser` companion object, without needing to duplicate it or tediously pass it around. That makes it very easy to write code that works with a generic type `T` as long as `T` has a suitable `StrParser`.

5.5.3.2 Context-Bound Syntax

This technique of taking an implicit parameter with a generic type is common enough that the Scala language provides dedicated syntax for it. The following method signature:

```scala
def parseFromString[T](s: String)(implicit parser: StrParser[T]) = ...
```

Can be written more concisely as:

```scala
def parseFromString[T: StrParser](s: String) = ...
```

This syntax is referred to as a *context bound*, and it is semantically equivalent to the `(implicit parser: StrParser[T])` syntax above. When using the context bound syntax, the implicit parameter isn't given a name, and so we cannot call `parser.parse` like we did earlier. Instead, we can resolve the implicit values via the `implicitly` function, e.g. `implicitly[StrParser[T]].parse`.

5.5.3.3 Compile-Time Implicit Safety

As Typeclass Inference uses the the same `implicit` language feature we saw earlier, mistakes such as attempting to call `parseFromConsole` with an invalid type produce a compile error:

```scala
@ val myDatagramSocket = parseFromConsole[java.net.DatagramSocket]
cmd19.sc:1: could not find implicit value for parameter parser:
          ammonite.$sess.cmd11.StrParser[java.net.DatagramSocket]
val myDatagramSocket = parseFromConsole[java.net.DatagramSocket]
                       ^
Compilation Failed
```
</> 5.46.scala

Similarly, if you try to call a method taking an `(implicit parser: StrParser[T])` from another method that does not have such an implicit available, the compiler will also raise an error:

```
@ def genericMethodWithoutImplicit[T](s: String) = parseFromString[T](s)
cmd2.sc:1: could not find implicit value for parameter parser:
          ammonite.$sess.cmd0.StrParser[T]
def genericMethodWithoutImplicit[T](s: String) = parseFromString[T](s)
                                                                    ^
```

Compilation Failed   </> *5.47.scala*

Most of the things we have done with Typeclass Inference could also be achieved using runtime reflection. However, relying on runtime reflection is fragile, and it is very easy for mistakes, bugs, or mis-configurations to make it to production before failing catastrophically. In contrast, Scala's `implicit` feature lets you achieve the same outcome but in a safe fashion: mistakes are caught early at compile-time, and you can fix them at your leisure rather than under the pressure of a ongoing production outage.

5.5.4 Recursive Typeclass Inference

We have already seen how we can use the typeclass technique to automatically pick which `StrParser` to use based on the type we want to parse to. This can also work for more complex types, where we tell the compiler we want a `Seq[Int]`, `(Int, Boolean)`, or even nested types like `Seq[(Int, Boolean)]`, and the compiler will automatically assemble the logic necessary to parse the type we want.

5.5.4.1 Parsing Sequences

For example, the following `ParseSeq` function provides a `StrParser[Seq[T]]` for any T which itself has an implicit `StrParser[T]` in scope:

```
implicit def ParseSeq[T](implicit p: StrParser[T]) = new StrParser[Seq[T]]{
  def parse(s: String) = s.split(',').toSeq.map(p.parse)
}
```
</> *5.48.scala*

Note that unlike the `implicit objects` we defined earlier which are singletons, here we have an `implicit def`. Depending on the type T, we would need a different `StrParser[T]`, and thus need a different `StrParser[Seq[T]]`. `implicit def ParseSeq` would thus return a different `StrParser` each time it is called with a different type T.

From this one defintion, we can now parse `Seq[Boolean]`s, `Seq[Int]`s, etc.

```
@ parseFromString[Seq[Boolean]]("true,false,true")
res99: Seq[Boolean] = ArraySeq(true, false, true)


@ parseFromString[Seq[Int]]("1,2,3,4")
res100: Seq[Int] = ArraySeq(1, 2, 3, 4)
```
</> *5.49.scala*

What we are effectively doing is teaching the compiler how to produce a `StrParser[Seq[T]]` for any type T as long as it has an implicit `StrParser[T]` available. Since we already have `StrParser[Int]`, `StrParser[Boolean]`, and `StrParser[Double]` available, the `ParseSeq` method gives `StrParser[Seq[Int]]`, `StrParser[Seq[Boolean]]`, and `StrParser[Seq[Double]]` for free.

The `StrParser[Seq[T]]` we are instantiating has a parse method that receives a parameter `s: String` and returns a `Seq[T]`. We just needed to implement the logic necessary to do that transformation, which we have done in the code snippet above.

5.5.4.2 Parsing Tuples

Similar to how we defined an `implicit def` to parse `Seq[T]`s, we could do the same to parse tuples. We do so below by assuming that tuples are represented by `key=value` pairs in the input string:

```scala
implicit def ParseTuple[T, V](implicit p1: StrParser[T], p2: StrParser[V]) =
  new StrParser[(T, V)]{
    def parse(s: String) = {
      val Array(left, right) = s.split('=')
      (p1.parse(left), p2.parse(right))
    }
  }
```
</> 5.50.scala

This definition produces a `StrParser[(T, V)]`, but only for a type `T` and type `V` for which there are `StrParser`s available. Now we can parse tuples, as `=`-separated pairs:

```scala
@ parseFromString[(Int, Boolean)]("123=true")
res102: (Int, Boolean) = (123, true)


@ parseFromString[(Boolean, Double)]("true=1.5")
res103: (Boolean, Double) = (true, 1.5)
```
</> 5.51.scala

5.5.4.3 Parsing Nested Structures

The two definitions above, `implicit def ParseSeq` and `implicit def ParseTuple`, are enough to let us also parse sequences of tuples, or tuples of sequences:

```scala
@ parseFromString[Seq[(Int, Boolean)]]("1=true,2=false,3=true,4=false")
res104: Seq[(Int, Boolean)] = ArraySeq((1, true), (2, false), (3, true), (4, false))


@ parseFromString[(Seq[Int], Seq[Boolean])]("1,2,3,4,5=true,false,true")
res105: (Seq[Int], Seq[Boolean]) = (ArraySeq(1, 2, 3, 4, 5), ArraySeq(true, false, true))
```
</> 5.52.scala

Note that in this case we cannot handle nested `Seq[Seq[T]]`s or nested tuples due to how we're naively splitting the input string. A more structured parser handles such cases without issues, allowing us to specify an arbitrarily complex output type and automatically inferring the necessary parser. We will use a serialization library that uses this technique in **Chapter 8: JSON and Binary Data Serialization**.

Most statically typed programming languages can infer types to some degree: even if not every expression is annotated with an explicit type, the compiler can still figure out the types based on the program structure. Typeclass derivation is effectively the reverse: by providing an explicit type, the compiler can infer the program structure necessary to provide a value of the type we are looking for.

In the example above, we just need to define how to handle the basic types - how to produce a StrParser[Boolean], StrParser[Int], StrParser[Seq[T]], StrParser[(T, V)] - and the compiler is able to figure out how to produce a StrParser[Seq[(Int, Boolean)]] when we need it.

See example 5.6 - TypeclassInference

5.6 Conclusion

In this chapter, we have explored some of the more unique features of Scala. Case Classes or Pattern Matching you will use on a daily basis, while By-Name Parameters, Implicit Parameters, or Typeclass Inference are more advanced tools that you might only use when dictated by a framework or library. Nevertheless, these are the features that make the Scala language what it is, providing a way to tackle difficult problems more elegantly than most mainstream languages allow.

We have walked through the basic motivation and use cases for these features in this chapter. You will get familiar with more use cases as we see the features in action throughout the rest of this book.

This chapter will be the last in which we discuss the Scala programming language in isolation: subsequent chapters will introduce you to much more complex topics like working with your operating system, remote services, and third-party libraries. The Scala language fundamentals you have learned so far will serve you well as you broaden your horizons, from learning about the Scala language itself to using the Scala language to solve real-world problems.

Exercise: Define a function that uses pattern matching on the Exprs we saw earlier to perform simple algebraic simplifications:

(1 + 1)   2

((1 + 1) * x)   (2 * x)

((2 - 1) * x)   x

(((1 + 1) * y) + ((1 - 1) * x))   (2 * y)

See example 5.7 - Simplify

Exercise: Modify the def retry function earlier that takes a by-name parameter and make it perform an exponential backoff, sleeping between retries, with a configurable initial delay in milliseconds:

```scala
retry(max = 50, delay = 100 /*milliseconds*/) {
  requests.get(s"$httpbin/status/200,400,500")
}
```
</> 5.53.scala

See example 5.8 - Backoff

Exercise: Modify the typeclass-based `parseFromString` method we saw earlier to take a JSON-like format, where lists are demarcated by square brackets with comma-separated elements. This should allow it to parse and construct arbitrarily deep nested data structures automatically via typeclass inference:

```scala
@ parseFromString[Seq[Boolean]]("[true,false,true]") // 1 layer of nesting
res1: Seq[Boolean] = List(true, false, true)


@ parseFromString[Seq[(Seq[Int], Seq[Boolean])]]( // 3 layers of nesting
    "[[[1],[true]],[[2,3],[false,true]],[[4,5,6],[false,true,false]]]"
  )
res2: Seq[(Seq[Int], Seq[Boolean])] = List(
  (List(1), List(true)),
  (List(2, 3), List(false, true)),
  (List(4, 5, 6), List(false, true, false))
)


@ parseFromString[Seq[(Seq[Int], Seq[(Boolean, Double)])]]( // 4 layers of nesting
    "[[[1],[[true,0.5]]],[[2,3],[[false,1.5],[true,2.5]]]]"
  )
res3: Seq[(Seq[Int], Seq[(Boolean, Double)])] = List(
  (List(1), List((true, 0.5))),
  (List(2, 3), List((false, 1.5), (true, 2.5)))
)
```
</> 5.54.scala

A production-ready version of this `parseFromString` method exists in `upickle.default.read`, which we will see in *Chapter 8: JSON and Binary Data Serialization*.

See example 5.9 - Deserialize

Exercise: How about using typeclasses to generate JSON, rather than parse it? Write a writeToString method that uses a StrWriter typeclass to take nested values parsed by parseFromString, and serialize them to the same strings they were parsed from.

```scala
@ writeToString[Seq[Boolean]](Seq(true, false, true))
res1: String = "[true,false,true]"
```

```scala
@ writeToString(Seq(true, false, true)) // type can be inferred
res2: String = "[true,false,true]"
```

```scala
@ writeToString[Seq[(Seq[Int], Seq[Boolean])]](
    Seq(
      (Seq(1), Seq(true)),
      (Seq(2, 3), Seq(false, true)),
      (Seq(4, 5, 6), Seq(false, true, false))
    )
  )
res3: String = "[[[1],[true]],[[2,3],[false,true]],[[4,5,6],[false,true,false]]]"
```

```scala
@ writeToString(
    Seq(
      (Seq(1), Seq((true, 0.5))),
      (Seq(2, 3), Seq((false, 1.5), (true, 2.5)))
    )
  )
res4: String = "[[[1],[[true,0.5]]],[[2,3],[[false,1.5],[true,2.5]]]]"</> 5.55.scala
```

See example 5.10 - Serialize

Discuss Chapter 5 online at https://www.handsonscala.com/discuss/5

Part II: Local Development

6 Implementing Algorithms in Scala   107

7 Files and Subprocesses   127

8 JSON and Binary Data Serialization   147

9 Self-Contained Scala Scripts   163

10 Static Build Pipelines   179

The second part of this book explores the core tools and techniques necessary for writing Scala applications that run on a single computer. We will cover algorithms, files and subprocess management, data serialization, scripts and build pipelines. This chapter builds towards a capstone project where we write an efficient incremental static site generator using the Scala language.

6

Implementing Algorithms in Scala

6.1 Merge Sort   108

6.2 Prefix Tries   112

6.3 Breadth First Search   118

6.4 Shortest Paths   121

```scala
def breadthFirstSearch[T](start: T, graph: Map[T, Seq[T]]): Set[T] = {
  val seen = collection.mutable.Set(start)
  val queue = collection.mutable.ArrayDeque(start)
  while (queue.nonEmpty) {
    val current = queue.removeHead()
    for (next <- graph(current) if !seen.contains(next)) {
      seen.add(next)
      queue.append(next)
    }
  }
  seen.toSet
}
```
</> 6.1.scala

Snippet 6.1: a simple breadth-first-search algorithm we will implement using Scala in this chapter

In this chapter, we will walk you through the implementation of a number of common algorithms using the Scala programming language. These algorithms are commonly taught in schools and tested at professional job interviews, so you have likely seen them before.

By implementing them in Scala, we aim to get you more familiar with using the Scala programming language to solve small problems in isolation. We will also see how some of the unique language features we saw in *Chapter 5: Notable Scala Features* can be applied to simplify the implementation of these well-known algorithms. This will prepare us for subsequent chapters which will expand in scope to include many different kinds of systems, APIs, tools and techniques.

6.1 Merge Sort

An Array is the simplest of data structures: a fixed length linear sequence of values. One of the most common thing you do with arrays is to sort them and search them. Merge Sort is one way to sort them, with a balance of speed and simplicity. The key steps in a merge sort are as follows:

- Take an unsorted array of items
- If the array has a single item, it is already sorted
- Otherwise, split the array in half
- Separately merge sort the two halves of the array
- Merge the two sorted halves into one combined sorted array

These steps are recursive: to sort each array with more than one item, we have to split it in half and sort the halves. We can visualize this as follows starting with the unsorted `Array(4, 0, 1, 5, 3, 2)`:

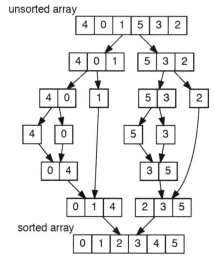

Because the array we are working with gets halved every split, there can only be $O(log\ n)$ levels of splitting for an array of size n. Each level takes $O(n)$ time to split and merge the arrays, resulting in a final algorithm which is of complexity $O(n\ log\ n)$. These steps translate into the following code:

```scala
def mergeSort(items: Array[Int]): Array[Int] = {      MergeSort.sc
  if (items.length <= 1) items
  else {
    val (left, right) = items.splitAt(items.length / 2)
    val (sortedLeft, sortedRight) = (mergeSort(left), mergeSort(right))
  }
}
```
</> 6.2.scala

The translation is relatively straightforward: we define a `mergeSort` function that takes in an `Array` (for now hardcoded to elements of type `Int`). If it has length 1, we return it. Otherwise, we split it in half, and sort both halves.

The only remaining bit of code is to merge the two halves back together. This can be done by reading items from both `sortedLeft` and `sortedRight`, one at a time, and adding the smaller of the two items to the output array. One step that merges two already-sorted arrays into one combined sorted array looks like this, with the elements of the combined array being filled in from left to right:

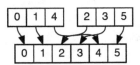

This can be implemented as follows:

```scala
    val (sortedLeft, sortedRight) = (mergeSort(left), mergeSort(right))      MergeSort.sc
+   var (leftIdx, rightIdx) = (0, 0)
+   val output = Array.newBuilder[Int]
+   while (leftIdx < sortedLeft.length || rightIdx < sortedRight.length) {
+     val takeLeft = (leftIdx < sortedLeft.length, rightIdx < sortedRight.length) match {
+       case (true, false) => true
+       case (false, true) => false
+       case (true, true) => sortedLeft(leftIdx) < sortedRight(rightIdx)
+     }
+     if (takeLeft) {
+       output += sortedLeft(leftIdx)
+       leftIdx += 1
+     } else {
+       output += sortedRight(rightIdx)
+       rightIdx += 1
+     }
+   }
+   output.result()
  }
```
</> 6.3.scala

We maintain indices into the left and right arrays. At every step, we check both sides to see if either side has run out of elements, to find an element to add to our output builder:

- If one side has run out, we always take from the other
- If neither side has run out, we take the element which is smaller
- If both sides have run out of elements, we are done

Our `MergeSort.sc` file containing this function can be tested in the REPL by loading it via `amm --predef`:

```
$ amm --predef MergeSort.sc
Welcome to the Ammonite Repl 2.2.0 (Scala 2.13.2 Java 11.0.7)
@ mergeSort(Array(1))
res0: Array[Int] = Array(1)


@ mergeSort(Array(2, 1))
res1: Array[Int] = Array(1, 2)


@ mergeSort(Array(4, 0, 1, 5, 2, 3))
res2: Array[Int] = Array(0, 1, 2, 3, 4, 5)
```
                                                                    </> 6.4.scala

See example 6.1 - MergeSort

6.1.1 Generic Merge Sort

The merge sort function we defined above is hardcoded to only work with `Array[Int]`s. However, we do not need to be limited to only that type:

- We could sort any `IndexedSeq`, not just `Array`, as we just need to look up elements by index
- We could sort any type that can be compared, not just `Int`.

To do so, we need to change the signature of `def mergeSort` as follows:

```
-def mergeSort(items: Array[Int]): Array[Int] = {
+def mergeSort[T: Ordering](items: IndexedSeq[T]): IndexedSeq[T] = {
```
                                                                    </> 6.5.scala

The new signature declares that we can take and return any `IndexedSeq`, not just `Array`s, and the items can be of any type `T` as long as there exists an implicit `Ordering[T]`. This `T: Ordering` is the *context bound* syntax we saw in **Chapter 5: Notable Scala Features**.

We also need to change our `output` builder from an `Array.newBuilder[Int]` to instead use `IndexedSeq.newBuilder[T]`, and replace `<` with the `Ordering`'s comparison function, which may not be the same `<` we've been using on `Int`s:

```
-val output = Array.newBuilder[Int]
+val output = IndexedSeq.newBuilder[T]
```
                                                                    </> 6.6.scala

```
-case (true, true) => sortedLeft(leftIdx) < sortedRight(rightIdx)
+case (true, true) => Ordering[T].lt(sortedLeft(leftIdx), sortedRight(rightIdx))
```
                                                                    </> 6.7.scala

If we restart out Ammonite REPL and load in our modified script, we can now sort `Array`s or `Vector`s of integers as well as non-integer types like `string`s:

```
@ mergeSort(Array(5, 3, 4, 2, 1))
res0: IndexedSeq[Int] = Vector(1, 2, 3, 4, 5)


@ mergeSort(Vector(5, 3, 4, 2, 1))
res1: IndexedSeq[Int] = Vector(1, 2, 3, 4, 5)


@ mergeSort(Vector("banana", "apple", "durian", "cabbage"))
res2: IndexedSeq[String] = Vector("apple", "banana", "cabbage", "durian")       </> 6.8.scala
```

If you have your own custom class you want to make sortable, you can also define a custom ordering for your class to allow sorting it. Note that in all these cases, mergeSort returns a Vector as that is the default implementation of IndexedSeq. The final code for the generic merge sort is as follows:

```
def mergeSort[T: Ordering](items: IndexedSeq[T]): IndexedSeq[T] = {          MergeSort.sc
  if (items.length <= 1) items
  else {
    val (left, right) = items.splitAt(items.length / 2)
    val (sortedLeft, sortedRight) = (mergeSort(left), mergeSort(right))
    var (leftIdx, rightIdx) = (0, 0)
    val output = IndexedSeq.newBuilder[T]
    while (leftIdx < sortedLeft.length || rightIdx < sortedRight.length) {
      val takeLeft = (leftIdx < sortedLeft.length, rightIdx < sortedRight.length) match {
        case (true, false) => true
        case (false, true) => false
        case (true, true) => Ordering[T].lt(sortedLeft(leftIdx), sortedRight(rightIdx))
      }
      if (takeLeft) {
        output += sortedLeft(leftIdx)
        leftIdx += 1
      } else {
        output += sortedRight(rightIdx)
        rightIdx += 1
      }
    }
    output.result()
  }
}                                                                            </> 6.9.scala
```

See example 6.2 - GenericMergeSort

6.2 Prefix Tries

Another common family of algorithms you may end up using is those operating on a Trie, or Prefix Tree. A Trie is a tree-shaped data structure that behaves similarly to a Set[String], providing .add(s: String) and .contains(s: String) methods, but has additional specialized functions that normal Sets do not:

- .prefixesMatchingString(s: String) efficiently finds all strings in the Trie which are a prefix of the string s. Useful for identifying words of varying length in a larger input string.

- .stringsMatchingPrefix(s: String) efficiently queries the Trie for all strings which contain a string s as a prefix. Useful for things like autocompletes, where you want to narrow down a set of possible completions given incomplete user input.

A Trie stores the strings it contains as a tree of characters. Words that share prefixes will share that portion of the tree. For example, a Trie for the following Set can be represented as a tree with the first few nodes shared between words:

Set("mango", "mandarin", "map", "man")

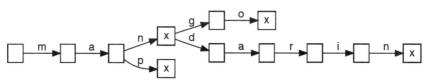

Each node in the Trie contains child nodes, each associated with a particular character. We use Xs to represent the nodes which correspond to the end of a string. Note that a string may be a prefix of another string, e.g. man being a prefix of mango and mandarin, thus Xs can appear in any node and not just the leaf nodes of the tree.

Tries come in both mutable and immutable flavors. For this chapter, we will be implementing a simple mutable Trie.

6.2.1 Trie Set Operations

A first sketch of our Trie data structure might look something like this:

```
class Trie() {                                                    Trie.sc
  class Node(var hasValue: Boolean,
            val children: collection.mutable.Map[Char, Node] = collection.mutable.Map())
  val root = new Node(false)
}
                                                             </> 6.10.scala
```

A Trie contains nodes, and each node has a map of characters to child nodes. The hasValue field represents the Xs in the diagram above, and indicates if the node is the last node in a string. Each Trie operation starts from a root node, which is defined as val root above.

6.2.1.1 Trie.add

To add an element to our Trie, we need to walk the added string character by character. For the parts of the string which already exist in the tree we do nothing, but for those that do not exist in the tree we need to construct nodes for them.

For example, to add the word manda to the Trie above, it suffices to walk down the m a n d a edges and then tag that node with an X:

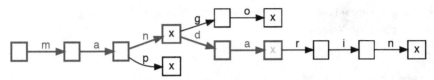

On the other hand, to add the word mandolin to the Trie, we need to walk down the m a n d edges, construct another set of o l i n edges and corresponding nodes, and finally tag the last node with an X:

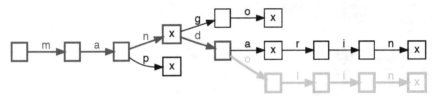

We can do that as follows:

```scala
  val root = new Node(false)                                              Trie.sc
+ def add(s: String) = {
+   var current = root
+   for (c <- s) current = current.children.getOrElseUpdate(c, new Node(false))
+   current.hasValue = true
+ }
}
                                                                    </> 6.11.scala
```

Essentially, we walk the characters of the input string, starting from the root of the Trie, and for each character we try to look up the corresponding child of the current node. If the child exists we look up the next character from that child, but if the child doesn't exist we create it and associate it with the current character. At the end of this walk, the current node is the node that corresponds to the entire string s, and so we set its hasValue = true

Note that the second argument of .getOrElseUpdate is a by-name parameter, which we discussed in **Chapter 5: Notable Scala Features**; that means we do not actually instantiate the new Node(false) unless the character c cannot be found in the children map.

6.2.1.2 Trie.contains

To complete our implementation of the basic Set API, we need to implement .contains. This is similar to add, except:

- We need to check if the final node we end up at has `hasValue` `==` `true`
- Instead of constructing the nodes in the tree if they do not exist, we terminate the traversal early and return `false`:

The following code would do this for us:

```
+ def contains(s: String): Boolean = {                                    Trie.sc
+   var current = Option(root)
+   for (c <- s if current.nonEmpty) current = current.get.children.get(c)
+   current.exists(_.hasValue)
+ }                                                                  </> 6.12.scala
```

Testing this in `amm` `--predef` `Trie.sc`, we can now use `add` and `contains`:

```
@ val t = new Trie()

@ t.add("mango")

@ t.add("mandarin")

@ t.add("map")

@ t.add("man")
```

```
@ t.contains("mango")
res5: Boolean = true

@ t.contains("mang")
res6: Boolean = false

@ t.contains("man")
res7: Boolean = true

@ t.contains("mandarin")
res8: Boolean = true

@ t.contains("mandarine")
res9: Boolean = false
```
`</> 6.13.scala`   `</> 6.14.scala`

Now that we have the basic Set operations working, the next step is to implement the methods that only Tries can efficiently support: `prefixesMatchingString` and `stringsMatchingPrefix`.

6.2.2 Trie Prefix Operations

6.2.2.1 Trie.prefixesMatchingString

- `.prefixesMatchingString(s: String)` efficiently finds all strings in the Trie which are a prefix of the string `s`.

Implementing this is similar to `contains`: we use the characters of `s` to walk the tree structure, but instead of just checking if the final node has `hasValue = true`, we aggregate all nodes we come across with `hasValue = true` and return them. For example, if we pass in `s = "mangosteen"` to the Trie we saw earlier, we'd expect a traversal that looks like this:

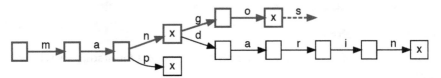

The traversal walks the nodes for mango, picks up the two xs after 3 and 5 steps, then then ends because it is unable to find the next character s. We thus find that the prefixes of mangosteen length 3 and 5 are present in the Trie, and those lengths correspond to the output strings Seq("man", "mango"). This traversal looks like this in code:

```
+ def prefixesMatchingString0(s: String): Set[Int] = {        Trie.scala
+     var current = Option(root)
+     val output = Set.newBuilder[Int]
+     for ((c, i) <- s.zipWithIndex if current.nonEmpty) {
+         if (current.get.hasValue) output += i
+         current = current.get.children.get(c)
+     }
+     if (current.exists(_.hasValue)) output += s.length
+     output.result()
+ }
                                                           </> 6.15.scala
```

Note how we are using the .zipWithIndex method on s: String in order to loop over every character together with its index. This is usually simpler than using Range(...) to loop over indices manually. For now, prefixesMatchingString0 returns a Set[Int] of the indices of the matching prefixes. We can test this on the same Trie we built earlier:

```
@ val t = new Trie(); t.add("mango"); t.add("mandarin"); t.add("map"); t.add("man")

@ t.prefixesMatchingString0("manible")
res1: Set[Int] = Set(3)

@ t.prefixesMatchingString0("mangosteen")
res2: Set[Int] = Set(3, 5)                                 </> 6.16.scala
```

If we want the prefixes as strings, we can get them by calling .substring on the input

```
+ def prefixesMatchingString(s: String): Set[String] = {    Trie.scala
+     prefixesMatchingString0(s).map(s.substring(0, _))
+ }
                                                           </> 6.17.scala
```

```
@ val t = new Trie(); t.add("mango"); t.add("mandarin"); t.add("map"); t.add("man")

@ t.prefixesMatchingString("mangosteen")
res3: Set[String] = Set("man", "mango")                    </> 6.18.scala
```

Next, let's look at stringsMatchingPrefix:

6.2.2.2 Trie.stringsMatchingPrefix

- .stringsMatchingPrefix(s: String) efficiently queries the Trie for all strings which contain a string s as a prefix.

In a normal Set[String], such as a hash-set, we can only look up elements by exact equality: to filter by prefix, we would need to iterate through every string in the set and check if the string has the given prefix. The structure of a Trie lets us do this more efficiently: we can use the input string s to navigate directly to the subtree we care about, and then just iterate over that subtree to find all entries with the given prefix.

For example, given a prefix man, we can visualize these two steps in the following diagrams: first an initial walk using the characters in s: String.

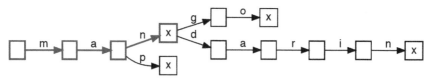

And then a recursive walk, starting where the initial walk left off

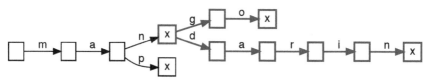

In this example, the recursive walk picks up the words man, mango and mandarin in the subtree of man, and thus we can conclude that those are the words in the Trie that contain man as a prefix. This can be implemented as follows:

```scala
def stringsMatchingPrefix(s: String): Set[String] = {
  var current = Option(root)
  for (c <- s if current.nonEmpty) current = current.get.children.get(c) // initial walk
  if (current.isEmpty) Set()
  else {
    val output = Set.newBuilder[String]
    def recurse(current: Node, path: List[Char]): Unit = {
      if (current.hasValue) output += (s + path.reverse.mkString)
      for ((c, n) <- current.children) recurse(n, c :: path)
    }
    recurse(current.get, Nil) // recursive walk
    output.result()
  }
}
```

Trie.scala

</> 6.19.scala

The *initial walk* and *recursive traversal* phases of this algorithm are marked with comments on the snippet above. Note that for the recursive traversal, we keep a `List[Char]` that represents the current path from the base of the recursion. Because `Lists` share their tails, creating a new list via `c :: path` is cheap and every call to `recurse` can have its own `List` of characters. On the other hand, because `Lists` only allow prepending nodes on the left hand side, we need to call `.reverse` to put the characters in the correct order before adding them to the `output`.

We can test this in the REPL as follows:

```
@ val t = new Trie(); t.add("mango"); t.add("mandarin"); t.add("map"); t.add("man")

@ t.stringsMatchingPrefix("man")
res1: Set[String] = Set("man", "mandarin", "mango")

@ t.stringsMatchingPrefix("ma")
res2: Set[String] = Set("map", "man", "mandarin", "mango")

@ t.stringsMatchingPrefix("map")
res3: Set[String] = Set("map")

@ t.stringsMatchingPrefix("mand")
res4: Set[String] = Set("mandarin")

@ t.stringsMatchingPrefix("mando")
res5: Set[String] = Set()
```
</> 6.20.scala

Our final Trie code looks like this:

```
class Trie() {                                                        Trie.sc
  class Node(var hasValue: Boolean,
             val children: collection.mutable.Map[Char, Node] = collection.mutable.Map())
  val root = new Node(false)
  def add(s: String) = {
    var current = root
    for (c <- s) current = current.children.getOrElseUpdate(c, new Node(false))
    current.hasValue = true
  }
  def contains(s: String): Boolean = {
    var current = Option(root)
    for (c <- s if current.nonEmpty) current = current.get.children.get(c)
    current.exists(_.hasValue)
  }
  def prefixesMatchingString0(s: String): Set[Int] = {
```

```scala
    var current = Option(root)
    val output = Set.newBuilder[Int]
    for ((c, i) <- s.zipWithIndex if current.nonEmpty) {
      if (current.get.hasValue) output += i
      current = current.get.children.get(c)
    }
    if (current.exists(_.hasValue)) output += s.length
    output.result()
  }
  def prefixesMatchingString(s: String): Set[String] = {
    prefixesMatchingString0(s).map(s.substring(0, _))
  }
  def stringsMatchingPrefix(s: String): Set[String] = {
    var current = Option(root)
    for (c <- s if current.nonEmpty) current = current.get.children.get(c) // initial walk
    if (current.isEmpty) Set()
    else {
      val output = Set.newBuilder[String]
      def recurse(current: Node, path: List[Char]): Unit = {
        if (current.hasValue) output += (s + path.reverse.mkString)
        for ((c, n) <- current.children) recurse(n, c :: path)
      }
      recurse(current.get, Nil) // recursive walk
      output.result()
    }
  }
}
```

</> 6.21.scala

There are many other Set and Trie operations not shown here, such as removing elements, iteration over all elements in the Trie, or treating the strings in the Trie as keys and associating values with them. Implementing those is left as an exercise for the reader.

See example 6.3 - Trie

6.3 Breadth First Search

The last kind of algorithms we will discuss are those that work on graphs. We will see how to implement a common directed graph algorithm in Scala: Breadth First Search.

There are many ways to represent directed graphs: as adjacency lists, adjacency matrices, edge lists, and so on. For the purpose of this exercise, we will represent the graph as a Map of nodes to the outgoing edges:

```scala
val graph = Map(
  "a" -> Seq("b", "c"),
  "b" -> Seq("a"),
  "c" -> Seq("b")
)
```

</> 6.22.scala

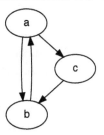

Directed graphs can have cycles: above, we see there is a cycle between a -> b -> a, as well as a cycle between a -> c -> b -> a. You can also have directed *acyclic* graphs, which do not have cycles:

```scala
val graph = Map(
  "a" -> Seq("b", "c"),
  "b" -> Seq("c", "d"),
  "c" -> Seq("d"),
  "d" -> Seq()
)
```

</> 6.23.scala

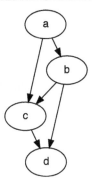

Breadth first search is a flexible algorithm that allows us to do many things given a directed graph:

- Find all nodes which are reachable from a particular starting node
- Find the shortest distance between a starting node and all other nodes
- Find the shortest path between two specific nodes

These are all pretty common things to do: e.g. a web crawler may want to find all the web pages that are reachable from a given starting page, while a car's navigator may want to find the shortest path on the road network from your location to your destination.

6.3.1 Implementing Breadth First Search

The key steps of breadth first search are as follows:

- Keep a seen set of all nodes you have seen so far, and a queue of nodes waiting to be processed
- Start with your starting node in both the seen set and queue
- While the queue is not empty, pull a node off the queue
- For every node which is reachable from the node you just pulled off the queue, if it isn't present in the seen set, add it to both the seen set and queue
- When the queue is empty, we have searched the entire graph

Translating these steps to Scala looks like this:

```scala
def search[T](start: T, graph: Map[T, Seq[T]]): Set[T] = {
  val seen = collection.mutable.Set(start)
  val queue = collection.mutable.ArrayDeque(start)
  while (queue.nonEmpty) {
    val current = queue.removeHead()
    for (next <- graph(current) if !seen.contains(next)) {
      seen.add(next)
      queue.append(next)
    }
  }
  seen.to(Set)
}
```
</> 6.24.scala

We can test this out in the REPL, on the graphs we saw earlier. In the first example graph we saw earlier, every node in the graph is connected to every other node, and thus starting from the node "c" we can reach nodes "a", "b", "c"

```scala
@ search(
    start = "c",
    graph = Map(
      "a" -> Seq("b", "c"),
      "b" -> Seq("a"),
      "c" -> Seq("b")
    )
  )
res0: Set[String] = Set("a", "b", "c")
```
</> 6.25.scala

Next, let's look at the acyclic graph, where each node was only connected to the nodes below it:

```
@ search(
    start = "a",
    graph = Map(
      "a" -> Seq("b", "c"),
      "b" -> Seq("c", "d"),
      "c" -> Seq("d"),
      "d" -> Seq()
    )
  )
res1: Set[String] = Set("a", "b", "c", "d")
                              </> 6.26.scala
```

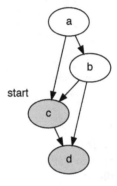

```
@ search(
    start = "c",
    graph = Map(
      "a" -> Seq("b", "c"),
      "b" -> Seq("c", "d"),
      "c" -> Seq("d"),
      "d" -> Seq()
    )
  )
res2: Set[String] = Set("c", "d")
                              </> 6.27.scala
```

Here, we can see starting from node "a" we can reach nodes "a", "b", "c", "d", but starting from node "c" we can only reach nodes "c", "d".

See example 6.4 - Search

6.4 Shortest Paths

So far, our breadth first search algorithm is able to find all nodes reachable from a starting point, but cannot tell us the shortest path between two nodes. However, since the breadth first search traverses the nodes in increasing distance from the start, the first path we find from our start node to our destination will be a shortest path between the two nodes.

For that, we will have to modify the algorithm slightly to track additional metadata. Rather than keeping a seen Set[T], we instead maintain a Map[T, List[T]] that keeps track of the path taken to each node:

```scala
def searchPaths[T](start: T, graph: Map[T, Seq[T]]): Map[T, List[T]] = {    Search.sc
  val seen = collection.mutable.Map(start -> List(start))
  val queue = collection.mutable.ArrayDeque(start -> List(start))
  while (queue.nonEmpty) {
    val (current, path) = queue.removeHead()
    for (next <- graph(current) if !seen.contains(next)) {
      val newPath = next :: path
      seen(next) = newPath
      queue.append((next, newPath))
    }
  }
  seen.toMap
}


def shortestPath[T](start: T, dest: T, graph: Map[T, Seq[T]]): Seq[T] = {
  val shortestReversedPaths = searchPaths(start, graph)
  shortestReversedPaths(dest).reverse
}
```
</> 6.28.scala

Each time we take an item off the queue and enqueue its downstream nodes, we also extend the path with that node and store the path in the seen map. This gives us a Map[T, List[T]] of every node in the graph reachable from the start, along with the path we took to get from start to the node in question:

```scala
@ searchPaths(
    start = "a",
    graph = Map(
      "a" -> Seq("b", "c"),
      "b" -> Seq("c", "d"),
      "c" -> Seq("d"),
      "d" -> Seq()
    )
  )
res0: Map[String, List[String]] = Map(
  "a" -> List("a"),
  "b" -> List("b", "a"),
  "c" -> List("c", "a"),
  "d" -> List("d", "b", "a")
)
```
</> 6.29.scala

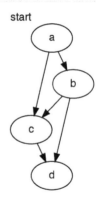

As we saw earlier when implementing Trie.stringsMatchingPrefix (*6.2.2.2*), `List`s which have identical tails can share them, and here we again take advantage of that. The linked list nodes of `List("a")` are shared between `List("b", "a")` and `List("c", "a")`, and the linked list nodes of `List("b", "a")` are shared with `List("d", "b", "a")`. Thus although we may appear to have $O(n)$ separate collections with $O(n)$ elements in each one, due to structural sharing they actually form a single tree structure that takes $O(n)$ memory overall:

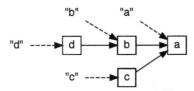

One subtlety about `List`s is that because `List`s share their *tail*, if we want to take advantage of sharing we have to build up the paths in reverse order by prepending new nodes to the left side of each list at every step. Thus to find the shortest path from `"a"` to `"d"`, we reverse the list in `def` `shortestPath` to get it in the right order.

And we're done:

```scala
@ shortestPath(
    start = "a",
    dest = "d",
    graph = Map(
      "a" -> Seq("b", "c"),
      "b" -> Seq("c", "d"),
      "c" -> Seq("d"),
      "d" -> Seq()
    )
  )
res1: Seq[String] = List("a", "b", "d")
                                      </> 6.30.scala
```

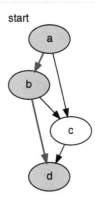

```
@ shortestPath(
    start = "a",
    dest = "c",
    graph = Map(
        "a" -> Seq("b", "c"),
        "b" -> Seq("c", "d"),
        "c" -> Seq("d"),
        "d" -> Seq()
    )
)
res2: Seq[String] = List("a", "c")
```
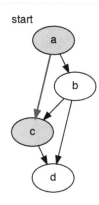

                        </> 6.31.scala

One of the shortest paths from `"a"` to `"d"` is indeed `"a"`, `"b"`, `"d"`, and the shortest path from `"a"` to `"c"` is directly `"a"`, `"c"`. By using a breadth-first search to traverse the graph, and `Map[T, List[T]]` to keep track of paths in an efficient manner (due to shared tails among the lists), we have written a function that efficiently gives us the shortest path from our start node to every other node in the graph, from which we can easily find the shortest path to the node we want.

See example 6.5 - SearchPaths

6.5 Conclusion

In this chapter, we have implemented common algorithms over three fundamental data structures: sorting Arrays, recursing over Trees, and traversing Graphs. In doing so, we have seen how to use the Scala programming language in detail: using common language features like variables, loops, functions, classes, recursion or library features like collections to implement non-trivial algorithms and data-structures.

We have also seen how a few of Scala's unique features can make algorithms cleaner to implement:

- How the by-name parameters of `.getOrElseUpdate` makes on-demand construction of a Trie trivial
- How the structural sharing of Scala's immutable `List` can make returning multiple paths on a trie or graph efficient

While you are unlikely to spend much of your professional career re-implementing basic algorithms, having experience working with them in Scala will form a good foundation for working in more complex real-world environments.

Exercise: Implement a simple binary search algorithm in Scala, to find an element within a sorted Array in $O(log\ n)$ time.

See example 6.6 - BinarySearch

Exercise: Define an `ImmutableTrie` class that has the same methods as the `Trie` class we discussed in this chapter, but instead of a `def` add method it should take a sequence of strings during construction and construct the data structure without any use of `var`s or mutable collections.

See example 6.7 - ImmutableTrie

Exercise: Convert the breadth-first-search based `shortestPath` method into a depth-first search.

See example 6.8 - DepthSearchPaths

Exercise: Write a sudoku solver that uses a depth-first search on the space of partially-filled grids to solve a sudoku puzzle like that shown below. You can modify the `def isValidSudoku` function we saw in *Chapter 4: Scala Collections* to constrain the search and avoid spending time on partially-filled grids that are already invalid.

```scala
val puzzle = Array(
  Array(3, 0, 6, 5, 0, 8, 4, 0, 0),
  Array(5, 2, 0, 0, 0, 0, 0, 0, 0),
  Array(0, 8, 7, 0, 0, 0, 0, 3, 1),
  Array(0, 0, 3, 0, 1, 0, 0, 8, 0),
  Array(9, 0, 0, 8, 6, 3, 0, 0, 5),
  Array(0, 5, 0, 0, 9, 0, 6, 0, 0),
  Array(1, 3, 0, 0, 0, 0, 2, 5, 0),
  Array(0, 0, 0, 0, 0, 0, 0, 7, 4),
  Array(0, 0, 5, 2, 0, 6, 3, 0, 0)
)                        </> 6.32.scala
```

```scala
val solution =  Array(
  Array(3, 1, 6, 5, 7, 8, 4, 9, 2),
  Array(5, 2, 9, 1, 3, 4, 7, 6, 8),
  Array(4, 8, 7, 6, 2, 9, 5, 3, 1),
  Array(2, 6, 3, 4, 1, 5, 9, 8, 7),
  Array(9, 7, 4, 8, 6, 3, 1, 2, 5),
  Array(8, 5, 1, 7, 9, 2, 6, 4, 3),
  Array(1, 3, 8, 9, 4, 7, 2, 5, 6),
  Array(6, 9, 2, 3, 5, 1, 8, 7, 4),
  Array(7, 4, 5, 2, 8, 6, 3, 1, 9)
)                        </> 6.33.scala
```

See example 6.9 - Sudoku

Exercise: Modify our `Trie` to be a generic Map-like data structure `Trie[T]` that can associate values of type T with each `String` that it stores. It should be usable as follows:

```scala
                                                      TestTrie2.sc
val t = new Trie[Int]()
t.add("mango", 1337); t.add("mandarin", 31337); t.add("map", 37); t.add("man", 7)
assert(t.get("mango") == Some(1337))
assert(t.prefixesMatchingString("mangosteen") == Map("man" -> 7, "mango" -> 1337))
assert(t.stringsMatchingPrefix("mand") == Map("mandarin" -> 31337))  </> 6.34.scala
```

See example 6.10 - TrieMap

Exercise: A *Flood Fill* is a common operation to perform on images: starting from a given pixel, search any adjacent pixels that are sufficiently "similar", repeating the process in a breadth or depth first fashion until there are no more pixels to search. Using the Java standard library, implement a `floodFill` function that can be called as follows to perform a flood fill on the image below, changing the color of the book cover from blue to black:

```scala
floodFill(                                                    TestFloodFill.sc
  src = "Raw.jpg", dest = "Filled.jpg", startX = 180, startY = 90,
  compareColors = { (a: java.awt.Color, b: java.awt.Color) =>
    def sqrDiff(f: java.awt.Color => Int) = math.pow(f(a) - f(b), 2)
    math.sqrt(sqrDiff(_.getBlue) + sqrDiff(_.getGreen) + sqrDiff(_.getRed)) < 25
  },
  fillColor = java.awt.Color.BLACK
)                                                             </> 6.35.scala
```

- Raw.jpg *(https://github.com/handsonscala/handsonscala/tree/v1/resources/6)*
- Filled.jpg *(https://github.com/handsonscala/handsonscala/tree/v1/resources/6)*

The main functionality that you need from the Java standard library is given below:

```scala
val raw = javax.imageio.ImageIO.read(new java.io.File("Raw.jpg"))   ExampleApiUsage.sc
val (x, y) = (90, 180)
val color = new java.awt.Color(raw.getRGB(x, y))
val (r, g, b) = (color.getRed, color.getGreen, color.getBlue)
raw.setRGB(x, y, java.awt.Color.BLACK.getRGB)
javax.imageio.ImageIO.write(raw, "jpg", new java.io.File("Out.jpg"))  </> 6.36.scala
```

See example 6.11 - FloodFill

Discuss Chapter 6 online at https://www.handsonscala.com/discuss/6

7

Files and Subprocesses

7.1 Paths   128

7.2 Filesystem Operations   130

7.3 Folder Syncing   135

7.4 Simple Subprocess Invocations   139

7.5 Interactive and Streaming Subprocesses   142

```scala
@ os.walk(os.pwd).filter(os.isFile).map(p => (os.size(p), p)).sortBy(-_._1).take(5)
res60: IndexedSeq[(Long, os.Path)] = ArrayBuffer(
  (6340270L, /Users/lihaoyi/test/post/Reimagining/GithubHistory.gif),
  (6008395L, /Users/lihaoyi/test/post/SmartNation/routes.json),
  (5499949L, /Users/lihaoyi/test/post/slides/Why-You-Might-Like-Scala.js.pdf),
  (5461595L, /Users/lihaoyi/test/post/slides/Cross-Platform-Development-in-Scala.js.pdf),
  (4576936L, /Users/lihaoyi/test/post/Reimagining/FluentSearch.gif)
)
                                                                    </> 7.1.scala
```

Snippet 7.1: a short Scala code snippet to find the five largest files in a directory tree

Working with files and subprocesses is one of the most common things you do in programming: from the Bash shell, to Python or Ruby scripts, to large applications written in a compiled language. At some point everyone will have to write to a file or talk to a subprocess. This chapter will walk you through how to perform basic file and subprocess operations in Scala.

This chapter finishes with two small projects: building a simple file synchronizer, and building a streaming subprocess pipeline. These projects will form the basis for *Chapter 17: Multi-Process Applications* and *Chapter 18: Building a Real-time File Synchronizer*

Throughout this chapter we will be using the OS-Lib library. OS-Lib comes bundled with Ammonite, and can be used within the REPL and *.sc script files. We will be using the Ammonite Scala REPL for most of the examples in this chapter. All functionality within this library comes from the os package.

We will be using the following sample folder full of files for these examples:

- sample-blog.zip *(https://github.com/handsonscala/handsonscala/tree/v1/resources/7)*

7.1 Paths

Most operations we will be working with involve filesystem paths: we read data from a path, write data to a path, copy files from one path to another, or list a folder path to see what files are inside. This is represented by the os.Path type, with separate os.RelPath and os.SubPath types to model relative paths and sub-paths respectively.

The separation between the different kinds of paths allows additional compile-time checks that help avoid common mistakes when working with files. This helps prevent both correctness bugs as well as security issues such as directory traversal attacks.

There are three paths that are built in to the os package: os.pwd, os.root, os.home. These refer to your process working directory, filesystem root, and user home folder respectively. You can also get the sequence of path segments using .segments, or the last segment of the path (usually the file or folder name), using .last.

```
@ os.pwd
res0: os.Path = /Users/lihaoyi/test
```

```
@ os.home.segments.toList
res3: List[String] = List(
  "Users",
  "lihaoyi",
)
```

```
@ os.root
res1: os.Path = /
```

```
@ os.home
res2: os.Path = /Users/lihaoyi        </> 7.2.scala
```

```
@ os.home.last
res4: String = "lihaoyi"              </> 7.3.scala
```

7.1.1 Constructing Paths

To create a new path based on an existing path, you can use the / operator provided by the library to add additional path segments. Note that you can only append single path segments to a path using the / operator on strings, e.g. adding multiple path segments via the string "Github/blog" is not allowed:

```
@ os.home / "Github" / "blog"
res5: os.Path = /Users/lihaoyi/Github/blog
                            </> 7.4.scala
```

```
@ os.home / "Github/blog"
os.PathError$InvalidSegment: [Github/blog]
is not a valid path segment.  </> 7.5.scala
```

If you want to treat the string as a relative path or subpath, need to use the os.RelPath (*7.1.2*) or os.SubPath (*7.1.3*) constructor in order to construct a relative path of more than one segment. This helps avoid confusion between working with individual path segments as `strings` and working with more general relative paths as os.SubPaths or os.RelPaths.

The special os.up path segment lets you move up one level:

```
@ os.pwd / os.up
res7: os.Path = /Users/lihaoyi</> 7.6.scala
```

```
@ os.pwd / os.up / os.up
res8: os.Path = /Users          </> 7.7.scala
```

os.Path(...) is used to parse os.Paths from strings. This is useful for paths coming in from elsewhere, e.g. read from a file or command-line arguments. Note that by default the os.Path(...) constructor only allows absolute paths. If you want to parse a string that is a relative path into an absolute os.Path, you have to provide a `base` path from which that relative path will begin at.

```
@ os.Path("/Users/lihaoyi")
res9: os.Path = /Users/lihaoyi
```

```
@ os.Path("post", base = os.pwd)
res11: os.Path = /Users/lihaoyi/test/post
```

```
@ os.Path("post")
java.lang.IllegalArgumentException:
post is not an absolute path  </> 7.8.scala
```

```
@ os.Path("../Ammonite", base = os.pwd)
res12: os.Path = /Users/lihaoyi/Ammonite
                              </> 7.9.scala
```

7.1.2 Relative Paths

To work with relative paths on disk, you can use os.RelPath:

```
@ os.RelPath("post")
res13: os.RelPath = post
                    </> 7.10.scala
```

```
@ os.RelPath("../hello/world")
res14: os.RelPath = ../hello/world
                              </> 7.11.scala
```

This helps ensure you do not mix up os.Paths which are always absolute and os.RelPaths which are always relative. To combine a relative path and an absolute path, you can use the same / operator. Relative paths themselves can also be combined using /, in any order, but trying to combine an absolute os.Path on the right side of a relative os.RelPath is a compile error:

```
@ val helloRelPath = os.RelPath("../hello")

@ os.home / helloRelPath
res16: os.Path = /Users/hello

@ helloRelPath / os.RelPath("post")
res17: os.RelPath = ../hello/post
                              </> 7.12.scala
```

```
@ helloRelPath / os.pwd
cmd4.sc:1: type mismatch;
 found    : os.Path
 required: os.PathChunk
val res4 = helloRelPath / os.pwd
                          ^
Compilation Failed
                              </> 7.13.scala
```

If you want the relative path between two absolute paths, you can use .relativeTo:

```
@ val githubPath = os.Path("/Users/lihaoyi/Github"); val usersPath = os.Path("/Users")

@ githubPath.relativeTo(usersPath)
res19: os.RelPath = lihaoyi/Github

@ usersPath.relativeTo(githubPath)
res20: os.RelPath = ../..
```
`</> 7.14.scala`

7.1.3 Sub Paths

os.SubPaths are a special case of relative paths, where there cannot be any .. segments at the start. Similar to relative paths, sub-paths can be created between absolute os.Paths using .subRelativeTo.

```
@ os.SubPath("post")
res21: os.SubPath = post


@ os.SubPath("../hello/world")
java.lang.IllegalArgumentException:
subpaths cannot start with ..
```
`</> 7.15.scala`

```
@ val p1 = os.Path("/Users/lihaoyi/Github")

@ val p2 = os.Path("/Users")

@ p1.subRelativeTo(p2)
res25: os.SubPath = lihaoyi/Github
```
`</> 7.16.scala`

os.SubPath is useful for cases where you have a relative path that should always be "within" a particular base folder. This can help rule out a whole class of directory traversal attacks where an unexpected .. in a relative path allows the attacker to read your /etc/passwd or some other sensitive files.

7.2 Filesystem Operations

This section will walk through the most commonly used filesystem operations that we will use throughout the rest of this book.

Note that most filesystem operations only accept absolute os.Paths. os.SubPaths or os.RelPaths must first be converted into an absolute os.Path before being used in such an operation. Many of these commands have variants that let you configure the operation, e.g. os.read lets you pass in an offset to read from and a count of characters to read, os.makeDir has os.makeDir.all to recursively create necessary folders, os.remove.all to recursively remove a folder and its contents, and so on.

7.2.1 Queries

7.2.1.1 os.list

```
@ os.list(os.pwd)
res26: IndexedSeq[os.Path] = ArraySeq(
  /Users/lihaoyi/test/.gitignore,
  /Users/lihaoyi/test/post
)                        </> 7.17.scala
```

os.list allows you to list out the direct children of a folder. Note that the order of results returned from os.list may vary depending on the filesystem your computer is using. If you need the results in a particular order, you should sort them yourself using .sorted on the returned collection.

7.2.1.2 os.walk

```
@ os.walk(os.pwd)
res27: IndexedSeq[os.Path] = ArraySeq(
  /Users/lihaoyi/test/.gitignore,
  /Users/lihaoyi/test/post,
  /Users/lihaoyi/test/post/Interview.md,
  /Users/lihaoyi/test/post/Hub,
  /Users/lihaoyi/test/post/Hub/Search.png,
...                      </> 7.18.scala
```

os.walk does a recursive listing. This may take a significant amount of time and memory for large folder trees; you can use os.walk.stream (7.2.4) to process the results in a streaming fashion.

7.2.1.3 os.stat

```
@ os.stat(os.pwd / ".gitignore")
res28: os.StatInfo = StatInfo(
  129L,
  2019-09-27T08:04:35.292056Z,
  2019-12-15T22:23:01.462598Z,
  2019-09-27T08:04:35Z,
  File
)                        </> 7.19.scala
```

os.stat fetches the filesystem metadata for an individual file or folder. You can also perform more specific queries such as os.isFile, os.isDir, os.mtime, os.size, etc. if you have a particular question you want to answer.

7.2.2 Actions

7.2.2.1 os.read, os.write

```
@ os.write(os.pwd / "new.txt", "Hello")
```

```
@ os.list(os.pwd)
res30: IndexedSeq[os.Path] = ArraySeq(
  /Users/lihaoyi/test/.gitignore,
  /Users/lihaoyi/test/post,
  /Users/lihaoyi/test/new.txt,
)
```

```
@ os.read(os.pwd / "new.txt")
res31: String = "Hello"          </> 7.20.scala
```

os.write writes to a file. You can write any datatype implementing the Writable interface: Strings, Array[Byte]s, or even the ujson.Values we will meet in **Chapter 8: JSON and Binary Data Serialization** and Scalatags HTML templates we will meet in **Chapter 9: Self-Contained Scala Scripts**.

os.read reads a file as a String. You also have os.read.lines to read the lines of a file as a IndexedSeq[String], and os.read.bytes to read a file as an Array[Byte]:

7.2.2.2 os.move

```
@ os.move(
    os.pwd / "new.txt",
    os.pwd / "newer.txt"
  )
```

```
@ os.list(os.pwd)
res32: IndexedSeq[os.Path] = ArraySeq(
  /Users/lihaoyi/test/.gitignore,
  /Users/lihaoyi/test/post,
  /Users/lihaoyi/test/newer.txt
)                        </> 7.21.scala
```

7.2.2.3 os.copy

```
@ os.copy(
    os.pwd / "newer.txt",
    os.pwd / "newer-2.txt"
  )
```

```
@ os.list(os.pwd)
res33: IndexedSeq[os.Path] = ArraySeq(
  /Users/lihaoyi/test/.gitignore,
  /Users/lihaoyi/test/post,
  /Users/lihaoyi/test/newer-2.txt,
  /Users/lihaoyi/test/newer.txt
)                        </> 7.22.scala
```

7.2.2.4 os.remove

```
@ os.remove(os.pwd / "newer.txt")
```

```
@ os.list(os.pwd)
res37: IndexedSeq[os.Path] = ArraySeq(
  /Users/lihaoyi/test/.gitignore,
  /Users/lihaoyi/test/post,
  /Users/lihaoyi/test/newer-2.txt
)                        </> 7.23.scala
```

7.2.2.5 os.makeDir

```
@ os.makeDir(os.pwd / "new-folder")
```

```
@ os.list(os.pwd)
res39: IndexedSeq[os.Path] = ArraySeq(
  /Users/lihaoyi/test/.gitignore,
  /Users/lihaoyi/test/post,
  /Users/lihaoyi/test/new-folder,
  /Users/lihaoyi/test/newer-2.txt
)                        </> 7.24.scala
```

7.2.3 Combining Operations

Many filesystem operations return collections of results: the files in a folder, the lines of a file, and so on. You can operate on these collections the same way we did in *Chapter 4: Scala Collections*, chaining together calls to `.map`/`.filter`/etc. to get the result we want.

For example, if we wanted to walk a folder recursively and find the largest files within it, we can do that as follows:

```
@ os.walk(os.pwd).filter(os.isFile).map(p => (os.size(p), p)).sortBy(-_._1).take(5)
res40: IndexedSeq[(Long, os.Path)] = ArraySeq(
  (6340270L, /Users/lihaoyi/test/post/Reimagining/GithubHistory.gif),
  (6008395L, /Users/lihaoyi/test/post/SmartNation/routes.json),
  (5499949L, /Users/lihaoyi/test/post/slides/Why-You-Might-Like-Scala.js.pdf),
  (5461595L, /Users/lihaoyi/test/post/slides/Cross-Platform-Development-in-Scala.js.pdf),
  (4576936L, /Users/lihaoyi/test/post/Reimagining/FluentSearch.gif)
)                                                                      </> 7.25.scala
```

See example 7.1 - LargestFiles

Note that this snippet loads all files into an in-memory data structure before filtering and transforming it. To avoid loading everything into memory, most such operations also provide a `.stream` variant.

7.2.4 Streaming

The `.stream` version of filesystem operations allows you to process their output in a streaming fashion, one element at a time, without all the output in-memory at once. This lets you process large results without running out of memory.

For example, you can use os.read.lines.stream to stream the lines of a file, or os.walk.stream to stream the recursive contents of a folder:

```
@ os.read.lines.stream(os.pwd / ".gitignore").foreach(println)
target/
*.iml
.idea
.settings
...
```

```
@ os.walk.stream(os.pwd).foreach(println)
/Users/lihaoyi/test/.gitignore
/Users/lihaoyi/test/post
/Users/lihaoyi/test/post/Programming Interview.md
/Users/lihaoyi/test/post/Hub
/Users/lihaoyi/test/post/Hub/Search.png
```
`</> 7.26.scala`

`*.stream` operations return a Generator type. These are similar to iterators, except they ensure that resources are always released after processing. Most collection operations like .foreach, .map, .filter, .toArray, etc. are available on Generators.

7.2.5 Transforming Streams

Like the Views we saw in **Chapter 4: Scala Collections**, Generators allow you to combine several transformations like .map, .filter, etc. into one traversal that runs when you finally call a method like .foreach or .toList. Here's an example that combines os.read.lines.stream, filter, and map to list out the lines in .gitignore which start with a "." character, with the "." stripped:

```
@ { os.read.lines.stream(os.pwd / ".gitignore")
      .filter(_.startsWith("."))
      .map(_.drop(1))
      .toList }
res43: List[String] = List(
  "idea",
  "settings",
  "classpath",
  ...
```
`</> 7.27.scala`

```
@ os.read.lines.stream(os.pwd / ".gitignore").collect{case s".$str" => str}.toList
res44: List[String] = List(
  "idea",
  "settings",
  "classpath",
  ...
```
`</> 7.28.scala`

Because we are using `.stream`, the reading/filtering/mapping occurs one line at a time. We do not accumulate the results in-memory until the end when we call `.toList`: this can be useful when the data being read is larger than can comfortably fit in memory all at once.

Now that we have gone through the basic filesystem operations, let's examine a use case.

7.3 Folder Syncing

For this use case, we will write a program that will take a source and destination folder, and efficiently update the destination folder to look like the source folder: adding any files that may be missing, and modifying files where necessary to make sure they have the same contents. For simplicity, we will ignore deletions and symbolic links. We will also assume that naively deleting the entire destination directory and re-copying the source over is too inefficient, and that we want to synchronize the two folders on a per-file/folder basis.

Let us start by defining the method signature of our folder synchronizer:

```scala
@ def sync(src: os.Path, dest: os.Path) = {
  }
```
</> 7.29.scala

7.3.1 Walking the Filesystem

The first thing we need to do is recursively walk all contents of the source folder, so we can see what we have on disk that we might need to sync:

```scala
@ def sync(src: os.Path, dest: os.Path) = {
+     for (srcSubPath <- os.walk(src)) {
+       val subPath = srcSubPath.subRelativeTo(src)
+       val destSubPath = dest / subPath
+       println((os.isDir(srcSubPath), os.isDir(destSubPath)))
+     }
  }
```
</> 7.30.scala

Running this on our source folder with files and destination folder without files, we get the following:

```scala
@ sync(os.pwd / "post", os.pwd / "post-copy")
(false, false)
(true, false)
(false, false)
(false, false)
...
```
</> 7.31.scala

For now, the destination folder doesn't exist, so `isDir` returns `false` on all of the paths.

7.3.2 Copying New Files Over

The next step is to start syncing over files. We walk over the `src` and the corresponding paths in `dest` together, and if they differ, copy the source sub-path over the destination sub-path:

```scala
@ def sync(src: os.Path, dest: os.Path) = {
    for (srcSubPath <- os.walk(src)) {
      val subPath = srcSubPath.subRelativeTo(src)
      val destSubPath = dest / subPath
-     println((os.isDir(srcSubPath), os.isDir(destSubPath)))
+     (os.isDir(srcSubPath), os.isDir(destSubPath)) match {
+       case (false, true) | (true, false) =>
+         os.copy.over(srcSubPath, destSubPath, createFolders = true)
+       case _ => // do nothing
+     }
    }
}
```
</> 7.32.scala

Since `isDir` returns `false` both when the path refers to a file as well as if the path is empty, the above snippet uses `.copy.over` to delete the destination path and copy over the contents of the source in the following circumstances:

- The source path contains a file and the destination path contains a folder
- The source path contains a folder and the destination path contains a file
- The source path contains a folder and the destination path is empty

There are three cases the above code does not support:

- If the source path is empty and the destination path contains a folder. This is a "delete" which we will ignore for now; supporting this is left as an exercise for the reader

- If the source path is a folder and the destination path is a folder. In this case doing nothing is fine: `os.walk` will enter the source path folder and process all the files within it recursively

- If the source path is a file and the destination path is a file, but they have different contents

We will handle the last case next.

7.3.3 Updating Files

The last case we need to support is when both source and destination paths contain files, but with different contents. We can do that by handling the `(false, false)` in our pattern match, but only if the destination path is empty or the destination path has a file with different contents than the source path:

```scala
@ def sync(src: os.Path, dest: os.Path) = {
    for (srcSubPath <- os.walk(src)) {
      val subPath = srcSubPath.subRelativeTo(src)
      val destSubPath = dest / subPath
      (os.isDir(srcSubPath), os.isDir(destSubPath)) match {
        case (false, true) | (true, false) =>
          os.copy.over(srcSubPath, destSubPath, createFolders = true)
+       case (false, false)
+       if !os.exists(destSubPath)
+       || !os.read.bytes(srcSubPath).sameElements(os.read.bytes(destSubPath)) =>
+
+         os.copy.over(srcSubPath, destSubPath, createFolders = true)

        case _ => // do nothing
      }
    }
}
```
</> 7.33.scala

See example 7.2 - FileSync

We are again using `os.copy.over`, which conveniently over-writes any file that was already at the destination path: a more fine-grained file syncer may want to update the file in place if only part of it has changed. We use `.sameElements` to compare the two `Arrays` rather than `==`, as `Arrays` in Scala use reference equality and so `==` will always return `false` for two different `Arrays` even if they have the same contents.

Note that we do not need to run `os.exists(srcSubPath)` to see if it exists, as the fact that it got picked up by `os.walk` tells us that it does. While the file may potentially get deleted between `os.walk` picking it up and `os.read.bytes` reading its contents, for now we ignore such race conditions and assume that the file system is static while the `sync` is ongoing. Dealing with such concurrent modification will be the topic of *Chapter 18: Building a Real-time File Synchronizer*.

7.3.4 Testing Our File Syncer

We can now run `sync` on our two folders, and then `os.walk` the `dest` path and see all our files in place:

```scala
@ sync(os.pwd / "post", os.pwd / "post-copy")


@ os.walk(os.pwd / "post-copy")
res51: IndexedSeq[os.Path] = ArraySeq(
  /Users/lihaoyi/test/post-copy/Optimizing Scala.md,
  /Users/lihaoyi/test/post-copy/Programming Interview.md,
  /Users/lihaoyi/test/post-copy/Scala Vectors.md,
  /Users/lihaoyi/test/post-copy/Reimagining/,
  /Users/lihaoyi/test/post-copy/Reimagining/GithubSearch.png,
...
```
</> 7.34.scala

To test incremental updates, we can try adding an entry to the `src` folder, run the `sync`, and then see that our file has been synced over to `dest`:

```scala
@ os.write(os.pwd / "post" / "ABC.txt", "Hello World")


@ sync(os.pwd / "post", os.pwd / "post-copy")


@ os.exists(os.pwd / "post-copy" / "ABC.txt")
res54: Boolean = true


@ os.read(os.pwd / "post-copy" / "ABC.txt")
res55: String = "Hello World"
```
</> 7.35.scala

By appending some content to one of the files in `src`, we can verify that modifications to that file also get synced over when `sync` is run:

```scala
@ os.write.append(os.pwd / "post" / "ABC.txt", "\nI am Cow")


@ sync(os.pwd / "post", os.pwd / "post-copy")


@ os.read(os.pwd / "post-copy" / "ABC.txt")
res58: String = """Hello World
I am Cow"""
```
</> 7.36.scala

This example is greatly simplified: we do not consider deletions, permissions, symbolic links, or concurrency/parallelism concerns. Our file synchronizer runs in-process on a single computer, and cannot be easily used to synchronize files over a network. Nevertheless, it should give you a good sense of how working with the filesystem via Scala's OS-Lib library works.

7.4 Simple Subprocess Invocations

The other major operating-system feature that you will likely use is process management. Most complex systems are made of multiple processes: often the tool you need is not usable as a library within your program, but can be easily started as a subprocess to accomplish the task at hand.

A common pattern is to spawn a subprocess, wait for it to complete, and process its output. This is done through the os.proc.call function:

```
os.proc(command: os.Shellable*)
  .call(cwd: Path = null,
        env: Map[String, String] = null,
        stdin: ProcessInput = os.Pipe,
        stdout: ProcessOutput = os.Pipe,
        stderr: ProcessOutput = os.Inherit,
        mergeErrIntoOut: Boolean = false,
        timeout: Long = Long.MaxValue,
        check: Boolean = true,
        propagateEnv: Boolean = true): os.CommandResult
```
</> 7.37.scala

os.proc.call takes a lot of optional parameters, but at its simplest you pass in the command you want to execute, and it returns you an os.CommandResult object, which contains the exit code, stdout, and stderr of the completed process. For example, we can run git status within a Git repository and receive the output of the Git subprocess:

```
@ val gitStatus = os.proc("git", "status").call()
gitStatus: os.CommandResult = CommandResult(
  0,
...


@ gitStatus.exitCode
res1: Int = 0


@ gitStatus.out.text()
res2: String = """On branch master
Your branch is up to date with 'origin/master'.
Changes to be committed:
...
```
</> 7.38.scala

Common things to customize include:

- cwd to set the location of the subprocess's current working directory; defaults to the os.pwd of the host process

- env to customize the environment variables passed to the subprocess; defaults to inheriting those of the host process

- stdin/stderr/stdout to pass data into the subprocess's standard input stream, and redirect where its standard output and error streams go. Defaults to not taking standard input, and collecting the output in the os.CommandResult, and forwarding any errors to the terminal

- check = false to avoid throwing an exception if the subprocess has a non-zero exit code

While here we are passing Strings into os.proc(), you can also pass Seq[String]s, Option[String]s, and os.Paths. We will now explore some simple use cases using os.proc.call to do useful work.

7.4.1 Use Case: remove non-current branches from a Git repo

Often, someone using the Git version control system ends up creating one branch for every task they are working on. After merging those branches into master, the branch names still hang around, and it can be tedious to run git branch -D over and over to remove them. Let's use Git subprocesses to help remove all branches except the current branch from the local Git repo.

To do this, first we run git branch to see the current branches, and get the output as a series of lines:

```scala
@ val gitBranchLines = os.proc("git", "branch").call().out.lines()
gitBranchLines: Vector[String] = Vector(
  "  561",
  "  571",
  "  595",
  "  599",
  "  600",
  "  609",
  "* master"
)
```
</> 7.39.scala

Next, we find all the branches whose lines start with " ", and remove the whitespace:

```scala
@ val otherBranches = gitBranchLines.filter(_.startsWith("  ")).map(_.drop(2))
otherBranches: Vector[String] = Vector("561", "571", "595", "599", "600", "609")
```
</> 7.40.scala

You can also write this using pattern matching and .collect, as:

```scala
@ val otherBranches = gitBranchLines.collect{case s"  $branchName" => branchName}
otherBranches: Vector[String] = Vector("561", "571", "595", "599", "600", "609")
```
</> 7.41.scala

Lastly, we run git branch -D on each such branch to remove them. We can then see only the current * master branch remaining:

```
@ for (branch <- otherBranches) os.proc("git", "branch", "-D", branch).call()

@ val gitBranchLines = os.proc("git", "branch").call().out.lines()
gitBranchLines: Vector[String] = Vector("* master")                        </> 7.42.scala
```

While everything we did here using subprocesses could also have been done in-process, e.g. using a library like JGit, it is sometimes easier use a command-line tool you are already familiar with rather than having to learn an entirely new programmatic API. In this case, the `git` command-line interface is something many developers use every day, and being able to easily re-use those same commands from within your Scala program is a great advantage in readability.

The full code for removing all non-current branches from a Git repo is as follows:

```
def gitBranchLines = os.proc("git", "branch").call().out.lines()        RemoveBranches.sc
pprint.log(gitBranchLines)

val otherBranches = gitBranchLines.collect{case s"  $branchName" => branchName}
for (branch <- otherBranches) os.proc("git", "branch", "-D", branch).call()
pprint.log(otherBranches)                                                </> 7.43.scala
```

See example 7.3 - RemoveBranches

7.4.2 Use Case: Curl to a local file

The previous example did not configure the subprocess' `stdin` or `stdout` streams at all: the `git branch` operations get all their necessary input from the command line arguments, and returned their output as `stdout` to the host process. In this next example, we will spawn a `curl` subprocess and configure `stdout` to send the output directly to a file without buffering in-memory.

`stdout` and `stderr` can be passed the following data types:

- `os.Pipe`: the default for `stdout`, aggregates the output into the `.out` field in the `CommandResult`

- `os.Inherit`: the default for `stderr`, forwards the output to the parent process' output. Useful for forwarding error messages or logs straight to your terminal

- `os.Path`: a file on disk to forward the output to, which we will use below

We can thus spawn a `curl` subprocess with the `stdout` redirected to a local file:

```
@ val url = "https://api.github.com/repos/lihaoyi/mill/releases"

@ os.proc("curl", url).call(stdout = os.pwd / "github.json")
res7: os.CommandResult = CommandResult(0, ArraySeq())                    </> 7.44.scala
```

After the `curl` completes, we can now spawn a `ls -lh` subprocess to get the metadata of the file we just downloaded:

```scala
@ os.proc("ls", "-lh", "github.json").call().out.text()
res8: String = """-rw-r--r--  1 lihaoyi  staff   607K Jun  3 13:16 github.json
"""
```
</> 7.45.scala

7.4.3 Streaming Gzip

`os.proc.call` allows you to set both the `stdin` as well as `stdout`, using the subprocess to process data from one file to another in a streaming fashion. Here, we are using the `gzip` command-line tool to compress the `github.json` file we downloaded earlier into a `github.json.gz`:

```scala
@ os.proc("gzip").call(stdin = os.pwd / "github.json", stdout = os.pwd / "github.json.gz")
res9: os.CommandResult = CommandResult(0, ArrayBuffer())

@ os.proc("ls", "-lh", "github.json.gz").call().out.text()
res10: String = """-rw-r--r--  1 lihaoyi  staff    23K Jun  3 13:30 github.json.gz
"""
```
</> 7.46.scala

This lets you use subprocesses to handle large files and large amounts of data without having to load either the input or the output into the host process's memory. This is useful if the files are large and memory is limited.

`os.proc.call` only allows you to spawn a single subprocess at a time, and only returns once that subprocess has completed. This is great for simple commands, like the `curl` and `git` commands we saw earlier, and can even be used for simple single-stage streaming commands like `gzip`. However, if we want more control over how the subprocess is used, or to wire up multiple subprocesses to form a multi-stage pipeline, we need `os.proc.spawn`.

7.5 Interactive and Streaming Subprocesses

```scala
os.proc(command: os.Shellable*)
  .spawn(cwd: Path = null,
         env: Map[String, String] = null,
         stdin: os.ProcessInput = os.Pipe,
         stdout: os.ProcessOutput = os.Pipe,
         stderr: os.ProcessOutput = os.Inherit,
         mergeErrIntoOut: Boolean = false,
         propagateEnv: Boolean = true): os.SubProcess
```
</> 7.47.scala

os.proc.spawn takes a similar set of arguments as `os.proc.call`, but instead of returning a completed `os.CommandResult`, it instead returns an `os.SubProcess` object. This represents a subprocess that runs in the background while your program continues to execute, and you can interact with it via its `stdin`, `stdout` and `stderr` streams.

7.5.1 Interacting with a Subprocess

The first big use case for `os.proc.spawn` is to spawn a long-lived worker process running concurrently with the host process. This background process may not be streaming large amounts of data, but simply has its own in-memory state you want to interact with and preserve between interactions.

A simple example of this is to keep a Python process running in the background:

```
@ val sub = os.proc("python", "-u", "-c", "while True: print(eval(raw_input()))").spawn()
sub: os.SubProcess = os.SubProcess@22a7d4a2                                    </> 7.48.scala
```

This tiny snippet of Python code in the `-c` parameter reads input lines from stdin, `eval`s them as Python code, and `print`s the result over `stdout` back to the host process. By spawning a subprocess, we can write `string`s to the subprocess' input streams using `sub.stdin.write` and `sub.stdin.writeLine`, and read `string` lines from its standard output using `sub.stdout.readLine()`:

```
@ sub.stdin.writeLine("1 + 2 + 4")            @ sub.stdin.writeLine("'1' + '2' + '4'")

@ sub.stdin.flush()                           @ sub.stdin.flush()

@ sub.stdout.readLine()                       @ sub.stdout.readLine()
res14: String = "7"           </> 7.49.scala  res17: String = "124"         </> 7.50.scala
```

`stdin` and `stdout` also support reading and writing binary data. When we are done with the subprocess, we can destroy it:

```
@ sub.isAlive()
res18: Boolean = true

@ sub.destroy()

@ sub.isAlive()
res20: Boolean = false                                                        </> 7.51.scala
```

See example 7.4 - InteractivePython

This usage pattern is handy in a few cases:

- The process you are delegating work to is slow to initialize, so you do not want to spawn a new one every time. e.g. a Python process can take 10s to 100s of milliseconds to start

- The process you are delegating work to has its own in-memory state that needs to be preserved, and throwing away the data by spawning a new subprocess each time simply doesn't work

- The work you are delegating is *untrusted*, and you want to run it in a subprocess to take advantage of the sandboxing and security features provided by the operating system

7.5.2 Streaming distinct contributors in a Git repo history

Apart from interactively exchanging data with a subprocess over `stdin` and `stdout`, the other common use case for `os.proc.spawn` is to connect multiple subprocesses via their standard input and standard output. This lets them exchange and process data in a streaming fashion.

The first streaming use case we will visit is to find the distinct contributors to a Git repository. To run these steps in parallel, in a streaming pipeline, you can use `os.proc.spawn` as follows:

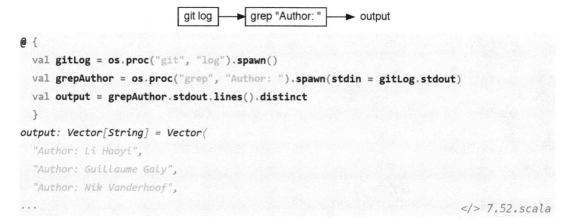

```scala
@ {
  val gitLog = os.proc("git", "log").spawn()
  val grepAuthor = os.proc("grep", "Author: ").spawn(stdin = gitLog.stdout)
  val output = grepAuthor.stdout.lines().distinct
}
output: Vector[String] = Vector(
  "Author: Li Haoyi",
  "Author: Guillaume Galy",
  "Author: Nik Vanderhoof",
  ...
```
</> 7.52.scala

Here, we spawn one `gitLog` subprocess, and pass the `stdout` of `gitLog` into the `stdin` of a `grepAuthor` subprocess. At that point, both `os.SubProcess`es are running in the background, the output of one feeding into the input of the other. The `grepAuthor` subprocess exposes a `grepAuthor.stdout` attribute that you can use to read the output, either interactively via `readLine` as we saw earlier, or in bulk via methods like `.text()` or `.lines()`.

7.5.3 Streaming Subprocess Pipelines

Subprocess pipelines do not need to start or end in-memory, or even on your local computer. Here is an example of downloading some data from `api.github.com`, and re-uploading it to `httpbin.org`, in a streaming fashion using `curl` on both ends:

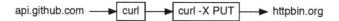

```
@ {
  val download = os
    .proc("curl", "https://api.github.com/repos/lihaoyi/mill/releases")
    .spawn()

  val upload = os
    .proc("curl", "-X", "PUT", "-d", "@-", "https://httpbin.org/anything")
    .spawn(stdin = download.stdout)

  val contentLength = upload.stdout.lines().filter(_.contains("Content-Length"))
}
contentLength: Vector[String] = Vector("    \"Content-Length\": \"609216\",</} 7.53.scala
```

See example 7.5 - StreamingDownloadProcessReupload1

Looking at the JSON output of the final `upload` response, we can see that the `"Content-Length"` of the output is 609,216 bytes which roughly matches the 607kb number we saw earlier. For now, we are just using a quick `.contains` check on `String`s to find the relevant line in the JSON: we will see how to do JSON processing in a more structured way later in **Chapter 8: JSON and Binary Data Serialization**.

As each subprocess doesn't know anything about its neighbours, it is easy to change the topology of the pipeline. For example, if we want to introduce `base64` and `gzip` steps in between the `curl` download and `curl -X PUT` upload, we could do that as follows:

api.github.com ⟶ [curl] ⟶ [base64] ⟶ [gzip] ⟶ [curl -X PUT] ⟶ httpbin.org

```
@ {
  val download = ...

+ val base64 = os.proc("base64").spawn(stdin = download.stdout)
+
+ val gzip = os.proc("gzip").spawn(stdin = base64.stdout)

  val upload = os
    .proc("curl", "-X", "PUT", "-d", "@-", "https://httpbin.org/anything")
-   .spawn(stdin = download.stdout)
+   .spawn(stdin = gzip.stdout)

  val contentLength = upload.stdout.lines().filter(_.contains("Content-Length"))
}
contentLength: Vector[String] = Vector("    \"Content-Length\": \"38517\",</} 7.54.scala
```

See example 7.6 - StreamingDownloadProcessReupload2

`os.proc.spawn` thus allows you to put together quite sophisticated subprocess pipelines in a straightforward manner. In the example above, all four stages run in parallel, with the download, base 64 encoding, gzip compression, and upload taking place concurrently in four separate subprocess. The data is processed in a streaming fashion as it is piped between the four processes, allowing us to perform the whole computation without ever accumulating the complete dataset in memory.

7.6 Conclusion

In this chapter, we have seen how we can use the os package to make working with the filesystem quick and easy, and how to conveniently set up subprocess pipelines to accomplish what you want. From synchronizing files to doing network data plumbing, all the tools you need are just a few lines of code away. We will be using this package to work with files and subprocesses throughout the rest of this book.

To use OS-Lib in a project built using Mill or another build tool, you need the following coordinates:

```
ivy"com.lihaoyi::os-lib:0.7.1"                                                    Mill
```

In the interest of time, the scope of this chapter is limited. The OS-Lib library documentation is a much more thorough reference:

- https://github.com/lihaoyi/os-lib

We will revisit the file synchronizer and subprocess pipelines we built in this chapter later in this book, in *Chapter 17: Multi-Process Applications* and *Chapter 18: Building a Real-time File Synchronizer*.

> **Exercise:** Modify the folder sync function we wrote earlier to support deletes: if a file or folder exists in the destination folder but not in the source folder, we should delete it from the destination folder when synchronizing them.
>
> **See example** 7.7 - FileSyncDelete

> **Exercise:** Add another stage to our streaming subprocess pipeline that uses tee to stream the compressed data to a local file while still uploading it to httpbin.org.
>
> **See example** 7.8 - StreamingDownloadProcessReuploadTee

> **Discuss Chapter 7 online at** https://www.handsonscala.com/discuss/7

8

JSON and Binary Data Serialization

8.1 Manipulating JSON   148

8.2 JSON Serialization of Scala Data Types   152

8.3 Writing your own Generic Serialization Methods   156

8.4 Binary Serialization   158

```scala
@ val output = ujson.Arr(
    ujson.Obj("hello" -> "world", "answer" -> 42),
    true
  )

@ output(0)("hello") = "goodbye"

@ output(0)("tags") = ujson.Arr("awesome", "yay", "wonderful")

@ println(output)
[{"hello":"goodbye","answer":42,"tags":["awesome","yay","wonderful"]},true]    </> 8.1.scala
```

Snippet 8.1: manipulating a JSON tree structure in the Scala REPL

Data serialization is an important tool in any programmer's toolbox. While variables and classes are enough to store data within a process, most data tends to outlive a single program process: whether saved to disk, exchanged between processes, or sent over the network. This chapter will cover how to serialize your Scala data structures to two common data formats - textual JSON and binary MessagePack - and how you can interact with the structured data in a variety of useful ways.

The JSON workflows we learn in this chapter will be used later in *Chapter 12: Working with HTTP APIs* and *Chapter 14: Simple Web and API Servers*, while the binary serialization techniques we learn here will be used later in *Chapter 17: Multi-Process Applications*.

The easiest way to work with JSON and binary serialization is through the uPickle library. uJson and uPickle come bundled with Ammonite, and can be used within the REPL and *.sc script files. To begin, first download the sample JSON data at:

- ammonite-releases.json *(https://github.com/handsonscala/handsonscala/tree/v1/resources/8)*

We will be using the Ammonite Scala REPL for most of the work in this chapter, which comes with uPickle built in. You can type ujson.<tab> and upickle.<tab> to see the listing of available operations.

8.1 Manipulating JSON

Given a JSON string, You can parse it into a ujson.Value using ujson.read:

```
@ val jsonString = os.read(os.pwd / "ammonite-releases.json")
jsonString: String = """[
  {
    "url": "https://api.github.com/repos/.../releases/17991367",
    "assets_url": "https://api.github.com/repos/.../releases/17991367/assets",
    "upload_url": "https://uploads.github.com/repos/.../releases/17991367/assets",
...


@ val data = ujson.read(jsonString)
data: ujson.Value = Arr(
  ArrayBuffer(
    Obj(
      LinkedHashMap(
        "url" -> Str("https://api.github.com/repos/.../releases/17991367"),
        "assets_url" -> Str("https://api.github.com/repos/.../releases/17991367/assets"),
...
```
</> 8.2.scala

You can also construct JSON data structures directly using the ujson.* constructors. The constructors for primitive types like numbers, strings, and booleans are optional and can be elided:

```
@ val small = ujson.Arr(
    ujson.Obj("hello" -> ujson.Str("world"), "answer" -> ujson.Num(42)),
    ujson.Bool(true)
  )


@ val small = ujson.Arr(
    ujson.Obj("hello" -> "world", "answer" -> 42),
    true
  )
```
</> 8.3.scala

These can be serialized back to a string using the `ujson.write` function, or written directly to a file without needing to first serialize it to a `string` in-memory:

```
@ println(ujson.write(small))
[{"hello":"world","answer":42},true]


@ os.write(os.pwd / "out.json", small)


@ os.read(os.pwd / "out.json")
res6: String = "[{\"hello\":\"world\",\"answer\":42},true]"                    </> 8.4.scala
```

> See example 8.1 - Create

8.1.1 The ujson.Value Data Type

A `ujson.Value` can be one of several types:

```
sealed trait Value

case class Str(value: String) extends Value
case class Obj(value: mutable.LinkedHashMap[String, Value]) extends Value
case class Arr(value: mutable.ArrayBuffer[Value]) extends Value
case class Num(value: Double) extends Value

sealed trait Bool extends Value
case object False extends Bool
case object True extends Bool
case object Null extends Value                                                 </> 8.5.scala
```

`Value` is a `sealed trait`, indicating that this set of classes and objects encompass all the possible JSON Values. You can conveniently cast a `ujson.Value` to a specific sub-type and get its internal data by using the `.bool`, `.num`, `.arr`, `.obj`, or `.str` methods:

```
@ data.
apply       bool        num         render      transform   value
arr         isNull      obj         str         update                        </> 8.6.scala
```

If you are working with your JSON as an opaque tree - indexing into it by index or key, updating elements by index or key - you can do that directly using the `data(...)` and `data(...) = ...` syntax.

8.1.2 Querying and Modifying JSON

You can look up entries in the JSON data structure using `data(...)` syntax, similar to how you look up entries in an `Array` or `Map`:

```
@ data(0)
res7: ujson.Value = Obj(
  LinkedHashMap(
    "url" -> Str("https://api.github.com/repos/.../releases/17991367"),
    "assets_url" -> Str("https://api.github.com/repos/.../releases/17991367/assets"),
...

@ data(0)("url")
res8: ujson.Value = Str("https://api.github.com/repos/.../releases/17991367")

@ data(0)("author")("id")
res9: ujson.Value = Num(2.0607116E7)                                    </> 8.7.scala
```

ujson.Values are mutable:

```
@ println(small)
[{"hello":"world","answer":42},true]

@ small(0)("hello") = "goodbye"

@ small(0)("tags") = ujson.Arr("awesome", "yay", "wonderful")

@ println(small)
[{"hello":"goodbye","answer":42,"tags":["awesome","yay","wonderful"]},true]  </> 8.8.scala
```

8.1.3 Extracting Typed Values

If you want to assume your JSON value is of a particular type and do type-specific operations like "*iterate over array*", "*get length of string*", or "*get keys of object*", you need to use `.arr`, `.str`, or `.obj` to cast your JSON structure to the specific type and extract the value.

For example, fetching and manipulating the fields of a `ujson.Obj` requires use of `.obj`:

```
@ small(0).obj.remove("hello")

@ small.arr.append(123)

@ println(small)
[{"answer":42,"tags":["awesome","yay","wonderful"]},true,123]          </> 8.9.scala
```

Extracting values as primitive types requires use of `.str` or `.num`. Note that `ujson.Nums` are stored as doubles. You can call `.toInt` to convert the `ujson.Nums` to integers:

```
@ data(0)("url").str
res17: String = "https://api.github.com/repos/.../releases/17991367"


@ data(0)("author")("id").num
res18: Double = 2.0607116E7


@ data(0)("author")("id").num.toInt
res19: Int = 20607116                                                    </> 8.10.scala
```

See example 8.2 - Manipulate

If the type of the JSON value is not parseable into the `str` or `num` type we are expecting, the call throws a runtime exception.

8.1.4 Traversing JSON

To traverse over the tree structure of the `ujson.Value` (*8.1.1*), we can use a recursive function. For example, here is one that recursively traverses the `data` we had parsed earlier, and collects all the `ujson.Str` nodes in the JSON structure.

```
@ def traverse(v: ujson.Value): Iterable[String] = v match {
    case a: ujson.Arr => a.arr.map(traverse).flatten
    case o: ujson.Obj => o.obj.values.map(traverse).flatten
    case s: ujson.Str => Seq(s.str)
    case _ => Nil
  }


@ traverse(data)
res21: Iterable[String] = ArrayBuffer(
  "https://api.github.com/repos/.../releases/17991367",
  "https://api.github.com/repos/.../releases/17991367/assets",
  "https://uploads.github.com/repos/.../releases/17991367/assets",
  "https://github.com/.../releases/tag/1.6.8",
...                                                                      </> 8.11.scala
```

See example 8.3 - Traverse

8.2 JSON Serialization of Scala Data Types

Often you do not just want dynamically-typed JSON trees: rather, you usually want Scala collections or `case` `class`es, with fields of known types. Serializing values of type T is done by looking up `implicit` serializers of type `ReadWriter[T]`. Some of these serializers are provided by the library, while others you have to define yourself in your own code.

8.2.1 Serializing Scala Builtins

Implicit `ReadWriters` are already defined for most common Scala data types: `Ints`, `Doubles`, `Strings`, `Seqs`, `Lists`, `Maps`, tuples, etc. You can thus serialize and deserialize collections of primitives and other builtin types automatically.

```
@ val numbers = upickle.default.read[Seq[Int]]("[1, 2, 3, 4]")
numbers: Seq[Int] = List(1, 2, 3, 4)

@ upickle.default.write(numbers)
res23: String = "[1,2,3,4]"

@ val tuples = upickle.default.read[Seq[(Int, Boolean)]]("[[1, true], [2, false]]")
tuples: Seq[(Int, Boolean)] = List((1, true), (2, false))

@ upickle.default.write(tuples)
res25: String = "[[1,true],[2,false]]"                              </> 8.12.scala
```

Serialization is done via the *Typeclass Inference* technique we covered in **Chapter 5: Notable Scala Features**, and thus can work for arbitrarily deep nested data structures:

```
@ val input = """{"weasel": ["i", "am"], "baboon": ["i", "r"]}"""

@ val parsed = upickle.default.read[Map[String, Seq[String]]](input)
parsed: Map[String, Seq[String]] = Map(
  "weasel" -> List("i", "am"),
  "baboon" -> List("i", "r")
)

@ upickle.default.write(parsed)
res28: String = "{\"weasel\":[\"i\",\"am\"],\"baboon\":[\"i\",\"r\"]}"   </> 8.13.scala
```

See example 8.4 - SerializationBuiltins

8.2.2 Serializing Case Classes

To convert a JSON structure into a `case class`, there are a few steps:

1. Define a `case class` representing the fields and types you expect to be present in the JSON
2. Define an implicit `upickle.default.ReadWriter` for that case class
3. Use `upickle.default.read` to deserialize the JSON structure.

For example, the `author` value in the JSON data we saw earlier has the following fields:

```scala
@ println(ujson.write(data(0)("author"), indent = 4))
{
    "login": "Ammonite-Bot",
    "id": 20607116,
    "node_id": "MDQ6VXNLcjIwNjA3MTE2",
    "gravatar_id": "",
    "type": "User",
    "site_admin": false,
    ...
}
```
</> 8.14.scala

Which can be (partially) modeled as the following `case class`:

```scala
@ case class Author(login: String, id: Int, site_admin: Boolean)

@ implicit val authorRW: upickle.default.ReadWriter[Author] = upickle.default.macroRW
```
</> 8.15.scala

For every `case class` you want to serialize, you have to define an implicit `upickle.default.ReadWriter` to mark it as serializable. For now we use `macroRW` which serializes and deserializes the `case class` with its field names mapped to corresponding JSON object keys, but you could also do it manually via a Mapped Serializer (*8.2.3*) if you need more flexibility or customization.

```
@ val author = upickle.default.read[Author](data(0)("author")) // read from JSON structure
author: Author = Author("Ammonite-Bot", 20607116, false)


@ author.login
res33: String = "Ammonite-Bot"


@ val author2 = upickle.default.read[Author](  // read directly from a String
    """{"login": "lihaoyi", "id": 313373, "site_admin": true}"""
  )
author2: Author = Author("Lihaoyi", 313373, true)


@ upickle.default.write(author2)
res35: String = "{\"login\":\"lihaoyi\",\"id\":313373,\"site_admin\":true}"</> 8.16.scala
```

Once you have defined a ReadWriter[Author], you can then also serialize and de-serialize Authors as part of any larger data structure:

```
@ upickle.default.read[Map[String, Author]]("""{
    "haoyi": {"login": "lihaoyi", "id": 1337, "site_admin": true},
    "bot": {"login": "ammonite-bot", "id": 31337, "site_admin": false}
  }""")
res36: Map[String, Author] = Map(
  "haoyi" -> Author("lihaoyi", 1337, true),
  "bot" -> Author("ammonite-bot", 31337, false)
)
                                                                    </> 8.17.scala
```

See example 8.5 - SerializationCaseClass

In general, you can serialize any arbitrarily nested tree of case classes, collections, and primitives, as long as every value within that structure is itself serializable.

8.2.3 Mapped Serializers

uPickle allows you to easily construct implicit serializers for new types based on existing ones. For example, by default uPickle does not have support for serializing os.Paths:

```
@ upickle.default.write(os.pwd)
cmd0.sc:1: could not find implicit value for evidence parameter
          of type upickle.default.Writer[os.Path]
val res0 = upickle.default.write(os.pwd)
                     ^
Compilation Failed
                                                                    </> 8.18.scala
```

However, because `os.Path`s can be trivially converted to and from `String`s, we can use the `bimap` function to construct a `ReadWriter[os.Path]` from the existing `ReadWriter[String]`:

```scala
@ implicit val pathRw = upickle.default.readwriter[String].bimap[os.Path](
    p => ... /* convert os.Path to String */,
    s => ... /* convert String to os.Path */
  )                                                                      </> 8.19.scala
```

`bimap` needs you to specify what your existing serializer is (here `String`), and what new type you want to serialize (`os.Path`), and provide conversion functions to convert back and forth between the two types. In this case, we could use the following converters:

```scala
@ implicit val pathRw = upickle.default.readwriter[String].bimap[os.Path](
    p => p.toString,
    s => os.Path(s)
  )                                                                      </> 8.20.scala
```

With this `implicit val pathRw` defined, we can now serialize and deserialize `os.Path`s. This applies recursively as well, so any `case class`es or collections contain `os.Path` can now be serialized as well:

```scala
@ val str = upickle.default.write(os.pwd)
str: String = "\"/Users/lihaoyi/test\""

@ upickle.default.read[os.Path](str)
res39: os.Path = /Users/lihaoyi/test

@ val str2 = upickle.default.write(Array(os.pwd, os.home, os.root))
str2: String = "[\"/Users/lihaoyi/test\",\"/Users/lihaoyi\",\"/\"]"

@ upickle.default.read[Array[os.Path]](str2)
res41: Array[os.Path] = Array(/Users/lihaoyi/test, /Users/lihaoyi, /)      </> 8.21.scala
```

If you want more flexibility in how your JSON is deserialized into your data type, you can use `upickle.default.readwriter[ujson.Value].bimap` to work with the raw `ujson.Value`s:

```scala
@ implicit val pathRw = upickle.default.readwriter[ujson.Value].bimap[Thing](
    p => ... /* convert a Thing to ujson.Value */,
    s => ... /* convert a ujson.Value to Thing */
  )                                                                      </> 8.22.scala
```

You then have full freedom in how you want to convert a `ujson.Value` into a `Thing`, and how you want to serialize the `Thing` back into a `ujson.Value`.

8.3 Writing your own Generic Serialization Methods

You can define your own methods that are able to serialize (or deserialize) values of various types by making them generic with a context bound of Reader, Writer, or ReadWriter.

8.3.1 uPickle Context Bounds

The key context bounds relevant to the uPickle serialization library are:

- def foo[T: upickle.default.Reader]: allows use of upickle.default.read[T]

- def foo[T: upickle.default.Writer]: allows use of upickle.default.write[T]

- def foo[T: upickle.default.ReadWriter]: allows use of both upickle.default.read[T] and upickle.default.write[T]

As we discussed in *Chapter 5: Notable Scala Features*, the context bound syntax above is equivalent to the following implicit parameter:

```scala
def foo[T](implicit reader: upickle.default.Reader[T])
```

This allows the compiler to infer the parameter if it is not explicitly provided, and saves us the inconvenience of having to pass serializers around manually.

8.3.2 Generic Serialization Methods

Using context bounds, we can write generic methods that can operate on any input type, as long as that type is JSON serializable. For example, if we want to write a method that serializes a value and prints out the JSON to the console, we can do that as follows:

```scala
@ case class Asset(id: Int, name: String)

@ implicit val assetRw = upickle.default.macroRW[Asset]

@ def myPrintJson[T: upickle.default.Writer](t: T) = println(upickle.default.write(t))
                                                                        </> 8.23.scala

@ myPrintJson(Asset(1, "hello"))
{"id":1,"name":"hello"}

@ myPrintJson(Seq(1, 2, 3))
[1,2,3]

@ myPrintJson(Seq(Asset(1, "hello"), Asset(2, "goodbye")))
[{"id":1,"name":"hello"},{"id":2,"name":"goodbye"}]          </> 8.24.scala
```

If we want to write a method that reads input from the console and parses it to JSON of a particular type, we can do that as well:

```scala
@ def myReadJson[T: upickle.default.Reader](): T = {
    print("Enter some JSON: ")
    upickle.default.read[T](Console.in.readLine())
  }

@ myReadJson[Seq[Int]]()
Enter some JSON: [1, 2, 3, 4, 5]
res49: Seq[Int] = List(1, 2, 3, 4, 5)

@ myReadJson[Author]()
Enter some JSON: {"login": "Haoyi", "id": 1337, "site_admin": true}
res50: Author = Author("Haoyi", 1337, true)                          </> 8.25.scala
```

Note that when calling `myReadJson()`, we have to pass in the type parameter `[Seq[Int]]` or `[Author]` explicitly, whereas when calling `myPrintJson()` the compiler can infer the type parameter based on the type of the given value `Asset(1, "hello")`, `Seq(1, 2, 3)`, etc.

In general, we do not need a context bound when we are writing code that operates on a single concrete type, as the compiler will already be able to infer the correct concrete serializer. We only need a context bound if the method is generic, to indicate to the compiler that it should be callable only with concrete types that have an implicit `Reader[T]` or `Writer[T]` available

We will be using this ability to write generic methods dealing with serialization and de-serialization to write generic RPC (Remote Procedure Call) logic in *Chapter 17: Multi-Process Applications*.

8.3.3 Why Context Bounds?

The advantage of using context bounds over other ways of serializing data types is that they allow the serialization logic to be inferred statically. That has three consequences:

8.3.3.1 Performance with Convenience

uPickle's serializers being resolved at compile time using Scala's `implicit`s gives you the convenience of reflection-based frameworks with the performance of hand-written serialization code.

Unlike hand-written serializers, the compiler does most of the busy-work constructing the serialization logic for you. You only need to teach it how to serialize and deserialize your basic primitives and collections and it will know how to serialize all combinations of these without additional boilerplate.

Unlike reflection-based serializers, uPickles serializers are fast: they avoid runtime reflection which has significant overhead in most languages, and can be optimized by the compiler to generate lean and efficient code to execute at run time.

8.3.3.2 Compile-Time Error Reporting

The compiler is able to reject non-serializable data types early during compilation, rather than blowing up later after the code has been deployed to production. For example, since we defined the `myPrintJson` earlier with a `T: upickle.default.Writer` context bound, the compiler helps prevents us from accidentally passing in an unserializable value.

For example, trying to serialize an open process output stream results in a compile error telling us exactly what we need to fix before the code can run:

```
@ myPrintJson(System.out)
cmd6.sc:1: could not find implicit value for evidence parameter of type
          upickle.default.Writer[java.io.PrintStream]
val res6 = myPrintJson(System.out)
                       ^
Compilation Failed                                              </> 8.26.scala
```

8.3.3.3 Security

Because every `upickle.default.read` call has a statically-specified type, we will never deserialize a value of unexpected type: this rules out a class of security issues where an attacker can force your code to accidentally deserialize an unsafe object able to compromise your application.

For example, if we accidentally try to deserialize a `sun.misc.Unsafe` instance from JSON, we get an immediate compile time error:

```
@ myReadJson[sun.misc.Unsafe]()
cmd12.sc:1: could not find implicit value for evidence parameter of type
          upickle.default.Reader[sun.misc.Unsafe]
val res12 = myReadJson[sun.misc.Unsafe]()
                       ^
Compilation Failed                                              </> 8.27.scala
```

In general, the Scala language allows you to check the serializability of your data structures at compile time, avoiding an entire class of bugs and security vulnerabilities. Rather than finding your serialization logic crashing or misbehaving in production due to an unexpected value appearing in your data structure, the Scala compiler surfaces these issues at compile time, making them much easier to diagnose and fix.

8.4 Binary Serialization

Apart from serializing Scala data types as JSON, uPickle also supports serializing them to compact MessagePack binary blobs. These are often more compact than JSON, especially for binary data that would need to be Base 64 encoded to fit in a JSON string, at the expense of losing human readability.

8.4.1 writeBinary and readBinary

Serializing data structures to binary blobs is done via the `writeBinary` and `readBinary` methods:

```
@ case class Author(login: String, id: Int, site_admin: Boolean)

@ implicit val authorRw = upickle.default.macroRW[Author]

@ val blob = upickle.default.writeBinary(Author("haoyi", 31337, true))
blob: Array[Byte] = Array(-125, -91, 108, 111, ...)

@ upickle.default.readBinary[Author](blob)
res54: Author = Author("haoyi", 31337, true)                    </> 8.28.scala
```

writeBinary and readBinary work on any Scala data type that can be converted to JSON, including compound data types. The following example demonstrates serialization and de-serialization of Map[Int, List[Author]]s:

```
@ val data = Map(
    1 -> Nil,
    2 -> List(Author("haoyi", 1337, true), Author("lihaoyi", 31337, true))
  )

@ val blob2 = upickle.default.writeBinary(data)
blob2: Array[Byte] = Array(-110, -110, 1, -112, ...)

@ upickle.default.readBinary[Map[Int, List[Author]]](blob2)
res57: Map[Int, List[Author]] = Map(
  1 -> List(),
  2 -> List(Author("haoyi", 1337, true), Author("lihaoyi", 31337, true))
)                                                               </> 8.29.scala
```

Unlike JSON, MessagePack binary blobs are not human readable by default: Array(-110, -110, 1, -112, ...) is not something you can quickly skim and see what it contains! If you are working with a third-party server returning MessagePack binaries with an unknown or unusual structure, this can make it difficult to understand what a MessagePack blob contains so you can properly deserialize it.

8.4.2 MessagePack Structures

To help work with the MessagePack blobs of unknown structure, uPickle comes with a uPack library that lets you read the blobs into an in-memory `upack.Msg` structure (similar to `ujson.Value`) that is easy to inspect:

```
@ upack.read(blob)
res58: upack.Msg = Obj(
  LinkedHashMap(
    Str("login") -> Str("haoyi"),
    Str("id") -> Int32(31337),
    Str("site_admin") -> True
  )
)
```
</> 8.30.scala

```
@ upack.read(blob2)
res59: upack.Msg = Arr(
  ArrayBuffer(
    Arr(ArrayBuffer(Int32(1), Arr(ArrayBuffer()))),
    Arr(
      ArrayBuffer(
        Int32(2),
        Arr(
          ArrayBuffer(
            Obj(
              LinkedHashMap(
                Str("login") -> Str("haoyi"),
                Str("id") -> Int32(1337),
                Str("site_admin") -> True
              )
            ),
...
```
</> 8.31.scala

Reading the binary blobs into `upack.Msgs` is a great debugging tool, and can help you figure out what is going on under the hood if your `writeBinary`/`readBinary` serialization is misbehaving.

Like `ujson.Values`, you can manually construct `upack.Msg` from scratch using their constituent parts `upack.Arr`, `upack.Obj`, `upack.Bool`, etc. This can be useful if you need to interact with some third-party systems and need full control of the MessagePack messages you are sending:

```
@ val msg = upack.Obj(
    upack.Str("login") -> upack.Str("haoyi"),
    upack.Str("id") -> upack.Int32(31337),
    upack.Str("site_admin") -> upack.True
  )

@ val blob3 = upack.write(msg)
blob3: Array[Byte] = Array(-125, -91, 108, 111, 111, ...)

@ val deserialized = upickle.default.readBinary[Author](blob3)
deserialized: Author = Author("haoyi", 31337, true)                    </> 8.32.scala
```

See example 8.6 - SerializationBinary

8.5 Conclusion

Serializing data is one of the core tools that any programmer needs to have. This chapter introduces you to the basics of working with data serialization in a Scala program, using the uPickle library. uPickle focuses on providing convenient serialization for built in data structures and user-defined `case class`es, though with Mapped Serializers (*8.2.3*) you can extend it yourself to support any arbitrary data type. For more details on using the uPickle serialization library to work with JSON or MessagePack data, you can refer to the reference documentation:

- http://www.lihaoyi.com/upickle

uPickle is also available for you to use in projects built using Mill or other build tools at the following coordinates:

```
ivy"com.lihaoyi::upickle:1.2.0"                                                 Mill
```

We will use the JSON APIs we learned in this chapter later in *Chapter 12: Working with HTTP APIs*, *Chapter 14: Simple Web and API Servers*, and use the MessagePack binary serialization techniques in *Chapter 17: Multi-Process Applications*.

While this chapter focuses on the uPickle library, there are many other JSON or binary serialization libraries in the Scala ecosystem:

- Circe JSON: https://github.com/circe/circe
- Play JSON: https://github.com/playframework/play-json
- ScalaPB: https://github.com/scalapb/ScalaPB

These other libraries make different sets of tradeoffs. You can try them out to see how they work and find if there is one you prefer, but for simplicity the rest of this book will be using uPickle.

This flow chart covers most of the common workflows working with textual JSON and binary MessagePack data in Scala:

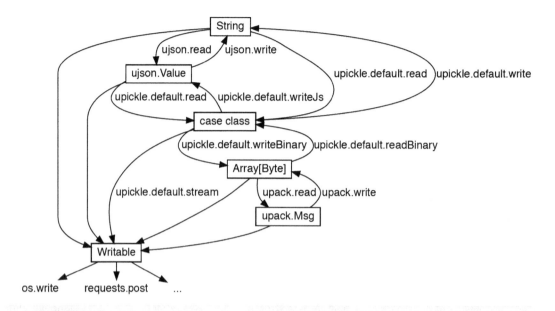

Exercise: Given a normal class `class Foo(val i: Int, val s: String)` with two public fields, using the `bimap` method we saw earlier to define an implicit `ReadWriter` for it to allow instances to be serialized to Javascript objects `{"i": ..., "s": ...}`.

See example 8.7 - BiMapClass

Exercise: Often JSON data structures have fields that you do not care about, and make skimming through the JSON verbose and tedious: e.g. the `ammonite-releases.json` we receive from Github comes loaded with lots of verbose and often-not-very-useful URLs shown below.

```
"followers_url": "https://api.github.com/users/Ammonite-Bot/followers",
"following_url": "https://api.github.com/users/Ammonite-Bot/following{/other_user}",
"gists_url": "https://api.github.com/users/Ammonite-Bot/gists{/gist_id}", </> 8.33.json
```

Write a method that takes a `ujson.Value`, and removes any values which are strings beginning with `"https://"`. You can do so either in a mutable or immutable style: either modifying the `ujson.Value` in place, or constructing and returning a new `ujson.Value` with those values elided.

See example 8.8 - TraverseFilter

Discuss Chapter 8 online at https://www.handsonscala.com/discuss/8

9

Self-Contained Scala Scripts

9.1 Reading Files Off Disk   164

9.2 Rendering HTML with Scalatags   165

9.3 Rendering Markdown with Commonmark-Java   167

9.4 Links and Bootstrap   172

9.5 Optionally Deploying the Static Site   175

```scala
os.write(
  os.pwd / "out" / "index.html",
  doctype("html")(
    html(
      body(
        h1("Blog"),
        for ((_, suffix, _) <- postInfo)
        yield h2(a(href := ("post/" + mdNameToHtml(suffix)))(suffix))
      )
    )
  )
)
```
</> 9.1.scala

Snippet 9.1: rendering a HTML page using the third-party Scalatags HTML library

Scala Scripts are a great way to write small programs. Each script is self-contained and can download its own dependencies when necessary, and make use of both Java and Scala libraries. This lets you write and distribute scripts without spending time fiddling with build configuration or library installation.

In this chapter, we will write a static site generator script that uses third-party libraries to process Markdown input files and generate a set of HTML output files, ready for deployment on any static file hosting service. This will form the foundation for **Chapter 10: Static Build Pipelines**, where we will turn the static site generator into an efficient incremental build pipeline by using the Mill build tool.

We will start from the simplest possible working script:

```
println("Hello!")                                                    Blog.sc
```

```
$ amm Blog.sc
Hello!                                                          </> 9.2.bash
```

Starting from this simple script, we will extend it to:

- Read markdown files from the filesystem
- Generate the HTML page skeleton using the Scalatags library
- Parse and render the markdown using the Atlassian Commonmark library
- Link our pages together using hyperlinks and add some CSS to make it look good
- Add an optional flag that deploys the static site to a Git repository

9.1 Reading Files Off Disk

Typically, static site generators take their input as markdown files, possibly with additional metadata, and use that to generate HTML. For this exercise, let's assume that there will be a post/ folder that contains any markdown files we want to convert into blog posts, and each one will be named following the convention:

- `1 - My First Post`.md
- `2 - My Second Post`.md
- `3 - My Third Post`.md
- etc.

The number before the `-` indicating the order of the blog post in the final site, while the text after indicates the title of the post. We can create some sample posts at the command line as follows:

```
$ mkdir post
$ touch "post/1 - My First Post.md"
$ touch "post/2 - My Second Post.md"
$ touch "post/3 - My Third Post.md"


$ ls
Blog.sc posts


$ ls post/
1 - My First Post.md    2 - My Second Post.md    3 - My Third Post.md    </> 9.3.bash
```

Finding these posts is easy with the filesystem operations provided by the os package:

```
interp.watch(os.pwd / "post")                                          Blog.sc
val postInfo = os
  .list(os.pwd / "post")
  .map{ p =>
    val s"$prefix - $suffix.md" = p.last
    (prefix, suffix, p)
  }
  .sortBy(_._1.toInt)


println("POSTS")
postInfo.foreach(println)                                          </> 9.4.scala
```

Here, we are listing all files in the `post/` folder, splitting their file names on `-`, and using the two segments to be the number and name of our blog posts. We can run the script to see that it is able to understand the layout of the blog posts, extract their number and name, and sort them in order.

```
$ amm Blog.sc
POSTS
(1,My First Post,/Users/haoyi/test/posts/1 - My First Post.md)
(2,My Second Post,/Users/haoyi/test/posts/2 - My Second Post.md)
(3,My Third Post,/Users/haoyi/test/posts/3 - My Third Post.md)    </> 9.5.bash
```

Note the `interp.watch` call. This is optional, and helps support the `--watch` flag. Normally `amm --watch` will watch the script you are running and re-run the script when it changes. `interp.watch` broadens that to also watch the `post/` folder, re-running the script if the contents of that folder changes. That can make iterating on the script or the files being processed a much smoother experience than having to re-run the script manually each time.

See example 9.1 - Printing

9.2 Rendering HTML with Scalatags

A static site generator needs to generate a static site, and static sites are made of HTML pages. We could generate HTML by stitching together strings like `"<div>" + content + "</div>"`, but doing so is tedious and unsafe, prone to XSS injection if we're not careful. Luckily, in Scala Scripts we can easily import whatever Java or Scala libraries we want: for now we will import the Scalatags HTML generation library:

- http://www.lihaoyi.com/scalatags/

```
+import $ivy.`com.lihaoyi::scalatags:0.9.1`, scalatags.Text.all._        Blog.sc
```

`import $ivy` is a special syntax available in the REPL and scripts for downloading a third-party dependency. In this case, we use it to download the Scalatags HTML library. After `import $ivy`, we then import `scalatags.Text.all._` to bring the necessary functions into scope, which lets us use Scalatags to generate our first HTML file:

```
-println("POSTS")                                                    Blog.sc
-postInfo.foreach(println)
+os.remove.all(os.pwd / "out")
+os.makeDir.all(os.pwd / "out" / "post")
+os.write(
+  os.pwd / "out" / "index.html",
+  doctype("html")(
+    html(
+      body(
+        h1("Blog"),
+        for ((_, suffix, _) <- postInfo)
+        yield h2(suffix)
+      )
+    )
+  )
+)
```
</> 9.6.scala

See example 9.2 - Index

This snippet writes a small HTML blob, with `<html>`, `<body>` and `<h1>`/`<h2>` tags to an out/index.html file. Each function call `html(...)`, `body(...)`, `h1(...)`, etc. defines a pair of opening/closing HTML tags, with the strings such as `"Blog"` becoming the textual contents of the enclosing tag. Put together, this constructs a scalatags fragment, or `Frag`. Scalatags `Frag`s satisfy the Writable interface, and can be directly written to a file via `os.write`, or serialized into an in-memory `String` via `.render`.

For now we will be using an out/ folder to store all our output HTML files, so every run we will first delete the out/ folder with `os.remove.all` and re-create the out/ and out/post/ folders with `os.makeDir.all` in preparation for writing the HTML files.

We can run the script to see it in action:

```
$ amm Blog.sc


$ cat out/index.html
<!DOCTYPE html><html><head></head><body>
<h1>Haoyi's Blog</h1><h2>My First Post.md</h2><h2>My Second Post.md</h2>
<h2>My Third Post.md</h2></body></html>
```
</> 9.7.bash

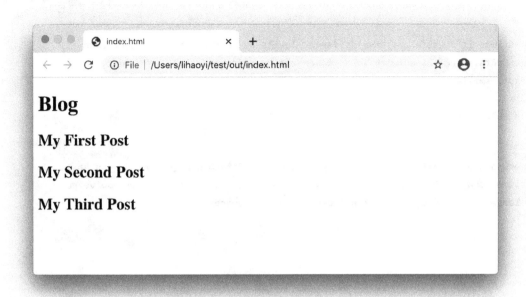

9.3 Rendering Markdown with Commonmark-Java

While the skeleton of the page is written in HTML using Scalatags, for long-form blog posts it is more convenient to write them in Markdown. As sample blog posts, we will take some generic text from the Github Markdown Guide:

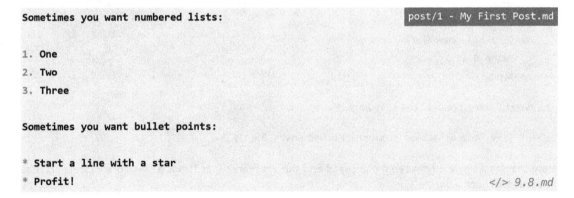

```
Sometimes you want numbered lists:                    post/1 - My First Post.md


1. One
2. Two
3. Three


Sometimes you want bullet points:


* Start a line with a star
* Profit!                                                        </> 9.8.md
```

```
# Structured documents                                          post/2 - My Second Post.md
```

Sometimes it's useful to have different levels of headings to structure your
documents. Start lines with a `#` to create headings. Multiple `##` in a row
denote smaller heading sizes.

```
### This is a third-tier heading                                              </> 9.9.md
```

```
                                                                post/3 - My Third Post.md
```
There are many different ways to style code with GitHub's markdown. If you have
inline code blocks, wrap them in backticks: `var example = true`. If you've got
a longer block of code, you can indent with four spaces:

```
    if (isAwesome) {
      return true
    }                                                                        </> 9.10.md
```

Perhaps not the most insightful thought-pieces, but they will do for now. The next question would be, how can we parse the markdown? There are perfectly good markdown parsers in Java, and we can pick any we want to use from Scala. For now, we will use the `atlassian/commonmark-java` library.

- https://github.com/atlassian/commonmark-java

The linked readme gives you the maven snippet necessary to use this parser:

```xml
<dependency>
    <groupId>com.atlassian.commonmark</groupId>
    <artifactId>commonmark</artifactId>
    <version>0.13.1</version>
</dependency>                                                                </> 9.11.xml
```

This directly corresponds to the $ivy import:

```
import $ivy.`com.atlassian.commonmark:commonmark:0.13.1`
```

Note that it's a single `:` between the `groupId` and the `artifactId`, as this is a Java library (Scala libraries like Scalatags need a double `::`)

9.3.1 Translating Java Snippets to Scala

The Commonmark-Java library gives us some Java sample code to get started using the library:

```
import org.commonmark.node.*;
import org.commonmark.parser.Parser;
import org.commonmark.renderer.html.HtmlRenderer;

Parser parser = Parser.builder().build();
Node document = parser.parse("This is *Sparta*");
HtmlRenderer renderer = HtmlRenderer.builder().build();
renderer.render(document);  // "<p>This is <em>Sparta</em></p>\n"        </> 9.12.java
```

Translating this Java code into Scala basically involves replacing all the local variables with `val`s. Using `import $ivy` in the Ammonite Scala REPL lets us easily test this:

```
@ import $ivy.`com.atlassian.commonmark:commonmark:0.13.1`

@ val parser = org.commonmark.parser.Parser.builder().build()

@ val document = parser.parse("This is *Sparta*")

@ val renderer = org.commonmark.renderer.html.HtmlRenderer.builder().build()

@ val output = renderer.render(document)
output: String = """<p>This is <em>Sparta</em></p>
"""                                                                       </> 9.13.scala
```

Now that we have it working, we can use this in our code: reading the `.md` files, transforming them into HTML and writing them into HTML files:

```
 import $ivy.`com.lihaoyi::scalatags:0.9.1`, scalatags.Text.all._       Blog.sc
+import $ivy.`com.atlassian.commonmark:commonmark:0.13.1`               </> 9.14.scala
```

```
+def mdNameToHtml(name: String) = name.replace(" ", "-").toLowerCase + ".html"    Blog.sc
+
+for ((_, suffix, path) <- postInfo) {
+  val parser = org.commonmark.parser.Parser.builder().build()
+  val document = parser.parse(os.read(path))
+  val renderer = org.commonmark.renderer.html.HtmlRenderer.builder().build()
+  val output = renderer.render(document)
+  os.write(
+    os.pwd / "out" / "post" / mdNameToHtml(suffix),
+    doctype("html")(
+      html(
+        body(
+          h1("Blog", " / ", suffix),
+          raw(output)
+        )
+      )
+    )
+  )
+}
```
</> 9.15.scala

You can see the new `for` loop in the middle with all the code adapted from the `atlassian/commonmark-java` docs, basically verbatim. We are converting the "raw" names of the files to URL-friendly names in the `mdNameToHtml` method. For now we will ignore the possibility of name collisions.

Note that we are including the generating HTML strings provided by `atlassian/commonmark-java` wrapped in `raw(...)`. By default any strings we include in Scalatags fragments are sanitized, which protects you from Cross-Site Scripting and other attacks that arise from unexpected HTML being present in the strings. However, in this case we *want* the HTML in the rendered markdown, and thus we use `raw(...)` to opt-in to including the rendered markdown un-sanitized.

9.3.2 Testing our Java Markdown Parser

Running this, it will download the `atlassian/commonmark-java` library the first time, and use it to render our markdown blog posts to HTML:

```
$ amm Blog.sc

$ find out -type f
out
out/index.html
out/post/my-first-post.html
out/post/my-second-post.html
out/post/my-third-post.html
```
</> 9.16.bash

We can see on the filesystem that our `my-first-post.html` and `my-second-post.html` files are all in place. We can browse the generated HTML below:

```
$ cat out/post/my-first-post.html
<!DOCTYPE html><html><body>
<h1>Blog / My First Post</h1>
<p>Sometimes you want numbered lists:</p>
<ol>
<li>One</li>
<li>Two</li>
<li>Three</li>
</ol>
<p>Sometimes you want bullet points:</p>
<ul>
<li>Start a line with a star</li>
<li>Profit!</li>
</ul>
</body></html>                                                    </> 9.17.xml
```

Or open them in the browser:

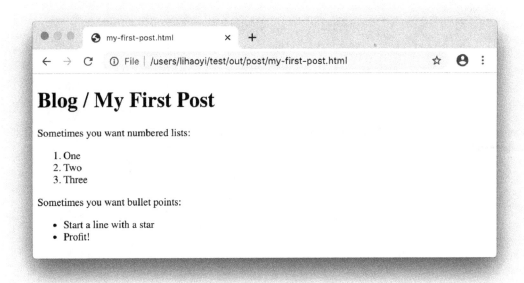

See example 9.3 - Markdown

9.4 Links and Bootstrap

9.4.1 Page Links

To turn our folder of generated HTML files into a proper static site, we need to add links between the pages. At the very least, we need links from the index.html page to each individual blog post, and a link from each post back to the index.html page. This is a matter of adding an `<a href>` tag inside the h2 header tags in index.html, with the href being the relative path to the HTML file of each individual blog post:

```
html(                                                              Blog.sc
  body(
    h1("Blog"),
    for ((_, suffix, _) <- postInfo)
-     yield h2(suffix)
+     yield h2(a(href := ("post/" + mdNameToHtml(suffix)), suffix))
  )
)                                                              </> 9.18.scala
```

:= is a custom operator provided by the Scalatags, and is used to specify HTML attributes and styles. We need to perform a similar change on each individual post's HTML page:

```
html(                                                              Blog.sc
  body(
-   h1("Blog", " / ", suffix),
+   h1(a(href := "../index.html")("Blog"), " / ", suffix),
    raw(output)
  )
)                                                              </> 9.19.scala
```

After re-generating the HTML files using `amm Blog.sc`, we can see that the post listing in index.html links to the respective post's HTML files:

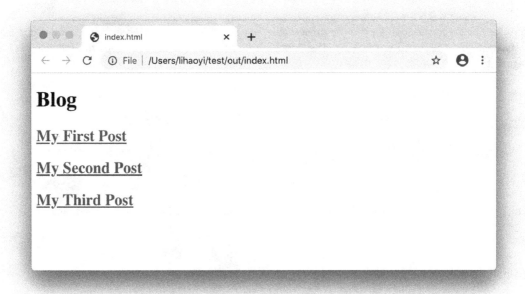

And each individual post has the `Blog` header at the top left link back to the `index.html` page:

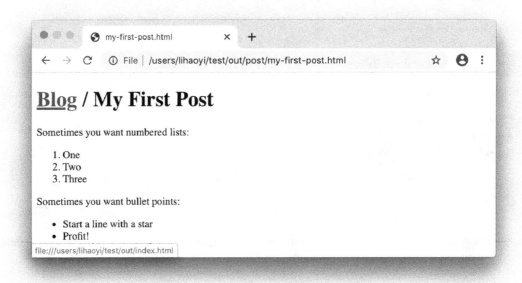

See example 9.4 - Links

9.4.2 Bootstrap

To make our static site look a bit more presentable, we can layer on some Bootstrap CSS over our ugly unstyled page, in order to pretty it up. The Bootstrap getting started page provides the following HTML fragment:

- http://getbootstrap.com/getting-started

```
<link
    rel="stylesheet"
    href="https://stackpath.bootstrapcdn.com/bootstrap/4.4.1/css/bootstrap.css"
>
```
`</>` *9.20.html*

Which translates into the following Scalatags fragments that we need to include in our head tag:

```
+val bootstrapCss = link(                                              Blog.sc
+   rel := "stylesheet",
+   href := "https://stackpath.bootstrapcdn.com/bootstrap/4.5.0/css/bootstrap.css"
+)
```
`</>` *9.21.scala*

```
  os.write(                                                           Blog.sc
    os.pwd / "out" / "post" / mdNameToHtml(suffix),
    doctype("html")(
      html(
+       head(bootstrapCss),
        body(
          h1(a("Blog", href := "../index.html"), " / ", suffix),      </> 9.22.scala
```

```
  os.write(                                                           Blog.sc
    os.pwd / "out" / "index.html",
    doctype("html")(
      html(
+       head(bootstrapCss),
        body(
          h1("Blog"),                                                 </> 9.23.scala
```

Here, we're including the link as described in the Bootstrap docs, converted it to Scalatags template syntax. We can see it take effect in the browser:

You can paste this into a `Blog.sc` file, put markdown files with the naming convention `1 - Hello.md` `2 - Post.md` in the `post/` folder, and run `amm Blog.sc` to generate the HTML pages. Once generated, those pages can go anywhere: viewed locally, pushed to github pages, or deployed elsewhere. The website we are generating is static and can be deployed on any static content host.

The first time you run the script, it will take 2-3 seconds to compile. After that first compile, executing the script should take about a second. You can edit the markdown files and the HTML pages will be re-generated quickly.

See example 9.5 - Bootstrap

9.5 Optionally Deploying the Static Site

Scala Scripts can take command line arguments via `@main def main(...)` methods, where the arguments to `main` are taken from the command line. We will define a `@main` method for our `Blog.sc` script that allows the user to specify a remote Git repository from the command line, and uses `os.proc` operations to push the static site to that repository.

This can be done as follows:

```
import $ivy.`com.lihaoyi::scalatags:0.9.1`, scalatags.Text.all._        Blog.sc
import $ivy.`com.atlassian.commonmark:commonmark:0.13.1`

+ @main def main(targetGitRepo: String = ""): Unit = {

    ...

+   if (targetGitRepo != "") {
+     os.proc("git", "init").call(cwd = os.pwd / "out")
+     os.proc("git", "add", "-A").call(cwd = os.pwd / "out")
+     os.proc("git", "commit", "-am", ".").call(cwd = os.pwd / "out")
+     os.proc("git", "push", targetGitRepo, "head", "-f").call(cwd = os.pwd / "out")
+   }
+ }
```
</> 9.24.scala

Rather than writing our code top-level, we put it inside a @main method that takes parameters. Parameter types can be simple primitives (Strings, Ints, Booleans, etc.) and parameters can have default values to make them optional. In this case, the default value targetGitRepo = "" simply skips the deployment step if the user does not pass in that argument from the command line.

Blog.sc can now be called as follows:

```
$ amm Blog.sc # Generate the static site, do not deploy it

$ amm Blog.sc git@github.com:lihaoyi/test.git # generate and deploy

$ amm Blog.sc --targetGitRepo git@github.com:lihaoyi/test.git # named-argument syntax
```
</> 9.25.bash

This code is suitable for deployment to a Github Pages site, where the static site content is hosted in a Git repository. If you want to deploy elsewhere, it should be straightforward to adapt to whatever deployment logic you need

The final static site now looks like this:

```
import $ivy.`com.lihaoyi::scalatags:0.9.1`, scalatags.Text.all._        Blog.sc
import $ivy.`com.atlassian.commonmark:commonmark:0.13.1`

@main def main(targetGitRepo: String = ""): Unit = {
  interp.watch(os.pwd / "post")
  val postInfo = os
    .list(os.pwd / "post")
    .map{ p =>
      val s"$prefix - $suffix.md" = p.last
```

```scala
      (prefix, suffix, p)
  }
  .sortBy(_._1.toInt)

def mdNameToHtml(name: String) = name.replace(" ", "-").toLowerCase + ".html"

val bootstrapCss = link(
  rel := "stylesheet",
  href := "https://stackpath.bootstrapcdn.com/bootstrap/4.5.0/css/bootstrap.css"
)

os.remove.all(os.pwd / "out")
os.makeDir.all(os.pwd / "out" / "post")

for ((_, suffix, path) <- postInfo) {
  val parser = org.commonmark.parser.Parser.builder().build()
  val document = parser.parse(os.read(path))
  val renderer = org.commonmark.renderer.html.HtmlRenderer.builder().build()
  val output = renderer.render(document)
  os.write(
    os.pwd / "out" / "post" / mdNameToHtml(suffix),
    doctype("html")(
      html(
        head(bootstrapCss),
        body(
          h1(a("Blog", href := "../index.html"), " / ", suffix),
          raw(output)
        )
      )
    )
  )
}

os.write(
  os.pwd / "out" / "index.html",
  doctype("html")(
    html(
      head(bootstrapCss),
      body(
        h1("Blog"),
        for ((_, suffix, _) <- postInfo)
```

```
          yield h2(a(href := ("post/" + mdNameToHtml(suffix)))(suffix))
       )
     )
   )
 )

 if (targetGitRepo != "") {
   os.proc("git", "init").call(cwd = os.pwd / "out")
   os.proc("git", "add", "-A").call(cwd = os.pwd / "out")
   os.proc("git", "commit", "-am", ".").call(cwd = os.pwd / "out")
   os.proc("git", "push", targetGitRepo, "HEAD", "-f").call(cwd = os.pwd / "out")
 }
}
                                                                    </> 9.26.scala
```

See example 9.6 - Deploy

9.6 Conclusion

In this chapter, we've written a Scala Script that implements a small static blog generator. It takes Markdown files in a folder and renders them into a HTML website we can host online. We used the filesystem APIs we learned about in *Chapter 7: Files and Subprocesses*, along with the third-party Scala library Scalatags to render HTML and the third-party Java library Atlassian Commonmark to parse and render the markdown. The end result was a single self-contained script that can download its own dependencies and run in any environment without prior setup. Scala scripts are a great way to "try out" third party libraries, testing them out without the complexity of a larger project or build system.

Next, in *Chapter 10: Static Build Pipelines*, we will re-visit this static site generator in order to make it incremental. This will allow us to re-use previously rendered HTML files, speeding up re-generation of the static site even as the number of posts and pages grows. We will re-visit the Scalatags HTML library in *Chapter 14: Simple Web and API Servers*, and use it to render the HTML of our interactive chat website.

Exercise: Use the filesystem last-modified timestamp for each blog post's .md file and use it to automatically provide a "*Written On YYYY-MM-DD*" annotation at the bottom of each blog post, as well as under each post's preview on the index page

See example 9.7 - DeployTimestamp

Discuss Chapter 9 online at https://www.handsonscala.com/discuss/9

10

Static Build Pipelines

10.1 Mill Build Pipelines   180

10.2 Mill Modules   185

10.3 Revisiting our Static Site Script   189

10.4 Conversion to a Mill Build Pipeline   190

10.5 Extending our Static Site Pipeline   194

```scala
import mill._


def srcs = T.source(millSourcePath / "src")


def concat = T{
  os.write(T.dest / "concat.txt",  os.list(srcs().path).map(os.read(_)))
  PathRef(T.dest / "concat.txt")
}
                                                              </> 10.1.scala
```

Snippet 10.1: the definition of a simple Mill build pipeline

Build pipelines are a common pattern, where you have files and assets you want to process but want to do so efficiently, incrementally, and in parallel. This usually means only re-processing files when they change, and re-using the already processed assets as much as possible. Whether you are compiling Scala, minifying Javascript, or compressing tarballs, many of these file-processing workflows can be slow. Parallelizing these workflows and avoiding unnecessary work can greatly speed up your development cycle.

This chapter will walk through how to use the Mill build tool to set up these build pipelines, and demonstrate the advantages of a build pipeline over a naive build script. We will take the the simple static site generator we wrote in *Chapter 9: Self-Contained Scala Scripts* and convert it into an efficient build pipeline that can incrementally update the static site as you make changes to the sources. We will be using the Mill build tool in several of the projects later in the book, starting with *Chapter 14: Simple Web and API Servers*.

10.1 Mill Build Pipelines

We will be using the Mill Build Tool to define our build pipelines. While Mill can be used to compile/test/package Scala code (which we will see in subsequent chapters) it can also be used as a general purpose tool for efficiently and incrementally keeping static assets up to date.

In this chapter we will be managing the compilation of markdown files into a HTML static site, but any workflow which you would like to do once and re-use can benefit from Mill. Minifying Javascript files, pre-processing CSS, generating source code, preparing tar or zip archives for deployment: these are all workflows which are slow enough you do not want to repeat them unnecessarily. Avoiding unnecessary re-processing is exactly what Mill helps you do.

10.1.1 Defining a Build Pipeline

To introduce the core concepts in Mill, we'll first look at a trivial Mill build that takes files in a source folder and concatenates them together:

```scala
import mill._                                                        build.sc

def srcs = T.source(millSourcePath / "src")

def concat = T{
  os.write(T.dest / "concat.txt", os.list(srcs().path).map(os.read(_)))
  PathRef(T.dest / "concat.txt")
}
                                                                </> 10.2.scala
```

You can read this snippet as follows:

- This `build.sc` file defines one set of sources, named `srcs`, and one downstream target named `concat`.

- We make use of `srcs` in the body of `concat` via the `srcs()` syntax, which tells Mill that `concat` depends on `srcs` and makes the value of `srcs` available to `concat`.

- Inside `concat`, we list the `src/` folder, read all the files, and concatenate their contents into a single file `concat.txt`.

- The final `concat.txt` file is wrapped in a `PathRef`, which tells Mill that we care not just about the name of the file, but also its contents.

This results in the following simple dependency graph

10.1.1.1 Targets

The Mill build tool is built around the concept of *targets*. Targets are the nodes within the build graph, and represent individual steps that make up your build pipeline.

Every target you define via the `def foo = T{...}` syntax gives you the following things for free:

- It is made available for you to run from the command line via `./mill foo`
- The return value of the `T{...}` block is made printable via `./mill show foo`
- It automatically evaluates any necessary upstream tasks, before its own `T{...}` block evaluates
- It automatically caches the computed result on disk, and only re-evaluates when its inputs change

In general, this helps automate a lot of the tedious book-keeping that is normally needed when writing incremental build scripts. Rather than spending your time writing command-line argument parsers or hand-rolling a caching and invalidation strategy, Mill handles all that for you and allows you to focus on the logical structure of your build.

10.1.1.2 Target Destination Folders

Note that the `concat.txt` file is created within the `concat` target's destination folder `T.dest`. Every target has its own destination folder, named after the fully-qualified path to the target (in this case, `out/concat/dest/`). This means that we do not have to worry about the `concat` target's files being accidentally over-written by other targets.

In general, any Mill target should only create and modify files within its own `T.dest`, to avoid collisions and interference with other targets. The contents of `T.dest` are deleted each time before the target evaluates, ensuring that the target always starts each evaluation with a fresh destination folder and isn't affected by the outcome of previous evaluations.

10.1.2 Using Your Build Pipeline

We can install Mill in the current folder via `curl`, and create a `src/` folder with some files inside:

```
$ curl -L https://github.com/lihaoyi/mill/releases/download/0.8.0/0.8.0 -o mill
$ chmod +x mill

$ mkdir src

$ echo "hear me moo" > src/iamcow.txt

$ echo "hello world" > src/hello.txt                                    </> 10.3.bash
```

We can now build the `concat` target, ask Mill to print the path to its output file, and inspect its contents:

```
$ ./mill concat

$ ./mill show concat
"ref:fd0201e7:/Users/lihaoyi/test/out/concat/dest/concat.txt"

$ cat out/concat/dest/concat.txt
hear me moo
hello world
```
</> 10.4.bash

Mill re-uses output files whenever possible: in this case, since the concat target only depends on srcs, calling ./mill concat repeatedly returns the already generated concat.txt file. However, if we change the contents of the srcs by adding a new file to the folder, Mill automatically re-builds concat.txt to take the new input into account:

```
$ echo "twice as much as you" > src/iweigh.txt

$ ./mill concat

$ cat out/concat/dest/concat.txt
hear me moo
twice as much as you
hello world
```
</> 10.5.scala

See example 10.1 - Simple

10.1.3 Non-linear Build Pipelines

While our build pipeline above only has one set of sources and one target, we can also define more complex builds. For example, here is an example build with 2 source folders (`src/` and `resources/`) and 3 targets (`concat`, `compress` and `zipped`):

```scala
import mill._                                                        build.sc
def srcs = T.source(millSourcePath / "src")
+def resources = T.source(millSourcePath / "resources")

def concat = T{
  os.write(T.dest / "concat.txt",  os.list(srcs().path).map(os.read(_)))
  PathRef(T.dest / "concat.txt")
}
+def compress = T{
+  for (p <- os.list(resources().path)) {
+    val copied = T.dest / p.relativeTo(resources().path)
+    os.copy(p, copied)
+    os.proc("gzip", copied).call()
+  }
+  PathRef(T.dest)
+}
+def zipped = T{
+  val temp = T.dest / "temp"
+  os.makeDir(temp)
+  os.copy(concat().path, temp / "concat.txt")
+  for (p <- os.list(compress().path)) os.copy(p, temp / p.relativeTo(compress().path))
+  os.proc("zip", "-r", T.dest / "out.zip", ".").call(cwd = temp)
+  PathRef(T.dest / "out.zip")
+}
```
</> 10.6.scala

In addition to concatenating files, we also `gzip` compress the contents of our `resources/` folder. We then take the concatenated sources and compressed resources and zip them all up into a final `out.zip` file:

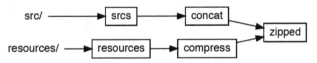

Given files in both `srcs/` and `resources/`:

```bash
$ mkdir resources

$ echo "# title" > resources/foo.md

$ echo "print(123)" > resources/thing.py
```
</> 10.7.bash

```scala
$ find . -type f | grep -v out
.
./build.sc
./mill
./resources/foo.md
./resources/thing.py
./src/iamcow.txt
./src/iweigh.txt
./src/hello.txt
```
</> 10.8.scala

We can run ./mill zipped and see the expected concat.txt and *.gz files in the output out.zip:

```
$ ./mill show zipped
"ref:a3771625:/Users/lihaoyi/test/out/zipped/dest/out.zip"


$ unzip -l out/zipped/dest/out.zip
Archive:  out/zipped/dest/out.zip
  Length      Date    Time    Name
---------  ---------- -----    ----
       35  11-30-2019 13:10   foo.md.gz
       45  11-30-2019 13:10   concat.txt
       40  11-30-2019 13:10   thing.py.gz
---------                     -------
      120                     3 files
```
</> 10.9.bash

10.1.4 Incremental Re-Computation

As shown earlier, out.zip is re-used as long as none of the inputs (src/ and resources/) change. However, because our pipeline has two branches, the concat and compress targets are independent: concat is only re-generated if the src/ folder changes:

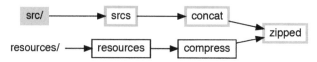

And the compress target is only re-generated if the resources/ folder changes:

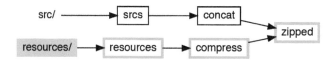

While in these examples our `T{...}` targets all returned `PathRefs` to files or folders, you can also define targets that return any JSON-serializable data type compatible with the uPickle library we went through in **Chapter 8: JSON and Binary Data Serialization**. Mill also supports a `-j <n>` flag to parallelize independent targets over multiple threads, e.g. `./mill -j 2 zipped` would spin up 2 threads to work through the two branches of the target graph in parallel.

See example 10.2 - Nonlinear

10.2 Mill Modules

Mill also supports the concept of *modules*. You can use modules to define repetitive sets of build targets.

It is very common for certain sets of targets to be duplicated within your build: perhaps for every folder of source files, you want to compile them, lint them, package them, test them, and publish them. By defining a `trait` that extends `Module`, you can apply the same set of targets to different folders on disk, making it easy to manage the build for larger and more complex projects.

Here we are taking the set of `srcs/resources` and `concat/compress/zipped` targets we defined earlier and wrapping them in a `trait` FooModule so they can be re-used:

```scala
                                                                    build.sc
import mill._
+ trait FooModule extends Module{
    def srcs = T.source(millSourcePath / "src")
    def resources = T.source(millSourcePath / "resources")

    def concat = T{ ... }
    def compress = T{ ... }
    def zipped = T{ ... }
+ }
+
+ object bar extends FooModule
+ object qux extends FooModule
                                                               </> 10.10.scala
```

`object` bar and `object` qux extend `trait` FooModule, and have `millSourcePaths` of bar/ and qux/ respectively. The srcs and resources definitions above thus point to the following folders:

- bar/src/
- bar/resources/
- qux/src/
- qux/resources/

You can ask Mill to list out the possible targets for you to build via `./mill resolve __` (that's two _s in a row):

```
$ ./mill resolve __
bar.compress
bar.concat
bar.resources
bar.srcs
bar.zipped
qux.compress
qux.concat
qux.resources
qux.srcs
qux.zipped
```
`</> 10.11.bash`

Any of the targets above can be built from the command line, e.g. via

```
$ mkdir -p bar/src bar/resources

$ echo "Hello" > bar/src/hello.txt; echo "World" > bar/src/world.txt

$ ./mill show bar.zipped
"ref:efdf1f3c:/Users/lihaoyi/test/out/bar/zipped/dest/out.zip"

$ unzip /Users/lihaoyi/test/out/bar/zipped/dest/out.zip
Archive:  /Users/lihaoyi/test/out/bar/zipped/dest/out.zip
 extracting: concat.txt

$ cat concat.txt
Hello
World
```
`</> 10.12.bash`

See example 10.3 - Modules

10.2.1 Nested Modules

Modules can also be nested to form arbitrary hierarchies:

```scala
import mill._                                                          build.sc

trait FooModule extends Module{
  def srcs = T.source(millSourcePath / "src")

  def concat = T{
    os.write(T.dest / "concat.txt",  os.list(srcs().path).map(os.read(_)))
    PathRef(T.dest / "concat.txt")
  }
}


object bar extends FooModule{
  object inner1 extends FooModule
  object inner2 extends FooModule
}
object wrapper extends Module{
  object qux extends FooModule
}                                                              </> 10.13.scala
```

Here we have four `FooModules`: `bar`, `bar.inner1`, `bar.inner2`, and `wrapper.qux`. This exposes the following source folders and targets:

Source Folders

- `bar/src/`
- `bar/inner1/src/`
- `bar/inner2/src/`
- `wrapper/qux/src/`

Targets

- `bar.concat`
- `bar.inner1.concat`
- `bar.inner2.concat`
- `wrapper.qux.concat`

Note that `wrapper` itself is a `Module` but not a `FooModule`, and thus does not itself define a `wrapper/src/` source folder or a `wrapper.concat` target. In general, every `object` in your module hierarchy needs to inherit from `Module`, although you can inherit from a custom subtype of `FooModule` if you want them to have some common targets already defined.

The `millSourcePath` made available within each module differs: while in the top-level build pipelines we saw earlier `millSourcePath` was always equal to `os.pwd`, within a module the `millSourcePath` reflects the module path, e.g. the `millSourcePath` of `bar` is `bar/`, the `millSourcePath` of `wrapper.qux` is `wrapper/qux/`, and so on.

10.2.2 Cross Modules

The last basic concept we will look at is *cross modules*. These are most useful when the number or layout of modules in your build isn't fixed, but can vary based on e.g. the files on the filesystem:

```scala
import mill._                                                          build.sc

val items = interp.watchValue{ os.list(millSourcePath / "foo").map(_.last) }

object foo extends Cross[FooModule](items:_*)
class FooModule(label: String) extends Module{
  def srcs = T.source(millSourcePath / "src")

  def concat = T{
    os.write(T.dest / "concat.txt",  os.list(srcs().path).map(os.read(_)))
    PathRef(T.dest / "concat.txt")
  }
}
```
</> 10.14.scala

Here, we define a cross module `foo` that takes a set of `items` found by listing the sub-folders in `foo/`. This set of `items` is dynamic, and can change if the folders on disk change, without needing to update the `build.sc` file for every change.

Note the `interp.watchValue` call; this is necessary to tell Mill to take note in case the number or layout of modules within the `foo/` folder changes. Without it, we would need to restart the Mill process using `./mill shutdown` to pick up changes in how many entries the cross-module contains.

The `Cross` class that `foo` inherits is a Mill builtin, that automatically generates a set of Mill modules corresponding to the items we passed in.

10.2.3 Modules Based on Folder Layout

As written, given a filesystem layout on the left, it results in the source folders and `concat` targets on the right:

```
$ mkdir -p foo/bar

$ mkdir -p foo/qux

$ find foo
foo
foo/bar
foo/qux
                                        </> 10.15.bash
```

sources

- `foo/bar/src`
- `foo/qux/src`

targets

```
$ ./mill resolve __.concat
foo[bar].concat
foo[qux].concat
                                        </> 10.16.bash
```

If we then add a new source folder via `mkdir -p`, Mill picks up the additional module and `concat` target:

```
$ mkdir -p foo/thing/src

$ ./mill resolve __.concat
foo[bar].concat
foo[qux].concat
foo[thing].concat
                                                            </> 10.17.bash
```

See example 10.5 - CrossModules

10.3 Revisiting our Static Site Script

We have now gone through the basics of how to use Mill to define simple asset pipelines to incrementally perform operations on a small set of files. Next, we will return to the `Blog.sc` static site script we wrote in **Chapter 9**, and see how we can use these techniques to make it incremental: to only re-build the pages of the static site whose inputs changed since the last time they were built.

While `Blog.sc` works fine in small cases, there is one big limitation: the entire script runs every time. Even if you only change one blog post's `.md` file, every file will need to be re-processed. This is wasteful, and can be slow as the number of blog posts grows. On a large blog, re-processing every post can take upwards of 20-30 seconds: a long time to wait every time you tweak some wording!

It is possible to manually keep track of which `.md` file was converted into which `.html` file, and thus avoid re-processing `.md` files unnecessarily. However, this kind of book-keeping is tedious and easy to get wrong. Luckily, this is the kind of book-keeping and incremental re-processing that Mill is good at!

10.4 Conversion to a Mill Build Pipeline

We will now walk through a step by step conversion of this `Blog.sc` script file into a Mill `build.sc`. First, we must rename `Blog.sc` into `build.sc` to convert it into a Mill build pipeline, and add the `import mill._` declaration:

```
import $ivy.`com.lihaoyi::scalatags:0.9.1`, scalatags.Text.all._        Blog.sc -> build.sc
import $ivy.`com.atlassian.commonmark:commonmark:0.13.1`
+import mill._                                                          </> 10.18.scala
```

Second, since we can rely on Mill invalidating and deleting stale files and folders as they fall out of date, we no longer need the `os.remove.all` and `os.makeDir.all` calls:

```
-os.remove.all(os.pwd / "out")                                         build.sc
-os.makeDir.all(os.pwd / "out" / "post")                               </> 10.19.scala
```

We will also remove the `@main` method wrapper and publishing code for now. Mill uses a different syntax for taking command-line arguments than raw Ammonite Scala Scripts do, and porting this functionality to our Mill build pipeline is left as an exercise at the end of the chapter.

```
- @main def main(targetGitRepo: String = ""): Unit = {                 build.sc
```

```
-   if (targetGitRepo != "") {                                         build.sc
-     os.proc("git", "init").call(cwd = os.pwd / "out")
-     os.proc("git", "add", "-A").call(cwd = os.pwd / "out")
-     os.proc("git", "commit", "-am", ".").call(cwd = os.pwd / "out")
-     os.proc("git", "push", targetGitRepo, "head", "-f").call(cwd = os.pwd / "out")
-   }
- }                                                                     </> 10.20.scala
```

10.4.1 For-Loop to Cross Modules

Third, we convert the `for`-loop that we previously used to iterate over the files in the `postInfo` list, and convert it into a cross module. That will allow every blog post's `.md` file to be processed, invalidated, and re-processed independently only if the original `.md` file changes:

```scala
-for ((_, suffix, path) <- postInfo) {                                    build.sc
+object post extends Cross[PostModule](postInfo.map(_._1):_*)
+class PostModule(number: String) extends Module{
+  val Some((_, suffix, markdownPath)) = postInfo.find(_._1 == number)
+  def path = T.source(markdownPath)
+  def render = T{
    val parser = org.commonmark.parser.Parser.builder().build()
-    val document = parser.parse(os.read(path))
+    val document = parser.parse(os.read(path().path))
    val renderer = org.commonmark.renderer.html.HtmlRenderer.builder().build()
    val output = renderer.render(document)
    os.write(
-      os.pwd / "out" / "post" / mdNameToHtml(suffix),
+      T.dest / mdNameToHtml(suffix),
      doctype("html")(
        ...
      )
    )
+    PathRef(T.dest / mdNameToHtml(suffix))
+  }
}                                                                      </> 10.21.scala
```

Note how the items in the `Cross[](...)` declaration is the number corresponding to each post in our `postInfo` list. For each item, we define a source `path` which is the source file itself, as well as a `def` `render` target which is a `PathRef` to the generated HTML. In the conversion from a hardcoded script to a Mill build pipeline, all the hardcoded references writing files `os.pwd` / `"out"` have been replaced by the `T.dest` of each target.

10.4.2 An Index Page Target

Fourth, we wrap the generation of the index.html file into a target as well:

```scala
+def links = T.input{ postInfo.map(_._2) }                              build.sc
+
+def index = T{
   os.write(
-    os.pwd / "out" / "index.html",
+    T.dest / "index.html",
     doctype("html")(
       html(
         head(bootstrapCss),
         body(
           h1("Blog"),
-          for ((_, suffix, _) <- postInfo)
+          for (suffix <- links())
           yield h2(a(href := ("post/" + mdNameToHtml(suffix)))(suffix))
         )
       )
     )
   )
+  PathRef(T.dest / "index.html")
+}                                                                    </> 10.22.scala
```

Note that we need to define a `def` `links` target that is a `T.input`: this tells Mill that the contents of the `postInfo.map` expression may change (since it depends on the files present on disk) and to make sure to re-evaluate it every time to check for changes. Again, the hardcoded references to `os.pwd / "out"` have been replaced by the `T.dest` of the individual target.

10.4.3 Arranging Files For Distribution

Lastly, we need to aggregate all our individual posts and the `index.html` file into a single target, which we will call `dist` (short for "distribution"):

```scala
+val posts = T.sequence(postInfo.map(_._1).map(post(_).render))            build.sc
+
+def dist = T {
+  for (post <- posts()) {
+    os.copy(post.path, T.dest / "post" / post.path.last, createFolders = true)
+  }
+  os.copy(index().path, T.dest / "index.html")
+
+  PathRef(T.dest)
+}                                                                    </> 10.23.scala
```

This is necessary because while previously we created the HTML files for the individual posts and index "in place", now they are each created in separate `T.dest` folders assigned by Mill so they can be separately invalidated and re-generated. Thus we need to copy them all into a single folder that we can open locally in the browser or upload to a static site host.

Note that we need to use the helper method `T.sequence` to turn the `Seq[T[PathRef]]` into a `T[Seq[PathRef]]` for us to use in `def dist`.

10.4.4 Using Your Static Build Pipeline

We now have a static site pipeline with the following shape:

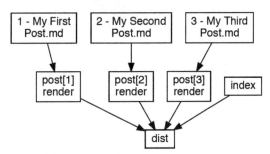

We can now take the same set of posts we used earlier, and build them into a static website using `./mill`. Note that the output is now in the `out/dist/dest/` folder, which is the `T.dest` folder for the `dist` target.

```
$ find post -type f
post/1 - My First Post.md
post/3 - My Third Post.md
post/2 - My Second Post.md

$ ./mill show dist
"ref:b33a3c95:/Users/lihaoyi/Github/blog/out/dist/dest"

$ find out/dist/dest -type f
out/dist/dest/index.html
out/dist/dest/post/my-first-post.html
out/dist/dest/post/my-second-post.html
out/dist/dest/post/my-third-post.html
```
</> 10.24.bash

We can then open the index.html in our browser to view the blog. Every time you run ./mill dist, Mill will only re-process the blog posts that have changed since you last ran it. You can also use ./mill --watch dist or ./mill -w dist to have Mill watch the filesystem and automatically re-process the files every time they change.

See example 10.6 - Blog

10.5 Extending our Static Site Pipeline

Now that we've defined a simple pipeline, let's consider two extensions:

- Download the bootstrap.css file at build time and bundle it with the static site, to avoid a dependency on the third party hosting service

- Extract a preview of each blog post and include it on the home page

10.5.1 Bundling Bootstrap

Bundling bootstrap is simple. We define a bootstrap target to download the file and include it in our `dist`:

```scala
- val bootstrapCss = link(
-   rel := "stylesheet",
-   href := "https://stackpath.bootstrapcdn.com/bootstrap/4.5.0/css/bootstrap.css"
- )
+ def bootstrap = T{
+   os.write(
+     T.dest / "bootstrap.css",
+     requests.get("https://stackpath.bootstrapcdn.com/bootstrap/4.5.0/css/bootstrap.css")
+   )
+   PathRef(T.dest / "bootstrap.css")
+ }
```
`build.sc`   `</> 10.25.scala`

```scala
def dist = T {
  for (post <- posts()) {
    os.copy(post.path, T.dest / "post" / post.path.last, createFolders = true)
  }
  os.copy(index().path, T.dest / "index.html")
+ os.copy(bootstrap().path, T.dest / "bootstrap.css")
  PathRef(T.dest)
}
```
`build.sc`   `</> 10.26.scala`

And then update our two `bootstrapCss` links to use a local URL:

```scala
- head(bootstrapCss),
+ head(link(rel := "stylesheet", href := "../bootstrap.css")),
```
`build.sc`   `</> 10.27.scala`

```scala
- head(bootstrapCss),
+ head(link(rel := "stylesheet", href := "bootstrap.css")),
```
`build.sc`   `</> 10.28.scala`

Now, when you run `./mill dist`, you can see that the `bootstrap.css` file is downloaded and bundled with your `dist` folder, and we can see in the browser that we are now using a locally-bundled version of Bootstrap:

```bash
$ find out/dist/dest -type f
out/dist/dest/bootstrap.css
out/dist/dest/index.html
out/dist/dest/post/my-first-post.html
out/dist/dest/post/my-second-post.html
out/dist/dest/post/my-third-post.html
```
`</> 10.29.bash`

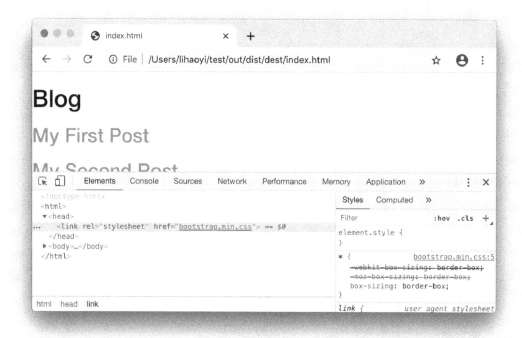

Since it does not depend on any `T.source`, the `bootstrap = T{}` target never invalidates. This is usually what you want when depending on a stable URL like `bootstrap/4.5.0`. If you are depending on something unstable that needs to be regenerated every build, define it as a `T.input{}` task.

We now have the following build pipeline, with the additional `bootstrap` step:

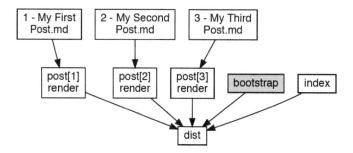

10.5.2 Post Previews

To render a paragraph preview of each blog post in the `index.html` page, the first step is to generate such a preview for each `PostModule`. We will simply take everything before the first empty line in the Markdown file, treat that as the "first paragraph" of the post, and feed it through our Markdown parser:

```scala
class PostModule(number: String) extends Module{                          build.sc
  val Some((_, suffix, path)) = postInfo.find(_._1 == number)
  def path = T.source(markdownPath)
+  def preview = T{
+    val parser = org.commonmark.parser.Parser.builder().build()
+    val firstPara = os.read.lines(path().path).takeWhile(_.nonEmpty)
+    val document = parser.parse(firstPara.mkString("\n"))
+    val renderer = org.commonmark.renderer.html.HtmlRenderer.builder().build()
+    val output = renderer.render(document)
+    output
+  }
  def render = T{                                                    </> 10.30.scala
```

Here we are leaving the preview as `output: String` rather than writing it to a file and using a `PathRef`.

Next, we need to aggregate the `previews` the same way we aggregated the `renders` earlier:

```scala
  def links = T.input{ postInfo.map(_._2) }                                build.sc
+ val previews = T.sequence(postInfo.map(_._1).map(post(_).preview))
  def index = T{                                                     </> 10.31.scala
```

Lastly, in `dist`, zip the preview together with the `postInfo` in order to render them:

```scala
- for (suffix <- links())                                                 build.sc
- yield h2(a(href := ("post/" + mdNameToHtml(suffix)))(suffix))
+ for ((suffix, preview) <- links().zip(previews()))
+ yield frag(
+   h2(a(href := ("post/" + mdNameToHtml(suffix)))(suffix)),
+   raw(preview) // include markdown-generated HTML "raw" without HTML-escaping it
+ )                                                                 </> 10.32.scala
```

Now we get pretty previews in `index.html`!

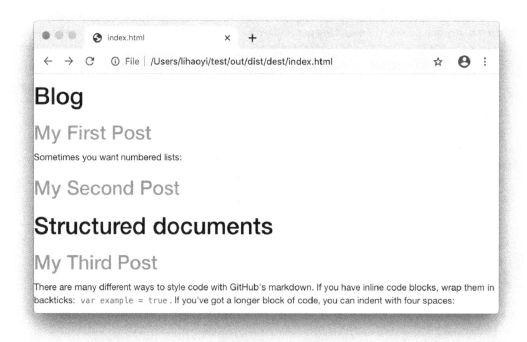

The build pipeline now looks like:

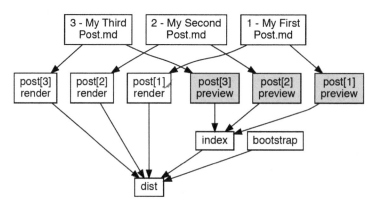

Note how we now have both `post[n].preview` and `post[n].render` targets, with the `preview` targets being used in `index` to generate the home page and the `render` targets only being used in the final `dist`. As we saw earlier, any change to a file only results in that file's downstream targets being re-generated. This saves time over naively re-generating the entire static site from scratch. It should also be clear the value that Mill Modules (*10.2*) bring, in allowing repetitive sets of targets like `preview` and `render` to be defined for all blog posts without boilerplate.

10.5.3 A Complete Static Site Pipeline

Here's the complete code, with the repetitive `org.commonmark.parser.Parser.builder()` code extracted into a shared `def` `renderMarkdown` function, and the repetitive HTML rendering code extracted into a shared `def` `renderHtmlPage` function:

```scala
import $ivy.`com.lihaoyi::scalatags:0.9.1`, scalatags.Text.all._    build.sc
import $ivy.`com.atlassian.commonmark:commonmark:0.13.1`
import mill._

def mdNameToHtml(name: String) = name.replace(" ", "-").toLowerCase + ".html"

val postInfo = interp.watchValue {
  os.list(os.pwd / "post")
    .map { p =>
      val s"$prefix - $suffix.md" = p.last
      (prefix, suffix, p)
    }
    .sortBy(_._1.toInt)
}
def bootstrap = T{
  os.write(
    T.dest / "bootstrap.css",
    requests.get("https://stackpath.bootstrapcdn.com/bootstrap/4.5.0/css/bootstrap.css")
  )
  PathRef(T.dest / "bootstrap.css")
}
def renderMarkdown(s: String) = {
  val parser = org.commonmark.parser.Parser.builder().build()
  val document = parser.parse(s)
  val renderer = org.commonmark.renderer.html.HtmlRenderer.builder().build()
  renderer.render(document)
}
def renderHtmlPage(dest: os.Path, bootstrapUrl: String, contents: Frag*) = {
  os.write(
    dest,
    doctype("html")(
      html(head(link(rel := "stylesheet", href := bootstrapUrl)), body(contents))
    )
  )
  PathRef(dest)
}
```

```scala
object post extends Cross[PostModule](postInfo.map(_._1):_*)
class PostModule(number: String) extends Module{
  val Some((_, suffix, markdownPath)) = postInfo.find(_._1 == number)
  def path = T.source(markdownPath)
  def preview = T{
    renderMarkdown(os.read.lines(path().path).takeWhile(_.nonEmpty).mkString("\n"))
  }
  def render = T{
    renderHtmlPage(
      T.dest / mdNameToHtml(suffix),
      "../bootstrap.css",
      h1(a(href := "../index.html")("Blog"), " / ", suffix),
      raw(renderMarkdown(os.read(path().path)))
    )
  }
}


def links = T.input{ postInfo.map(_._2) }
val posts = T.sequence(postInfo.map(_._1).map(post(_).render))
val previews = T.sequence(postInfo.map(_._1).map(post(_).preview))

def index = T {
  renderHtmlPage(
    T.dest / "index.html",
    "bootstrap.css",
    h1("Blog"),
    for ((suffix, preview) <- links().zip(previews()))
    yield frag(
      h2(a(href := ("post/" + mdNameToHtml(suffix)))(suffix)),
      raw(preview) // include markdown-generated HTML "raw" without HTML-escaping it
    )
  )
}
def dist = T {
  for (post <- posts()) {
    os.copy(post.path, T.dest / "post" / post.path.last, createFolders = true)
  }
  os.copy(index().path, T.dest / "index.html")
  os.copy(bootstrap().path, T.dest / "bootstrap.css")
  PathRef(T.dest)
}
```

</> 10.33.scala

10.6 Conclusion

In this chapter, we have learned how to define simple incremental build pipelines using Mill. We then took the script in *Chapter 9: Self-Contained Scala Scripts* and converted it into a Mill build pipeline. Unlike a naive script, this pipeline allows fast incremental updates whenever the underlying sources change, along with easy parallelization, all in less than 90 lines of code. We have also seen how to extend the Mill build pipeline, adding additional build steps to do things like bundling CSS files or showing post previews, all while preserving the efficient incremental nature of the build pipeline.

Mill is a general-purpose build tool and can be used to create general-purpose build pipelines for all sorts of data. In later chapters we will be using the Mill build tool to compile Java and Scala source code into executables. For a more thorough reference, you can browse the Mill online documentation:

- http://www.lihaoyi.com/mill

This chapter marks the end of the second section of this book: **Part II Local Development**. You should hopefully be confident using the Scala programming language to perform general housekeeping tasks on a single machine, manipulating files, subprocesses, and structured data to accomplish your goals. The next section of this book, **Part III Web Services**, will explore using Scala in a networked, distributed world: where your fundamental tools are not files and folders, but HTTP APIs, servers, and databases.

> **Exercise:** Mill builds can take also command line arguments, by defining `def main(...) = T.command{...}` methods. Similar to `@main` methods in Scala scripts, the arguments to `main` are taken from the command line. Define an `T.command` in our `build.sc` that allows the user to specify a remote git repository from the command line, and uses `os.proc` operations to push the static site to that repository.
>
> See example 10.8 - Push

Exercise: You can use the Puppeteer Javascript library to convert HTML web pages into PDFs, e.g. for printing or publishing as a book. Integrate Puppeteer into our static blog, using the subprocess techniques we learned in *Chapter 7: Files and Subprocesses*, to add a ./mill pdfs target that creates a PDF version of each of our blog posts.

Puppeteer can be installed via npm, and its docs can be found at:

- https://github.com/puppeteer/puppeteer

The following script can be run via node, assuming you have the puppeteer library installed via NPM, and takes a src HTML file path and dest output PDF path as command line arguments to perform the conversion from HTML to PDF:

```javascript
const puppeteer = require('puppeteer');
const [src, dest] = process.argv.slice(2)
puppeteer.launch().then(async function(browser){
  const page = await browser.newPage();
  await page.goto("file://" + src, {waitUntil: 'load'});
  await page.pdf({path: dest, format: 'A4'});
  process.exit(0)
})
```
</> 10.34.javascript

See example 10.9 - PostPdf

Exercise: The Apache PDFBox library is a convenient way to manipulate PDFs from Java or Scala code, and can easily be import $ivyed for use in your REPL or scripts via the coordinates org.apache.pdfbox:pdfbox:2.0.18. Add a new target to our build pipeline that uses the class org.apache.pdfbox.multipdf.PDFMergerUtility from PDFBox to concatenate the PDFs for each individual blog post into one long multi-page PDF that contains all of the blog posts one after another.

See example 10.10 - ConcatPdf

Discuss Chapter 10 online at https://www.handsonscala.com/discuss/10

Part III: Web Services

11 Scraping Websites   205

12 Working with HTTP APIs   221

13 Fork-Join Parallelism with Futures   239

14 Simple Web and API Servers   261

15 Querying SQL Databases   287

The third part of this book covers using Scala in a world of servers and clients, systems and services. We will explore using Scala both as a client and as a server, exchanging HTML and JSON over HTTP or Websockets. This part builds towards two capstone projects: a parallel web crawler and an interactive chat website, each representing common use cases you are likely to encounter using Scala in a networked, distributed environment.

11

Scraping Websites

11.1 Scraping Wikipedia   206

11.2 MDN Web Documentation   210

11.3 Scraping MDN   212

11.4 Putting it Together   217

```
@ val doc = Jsoup.connect("http://en.wikipedia.org/").get()

@ doc.title()
res2: String = "Wikipedia, the free encyclopedia"

@ val headlines = doc.select("#mp-itn b a")
headlines: select.Elements =
<a href="/wiki/Bek_Air_Flight_2100" title="Bek Air Flight 2100">Bek Air Flight 2100</a>
<a href="/wiki/Assassination_of_..." title="Assassination of ...">2018 killing</a>
<a href="/wiki/State_of_the_..." title="State of the...">upholds a ruling</a>
...                                                                     </> 11.1.scala
```

Snippet 11.1: scraping Wikipedia's front-page links using the Jsoup third-party library in the Scala REPL

The user-facing interface of most networked systems is a website. In fact, often that is the *only* interface! This chapter will walk you through using the Jsoup library from Scala to scrape human-readable HTML pages, unlocking the ability to extract data from websites that do not provide access via an API.

Apart from third-party scraping websites, Jsoup is also a useful tool for testing the HTML user interfaces that we will encounter in *Chapter 14: Simple Web and API Servers*. This chapter is also a chance to get more familiar with using Java libraries from Scala, a necessary skill to take advantage of the broad and deep Java ecosystem. Lastly, it is an exercise in doing non-trivial interactive development in the Scala REPL, which is a great place to prototype and try out pieces of code that are not ready to be saved in a script or project.

The examples in this chapter will use the Jsoup HTML query library in the Ammonite Scala REPL:

```
$ amm
Loading...
Welcome to the Ammonite Repl 2.2.0 (Scala 2.13.2 Java 11.0.7)
@ import $ivy.`org.jsoup:jsoup:1.13.1`, org.jsoup._          </> 11.2.scala
```

11.1 Scraping Wikipedia

To get started with Jsoup, we can follow the first example in the Jsoup documentation:

- https://jsoup.org

The example snippet downloads the front page of Wikipedia as a HTML document, then extracts the links and titles of the "In the News" articles. Although Jsoup is a Java library, translating their usage examples from Java to Scala code is straightforward, like what we saw earlier in **Chapter 9: Self-Contained Scala Scripts**.

First, we need to call `org.jsoup.Jsoup.connect` in order to download a simple web page to get started:

```
@ val doc = Jsoup.connect("http://en.wikipedia.org/").get()
doc: nodes.Document = <!doctype html>
<html class="client-nojs" lang="en" dir="ltr">
 <head>
  <meta charset="UTF-8">
  <title>Wikipedia, the free encyclopedia</title>
...                                                          </> 11.3.scala
```

Most functionality in the Jsoup library lives in the `org.jsoup.Jsoup` class. Above we used `.connect` to ask Jsoup to download a HTML page from a URL and parse it for us, but we can also use `.parse` to parse a string available locally. This could be useful if we already downloaded the HTML files ahead of time, and just need to do the parsing without any fetching. The Wikipedia front page at the time of writing has been saved as:

- Wikipedia.html *(https://github.com/handsonscala/handsonscala/tree/v1/resources/11)*

You can download it manually and parse it offline, without relying on the online `en.wikipedia.org` website being available:

```
@ val doc = Jsoup.parse(os.read(os.pwd / "Wikipedia.html"))
doc: nodes.Document = <!doctype html>
<html class="client-nojs" lang="en" dir="ltr">
 <head>
  <meta charset="UTF-8">
  <title>Wikipedia, the free encyclopedia</title>
...                                                          </> 11.4.scala
```

While Jsoup provides a myriad of different ways for querying and modifying a document, we will focus on just a few: .select, .text, and .attr

11.1.1 Selection

.select is the main way you can query for data within a HTML document. It takes a CSS Selector string, and uses that to select one or more elements within the document that you may be interested in. Note that we use import JavaConverters._ to enable the .asScala extension method: this makes it more convenient to convert between the Java collections that the Jsoup library uses and the Scala collections in our Scala REPL.

```
@ import collection.JavaConverters._
import collection.JavaConverters._

@ val headlines = doc.select("#mp-itn b a").asScala
headlines: collection.mutable.Buffer[nodes.Element] = Buffer(
  <a href="/wiki/Bek_Air_Flight_2100" title="Bek Air Flight 2100">Bek Air Flight 2100</a>,
  <a href="/wiki/Assassination_of_..." title="Assassination of ...">2018 killing</a>,
  <a href="/wiki/State_of_the_..." title="State of the...">upholds a ruling</a>,
...                                                          </> 11.5.scala
```

The basics of CSS selectors are as follows:

11.1.2 CSS Selector Cheat Sheet

foo	Selects all elements with that tag name, e.g.

```
<foo />
```

#foo	Selects all elements with that ID, e.g.

```
<div id="foo" />
```

.foo	Selects all elements with that class, e.g.

```
<div class="foo" />
<div class="foo bar qux" />                              </> 11.6.xml
```

foo#bar.qux	Selectors combined *without* spaces find elements matching all of them, e.g.

```
<foo id="bar" class="qux" />
```

foo #bar .qux   Selectors combined *with* spaces find elements that support the leftmost selector, then any (possibly nested) child elements that support the next selector, and so forth. e.g. this would match the innermost div in:

```
<foo><div id="bar"><div class="qux" /></div></foo>
```

foo > #bar > .qux   Selectors combined with > match only *direct* children, e.g. the inner div in:

```
<foo><div id="bar"><div class="qux" /></div></foo>
```

But not the inner div below, due to the ‹span› between the outer ‹foo› and the ‹div id="bar"›:

```
<foo><span><div id="bar"><div class="qux" /></div></span></foo>
```

11.1.3 Choosing Selectors via Inspect Element

To come up with the selector that would give us the `In the News` articles, we can go to Wikipedia in the browser and right-click `Inspect` on the part of the page we are interested in:

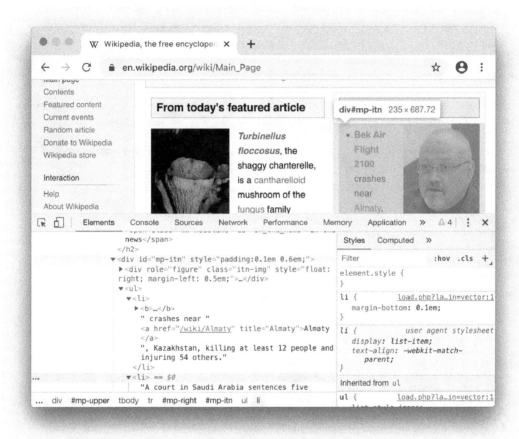

In the `Elements` tab of the developer tools pane above, we can see

- The `<div>` enclosing that part of the page has `id="mp-itn"`, so we can select it using `#mp-itn`.

- Within that `<div>`, we have an `<ul>` unordered list full of `<li>` list items.

- Within each list item is a mix of text and other tags, but we can see that the links to each article are always bolded in a `<b>` tag, and inside the `<b>` there is an `<a>` link tag

To select those links, we can thus combine `#mp-itn b` and `a` into a single `doc.select("#mp-itn b a")`. Apart from `.select`, there are other methods like `.next`, `.nextAll`, `.nextSibling`, `.nextElementSibling`, etc. to help find what you want within the HTML. These will be useful later.

11.1.4 Extracting data

Now that we've gotten the elements we want, the next step would be to retrieve the data we want from each element. HTML elements have three main things we care about:

- Attributes of the form `foo="bar"`, which Jsoup gives you via `.attr("foo")`

- Text contents, e.g. `<foo>hello world</foo>`, which Jsoup gives you via `.text`

- Direct child elements, which Jsoup gives you via `.children`.

We can iterate over the `headlines` elements and pick out the parts we want, whether attributes like the mouse-over `title` or the link target `href`, or the `.text` that the user will see on screen:

```scala
@ for (headline <- headlines) yield (headline.attr("title"), headline.attr("href"))
res4: collection.mutable.Buffer[(String, String)] = ArrayBuffer(
  ("Bek Air Flight 2100", "/wiki/Bek_Air_Flight_2100"),
  ("Assassination of ...", "/wiki/Assassination_of_..."),
  ("State of the...", "/wiki/State_of_the_..."),
...


@ for (headline <- headlines) yield headline.text
res5: collection.mutable.Buffer[String] = ArrayBuffer(
  "Bek Air Flight 2100",
  "2018 killing",
  "upholds a ruling",
...
                                                                           </> 11.7.scala
```

Thus, we are able to pick out the names of the *In the News* Wikipedia articles, and their titles and URLs, by using Jsoup to scrape the Wikipedia front page.

> See example **11.1** - ScrapingWiki

11.2 MDN Web Documentation

For the next exercise in this chapter, we will be using Jsoup to scrape the online Mozilla Development Network Web API documentation. Let us assume we want to fetch the first paragraph of documentation, as well as the list of methods and method descriptions, for every interface on the following page:

- https://developer.mozilla.org/en-US/docs/Web/API#Interfaces

This website contains manually curated documentation for the plethora of APIs available when writing JavaScript code in the browser, under the `Interfaces` section shown below. Each link brings you to the documentation of a single JavaScript class, which has a short description for the class and a list of properties and methods, each with their own description:

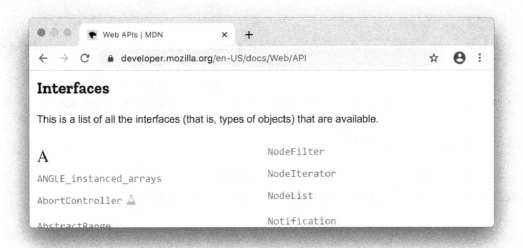

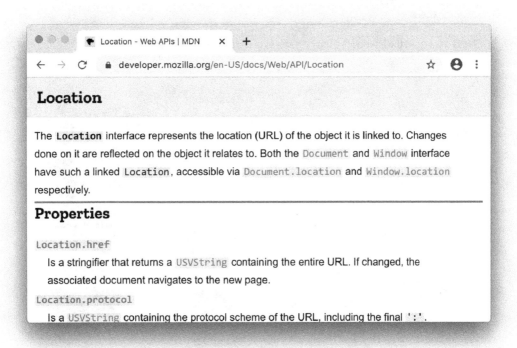

This content is only semi-structured: as it is hand-written, not every page follows exactly the same layout. Nevertheless, this semi-structured information can still be very useful: perhaps you want to integrate it into your editor to automatically provide some hints and tips while you are working on your own JavaScript code.

Our approach to convert this semi-structured website into something structured and machine-readable will be as follows:

- Scrape the main index page at `https://developer.mozilla.org/en-US/docs/Web/API` to find a list of URLs to all other pages we might be interested in
- Loop through the content of each individual URL and scrape the relevant summary documentation
- Aggregate all the scraped summary documentation and save it to a JSON file for use later.

11.3 Scraping MDN

11.3.1 Scraping The Documentation Index

We can right-click and `Inspect` the top-level index containing the links to each individual page:

From the `Elements` pane, we can see that the `<h2 id="Interfaces">` header can be used to identify the section we care about, since all of the `<a>` links are under the `<div class="index" ...>` below it. We can thus select all those links via:

```scala
@ val doc = Jsoup.connect("https://developer.mozilla.org/en-US/docs/Web/API").get()
doc: nodes.Document = <!doctype html>
<html lang="en" dir="ltr" class="no-js">
 <head prefix="og: http://ogp.me/ns#">
 ...
```

```scala
@ val links = doc.select("h2#Interfaces").nextAll.select("div.index a").asScala
links: collection.mutable.Buffer[nodes.Element] = Buffer(
  <a href="/en-US/docs/Web/API/ANGLE_instanced_arrays"><code>ANGLE_in...</code></a>,
  <a href="/en-US/docs/Web/API/AbortController"><code>AbortController</code></a>,
  ...
                                                                       </> 11.8.scala
```

From these elements, we can then extract the high-level information we want from each link: the URL, the mouse-over `title`, and the name of the page:

```scala
@ val linkData = links.map(link => (link.attr("href"), link.attr("title"), link.text))
linkData: collection.mutable.Buffer[(String, String, String)] = ArrayBuffer(
  (
    "/en-US/docs/Web/API/ANGLE_instanced_arrays",
    "The ANGLE_instanced_arrays extension is part of the WebGL API and allows to...",
    "ANGLE_instanced_arrays"
  ),
  ...
                                                                       </> 11.9.scala
```

From there, we can look into scraping each individual page.

11.3.2 Scraping Each Documentation Page

Let's go back to the `Location` page we saw earlier:

- https://developer.mozilla.org/en-US/docs/Web/API/Location

First, we can connect to that URL to download the HTML and parse it into a Jsoup `Document` ready for us to query:

```
@ val url = "https://developer.mozilla.org/en-US/docs/Web/API/Location"

@ val doc = Jsoup.connect(url).get()
doc: nodes.Document = <!doctype html>
<html lang="en" dir="ltr" class="no-js">
 <head prefix="og: http://ogp.me/ns#">
...
```
<div align="right"><i></> 11.10.scala</i></div>

11.3.2.1 Finding the First Paragraph

If we inspect the HTML of the page, we can see that the main page content is within an `<article id="wikiArticle">` tag, and the summary text for this `Location` page is simply the first `<p>` paragraph tag within:

We can use the `article#wikiArticle > p` selector to find all relevant paragraphs (Note we only want the *direct* children of #wikiArticle, hence the `>`) and use `.head` to find the first paragraph:

```
@ doc.select("article#wikiArticle > p").asScala.head.text
res39: String = "The Location interface represents the Location (URL) of the object..."
```
<div align="right"><i></> 11.11.scala</i></div>

11.3.2.2 Finding Property and Method Docs

Inspecting the list of properties and methods, we can see that the name and text for each property and method are within a `<dl>` definition list, as pairs of `<dt>` and `<dd>` tags:

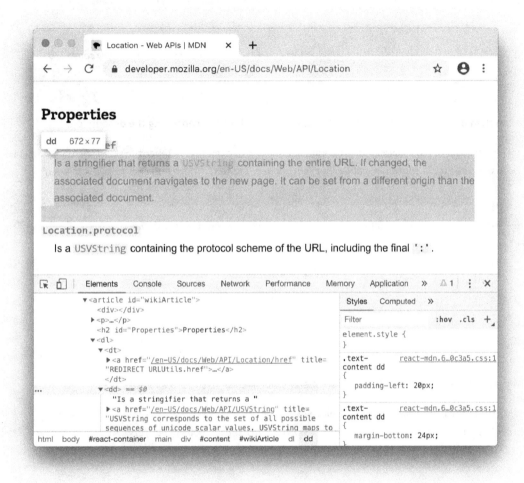

We can use the `article#wikiArticle dl dt` selector to find all the tags containing the name of a property or method:

```scala
@ val nameElements = doc.select("article#wikiArticle dl dt").asScala
nameElements: collection.mutable.Buffer[nodes.Element] = Buffer(
  <dt>
 <a href="/en-US/docs/Web/API/Location/href"><code>Location.href</code></a>
</dt>,
  <dt>
 <a href="/en-US/docs/Web/API/Location/protocol"><code>Location.protocol</code></a>
</dt>,
...
```
</> 11.12.scala

We can then use the .nextElementSibling of each to find the tag containing the description:

```scala
@ val nameDescPairs = nameElements.map(element => (element, element.nextElementSibling))
nameDescPairs: collection.mutable.Buffer[(nodes.Element, nodes.Element)] = ArrayBuffer(
  (
    <dt>
 <a href="/en-US/docs/Web/API/Location/href"><code>Location.href</code></a>
</dt>,
    <dd>
 Is a stringifier that returns a
 <a href="/en-US/docs/Web/API/USVString"><code>USVString</code></a>
</dd>
  ),
...
```
</> 11.13.scala

Lastly, to retrieve the text within each pair of elements, we can use the .text attribute:

```scala
@ val textPairs = nameDescPairs.map{case (k, v) => (k.text, v.text)}
textPairs: collection.mutable.Buffer[(String, String)] = ArrayBuffer(
  (
    "Location.href",
    "Is a stringifier that returns a USVString containing the entire URL. ..."
  ),
...
```
</> 11.14.scala

11.4 Putting it Together

Putting together the code we have written so far in the REPL gives us the following script:

```scala
import $ivy.`org.jsoup:jsoup:1.13.1`, org.jsoup._          ScrapingDocs.sc
import collection.JavaConverters._
val indexDoc = Jsoup.connect("https://developer.mozilla.org/en-US/docs/Web/API").get()
val links = indexDoc.select("h2#Interfaces").nextAll.select("div.index a").asScala
val linkData = links.map(link => (link.attr("href"), link.attr("title"), link.text))
val articles = for ((url, tooltip, name) <- linkData) yield {
  println("Scraping " + name)
  val doc = Jsoup.connect("https://developer.mozilla.org" + url).get()
  val summary = doc.select("article#wikiArticle > p").asScala.headOption match {
    case Some(n) => n.text; case None => ""
  }
  val methodsAndProperties = doc
    .select("article#wikiArticle dl dt")
    .asScala
    .map(el => (el.text, el.nextElementSibling match {case null => ""; case x => x.text}))
  (url, tooltip, name, summary, methodsAndProperties)
}                                                             </> 11.15.scala
```

See example 11.2 - ScrapingDocs

Note that we added a bit of error handling in here: rather than fetching the summary text via .head.text, we match on .headOption to account for the possibility that there is no summary paragraph. Similarly, we check .nextElementSibling to see if it is null before calling .text to fetch its contents. Other than that, it is essentially the same as the snippets we saw earlier. This should take a few minutes to run, as it has to fetch every page individually to parse and extract the data we want, producing the following output:

```scala
articles: Buffer[(String, String, String, String, Buffer[(String, String)])] = Buffer(
  (
    "/en-US/docs/Web/API/ANGLE_instanced_arrays",
    "The ANGLE_instanced_arrays extension is part of the WebGL API and allows to...",
    "ANGLE_instanced_arrays",
    "The ANGLE_instanced_arrays extension is part of the WebGL API and allows to...",
    ArrayBuffer(
      (
        "ext.VERTEX_ATTRIB_ARRAY_DIVISOR_ANGLE",
        "Returns a GLint describing the frequency divisor used for instanced..."
      ),
      (
        "ext.drawArraysInstancedANGLE()",
...
```
`</> 11.16.output-scala`

`articles` contains the first-paragraph summary of every documentation. We can see how many articles we have scraped in total, as well as how many member and property documentation snippets we have fetched. Lastly, if we need to use this information elsewhere, it is easy to dump to a JSON file that can be accessed later, perhaps from some other process.

```scala
@ articles.length
res15: Int = 917

@ articles.map(_._5.length).sum
res16: Int = 16583

@ os.write.over(os.pwd / "docs.json", upickle.default.write(articles, indent = 4))

@ os.read(os.pwd / "docs.json")
res65: String = """[
    [
        "/en-US/docs/Web/API/ANGLE_instanced_arrays",
        "The ANGLE_instanced_arrays extension is part of the WebGL API and allows...",
...
```
`</> 11.17.scala`

11.5 Conclusion

In this chapter, we walked through the basics of using the Jsoup HTML parser to scrape semi-structured data from Wikipedia's human-readable HTML pages. We then took the well-known MDN Web API Documentation and extracted summary documentation for every interface, method and property documented within it. We did our scraping interactively in the REPL, and were able to explore the data we scraped to make sure we were getting what we wanted. For re-usability, we saved the code in a Scala Script that we can easily run later.

Scraping websites is a core tool that every software engineer should have in their toolbox. Almost every third-party system or service exposes a web interface, and knowing how to scrape their interface opens up a host of possibilities in integrating these systems into your own programs and data processing.

This chapter only covers the basics of web scraping: for websites that need user accounts or have front-end Javascript, you may need to use Requests-Scala, or a more full-featured browser automation environment like Selenium. Nevertheless, this should be enough to get you started with the basic concepts of fetching, navigating and scraping HTML websites using Scala.

In the next chapter, ***Chapter 12: Working with HTTP APIs***, we will look at how we can take advantage of the structued HTTP/JSON APIs that some systems expose for third party code to integrate with.

Exercise: The MDN Web APIs page (https://developer.mozilla.org/en-US/docs/Web/API) has annotations marking the APIs which are deprecated, experimental, not yet standardized, and so on. Use Jsoup to scrape the annotations for every Web API and store them in a JSON file for later use.

See example 11.3 - ApiStatus

Exercise: Link rot is a common problem in any website, where URLs that were previously valid become invalid over time. Write a script that uses Jsoup to traverse the graph of .html pages and links on https://www.lihaoyi.com and returns a list of all internal and external links, so they can be checked for validity. You can use java.net.URI to help normalize the URLs and ensure you do not process the same page more than once.

See example 11.4 - ExternalLinks

Exercise: Many modern discussion forums have "threaded" discussions, meaning the discussion takes place in a tree-like format rather than in a linear sequence of comments. Use Jsoup to scrape the discussion off the following HTML web page from the https://lobste.rs/ discussion forum, converting it into a tree-like data structure defined by the `case class` below.

- Lobsters.html *(https://github.com/handsonscala/handsonscala/tree/v1/resources/11)*

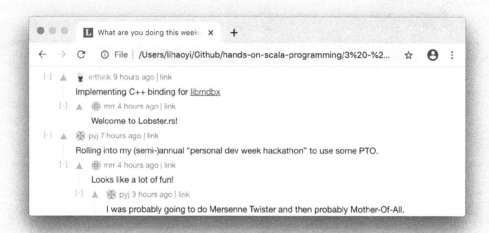

```scala
Comment("erthink", "Implementing C++ binding for libmdbx",
  List(Comment("mrr", "Welcome to Lobster.rs!", List()))
),
Comment("pyj", "Rolling into my (semi-)annual...",
  List(
    Comment("mrr", "Looks like a lot of fun!",
      List(
        Comment("pyj", "I was probably going to do...", List(...))
      )
    )
  )
),
```
</> 11.18.scala

See example 11.5 - ScrapingTrees

Discuss Chapter 11 online at https://www.handsonscala.com/discuss/11

12

Working with HTTP APIs

12.1 The Task: Github Issue Migrator   222

12.2 Creating Issues and Comments   224

12.3 Fetching Issues and Comments   226

12.4 Migrating Issues and Comments   232

```scala
@ requests.post(
    "https://api.github.com/repos/lihaoyi/test/issues",
    data = ujson.Obj("title" -> "hello"),
    headers = Map("Authorization" -> s"token $token")
  )
res1: requests.Response = Response(
  "https://api.github.com/repos/lihaoyi/test/issues",
  201,
  "Created",
...                                                    </> 12.1.scala
```

Snippet 12.1: interacting with Github's HTTP API from the Scala REPL

HTTP APIs have become the standard for any organization that wants to let external developers integrate with their systems. This chapter will walk you through how to access HTTP APIs in Scala, building up to a simple use case: migrating Github issues from one repository to another using Github's public API.

We will build upon techniques learned in this chapter in *Chapter 13: Fork-Join Parallelism with Futures*, where we will be writing a parallel web crawler using the Wikipedia JSON API to walk the graph of articles and the links between them.

The easiest way to work with HTTP JSON APIs is through the Requests-Scala library for HTTP, and uJson for JSON processing. Both libraries come bundled with Ammonite, which we will use throughout this chapter. *Chapter 8: JSON and Binary Data Serialization* covers in detail how to use the uJson library for parsing, modifying, querying and generating JSON data. The only new library we need for this chapter is Requests-Scala:

```
@ val r = requests.get("https://api.github.com/users/lihaoyi")

@ r.statusCode
res1: Int = 200

@ r.headers("content-type")
res2: Seq[String] = List("application/json; charset=utf-8")

@ r.text
res3: String = "{\"login\":\"Lihaoyi\",\"id\":934140,\"node_id\":\"MDQ6VXNLcjkzNDE0MA..."
```
</> 12.2.scala

Requests-Scala exposes the `requests.*` functions to make HTTP requests to a URL. Above we see the usage of `requests.get` to make a GET request, but we also have `requests.post`, `requests.put`, and many other methods each one corresponding to a kind of HTTP action:

```
val r = requests.post("http://httpbin.org/post", data = Map("key" -> "value"))

val r = requests.put("http://httpbin.org/put", data = Map("key" -> "value"))

val r = requests.delete("http://httpbin.org/delete")

val r = requests.options("http://httpbin.org/get")
```
</> 12.3.scala

The Requests-Scala documentation will have more details on how it can be used: uploading different kinds of data, setting headers, managing cookies, and so on. For now let us get on with our task, and we will learn the various features when they become necessary.

12.1 The Task: Github Issue Migrator

Our project for this chapter is to migrate a set of *Github Issues* from one repository to another. While Github easily lets you pull the source code history using `git pull` and push it to a new repository using `git push`, the issues are not so easy to move over.

There are a number of reasons why we may want to migrate our issues between repositories:

- Perhaps the original repository owner has gone missing, and the community wants to move development onto a new repository.

- Perhaps we wish to change platforms entirely: when Github became popular many people migrated their issue tracker history to Github from places like JIRA or Bitbucket, and we may want to migrate our issues elsewhere in future.

For now, let us stick with a simple case: we want to perform a one-off, one-way migration of Github issues from one existing Github repo to another, brand new one:

12.1.1 Old Existing Repository

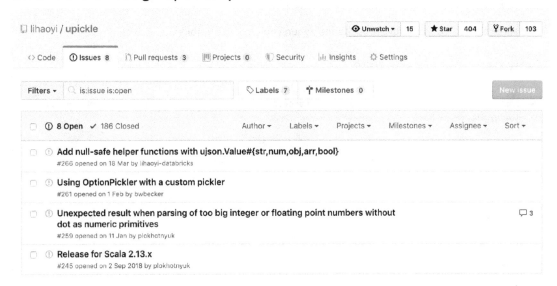

12.1.2 Brand New Repository

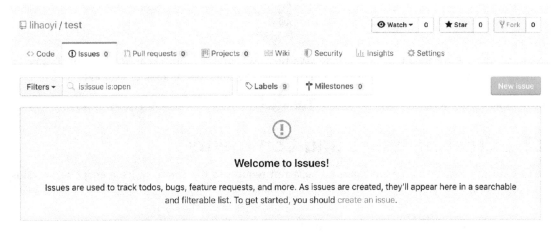

If you are going to run through this exercise on a real repository, make your new repository *Private* so you can work without worrying about other Github users interacting with it.

To limit the scope of the chapter, we will only be migrating over issues and comments, without consideration for other metadata like open/closed status, milestones, labels, and so on. Extending the migration code to handle those cases is left as an exercise to the reader.

We need to get an access token that gives our code read/write access to Github's data on our own repositories. The easiest way for a one-off project like this is to use a Personal Access Token, that you can create at:

- https://github.com/settings/tokens/new

Make sure you tick "Access public repositories" when you create your token:

New personal access token

Personal access tokens function like ordinary OAuth access tokens. They can be used instead of a password for Git over HTTPS, or can be used to authenticate to the API over Basic Authentication.

Note

Test Token

What's this token for?

Select scopes

Scopes define the access for personal tokens. Read more about OAuth scopes.

☐ **repo**	Full control of private repositories
☐ repo:status	Access commit status
☐ repo_deployment	Access deployment status
☑ public_repo	Access public repositories
☐ repo:invite	Access repository invitations

Once the token is generated, make sure you save the token to a file on disk, as you will not be able to retrieve it from the Github website later on. You can then read it into our Ammonite Scala REPL for use:

```
@ val token = os.read(os.home / "github_token.txt").trim() // strip any whitespace
```

12.2 Creating Issues and Comments

To test out this new token, we can make a simple test request to the *Create an Issue* endpoint, which is documented here:

- REST API V3: Create an Issue
- https://developer.github.com/v3/issues/#create-an-issue

```
@ requests.post(
    "https://api.github.com/repos/lihaoyi/test/issues",
    data = ujson.Obj("title" -> "hello"),
    headers = Map("Authorization" -> s"token $token")
  )
res1: requests.Response = Response(
  "https://api.github.com/repos/lihaoyi/test/issues",
  201,
  "Created",
  {"url":"https://api.github.com/repos/lihaoyi/test/issues/1", ...        </> 12.4.scala
```

Our request contained a small JSON payload, ujson.Obj("title" -> "hello"), which corresponds to the {"title": "hello"} JSON dictionary. Github responded to this request with a HTTP 201 code, which indicates the request was successful. Going to the issues page, we can see our new issue has been created:

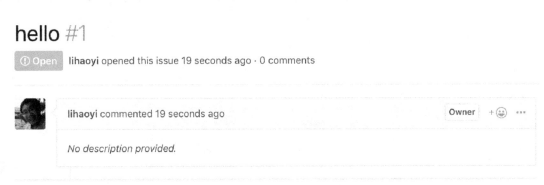

We can also try creating a comment, using the *Create a Comment* endpoint, documented here:

- REST API V3: Create a Comment
- https://developer.github.com/v3/issues/comments/#create-a-comment

```
@ requests.post(
    "https://api.github.com/repos/lihaoyi/test/issues/1/comments",
    data = ujson.Obj("body" -> "world"),
    headers = Map("Authorization" -> s"token $token")
  )
res2: requests.Response = Response(
  "https://api.github.com/repos/lihaoyi/test/issues/1/comments",
  201,
  "Created",
  {"url":"https://api.github.com/repos/lihaoyi/test/issues/comments/573959489", ...
                                                                        </> 12.5.scala
```

We can then open up the issue in the UI to see that the comment has been created:

12.3 Fetching Issues and Comments

For fetching issues, Github provides a public HTTP JSON API:

- REST API V3: List Issues for a Repository
- https://developer.github.com/v3/issues/#list-issues-for-a-repository

This tells us that we can make a HTTP request in the following format:

```
GET /repos/:owner/:repo/issues
```

Many parameters can be passed in to filter the returned collection: by `milestone`, `state`, `assignee`, `creator`, `mentioned`, `labels`, etc. For now we just want to get a list of all issues for us to migrate to the new repository. We can set `state=all` to fetch all issues both open and closed. The documentation tells us that we can expect a JSON response in the following format:

```json
[
  {
    "id": 1,
    "number": 1347,
    "state": "open",
    "title": "Found a bug",
    "body": "I'm having a problem with this.",
    "user": { "login": "octocat", "id": 1 },
    "labels": [],
    "assignee": { "login": "octocat", "id": 1 },
    "assignees": [],
    "milestone": { ... },
    "locked": true
  }
]
```
</> 12.6.json

This snippet is simplified, with many fields omitted for brevity. Nevertheless, this gives us a good idea of what we can expect: each issue has an ID, a state, a title, a body, and other metadata: creator, labels, assignees, milestone, and so on. To access this data programmatically, we can use Requests-Scala to make a HTTP GET request to this API endpoint to fetch data on the `lihaoyi/upickle` repository, and see the JSON string returned by the endpoint:

```scala
@ val resp = requests.get(
    "https://api.github.com/repos/lihaoyi/upickle/issues",
    params = Map("state" -> "all"),
    headers = Map("Authorization" -> s"token $token")
)
resp: requests.Response = Response(
  "https://api.github.com/repos/lihaoyi/upickle/issues",
  200,
  "OK",
  [{"url":"https://api.github.com/repos/lihaoyi/upickle/issues/294","repository_url": ...

@ resp.text()
res4: String = "[{\"url\":\"https://api.github.com/repos/lihaoyi/upickle/issues/620\"..."
```
</> 12.7.scala

Is is straightforward to parse this string into a JSON structure using the `ujson.read` method we saw in **Chapter 8: JSON and Binary Data Serialization**. This lets us easily traverse the structure, or pretty-print it in a reasonable way:

```
@ val parsed = ujson.read(resp)
parsed: ujson.Value.Value = Arr(
  ArrayBuffer(
    Obj(
      Map(
        "url" -> Str("https://api.github.com/repos/lihaoyi/upickle/issues/620"),
        "repository_url" -> Str("https://api.github.com/repos/lihaoyi/upickle"),

...

@ println(parsed.render(indent = 4))
[
    {
        "id": 449398451,
        "number": 620,
        "title": "Issue with custom repositories when trying to use Scoverage",
        "user": {
            "login": "jacarey",
            "id": 6933549,
```

... </> 12.8.scala

We now have the raw JSON data from Github in a reasonable format that we can work with. Next we will analyze the data and extract the bits of information we care about.

12.3.1 Pagination

The first thing to notice is that the returned issues collection is only 30 items long:

```
@ parsed.arr.length
res7: Int = 30
```
</> 12.9.scala

This seems incomplete, since we earlier saw that the lihaoyi/upickle repository has 8 open issues and 186 closed issues. On a closer reading of the documentation, we find out that this 30-item cutoff is due to pagination:

- https://developer.github.com/v3/#pagination

The relevant line is as follows:

Requests that return multiple items will be paginated to 30 items by default. You can specify further pages with the ?page parameter.

In order to fetch all the items, we have to pass a ?page parameter to fetch subsequent pages: ?page=1, ? page=2, ?page=3, stopping when there are no more pages to fetch. We can do that with a simple while loop, passing in page in the request params:

```scala
@ def fetchPaginated(url: String, params: (String, String)*) = {
    var done = false
    var page = 1
    val responses = collection.mutable.Buffer.empty[ujson.Value]
    while (!done) {
      println("page " + page + "...")
      val resp = requests.get(
        url,
        params = Map("page" -> page.toString) ++ params,
        headers = Map("Authorization" -> s"token $token")
      )
      val parsed = ujson.read(resp).arr
      if (parsed.length == 0) done = true
      else responses.appendAll(parsed)
      page += 1
    }
    responses
  }

@ val issues = fetchPaginated(
    "https://api.github.com/repos/lihaoyi/upickle/issues",
    "state" -> "all"
  )
page 1...
page 2...
page 3...                                                        </> 12.10.scala
```

Here, we parse each JSON response, cast it to a JSON array via `.arr`, and then check if the array has issues. If the array is not empty, we append all those issues to a `responses` buffer. If the array is empty, that means we're done.

Note that by making `fetchPaginated`'s take `params` as a variable argument list of tuples, that allows us to call `fetchPaginated` with the same `"key" -> "value"` syntax that we use for constructing `Maps` via `Map("key" -> "values")`. `"key" -> "value"` is a shorthand syntax for a tuple `("key", "value")`. Making `fetchPaginated` take `(String, String)*` lets us pass in an arbitrary number of key-value tuples to `fetchPaginated` without needing to manually wrap them in a `Seq`.

We can verify that we got all the issues we want by running:

```scala
@ issues.length
res10: Int = 272                                                 </> 12.11.scala
```

This matches what we would expect, with 8 open issues, 186 closed issues, 3 open pull requests, and 75 closed pull requests adding up to 272 issues in total.

12.3.2 Picking the data we want

Github by default treats issues and pull requests pretty similarly, but for the purpose of this exercise, let us assume we only want to migrate the issues. We'll also assume we don't need *all* the information on each issue: just the title, description, original author, and the text/author of each of the comments.

Looking through the JSON manually, we see that the JSON objects with the `pull_request` key represent pull requests, while those without represent issues. Since for now we only want to focus on issues, we can filter out the pull requests:

```scala
@ val nonPullRequests = issues.filter(!_.obj.contains("pull_request"))

@ nonPullRequests.length
res12: Int = 194
```
`</> 12.12.scala`

For each issue, we can pick out the number, title, body, and author from the `ujson.Value` using the `issue("...")` syntax:

```scala
@ val issueData = for (issue <- nonPullRequests) yield (
    issue("number").num.toInt,
    issue("title").str,
    issue("body").str,
    issue("user")("login").str
  )
issueData: collection.mutable.Buffer[(Int, String, String, String)] = ArrayBuffer(
  (
    272,
    "Custom pickling for sealed hierarchies",
    """Citing the manual, "sealed hierarchies are serialized as tagged values,
...
```
`</> 12.13.scala`

Now, we have the metadata around each top-level issue. However, one piece of information is still missing, and doesn't seem to appear at all in these responses: where are the issue comments?

12.3.3 Issue Comments

It turns out that Github has a separate HTTP JSON API endpoint for fetching the comments of an issue:

- REST API V3: List comments in a repository
- https://developer.github.com/v3/issues/comments/#list-comments-in-a-repository

Since there may be more than 30 comments, we need to paginate through the list-comments endpoint the same way we paginated through the list-issues endpoint. The endpoints are similar enough we can re-use the `fetchPaginated` function we defined earlier:

```scala
@ val comments =
    fetchPaginated("https://api.github.com/repos/lihaoyi/upickle/issues/comments")

@ println(comments(0).render(indent = 4))
{
    "url": "https://api.github.com/repos/lihaoyi/upickle/issues/comments/46443901",
    "html_url": "https://github.com/lihaoyi/upickle/issues/1#issuecomment-46443901",
    "issue_url": "https://api.github.com/repos/lihaoyi/upickle/issues/1",
    "id": 46443901,
    "user": { "login": "lihaoyi", ... },
    "created_at": "2014-06-18T14:38:49Z",
    "updated_at": "2014-06-18T14:38:49Z",
    "author_association": "OWNER",
    "body": "Oops, fixed it in trunk, so it'll be fixed next time I publish\n"
}
```
</> *12.14.scala*

From this data, it's quite easy to extract the issue each comment is tied to, along with the author and body text:

```scala
@ val commentData = for (comment <- comments) yield (
    comment("issue_url").str match {
      case s"https://api.github.com/repos/lihaoyi/$repo/issues/$id" => id.toInt
    },
    comment("user")("login").str,
    comment("body").str
  )
commentData: collection.mutable.Buffer[(Int, String, String)] = ArrayBuffer(
  (1, "lihaoyi", "Oops, fixed it in trunk, so it'll be fixed next time I publish"),
  (2, "lihaoyi", "Was a mistake, just published it, will show up on maven central..."),
...
```
</> *12.15.scala*

Note that in both `commentData` and `issueData`, we are manually extracting the fields we want from the JSON and constructing a collection of tuples representing the data we want. If the number of fields grows and the tuples get inconvenient to work with, it might be worth defining a case class representing the records and de-serializing to a collection of case class instances instead.

12.4 Migrating Issues and Comments

Now that we've got all the data from the old repository `lihaoyi/upickle`, and have the ability to post issues and comments to the new repository `lihaoyi/test`, it's time to do the migration!

We want:

- One new issue per old issue, with the same title and description, with the old issue's Author and ID as part of the new issue's description

- One new comment per old comment, with the same body, and the old comment's author included.

12.4.1 One new issue per old issue

Creating a new issue per old issue is simple:

- Sort the `issueData` we accumulated earlier
- Loop over the issues in sorted order
- Call the create-issue endpoint once per issue we want to create with the relevant `title` and `body`

```scala
@ val issueNums = for ((number, title, body, user) <- issueData.sortBy(_._1)) yield {
    println(s"Creating issue $number")
    val resp = requests.post(
      s"https://api.github.com/repos/lihaoyi/test/issues",
      data = ujson.Obj(
        "title" -> title,
        "body" -> s"$body\nID: $number\nOriginal Author: $user"
      ),
      headers = Map("Authorization" -> s"token $token")
    )
    val newIssueNumber = ujson.read(resp)("number").num.toInt
    (number, newIssueNumber)
  }
Creating issue 1
Creating issue 2
...
Creating issue 272                                              </> 12.16.scala
```

This creates all the issues we want:

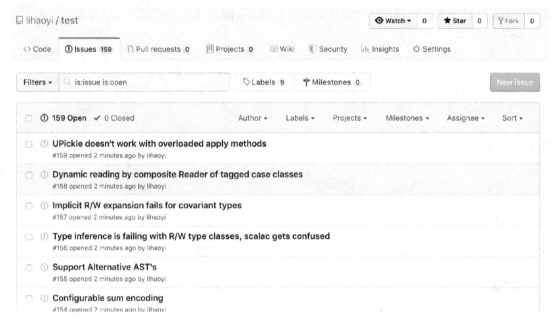

Note that we store the `newIssueNum` of each newly created issue, along with the `number` of the original issue. This will let us easily find the corresponding new issue for each old issue, and vice versa.

12.4.2 One new comment per old comment

Creating comments is similar: we loop over all the old comments and post a new comment to the relevant issue. We can use the `issueNums` we stored earlier to compute an `issueNumMap` for easy lookup:

```scala
@  val issueNumMap = issueNums.toMap
issueNumMap: Map[Int, Int] = Map(
  101 -> 118,
  88 -> 127,
  170 -> 66,
...                                                    </> 12.17.scala
```

This map lets us easily look up what the new issue number is for each of the old issues, so we can make sure the comments on each old issue get attached to the correct new issue. We can manually inspect the two repositories' issues to verify that that the title of each issue is the same for each pair of indices into the old and new repository's issue tracker.

Using `issueNumMap`, we can then loop over the comments on the old repository's issues and use `requests.post` to create comments on the new repository's issues:

```
@ for ((issueId, user, body) <- commentData; newIssueId <- issueNumMap.get(issueId)) {
    println(s"Commenting on issue old_id=$issueId new_id=$newIssueId")
    val resp = requests.post(
        s"https://api.github.com/repos/lihaoyi/test/issues/$newIssueId/comments",
        data = ujson.Obj("body" -> s"$body\nOriginal Author:$user"),
        headers = Map("Authorization" -> s"token $token")
    )
}
Commenting on issue old_id=1 new_id=1
Commenting on issue old_id=2 new_id=2
...
Commenting on issue old_id=272 new_id=194                          </> 12.18.scala
```

Now, we can see that all our issues have been populated with their respective comments:

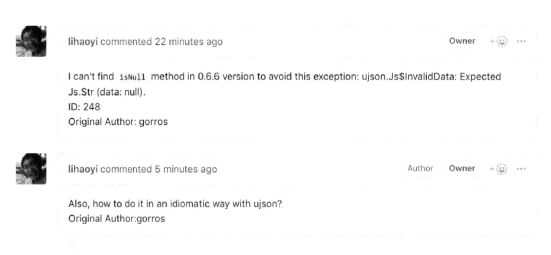

And we're done! All issues from the old repository have been migrated over to the new repository, and all comments on those issues have been migrated as well.

The issue migrator we have walked through here is deliberately simplified: we only migrate issues, do not handle open/closed status or other metadata, and do not migrate pull requests. Extending the issue migrator to handle those cases is left as an exercise for the reader.

To wrap up, here's all the code for our Github Issue Migrator, wrapped in a `@main` method to allow it be called via the command line as `amm IssueMigrator.sc lihaoyi/upickle lihaoyi/test`. Note that `lihaoyi/upickle` is has enough issues and comments that running this script might take a while; to speed things up, consider testing it out on a smaller repository such as `lihaoyi/requests-scala`.

```scala
@main def main(srcRepo: String, destRepo: String) = {                    IssueMigrator.sc
  val token = os.read(os.home / "github_token.txt").trim


  def fetchPaginated(url: String, params: (String, String)*) = {
    var done = false
    var page = 1
    val responses = collection.mutable.Buffer.empty[ujson.Value]
    while (!done) {
      println("page " + page + "...")
      val resp = requests.get(
        url,
        params = Map("page" -> page.toString) ++ params,
        headers = Map("Authorization" -> s"token $token")
      )
      val parsed = ujson.read(resp).arr
      if (parsed.length == 0) done = true
      else responses.appendAll(parsed)
      page += 1
    }
    responses
  }


  val issues =
    fetchPaginated(s"https://api.github.com/repos/$srcRepo/issues", "state" -> "all")


  val nonPullRequests = issues.filter(!_.obj.contains("pull_request"))


  val issueData = for (issue <- nonPullRequests) yield (
    issue("number").num.toInt,
    issue("title").str,
    issue("body").str,
    issue("user")("login").str
  )


  val comments =
    fetchPaginated(s"https://api.github.com/repos/$srcRepo/issues/comments")


  val commentData = for (comment <- comments) yield (
    comment("issue_url").str match {
      case s"https://api.github.com/repos/lihaoyi/$repo/issues/$id" => id.toInt
    },
```

```scala
    comment("user")("login").str,
    comment("body").str
  )


  val issueNums = for ((number, title, body, user) <- issueData.sortBy(_._1)) yield {
    println(s"Creating issue $number")
    val resp = requests.post(
      s"https://api.github.com/repos/$destRepo/issues",
      data = ujson.Obj(
        "title" -> title,
        "body" -> s"$body\nID: $number\nOriginal Author: $user"
      ),
      headers = Map("Authorization" -> s"token $token")
    )
    println(resp.statusCode)
    val newIssueNumber = ujson.read(resp)("number").num.toInt
    (number, newIssueNumber)
  }


  val issueNumMap = issueNums.toMap

  for ((issueId, user, body) <- commentData; newIssueId <- issueNumMap.get(issueId)) {
    println(s"Commenting on issue old_id=$issueId new_id=$newIssueId")
    val resp = requests.post(
      s"https://api.github.com/repos/lihaoyi/test/issues/$newIssueId/comments",
      data = ujson.Obj("body" -> s"$body\nOriginal Author:$user"),
      headers = Map("Authorization" -> s"token $token")
    )
    println(resp.statusCode)
  }
}
```

</> 12.19.scala

See example 12.1 - IssueMigrator

12.5 Conclusion

This chapter has gone through how to use `requests.get` to access data you need from a third party service, `ujson` to manipulate the JSON payloads, and `requests.post` to send commands back up. Note that the techniques covered in this chapter only work with third party services which expose HTTP JSON APIs that are designed for programmatic use.

`ujson` and `requests` can be used in projects built with Mill or other build tools via the following coordinates:

```
ivy"com.lihaoyi::ujson:1.2.0"                                              Mill
ivy"com.lihaoyi::requests:0.6.5"                                  </> 12.20.scala
```

The documentation for Requests-Scala has more detail, if you wish to dive deeper into the library:

- https://github.com/lihaoyi/requests-scala

While we will be using Requests-Scala throughout this book, the Scala ecosystem has several alternate HTTP clients you may encounter in the wild. The syntax for each library will differ, but the concepts involved in all of them are similar:

- STTP: https://github.com/softwaremill/sttp
- Akka HTTP: https://github.com/akka/akka-http
- HTTP4S: https://github.com/http4s/http4s
- AsyncHttpClient: https://github.com/AsyncHttpClient/async-http-client

We will re-visit Requests-Scala in *Chapter 13: Fork-Join Parallelism with Futures*, where we will use it along with AsyncHttpClient to recursively crawl the graph of Wikipedia articles.

> **Exercise:** Make the issue migrator add a link in every new issue's description back to the old github issue that it was created from.
>
> **See example 12.2 - IssueMigratorLink**

> **Exercise:** Migrate the open-closed status of each issue, such that the new issues are automatically closed if the old issue was closed.
>
> **See example 12.3 - IssueMigratorClosed**

> **Discuss Chapter 12 online at** https://www.handsonscala.com/discuss/12

13

Fork-Join Parallelism with Futures

13.1 Parallel Computation using Futures   240

13.2 N-Ways Parallelism   243

13.3 Parallel Web Crawling   246

13.4 Asynchronous Futures   252

13.5 Asynchronous Web Crawling   255

```scala
def fetchAllLinksParallel(startTitle: String, depth: Int): Set[String] = {
  var seen = Set(startTitle)
  var current = Set(startTitle)
  for (i <- Range(0, depth)) {
    val futures = for (title <- current) yield Future{ fetchLinks(title) }
    val nextTitleLists = futures.map(Await.result(_, Inf))
    current = nextTitleLists.flatten.filter(!seen.contains(_))
    seen = seen ++ current
  }
  seen
}
```
</> 13.1.scala

Snippet 13.1: a simple parallel web-crawler implemented using Scala Futures

The Scala programming language comes with a Futures API. Futures make parallel and asynchronous programming much easier to handle than working with traditional techniques of threads, locks, and callbacks.

This chapter dives into Scala's Futures: how to use them, how they work, and how you can use them to parallelize data processing workflows. It culminates in using Futures together with the techniques we learned in *Chapter 12: Working with HTTP APIs* to write a high-performance concurrent web crawler in a straightforward and intuitive way.

For this chapter, we will use the Ammonite Scala REPL with the `--class-based` flag:

```
$ amm --class-based
Loading...
Welcome to the Ammonite Repl 2.2.0 (Scala 2.13.2 Java 11.0.7)
@ import scala.concurrent._, duration.Duration.Inf, java.util.concurrent.Executors

@ implicit val ec = ExecutionContext.fromExecutorService(Executors.newFixedThreadPool(8))
                                                                          </> 13.2.scala
```

The `--class-based` flag is necessary in order to use Futures and other multi-threading constructs in the REPL due to implementation limitations. This flag is not necessary when using Scala projects built with Mill or other build tools.

We import the common classes and functions to let us work with Futures from the `scala.concurrent` package. We also import the duration `scala.concurrent.duration.Inf`, and construct an `ExecutionContext` using a `newFixedThreadPool` with 8 threads as a reasonable default to get started with. You can control the level of parallelism by changing the number of threads. There are also other kinds of `ExecutionContext` available for more advanced use cases.

Note that in a larger application, `ExecutionContext`s created from thread pools need to be explicitly terminated using `.shutdown()` when no longer needed (e.g. in a `finally` block at the end of the method in which they are used, or at the end of the `main` method if they are global). Thread pools are somewhat expensive to instantiate, so where possible you typically want to share them throughout your program rather than re-instantiating them everywhere they are needed.

13.1 Parallel Computation using Futures

As an example computation we can parallelize using Futures, we will be using an implementation of the BCrypt hash function from the following repository. We can load this into our Ammonite Scala REPL and define a `def` hash function that we can use to hash files.

- https://github.com/patrickfav/bcrypt

```
@ import $ivy.`at.favre.lib:bcrypt:0.9.0`

@ import at.favre.lib.crypto.bcrypt.{BCrypt, LongPasswordStrategies}

@ val hasher = BCrypt.`with`(LongPasswordStrategies.hashSha512(BCrypt.Version.VERSION_2A))

@ def hash(name: String) = {
    val salt = name.take(16).padTo(16, ' ').getBytes
    val bytes = hasher.hash(/*difficulty*/ 17, salt, os.read.bytes(os.pwd / name))
    new String(bytes)
  }
                                                                          </> 13.3.scala
```

We will be using the four following files as the data we will hash throughout this chapter:

- Chinatown.jpg *(https://github.com/handsonscala/handsonscala/tree/v1/resources/13)*
- Kresge.jpg *(https://github.com/handsonscala/handsonscala/tree/v1/resources/13)*
- Memorial.jpg *(https://github.com/handsonscala/handsonscala/tree/v1/resources/13)*
- ZCenter.jpg *(https://github.com/handsonscala/handsonscala/tree/v1/resources/13)*

With the difficulty level of hashing set to `17`, hashing one of these files takes a significant amount of time to complete. This is clear when we run `hash` on e.g. `Chinatown.jpg`:

```
@ time{ hash("Chinatown.jpg") }
res5: (String, FiniteDuration = (
  "$2a$17$O0fnZkDyZ1bsJknuXw.eG.9Mesh9W03ZnVPefgcTVP7sc2rYBdPb2",
  10942495521 nanoseconds
)
```
</> 13.4.scala

Using the `time{}` REPL builtin, we can see that this takes about 10 seconds to complete, depending on the hardware you are running on.

13.1.1 Sequential Code

Consider the following code that executes two call to `hash` sequentially. We can see that this takes about 20 seconds to run:

```
@ time{
    println(hash("Chinatown.jpg"))
    println(hash("ZCenter.jpg"))
  }
$2a$17$O0fnZkDyZ1bsJknuXw.eG.9Mesh9W03ZnVPefgcTVP7sc2rYBdPb2
$2a$17$UiLjZLPjag3oaEaeGA.eG.8KLuk3HS0iqPGaRJPdp1BjL4zjhQLWi
res6: (Unit, FiniteDuration) = ((), 20273416425 nanoseconds)
```
</> 13.5.scala

Typical Scala code, like most programming languages, executes sequentially: line by line from top to bottom, left to right within each line. If we can run both `hash` calls in parallel, we should be able to do it in half the time: about 10 seconds. That is where Futures come in.

13.1.2 Spawning Futures

The basic building block is `scala.concurrent.Future`, which we have imported as simply `Future`. Futures define lightweight tasks that run on a thread pool, perform some computation, and return a value. We construct a simple thread pool earlier (`Executors.newFixedThreadPool(8)`), but there a range of options you can choose from (`newWorkStealingPool`, `newSingleThreadExecutor`, etc.).

To create a future, use the `Future{ ... }` syntax:

```
@ val f1 = Future{ "hello" + 123 + "world" }
f1: Future[String] = Future(Success(hello123world))


@ val f2 = Future{ hash("Chinatown.jpg") }
f2: Future[String] = Future(<not completed>)                          </> 13.6.scala
```

We can see that the first Future f1 is already completed when printed out. That makes sense, as the computation is simple and would complete almost instantly, even before the result is printed to the console. The second Future f2 uses the hash function we defined earlier, and therefore takes longer and is listed as <not completed>. However, both lines val f1 = and val f2 = complete instantly! This is because when we create a Future, it runs in the background on a thread pool and we can continue doing other things while it is working.

If we wait about 10 seconds and ask for f2 again, we will see it complete and print out the hash of the file:

```
@ f2
res8: Future[String] = Future(Success($2a$17$O0fnZkDyZ1bsJknuXw.eG.9Mesh9W03ZnVPefgcTV...
                                                                     </> 13.7.scala
```

13.1.3 Offloading Work from the Main Thread

A Future's computation returns the single value at the end of the Future{ ... } block. When we want the return value of the Future, we can use Await.result to get it:

```
@ val f = Future{ hash("Chinatown.jpg") }
f: Future[String] = Future(<not completed>)


@ Await.result(f, Inf)
res11: String = "$2a$17$O0fnZkDyZ1bsJinOPw.eG.H80jYKe4v1rAF8k5sH9uRue4tma50...</> 13.8.scala
```

Even just creating a single Future to run in the background can be useful, as you can have your code do other things while the Future is running. For example, we can run one hash call inside the Future, do another hash call on the main thread, and then use Await.result to wait for the background call to complete:

```
@ val f = Future{ hash("Chinatown.jpg") }
f: Future[String] = Future(<not completed>)


@ val result = hash("ZCenter.jpg")
result: String = "$2a$17$U1LjZLPjag3oaEaeGA.eG.8KLuk3HS0iqPGaRJPdp1BjL4zjhQLWi"


@ val backgroundResult = Await.result(f, Inf)
backgroundResult: String = "$2a$17$O0fnZkDyZ1bsJknuXw.eG.9Mesh9W03ZnVPefgcTVP7sc2rYBdPb2"
                                                                     </> 13.9.scala
```

We can visualize the execution of the main thread and future as follows:

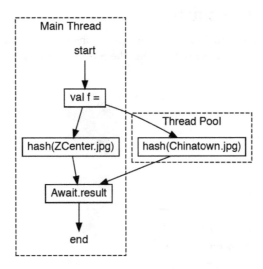

What `Await.result` does depends on whether the Future is completed when the `Await.result` is called on the main thread:

- If the Future is already completed, then `Await.result` immediately returns the value computed by the Future for you to use

- If the Future has not yet completed, then `Await.result` will wait until the value is ready before returning it

In both cases, you do not need to worry about using mutable variables, locking, or race conditions when transferring the result of the background Future back to the main thread: the `Await.result` function does that for you automatically, ensuring that your main thread will be given the `backgroundResult` value to use once it is ready.

13.2 N-Ways Parallelism

We have so far looked at two cases:

1. Sequential code
2. Running one half the work in a background Future and one half on the main thread

Let's now consider a third case: splitting a trivially-parallel computation into N parts, and running it N-ways parallel in the background.

13.2.1 N Sequential Computations

First, consider the following sequential computation, which runs our `def` `hash` function over every file in the process working directory. Below, we can see that the process overall takes about 39 seconds, running sequentially in a `for`-comprehension:

```scala
@ val (hashes, duration) = time{
    for (p <- os.list(os.pwd)) yield {
      println("Hashing " + p)
      hash(p.last)
    }
  }
Hashing /Users/lihaoyi/test/Chinatown.jpg
Hashing /Users/lihaoyi/test/Kresge.jpg
Hashing /Users/lihaoyi/test/Memorial.jpg
Hashing /Users/lihaoyi/test/ZCenter.jpg
hashes: IndexedSeq[String] = ArraySeq(
  "$2a$17$00fnZkDyZ1bsJknuXw.eG.9Mesh9W03ZnVPefgcTVP7sc2rYBdPb2",
  "$2a$17$Q1Hja0bjJknuXw.eGA.eG.KQ7bQL8kQbzR4sTBdT97icinfz5xh66",
  "$2a$17$RUTrZ1HnWUusYl/lGA.eG.TK2UsZfBYw6mLhDyORr659FFz2lPwZK",
  "$2a$17$UiLjZLPjag3oaEaeGA.eG.8KLuk3HS0iqPGaRJPdp1Bjl4zjhQLWi"
)
duration: FiniteDuration = 38949493436 nanoseconds                  </> 13.10.scala
```

13.2.2 N Parallel Computations

Because hashing one file is totally independent of hashing any other file, this computation is trivially parallelizable, and we can use Futures to utilize multiple cores to do the hashing in parallel. This involves kicking off a separate `Future{...}` block for every file we want to hash, and then waiting for all the results at the end:

```scala
  val (hashes, duration) = time{
-   for (p <- os.list(os.pwd)) yield {
+   val futures = for (p <- os.list(os.pwd)) yield Future{
      println("Hashing " + p)
      hash(p.last)
    }
+   futures.map(Await.result(_, Inf))
  }
                                                                    </> 13.11.scala
```

When we run this parallelized code snippet in the REPL, it produces the following output:

```
Hashing /Users/lihaoyi/test/Chinatown.jpg
Hashing /Users/lihaoyi/test/Kresge.jpg
Hashing /Users/lihaoyi/test/ZCenter.jpg
Hashing /Users/lihaoyi/test/Memorial.jpg
hashes: IndexedSeq[String] = ArraySeq(
  "$2a$17$O0fnZkDyZIbsJknuXw.eG.9Mesh9W03ZnVPefgcTVP7sc2rYBdPb2",
  "$2a$17$Q1Hja0bjJknuXw.eGA.eG.KQ7bQL8kQbzR4sTBdT97icinfz5xh66",
  "$2a$17$RUTrZ1HnWUusYL/LGA.eG.TK2UsZfBYw6mLhDyORr659FFz2LPwZK",
  "$2a$17$UiLjZLPjag3oaEaeGA.eG.8KLuk3HS0iqPGaRJPdp1BjL4zjhQLWi"
)
duration: FiniteDuration = 10292549149 nanoseconds            </> 13.12.output-scala
```

While earlier we had two Futures which we `Awaited` on individually, now we have a whole list of Futures (`val futures`) that we map over to await on all of them.

Note that the order in which the independent Futures are executed is arbitrary: the four `Hashing ...` messages printed by our parallel hashing code are in a different order than our previous sequential execution, and may be in different orders if we re-run the parallel hashing multiple times. However, when we run `futures.map(Await.result(_, Inf))`, the final collection of hashes will be assembled in the same order the Futures were created regardless of which order the hashing actually happened.

We can see that the total is down from 39 seconds to 10 seconds (10,292,549,149 nanoseconds). This is expected, since the Futures running on a background threadpool utilizes all CPU cores to run in parallel:

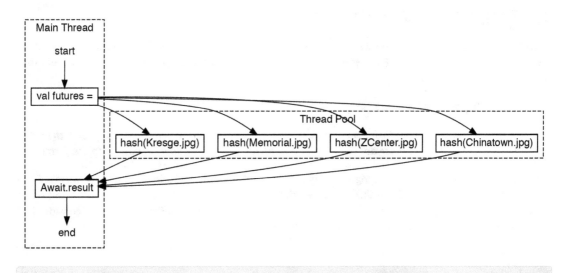

See example 13.1 - Hashing

13.2.3 Futures vs Threads

Unlike Threads, using Futures is often an easy way to make use of parallelism for minimal extra effort: here a three-line code change! You do not need to deal with the error-prone locks, queues, volatiles and atomics that typically permeate multi-threaded code. These construct are still used under the hood, but the Futures framework encapsulates it so you usually do not need to work with them directly.

Futures are also much cheaper than threads, and can be used much more freely:

- The memory overhead of a thread is typically has several megabytes, while that of a Future is less than a kilobyte

- Switching between threads thread takes several microseconds, while switching between Futures takes a tenth of a microsecond

As a result, while you generally want to stay below 1,000 threads due to performance and memory concerns, you can easily have 100,000s or 1,000,000s of Futures without issue. In this case, even if the folder had a large number of files within it, creating one Future per file is unlikely to cause issues.

Like Threads, the order in which Futures evaluate is arbitrary, and may differ between runs of your program. However, as long as the value being evaluated by each Future does not have side effects, the non-deterministic order of evaluation will not affect the behavior or correctness of your code. You thus should ensure the computations you are parallelizing with Futures are "pure" and only return a value with no observable side effects: if not, the side effects may occur in a different order each time your code runs, resulting in confusing and non-deterministic bugs.

13.3 Parallel Web Crawling

Apart from parallelizing CPU-bound code, Futures can also be useful for parallelizing network-bound code. We will now explore how to use Futures to parallelize a common task (and a common interview exercise!): writing a parallel *web crawler*.

Let us assume the task is as follows:

Given the title of a page on Wikipedia (e.g. "Albert Einstein"), write a program that will fetch the set of all pages within a certain number depth of links from the root page, and do so in parallel for performance.

There are several ways of approaching this exercise, which is essentially to implement a traversal of the graph of Wikipedia pages and the links between them. You can do the traversal either breadth-first or depth-first, and then there are many ways you could implement parallelism. For now we will consider just one approach: a breadth first traversal, parallelized using Futures.

13.3.1 A Single HTTP Request

For example, consider the following code to make a HTTP request and fetch all the links on a Wikipedia page:

```scala
def fetchLinks(title: String): Seq[String] = {
  val resp = requests.get(
    "https://en.wikipedia.org/w/api.php",
    params = Seq(
      "action" -> "query",
      "titles" -> title,
      "prop" -> "links",
      "format" -> "json"
    )
  )
  for{
    page <- ujson.read(resp)("query")("pages").obj.values.toSeq
    links <- page.obj.get("links").toSeq
    link <- links.arr
  } yield link("title").str
}
```
FetchLinks.sc

`</> 13.13.scala`

This makes use of the `requests` library to fetch the data from Wikipedia, and the `ujson` library to parse it, similar to what we did in **Chapter 12: Working with HTTP APIs**. You can add a `println(resp.text())` if you would like to see the raw response from Wikipedia, but for this chapter it is enough to know that this function can be called on any Wikipedia page to return a list of pages that are linked from it:

```scala
@ val links = fetchLinks("Albert Einstein")
links: Seq[String] = Seq(
  "20th Century Press Archives",
  "2dF Galaxy Redshift Survey",
  "A priori and a posteriori",
  "Aage Bohr",
  "Aarau",
  "Aargau",
  "Abba Eban",
  "Abdominal aortic aneurysm",
  "Abdus Salam",
  "Absent-minded professor"
)
```

`</> 13.14.scala`

For simplicity, let's ignore the fact that Wikipedia only returns the first 10 links on each page by default, and requires pagination to access the full list. This `fetchLinks` function will be the foundation on which we build our Wikipedia crawler.

13.3.2 Sequential Crawling

First, let us write the function that does a simple breadth-first traversal of the page-link graph:

```scala
import $file.FetchLinks, FetchLinks._                          Crawler.sc
def fetchAllLinks(startTitle: String, depth: Int): Set[String] = {
  var seen = Set(startTitle)
  var current = Set(startTitle)
  for (i <- Range(0, depth)) {
    val nextTitleLists = for (title <- current) yield fetchLinks(title)
    current = nextTitleLists.flatten.filter(!seen.contains(_))
    seen = seen ++ current
  }
  seen
}
```
</> 13.15.scala

See example 13.2 - Crawler

Unlike the breadth-first search we implemented in ***Chapter 6: Implementing Algorithms in Scala***, we do not maintain an explicit queue of links to process, and instead simply process all depth 1 links, then all depth 2 links, etc. until we get to the depth we want. The `current` set keeps track of what pages belong to the current depth, and the `seen` set prevents us from redundantly processing a page more than once. Loading this into the REPL using `amm --class-based --predef Crawler.sc`, we can call `fetchAllLinks` to traverse the page-link graph to various depths:

```scala
@ fetchAllLinks("Singapore", 2)
res21: Set[String] = HashSet(
  "Telephone numbers in Singapore",
  "14th G-15 summit",
  "2007 Iranian petrol rationing riots",
  "Cougar",
  "1915 Singapore Mutiny",
...
```
</> 13.16.scala

13.3.3 Parallel Crawling

Adding parallelism is as simple as performing each batch of fetches in parallel using `Future{ ... }`, then aggregating the results using `Await.result`:

```
-        val nextTitleLists = for (title <- current) yield fetchLinks(title)
+        val futures = for (title <- current) yield Future{ fetchLinks(title) }
+        val nextTitleLists = futures.map(Await.result(_, Inf))          </> 13.17.scala
```

The final code looks like this:

```
import $file.FetchLinks, FetchLinks._                              Crawler.sc
import scala.concurrent._, duration.Duration.Inf, java.util.concurrent.Executors
implicit val ec = ExecutionContext.fromExecutorService(Executors.newFixedThreadPool(8))
def fetchAllLinksParallel(startTitle: String, depth: Int): Set[String] = {
  var seen = Set(startTitle)
  var current = Set(startTitle)
  for (i <- Range(0, depth)) {
    val futures = for (title <- current) yield Future{ fetchLinks(title) }
    val nextTitleLists = futures.map(Await.result(_, Inf))
    current = nextTitleLists.flatten.filter(!seen.contains(_))
    seen = seen ++ current
  }
  seen
}                                                                  </> 13.18.scala
```

See example 13.3 - ParallelCrawler

This parallelizes each batch of `fetchLinks` calls, waiting until all calls in that batch complete before aggregating the results to prepare the next batch. We can then use this function the same way as the non-parallel version, returning the same results:

```
@ fetchAllLinksParallel("Singapore", 2)
res24: Set[String] = HashSet(
  "Telephone numbers in Singapore",
  "14th G-15 summit",
  "2007 Iranian petrol rationing riots",
  "Cougar",
  "1915 Singapore Mutiny",
...                                                                </> 13.19.scala
```

`fetchAllLinksParallel` executes as follows:

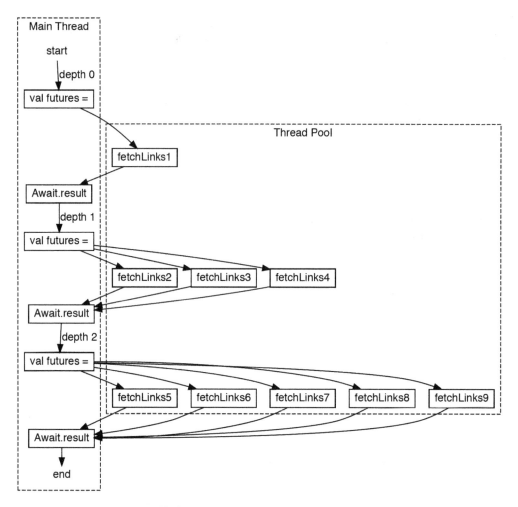

13.3.4 Testing our Parallel Webcrawler

Comparing the output of `fetchAllLinks` and `fetchAllLinksParallel`, it is easy to verify that the output of the two functions is identical:

```
@ fetchAllLinks("Singapore", 2) == fetchAllLinksParallel("Singapore", 2)
res26: Boolean = true


@ fetchAllLinks("Singapore", 3) == fetchAllLinksParallel("Singapore", 3)
res27: Boolean = true                                              </> 13.20.scala
```

Using the `time{}` REPL builtin, we can see that the parallel version completes significantly faster:

```
@ time{fetchAllLinks("Singapore", 2)}._2
res28: FiniteDuration = 4719789996 nanoseconds

@ time{fetchAllLinksParallel("Singapore", 2)}._2
res29: FiniteDuration = 1342978751 nanoseconds                    </> 13.21.scala

@ time{fetchAllLinks("Singapore", 3)}._2
res30: FiniteDuration = 31061249346 nanoseconds

@ time{fetchAllLinksParallel("Singapore", 3)}._2
res31: FiniteDuration = 4569134866 nanoseconds                    </> 13.22.scala
```

At depth 2, the parallel crawler takes 1.3s instead of 4.7s. At depth 3, the parallel crawler takes 4.6s instead of 31.0s. This is a significant speedup for just a three-line code change!

13.3.5 Thread Pool and Parallelism Limits

In this case, we are getting a maximum of about 8x parallelism because the thread pool we constructed has 8 threads.

As a rule of thumb, you generally want to keep the number of threads less than 1,000 to limit resource usage and thread contention. Here the `requests.get` method we use in `fetchAllLinks` is blocking - it needs at least one thread per open HTTP request - and thus we are limited in how many requests we can send in parallel. Higher levels of concurrency can be achieved by using Futures asynchronously, which we will cover later when we discuss Asynchronous Futures (*13.4*).

Another limitation may be the service you are querying, in this case Wikipedia. Most third-party services have rate limits meant to stop you from flooding them with requests, and even for those that don't you generally still want to avoid overloading their backend systems. By changing the size of the thread pool, you can control the degree of parallelism to avoid causing issues in the service you are interacting with.

As written, the amount of parallelism we can get is still sub-optimal: If one HTTP request takes a long time, it prevents the next batch from starting even if all other parallel HTTP requests have already completed. This is inherent in the batch-by-batch way we are doing parallelism. Improving `fetchAllLinksParallel` to better handle this case is left as an exercise to the reader, and can be done using techniques from **Chapter 16: Message-based Parallelism with Actors**.

13.4 Asynchronous Futures

So far we have been using `Await.result` to wait for a Future to complete before we can make use of its result. This makes it convenient to pass results between our parallel Futures, but requires the system thread calling `Await.result` to stop and wait for the Future to complete. Threads have overhead, so while 10 or 100 threads waiting around is not an issue, in high-concurrency systems having 1,000s of threads doing nothing is a significant waste of memory and other resources.

Futures can also work asynchronously: we can schedule work and interface with asynchronous callbacks without wasting a thread waiting for a result. This can greatly improve performance in high-concurrency scenarios.

There are two main ways to work with Futures asynchronously: interfacing with external callback-based APIs using Promises, and via asynchronous operators such as the `map`, `foreach`, `zip`, `sequence`, and `flatMap` and operations. We will cover both of them in this section.

13.4.1 Futures and Promises

So far we have only been creating Futures via `Future{ ... }` blocks, which schedules the code in the block to run on a background thread pool. Another way to create Futures is via `scala.concurrent.Promise`:

```scala
@ def doThing(succeed: Boolean) = {
    val p: Promise[String] = Promise[String]
    val f: Future[String] = p.future
    f.onComplete{
      case scala.util.Success(res) => println(s"Success! $res")
      case scala.util.Failure(exception) => println(s"Failure :( $exception")
    }
    if (succeed) p.success("Yay!")
    else p.failure(new Exception("boom"))
  }

@ doThing(succeed = true)
Success! Yay!

@ doThing(succeed = false)
Failure :( java.lang.Exception: boom
```
</> 13.23.scala

A Promise is like the "write" side of a Future, while the Future is the "read" side. Completing the `Promise` using `.success` or `.failure`, does two things:

- Passes the value to anyone waiting on the Future via `Await.result`
- Triggers any callbacks attached to the Future via `.onComplete`

Note that Futures and Promises can complete either successfully with a result or fail with an exception: in the failure case `Await.result` simply re-throws the exception, while `onComplete` requires you to handle both cases.

Using `Promises` to trigger `Futures` demonstrates that a `Future` is not necessarily a background task running on a thread pool: it is a more general construct, an operation that may complete asynchronously some time later. A task running on a thread pool is one such operation, but any operation with some kind of "on success" callback can also be modeled using `Future`.

13.4.2 Interfacing with Callbacks using Promises

Futures and Promises are equivalent to callbacks. Any function that takes success and error callbacks can be mechanically converted to a function that returns a Future, and vice versa:

13.4.2.1 Converting Futures to Callbacks

```scala
def futureFunc(): Future[String] = { ... }


def callbackFunc(onSuccess: String => Unit, onError: Throwable => Unit): Unit = {
  futureFunc().onComplete{
    case scala.util.Success(str) => onSuccess(str)
    case scala.util.Failure(ex) => onError(ex)
  }
}
```
</> 13.24.scala

13.4.2.2 Converting Callbacks to Futures

```scala
def futureFunc(): Future[String] = {
  val p = Promise[String]
  callbackFunc(
    onSuccess = str => p.success(str),
    onError = ex => p.failure(ex)
  )
  p.future
}


def callbackFunc(onSuccess: String => Unit, onError: Throwable => Unit): Unit = { ... }
```
</> 13.25.scala

While much of the Scala ecosystem uses Futures, the broader Java ecosystem has many libraries that design their asynchronous interfaces around callbacks. This inter-operability makes it straightforward to wrap any sort of asynchronous operation in a Future, allowing you to use it seamlessly from your Future-using code. We will see an example of this later, when we explore Asynchronous Web Crawling (*13.5*).

13.4.3 Asynchronous Operators

If we are working with Futures asynchronously, we generally want to avoid using `Await.result` to pass the result of one Future to another. While we can chain together Futures using callbacks, doing so is often inconvenient and error-prone. Scala's `Future` data type contains some useful methods that allow you to combine and transform the result of your Futures in a few common ways, making asynchronous computations both efficient and convenient.

In this section, we look at a few synchronous usages of Futures via `Await.result` (left) and see how we can instead write the code using asynchronous operators (right) to do the same computation but without blocking a thread waiting for results.

13.4.3.1 map, foreach

`map` lets you transform the result of a Future using a function, while `foreach` is similar to the `onComplete` method we saw earlier, except it only handles successful results. For example, rather than using `Await.result` to wait for the value of the hash and then calling `length` before printing it, we can instead use `map` to schedule the `length` call to happen whenever the hashing Future completes, and then `foreach` to schedule the `println` to happen after `length` computation completes:

```
                                 sync
 val fut = Future{ hash("Chinatown.jpg") }
-val res = Await.result(fut, Inf).length
-println(res)                      </> 13.26.scala
```

```
                                 async
 val fut = Future{ hash("Chinatown.jpg") }
+val res = fut.map(_.length)
+res.foreach(println)             </> 13.27.scala
```

This allows us to perform our `length` computation and `println` action asynchronously, without blocking the main thread. Just like how the call to `Future{ ... }` returns immediately even if the background computation has not yet completed, the `.map` and `.foreach` calls also return immediately and free up the calling thread to do other things.

13.4.3.2 zip

```
                                 sync
 val fut1 = Future{ hash("Chinatown.jpg") }
 val fut2 = Future{ hash("ZCenter.jpg") }
-val hash1 = Await.result(fut1, Inf)
-val hash2 = Await.result(fut2, Inf)
-val joined = s"$hash1 $hash2"
-println(joined)
                                  </> 13.28.scala
```

```
                                 async
 val fut1 = Future{ hash("Chinatown.jpg") }
 val fut2 = Future{ hash("ZCenter.jpg") }
+val zipped = fut1.zip(fut2)
+val joined = zipped.map{
+   case (hash1, hash2) => s"$hash1 $hash2"
+}
+joined.foreach(println)          </> 13.29.scala
```

The `zip` operator lets you combine a `Future[T]` and a `Future[V]` into a `Future[(T, V)]` that returns a tuple. We can then `map` on it to process the tuple, and `foreach` to print the result. In general, where we were previously using `Await.result` on multiple different Futures before proceeding with our computation, we can instead use `zip` and `map` to perform the same logic asynchronously.

```
                                                    sync
val files = Seq(
  "Chinatown.jpg", "ZCenter.jpg",
  "Kresge.jpg", "Memorial.jpg"
)
-val futs = files.map(s => Future{hash(s)})
-val hashes = futs.map(Await.result(_, Inf))
-val joined = hashes.mkString(" ")
-println(joined)                    </> 13.30.scala
```

```
                                                   async
val files = Seq(
  "Chinatown.jpg", "ZCenter.jpg",
  "Kresge.jpg", "Memorial.jpg"
)
+val futs = files.map(s => Future{hash(s)})
+val hashes = Future.sequence(futs)
+val joined = hashes.map(_.mkString(" "))
+joined.foreach(println)            </> 13.31.scala
```

`Future.sequence` lets you convert a collection of Futures `Seq[Future[T]]` into a Future returning a collection `Future[Seq[T]]`. Where we previous used `.map(Await.result(_, Inf))` to aggregate a sequence of asynchronous results, `Future.sequence` lets us do the aggregation asynchronously. We can then use `map` or `foreach` to further process the `Seq[T]` that the sequenced Future computes.

13.5 Asynchronous Web Crawling

To make use of what we have learned about asynchronous Futures, let us convert the parallel-but-synchronous web crawler we wrote earlier in Parallel Web Crawling (*13.3*) to make it asynchronous. We want to avoid using a thread for every HTTP request, and avoid blocking the main thread using `Await.result`. This will allow us to ramp up the concurrency: we could make thousands of concurrent web requests, as many as the network bandwidth will allow, without worrying about per-thread overhead.

13.5.1 Web Crawling via Recursion

The first step to asynchronous crawling is to convert our `for`-loop into a recursive function. We need to do this as `for`-loops are inherently synchronous, whereas recursion gives us the flexibility to evaluate either synchronously or asynchronously. We can do that conversion as follows:

```
import $file.FetchLinks, FetchLinks._                         Crawler.sc
import scala.concurrent._, duration.Duration.Inf, java.util.concurrent.Executors
implicit val ec = ExecutionContext.fromExecutorService(Executors.newFixedThreadPool(8))
def fetchAllLinksRec(startTitle: String, depth: Int): Set[String] = {
  def rec(current: Set[String], seen: Set[String], recDepth: Int): Set[String] = {
    if (recDepth >= depth) seen
    else {
      val futures = for (title <- current) yield Future{ fetchLinks(title) }
      val nextTitles = futures.map(Await.result(_, Inf)).flatten
      rec(nextTitles.filter(!seen.contains(_)), seen ++ nextTitles, recDepth + 1)
    }
  }
  rec(Set(startTitle), Set(startTitle), 0)
}                                                            </> 13.32.scala
```

For now, we are simply converting the `fetchAllLinksParallel` implementation from using a loop to using recursion, while preserving its existing behavior. In the conversion from a loop to recursion, there are a few major changes:

- The `for`-loop has now become a recursive function `rec` whose implementation contains most of the logic that was previously in the loop body

- We call `rec` once at the bottom of `fetchAllLinksRec` in order to start the recursion

- The `current` and `seen` variables are now instead parameters of `rec`, which is a recursive function defined within `fetchAllLinksAsync`

- We now need to keep track of `recDepth` of each recursion ourselves and terminate the recursion once the desired `depth` has been reached

- If we do not wish the recursion to terminate, we call `rec` recursively to make it execute another time

This conversion of a loop to recursion is a bit tricky, but sometimes necessary. Here it lets us make the looping logic asynchronous. For now, `fetchAllLinksRec` should behave in exactly the same way as our earlier `fetchAllLinksParallel` function: it is still synchronous, and still calls the same synchronous `fetchLinks` function we defined earlier. The only difference is that we converted the `for`-loop to recursion. Next, we will look at converting this to allow asynchronous crawling.

13.5.2 Asynchronous Link Fetching with AsyncHttpClient

Next, we need to make our `fetchLinks` function asynchronous. The `requests` package we were using earlier is optimized for simple synchronous operation, so we need to find a replacement. Luckily, the Java ecosystem has a wealth of such libraries, such as the popular AsyncHttpClient library:

- https://github.com/AsyncHttpClient/async-http-client

While this is a Java library, it is straightforward to use it from our Scala code. Going through the documentation, we first need to create a `asyncHttpClient()`, and after that it's straightforward to turn our `requests.get` call into a `asyncHttpClient.execute()`:

```
import $ivy.`org.asynchttpclient:async-http-client:2.5.2`              FetchLinksAsync.sc
import scala.concurrent._


val asyncHttpClient = org.asynchttpclient.Dsl.asyncHttpClient()


def fetchLinksAsync(title: String)(implicit ec: ExecutionContext): Future[Seq[String]] = {
  val p = Promise[String]
  val listenableFut = asyncHttpClient.prepareGet("https://en.wikipedia.org/w/api.php")
    .addQueryParam("action", "query").addQueryParam("titles", title)
    .addQueryParam("prop", "links").addQueryParam("format", "json")
    .execute()

  listenableFut.addListener(() => p.success(listenableFut.get().getResponseBody), null)
  val scalaFut: Future[String] = p.future
  scalaFut.map{ responseBody =>
    for{
      page <- ujson.read(responseBody)("query")("pages").obj.values.toSeq
      links <- page.obj.get("links").toSeq
      link <- links.arr
    } yield link("title").str
  }
}
```

</> 13.33.scala

Note that while `execute` returns a Java `org.asynchttpclient.ListenableFuture`, which is different from the `scala.concurrent.Future`s we have been using so far, it is straightforward to use Interfacing with Callbacks using Promises (*13.4.2*) to convert it into a Scala future `scalaFut`. We then use `map` on `scalaFut` to take the response body `String` and extract the `titles`, like what we saw earlier. `fetchAllLinksAsync` then returns a `Future[Seq[String]]`, indicating that the results are not available immediately when the function call returns, but will be made available some time in the future.

The `fetchLinksAsync` method above is defined to take an `implicit ec: ExecutionContext` as a parameter. This ensures that any asynchronous operations `fetchLinksAsync` performs share thread pool of whichever method is calling it. Typically, an application will only instantiate one thread pool and share it throughout all methods that need it via an `implicit` parameter. Thread pools are relatively expensive to instantiate, so you generally want to share them rather than re-instantiating a separate one for every method.

Sharing a common thread pool also makes your application convenient to re-configure: if you find yourself deploying your application on more powerful hardware, it is easy to change the number to threads a the shared thread pool uses in one place. Similarly, if you want to run your application single-threaded to help narrow down a tricky bug, you can make your entire application run on a `newSingleThreadExecutor` to eliminate any parallelism-related complexity.

13.5.3 Asynchronous Recursive Web Crawling

Lastly, we can combine our asynchronous `fetchAllLinksAsync` method with our recursive `fetchAllLinksRec` method to produce a `fetchAllLinksAsync` method that does an asynchronous crawl of the Wikipedia API:

```scala
import $file.FetchLinksAsync, FetchLinksAsync._                         Crawler.sc
import scala.concurrent._, java.util.concurrent.Executors
implicit val ec = ExecutionContext.fromExecutorService(Executors.newFixedThreadPool(8))


def fetchAllLinksAsync(startTitle: String, depth: Int): Future[Set[String]] = {
  def rec(current: Set[String], seen: Set[String], recDepth: Int): Future[Set[String]] = {
    if (recDepth >= depth) Future.successful(seen)
    else {
      val futures = for (title <- current) yield fetchLinksAsync(title)
      Future.sequence(futures).map{nextTitleLists =>
        val nextTitles = nextTitleLists.flatten
        rec(nextTitles.filter(!seen.contains(_)), seen ++ nextTitles, recDepth + 1)
      }.flatten
    }
  }
  rec(Set(startTitle), Set(startTitle), 0)
}
```
</> 13.34.scala

See example 13.5 - AsyncCrawler

The above definition of `fetchAllLinksAsync` is a modified version of `fetchAllLinksRec`. In making our Wikipedia crawler asynchronous, there are the following major changes:

- `fetchAllLinksAsync` now both return `Future[Set[String]]`, as does `rec`

- Rather than spawning a bunch of Futures using `Future{ ... }` blocks, we now directly call `fetchLinksAsync` on every value in `current`

- We use `Future.sequence` to aggregate each batch of results, rather than calling `Await.result` of every item, and use `map` to perform the further computation.

- In order to ensure that all branches of `rec` return a `Future[Set[String]]`, we need to wrap the base case `seen` in a `Future.successful(...)` so we don't return a bare `Set[String]`, and call `.flatten` on the recursive case so we don't return a nested `Future[Future[Set[String]]]`

Note that the `.map{...}.flatten` pattern can also be written as a single `.flatMap{...}`, which is a common operator when working with asynchronous workflows using Futures.

We can now run this and print the results follows:

```scala
@ fetchAllLinksAsync("Singapore", 3).foreach(println)
HashSet(1895 Singaporean Municipal Commission election, November 2015 Paris attacks, ...
                                                                    </> 13.35.scala
```

The call to `fetchAllLinksAsync` returns instantly, returning the `Future[Set[String]]`. Here we use `foreach` to `println` on the result when it is ready, but we can also combine it into a larger asynchronous Futures workflow using the same `map`, `zip` and `sequence` operations we saw earlier.

Now that we are no longer limited in parallelism by the number of threads available, deeper crawls with a lot more potential concurrency finish far quicker. With a crawl depth of 4, `fetchAllLinksParallel` finishes in about 11.3 seconds while `fetchAllLinksAsync` finishes in 2.6 seconds:

```scala
@ val (results, dur) = time { fetchAllLinksParallel("Singapore", 4) }
results: Set[String] = HashSet("Airbus", "10,000 Maniacs", "2004 in film", ...
dur: duration.FiniteDuration = 11358217828 nanoseconds

@ val (results, dur) = time { Await.result(fetchAllLinksAsync("Singapore", 4), Inf) }
results: Set[String] = HashSet("Airbus", "10,000 Maniacs", "2004 in film", ...
dur: duration.FiniteDuration = 2620180174 nanoseconds          </> 13.36.scala
```

In general, asynchronous concurrency allows a much greater degree of concurrency than blocking parallelism, but only for non-CPU-bound code such as the HTTP requests we are making above. Your system may still be bottle-necked in other places - network bandwidth, server rate-limiting, etc. - but it will no longer be limited by the number of threads available. While this asynchronous implementation is not necessary for small-scale crawlers, it can be useful when the number of web pages is large, and allow a single computer to crawl thousands of web pages at a time.

The implementation of `fetchAllLinksAsync` might look a bit unusual, but it is a relatively simple piece of code: 20 lines of code to make asynchronous HTTP requests, and 15 lines of code for the traversal logic. If we had implemented this using threads, or directly using the callbacks provided by AsyncHttpClient, we would need orders of magnitude more code to implement our parallel, asynchronous, breadth-first traversal of the graph of Wikipedia articles over the network.

13.6 Conclusion

In this chapter, we have introduced the usage of Scala's Futures as a way of easily starting parallel background tasks and aggregating their results, as well as a way of scheduling asynchronous workflows. We have covered:

- Creating and waiting on Futures
- Using Futures to parallelize compute-bound code (hashing files)
- Writing a parallel web crawler that performs a breadth-first traversal of Wikipedia's page-link graph
- Writing asynchronous code using Futures: interfacing with callbacks and asynchronous operators

Futures fit best in a "fork-join" model of parallelism: we split off independent tasks, run them in parallel, and then aggregate the results. This works best when each task is independent and pure, without internal state, and indifferent to what order it happens in. In other cases, there is still parallelism to be had: we will cover such scenarios later, in *Chapter 16: Message-based Parallelism with Actors*.

We have now spent the last three chapters interacting with HTTP servers and services from a client's perspective. The next two chapters, we will see it from the server's point of view: how to set up the HTML websites, JSON APIs, and backing databases that make up a typical web service looks like today.

Exercise: Use Futures to parallelize the MDN Web API Documentation scraper we wrote in *Chapter 11: Scraping Websites*, allowing it to run N ways parallel on the background thread pool.

See example 13.6 - ParallelScrapingDocs

Exercise: Take the generic merge sort from *Chapter 6: Implementing Algorithms in Scala* and parallelize it using `Futures`. As the number of `Futures` may be large, we should avoid blocking threads using `Await` and instead use Asynchronous Operators (*13.4.3*) where possible. Compare the performance of the parallel and sequential merge sorts: is the parallel merge sort faster? How is the speed affected if we fall back to sequential merge sorts when the sequences become small?

See example 13.7 - ParallelMergeSort

Exercise: Modify our asynchronous wikipedia crawler to limit the concurrent requests it makes to a configurable number, e.g. 32, to avoid being rate-limited or overloading the server we are fetching data from.

See example 13.8 - AsyncCrawlerThrottled

Exercise: Make use of the `AsyncHttpClient` we used in this chapter, together with the `Jsoup.parse` function we saw in *Chapter 11: Scraping Websites*, to write an asynchronous MDN Web API Documentation scraper that can run in parallel without being limited by the number of threads. To avoid overloading the network or server, limit the number of concurrent requests to 32.

See example 13.9 - AsyncThrottledScrapingDocs

Discuss Chapter 13 online at https://www.handsonscala.com/discuss/13

14

Simple Web and API Servers

14.1 A Minimal Webserver   262

14.2 Serving HTML   266

14.3 Forms and Dynamic Data   268

14.4 Dynamic Page Updates via API Requests   275

14.5 Real-time Updates with Websockets   280

```scala
object MinimalApplication extends cask.MainRoutes {
  @cask.get("/")
  def hello() = {
    "Hello World!"
  }


  @cask.post("/do-thing")
  def doThing(request: cask.Request) = {
    request.text().reverse
  }


  initialize()
}                                                         </> 14.1.scala
```

Snippet 14.1: a minimal Scala web application, using the Cask web framework

Web and API servers are the backbone of internet systems. While in the last few chapters we learned to access these systems from a *client's* perspective, this chapter will teach you how to provide such APIs and Websites from the *server's* perspective. We will walk through a complete example of building a simple real-time chat website serving both HTML web pages and JSON API endpoints. We will re-visit this website in **Chapter 15: Querying SQL Databases**, where we will convert its simple in-memory datastore into a proper SQL database.

In this chapter, we will work towards setting up a simple chat website. This will allow users to post chat messages for other users to see. For simplicity, we will ignore concerns such as authentication, performance, user management, and database persistence. Nevertheless, this chapter should be enough for you to get started building web and API servers in Scala, and provide a foundation you can build upon to create servers fit to deploy to a production environment.

We are going to use the Cask web framework. Cask is a Scala HTTP micro-framework that lets you get a simple website up and running quickly.

14.1 A Minimal Webserver

To begin working with Cask, download and unzip the example application:

```
$ curl -L \
  https://github.com/lihaoyi/cask/releases/download/0.7.4/minimalApplication-0.7.4.zip \
  -o cask.zip


$ unzip cask.zip


$ cd minimalApplication-0.7.4                                         </> 14.2.bash
```

14.1.1 Application Code

We can run find to see what we have available:

```
$ find . -type f
./build.sc
./app/test/src/ExampleTests.scala
./app/src/MinimalApplication.scala
./mill                                                                </> 14.3.bash
```

Most of what we're interested in lives in app/src/MinimalApplication.scala:

```scala
package app                                    app/src/MinimalApplication.scala
object MinimalApplication extends cask.MainRoutes {
  @cask.get("/")
  def hello() = {
    "Hello World!"
  }

  @cask.post("/do-thing")
  def doThing(request: cask.Request) = {
    request.text().reverse
  }

  initialize()
}                                                            </> 14.4.scala
```

Cask works by specifying the endpoints of your web server via the @cask annotations in a cask.MainRoutes object: @cask.get, @cask.post, and so on. The Cask documentation linked at the end of this chapter goes through the full range of different annotations. Each annotation specifies a URL route which the annotated endpoint function will handle.

Inheriting from cask.MainRoutes defines the standard JVM main method that launches the webserver and serves as the entry point of your program. You can override def main if you want to customize the startup and initialization logic.

Above we see that requests to the root URL / is handled by the hello() endpoint, while requests to the /do-thing URL are handled by the doThing() endpoint. All endpoints can optionally take a request: cask.Request argument representing the entire incoming HTTP request. Additional parameters can represent wildcard URL segments or values deserialized from the request in a decorator-specific fashion (e.g. @cask.get parameters come from URL query params, @cask.post parameters from a form encoded request body).

14.1.2 Webserver Build Configuration

The Cask application is built using Mill, configured via a `build.sc` file:

```scala
import mill._, scalalib._                                          build.sc

object app extends ScalaModule {
  def scalaVersion = "2.13.2"
  def ivyDeps = Agg(
    ivy"com.lihaoyi::cask:0.7.4"
  )
  object test extends Tests {
    def testFrameworks = Seq("utest.runner.Framework")

    def ivyDeps = Agg(
      ivy"com.lihaoyi::utest:0.7.4",
      ivy"com.lihaoyi::requests:0.6.5",
    )
  }
}
```

</> 14.5.scala

If you are using Intellij, you can run the following command to set up the Intelij project configuration. This will let you open up `minimalApplication-0.7.4/` in Intellij and see it indexed and ready for editing:

```
$ ./mill mill.scalalib.GenIdea/idea
```

If you are using VSCode within a Mill build, we need to create the `.mill-version` file before we can open the folder and select `Import build`:

```
$ echo "0.8.0" > .mill-version
```

14.1.3 Running and Testing our Webserver

We can run this program with the Mill build tool, using the `./mill` executable:

```
$ ./mill -w app.runBackground
```

`.runBackground` is similar to `.run`, except it allows you to do other things at the terminal, or use `-w/--watch` to watch for changes and reload the program running in the background. This background process keeps running indefinitely, until you use use `./mill clean app.runBackground` to shut it down.

We can then navigate to the server in the browser, by default at `localhost:8080`:

There is also a POST endpoint at /do-thing we can try out by running `curl` in another terminal window, or by running the automated tests in app/test/src/ExampleTests.scala using Mill:

```
$ curl -X POST --data hello http://localhost:8080/do-thing
olleh

$ ./mill app.test
[50/56] app.test.compile
[info] Compiling 1 Scala source to...
[info] Done compiling.
[56/56] app.test.test
-------------------------------- Running Tests --------------------------------
+ app.ExampleTests.MinimalApplication 629ms
```
</> 14.6.bash

Now let's get the webserver watching for changes again and get started with our chat website!

```
$ ./mill -w app.runBackground
```

14.2 Serving HTML

The first thing to do is to convert our plain-text `"Hello World!"` website into a HTML web page. The easiest way to do this is via the Scalatags HTML generation library, the same one we used in *Chapter 9: Self-Contained Scala Scripts*. To use Scalatags in this project, add it as a dependency to your `build.sc` file:

```
def ivyDeps = Agg(                                                          build.sc
+   ivy"com.lihaoyi::scalatags:0.9.1",
    ivy"com.lihaoyi::cask:0.7.4"
)                                                                       </> 14.7.scala
```

If using Intellij, you'll have to run the `./mill mill.scalalib.GenIdea/idea` command again to pick up the changes in your dependencies, followed by `./mill -w app.runBackground` to get the webserver listening for changes again. We can then import Scalatags into our `MinimalApplication.scala` file:

```
package app                                             app/src/MinimalApplication.scala
+import scalatags.Text.all._
object MinimalApplication extends cask.MainRoutes {                      </> 14.8.scala
```

And replace the `"Hello World!"` string with a minimal Scalatags HTML template using the same Bootstrap CSS we used in *Chapter 9: Self-Contained Scala Scripts*:

```
                                                        app/src/MinimalApplication.scala
+   val bootstrap = "https://stackpath.bootstrapcdn.com/bootstrap/4.5.0/css/bootstrap.css"

    @cask.get("/")
-   def hello() = {
-     "Hello World!"
-   }
+   def hello() = doctype("html")(
+     html(
+       head(link(rel := "stylesheet", href := bootstrap)),
+       body(
+         div(cls := "container")(
+           h1("Hello!"),
+           p("World")
+         )
+       )
+     )
+   )                                                                    </> 14.9.scala
```

We should see the `./mill -w app.runBackground` command re-compile our code and restart the server. We can then refresh the page to see our plain text response has been replaced by a basic HTML page:

14.2.1 A Mock Chat Website

To finish off this section, let's flesh out our Scalatags HTML template to look like a mock chat application: with hardcoded chats and dummy input boxes.

```scala
                                                          app/src/MinimalApplication.scala
    div(cls := "container")(
-     h1("Hello!"),
-     p("World")
+     h1("Scala Chat!"),
+     div(
+       p(b("alice"), " ", "Hello World!"),
+       p(b("bob"), " ", "I am cow, hear me moo")
+     ),
+     div(
+       input(`type` := "text", placeholder := "User name"),
+       input(`type` := "text", placeholder := "Write a message!")
+     )
    )
                                                          </> 14.10.scala
```

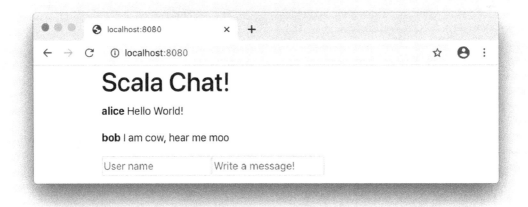

See example 14.1 - Mock

We now have a simple static website, serving HTML pages, using the Cask web framework and the Scalatags HTML library. The full code, along with a simple test suite, can be found in the online example linked above. This test suite uses the `requests` package we learned about in **Chapter 12: Working with HTTP APIs** to interact with the webserver and assert on its behavior. Subsequent examples of this chapter will also provide a test suite in the online sample code, for you to browse if interested.

Next, let's look at making this website actually work interactively!

14.3 Forms and Dynamic Data

Our first attempt at making this website interactive will be to use HTML forms. With HTML forms, the first browser request loads the initial HTML page, and every interaction does a POST back to the server that reloads the entire page:

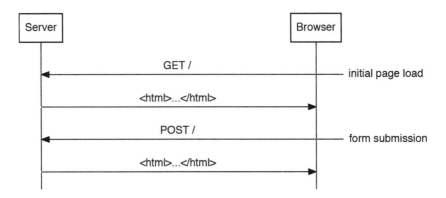

14.3.1 Dynamic Page Rendering

First we need to remove the hardcoded list of messages and instead render the HTML page based on data:

```scala
object MinimalApplication extends cask.MainRoutes {          app/src/MinimalApplication.scala
+ var messages = Vector(("alice", "Hello World!"), ("bob", "I am cow, hear me moo"))
  val bootstrap = "https://stackpath.bootstrapcdn.com/bootstrap/4.5.0/css/bootstrap.css"


  @cask.get("/")                                                          </> 14.11.scala
```

```scala
      div(                                                    app/src/MinimalApplication.scala
-       p(b("alice"), " ", "Hello World!"),
-       p(b("bob"), " ", "I am cow, hear me moo"),
+       for ((name, msg) <- messages) yield p(b(name), " ", msg)
      ),                                                                  </> 14.12.scala
```

For now, we will use a `Vector[(String, String)]` as our simple in-memory `messages` store. Storing our messages in a proper database is something we will cover later in **Chapter 15: Querying SQL Databases**.

14.3.2 Form Handling

To make the two `input`s at the bottom of the page interactive, we need to wrap them in a `form`:

```scala
-     div(                                                    app/src/MinimalApplication.scala
-       input(`type` := "text", placeholder := "User name"),
-       input(`type` := "text", placeholder := "Write a message!", width := "100%")
+     form(action := "/", method := "post")(
+       input(`type` := "text", name := "name", placeholder := "User name"),
+       input(`type` := "text", name := "msg", placeholder := "Write a message!"),
+       input(`type` := "submit")
      )                                                                   </> 14.13.scala
```

This gives us an interactive form that looks similar to the mock we had earlier. However, submitting the form gives us an `Error 404: Not Found` page: this is expected because we still haven't wired up the server to handle the form submission and receive the new chat message. We can do so as follows:

```scala
-   @cask.post("/do-thing")                                   app/src/MinimalApplication.scala
-   def doThing(request: cask.Request) = {
-     request.text().reverse
-   }
+   @cask.postForm("/")
+   def postChatMsg(name: String, msg: String) = {
+     messages = messages :+ (name -> msg)
+     hello()
+   }                                                                     </> 14.14.scala
```

This `@cask.postForm` definition adds another endpoint for the root `/` URL, except this one handles POST requests instead of GET requests. Now we can enter a user name and message, and post a message:

14.3.3 Validation

So far, we have allowed users to post arbitrary comments with arbitrary names. However, not all comments and names are valid: at the bare minimum we want to ensure the comment and name fields are not empty. We can do this via:

```scala
def postChatMsg(name: String, msg: String) = {        app/src/MinimalApplication.scala
-    messages = messages :+ (name -> msg)
+    if (name != "" && msg != "") messages = messages :+ (name -> msg)
    hello()
}                                                                      </> 14.15.scala
```

This blocks users from entering invalid `names` and `msgs`, but has another issue: a user with an invalid name or message will submit it, have it disappear, and have no feedback what went wrong. We can solve this by rendering an optional error message in the `hello()` page:

```scala
def postChatMsg(name: String, msg: String) = {        app/src/MinimalApplication.scala
-    if (name != "" && msg != "") messages = messages :+ (name -> msg)
-    hello()
+    if (name == "") hello(Some("Name cannot be empty"))
+    else if (msg == "") hello(Some("Message cannot be empty"))
+    else {
+      messages = messages :+ (name -> msg)
+      hello()
+    }
}                                                                      </> 14.16.scala
```

```scala
@cask.get("/")                                        app/src/MinimalApplication.scala
- def hello() = doctype("html")(
+ def hello(errorOpt: Option[String] = None) = doctype("html")(
    html(                                                              </> 14.17.scala
```

```scala
                                                      app/src/MinimalApplication.scala
        div(for ((name, msg) <- messages) yield p(b(name), " ", msg)),
+       for (error <- errorOpt) yield i(color.red)(error),
        form(action := "/", method := "post")(                        </> 14.18.scala
```

Now, an error message shows up when the name or message are invalid, which goes away on the next successful action:

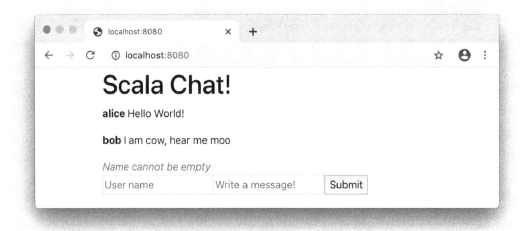

14.3.4 Remembering Names and Messages

One annoyance so far is that every time you post a message to the chat room, you need to re-enter your user name. Also, if your user name or message are invalid, it gets deleted and you have to type it out all over again to re-submit it. We can fix that by letting the `hello` page endpoint optionally fill in these fields for you:

```scala
@cask.get("/")
-  def hello(errorOpt: Option[String] = None) = doctype("html")(
+  def hello(errorOpt: Option[String] = None,
+            userName: Option[String] = None,
+            msg: Option[String] = None) = doctype("html")(
    html(
```

app/src/MinimalApplication.scala

</> 14.19.scala

```scala
        form(action := "/", method := "post")(        app/src/MinimalApplication.scala
-            input(`type` := "text", name := "name", placeholder := "User name"),
-            input(`type` := "text", name := "msg", placeholder := "Write a message!"),
+            input(
+              `type` := "text",
+              name := "name",
+              placeholder := "User name",
+              userName.map(value := _)
+            ),
+            input(
+              `type` := "text",
+              name := "msg",
+              placeholder := "Write a message!",
+              msg.map(value := _)
+            ),
            input(`type` := "submit")                         </> 14.20.scala
```

We add optional `userName` and `msg` query parameters to the root web page endpoint, and if they are present we include them as the default `value` of the HTML `input` tags. We also need to fill in the `userName` and `msg` in the `postChatMsg` endpoint when rendering the page back to the user:

```scala
  def postChatMsg(name: String, msg: String) = {        app/src/MinimalApplication.scala
-    if (name == "") hello(Some("Name cannot be empty"))
-    else if (msg == "") hello(Some("Message cannot be empty"))
+    if (name == "") hello(Some("Name cannot be empty"), Some(name), Some(msg))
+    else if (msg == "") hello(Some("Message cannot be empty"), Some(name), Some(msg))
    else {
      messages = messages :+ (name -> msg)
-      hello()
+      hello(None, Some(name), None)
    }
  }                                                          </> 14.21.scala
```

Now, whenever we submit a form to the def `postChatMsg` endpoint, it always renders the HTML page with your name already filled in. Furthermore, if there was an error, we also render the HTML page with the message already filled in:

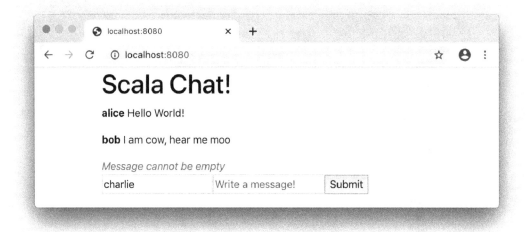

We only expect the user to need to edit or re-submit the message if there was a failure, whereas if the message was successfully posted we do not expect them to want to post it again.

The complete code for `MinimalApplication.scala` is now as follows:

```scala
package app                                          app/src/MinimalApplication.scala
import scalatags.Text.all._
object MinimalApplication extends cask.MainRoutes {
  var messages = Vector(("alice", "Hello World!"), ("bob", "I am cow, hear me moo"))
  val bootstrap = "https://stackpath.bootstrapcdn.com/bootstrap/4.5.0/css/bootstrap.css"

  @cask.get("/")
  def hello(errorOpt: Option[String] = None,
            userName: Option[String] = None,
            msg: Option[String] = None) = doctype("html")(
    html(
      head(link(rel := "stylesheet", href := bootstrap)),
      body(
        div(cls := "container")(
          h1("Scala Chat!"),
          div(for ((name, msg) <- messages) yield p(b(name), " ", msg)),
          for (error <- errorOpt) yield i(color.red)(error),
          form(action := "/", method := "post")(
            input(
              `type` := "text",
              name := "name",
```

```scala
            placeholder := "User name",
            userName.map(value := _)
          ),
          input(
            `type` := "text",
            name := "msg",
            placeholder := "Write a message!",
            msg.map(value := _)
          ),
          input(`type` := "submit")
        )
      )
    )
  )
)


@cask.postForm("/")
def postChatMsg(name: String, msg: String) = {
  if (name == "") hello(Some("Name cannot be empty"), Some(name), Some(msg))
  else if (msg == "") hello(Some("Message cannot be empty"), Some(name), Some(msg))
  else {
    messages = messages :+ (name -> msg)
    hello(None, Some(name), None)
  }
}

initialize()
}
```
</> 14.22.scala

See example 14.2 - Forms

14.4 Dynamic Page Updates via API Requests

We now have a simple form-based chat website, where users can post messages and other users who load the page can see the messages that were posted. The next step is to make the page updates *dynamic*, so users can post messages and see updates without needing to refresh the page.

To do this, we need to do two things:

- Allow the HTTP server to serve partial web pages, e.g. receiving messages and rendering the message list without rendering the entire page

- Add a small amount of JavaScript to submit the form data manually.

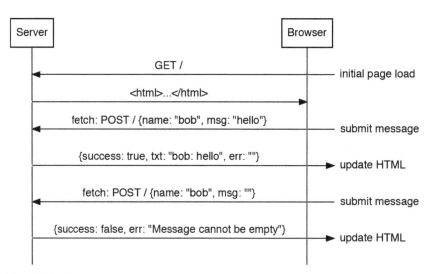

Note that although the first HTTP GET request fetches the entire HTML page, subsequent requests are done via the browser's `fetch` API and return JSON. This allows it to perform the HTTP POST without needing to refresh the page, and to process the returned data in Javascript to update the page in the browser.

14.4.1 Rendering Partial Pages

To render just the part of the page that needs to be updated, we refactor our code to extract a `messageList` helper function from the main `hello` page endpoint:

```
  )                                                          app/src/MinimalApplication.scala

+ def messageList() = frag(for ((name, msg) <- messages) yield p(b(name), " ", msg))


  @cask.postForm("/")                                                         </> 14.23.scala
```

```
                                                            app/src/MinimalApplication.scala
-       div(for ((name, msg) <- messages) yield p(b(name), " ", msg))
+       div(id := "messageList")(messageList()),                              </> 14.24.scala
```

Next, we will modify the `postChatMsg` endpoint so that instead of re-rendering the entire page, it only re-renders the `messageList` that might have changed. Note how we replace the old `@cask.postForm` endpoint with a `@cask.postJson`. Instead of calling `hello()` to re-render the entire page, we instead return a small JSON structure `ujson.Obj` that the browser JavaScript code can then use to update the HTML page. The `ujson.Obj` data type is provided by the same uJson library we saw learned in **Chapter 8: JSON and Binary Data Serialization**.

```
-  @cask.postForm("/")                                            app/src/MinimalApplication.scala
+  @cask.postJson("/")
   def postChatMsg(name: String, msg: String) = {
-    if (name == "") hello(Some("Name cannot be empty"), Some(name), Some(msg))
-    else if (msg == "") hello(Some("Message cannot be empty"), Some(name), Some(msg))
+    if (name == "") ujson.Obj("success" -> false, "err" -> "Name cannot be empty")
+    else if (msg == "") ujson.Obj("success" -> false, "err" -> "Message cannot be empty")
     else {
       messages = messages :+ (name -> msg)
-      hello(None, Some(name), None)
+      ujson.Obj("success" -> true, "txt" -> messageList().render, "err" -> "")
     }
   }
                                                                           </> 14.25.scala
```

Since we will be relying on JavaScript to populate and clear the `input` fields, we no longer need to populate them by setting their `msg` and `userName` values on the server. We can also remove them from our `def hello` endpoint:

```
   @cask.get("/")                                                  app/src/MinimalApplication.scala
-  def hello(errorOpt: Option[String] = None,
-            userName: Option[String] = None,
-            msg: Option[String] = None) = doctype("html")(
+  def hello() = doctype("html")(
                                                                           </> 14.26.scala
```

Now that we have the server side of things settled, let's wire up the relevant client-side code to send JSON requests to the server, receive the JSON response, and use it to update the HTML interface. To handle this client-side logic, we are going to give IDs to some of our key HTML elements so we can reference them in the JavaScript:

```scala
                                                      app/src/MinimalApplication.scala
-         for (error <- errorOpt) yield i(color.red)(error),
+         div(id := "errorDiv", color.red),
          form(action := "/", method := "post")(
-           input(
-             `type` := "text",
-             name := "name",
-             placeholder := "User name",
-             userName.map(value := _)
-           ),
+           input(`type` := "text", id := "nameInput", placeholder := "User name"),
-           input(
-             `type` := "text",
-             name := "msg",
-             placeholder := "Write a message!",
-             msg.map(value := _)
-           ),
+           input(`type` := "text", id := "msgInput", placeholder := "Write a message!"),
            input(`type` := "submit")
          )
                                                                        </> 14.27.scala
```

14.4.2 Page Updates with JavaScript

Next, we need to include some Javascript. This JavaScript snippet defines a function that lets us post the current form contents to the server using the browser's fetch API. We receive the JSON response, on success we use it to re-render the messageList, on failure we update the errorDiv:

```js
function submitForm() {                               app/resources/static/app.js
  fetch(
    "/",
    {method: "POST", body: JSON.stringify({name: nameInput.value, msg: msgInput.value})}
  ).then(response => response.json())
   .then(json => {
   if (json["success"]) {
     messageList.innerHTML = json["txt"]
     msgInput.value = ""
   }
   errorDiv.innerText = json["err"]
  })
}
                                                                        </> 14.28.js
```

```
  val bootstrap = "https://stackpath.bootstrapcdn.com/bootstrap/4.5.0/css/bootstrap.css"

+ @cask.staticResources("/static")
+ def staticResourceRoutes() = "static"


  @cask.get("/")
  def hello() = doctype("html")(                                          </> 14.29.scala
```

For now we are writing Javascript in a `static/app.js` file in the `resources/` folder of our `app` module. `resources/` contains files that are zipped into the executable `assembly` at compile time. These can then be served using a `@cask.staticResources` endpoint: the annotation's parameter specifies the HTTP route that serves these static files, and the return value specifies the path in the `resources/` folder that the files will be served from.

To wire up this JavaScript function with our form, we need to include it in the page using a `script` tag, and then replace the form's `action` attribute with an `onsubmit` attribute to call the function defined above:

```
  head(                                                     app/src/MinimalApplication.scala
    link(rel := "stylesheet", href := bootstrap),
+   script(src := "/static/app.js")
  ),                                                                      </> 14.30.scala
```

```
-   form(action := "/", method := "post")(                  app/src/MinimalApplication.scala
+   form(onsubmit := "submitForm(); return false")(                      </> 14.31.scala
```

With this, you can now add comments to the chat website, have them become immediately visible on your page, and then anyone loading the page after will see them as well.

Note that although the messages you leave are immediately visible to you, they are not visible to other people on the chat website unless they either refresh the page or leave their own comment to force their `messageList` to be reloaded. Making your messages immediately visible to other viewers without refreshing the page will be the last section of this chapter.

See example 14.3 - Ajax

14.5 Real-time Updates with Websockets

The concept of push updates is simple: every time a new message is submitted, we "push" it to every browser that is listening, rather than waiting for the browser to refresh and "pull" the updated data. There are many techniques we can use to accomplish this goal. For this chapter, we will be using one called Websockets.

Websockets allow the browser and the server to send messages to each other, outside the normal request-response flow of a HTTP request. Once a connection is established, either side can send messages any time, each of which contains an arbitrary payload string or bytes.

The workflow we will implement is as follows:

1. When the website loads, the browser will make a websocket connection to the server.

2. Once the connection is established, the server will respond with an initial txt containing the rendered messages, as HTML.

3. Any future server-side updates will be sent to the browser over the open connection.

4. If the connection is broken for any reason, the browser will re-establish it via step (1), the HTML will be brought up to date by the message in step (2) and be ready to receive future updates in step (3).

Each time a browser connects via websockets, the server sends a websocket message for it to bring its HTML up to date, and each time a chat message is posted to the server, the server broadcasts a websocket message to update all the clients. It doesn't matter whose browser sent a chat message: all connected browsers will be sent a websocket message to bring their HTML up to date.

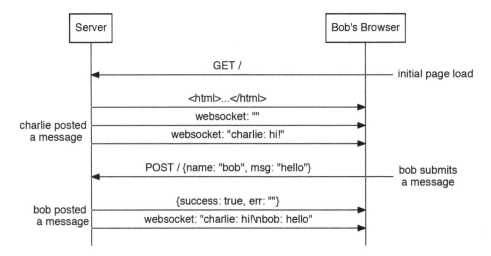

14.5.1 Server-side Websocket Support

The key to implementing this on the server is to maintain a set of `openConnections`, and a `@cask.websocket` endpoint to receive the incoming websocket connections and handle them:

```
+ var openConnections = Set.empty[cask.WsChannelActor]    app/src/MinimalApplication.scala
```

```
+ @cask.websocket("/subscribe")                           app/src/MinimalApplication.scala
+ def subscribe() = cask.WsHandler { connection =>
+   connection.send(cask.Ws.Text(messageList().render))
+   openConnections += connection
+   cask.WsActor { case cask.Ws.Close(_, _) => openConnections -= connection }
+ }                                                                     </> 14.32.scala
```

The Cask web framework models Websocket connections as *Actors*: these are effectively a sort of callback handler that you can `.send` messages to, and processes them in a single-threaded fashion. This is a good fit for Websocket connections which also involve sending and receiving messages: in the `cask.WsHandler` above, `connection` is an actor the server can `.send` messages destined for the browser, and the `cask.WsActor` we return is an actor that will handle messages the browser sends to the server. We will learn more about actors in **Chapter 16: Message-based Parallelism with Actors**

`subscribe` receives an incoming websocket connection from a browser, immediately responds with the current rendered `messageList`, and then registers the connection with `openConnections` to respond later. We then need to change the `postChatMsg` endpoint, to publish an update to all open connections every time a new message is posted:

```
      messages = messages :+ (name -> msg)              app/src/MinimalApplication.scala
-     ujson.Obj("success" -> true, "txt" -> messageList().render, "err" -> "")
+     for (conn <- openConnections) conn.send(cask.Ws.Text(messageList().render))
+     ujson.Obj("success" -> true, "err" -> "")                         </> 14.33.scala
```

Whenever a new chat message is posted, we send a message to all the open connections to notify them. Note that we no longer need to return the `txt` field in the response JSON, as it will already be properly propagated by the `connection.send` call above.

14.5.2 Browser-side Websocket Support

Lastly, we need to modify the JavaScript code in order to open up the Websocket connection and handle this exchange of messages:

```
                                                            app/resources/static/app.js
function submitForm() {
  fetch(
    "/",
    {method: "POST", body: JSON.stringify({name: nameInput.value, msg: msgInput.value})}
  ).then(response => response.json())
   .then(json => {
-    if (json["success"]) {
-      messageList.innerHTML = json["txt"]
-      msgInput.value = ""
-    }
+    if (json["success"]) msgInput.value = ""
     errorDiv.innerText = json["err"]
   })
}
+ var socket = new WebSocket("ws://" + location.host + "/subscribe");
+ socket.onmessage = function(ev) { messageList.innerHTML = ev.data }/> 14.34.javascript
```

Every time a new update is received, we render the ev.data in the messageList. Note that we no longer need to update the messageList element in the fetch callback, since the socket.onmessage callback will do that for us. Now, when we open up two browsers side by side, we can see the chat messages we leave in one of them immediately reflected in the other!

The complete server-side code for this section is as follows:

```
                                                            app/src/MinimalApplication.scala
package app
import scalatags.Text.all._
object MinimalApplication extends cask.MainRoutes {
  var messages = Vector(("alice", "Hello World!"), ("bob", "I am cow, hear me moo"))
  var openConnections = Set.empty[cask.WsChannelActor]
  val bootstrap = "https://stackpath.bootstrapcdn.com/bootstrap/4.5.0/css/bootstrap.css"

  @cask.staticResources("/static")
  def staticResourceRoutes() = "static"

  @cask.get("/")
  def hello() = doctype("html")(
    html(
      head(
```

```scala
        link(rel := "stylesheet", href := bootstrap),
        script(src := "/static/app.js")
      ),
      body(
        div(cls := "container")(
          h1("Scala Chat!"),
          div(id := "messageList")(messageList()),
          div(id := "errorDiv", color.red),
          form(onsubmit := "submitForm(); return false")(
            input(`type` := "text", id := "nameInput", placeholder := "User name"),
            input(`type` := "text", id := "msgInput", placeholder := "Write a message!"),
            input(`type` := "submit")
          )
        )
      )
    )
  )
)

def messageList() = frag(for ((name, msg) <- messages) yield p(b(name), " ", msg))

@cask.postJson("/")
def postChatMsg(name: String, msg: String) = {
  if (name == "") ujson.Obj("success" -> false, "err" -> "Name cannot be empty")
  else if (msg == "") ujson.Obj("success" -> false, "err" -> "Message cannot be empty")
  else {
    messages = messages :+ (name -> msg)
    for (conn <- openConnections) conn.send(cask.Ws.Text(messageList().render))
    ujson.Obj("success" -> true, "err" -> "")
  }
}

@cask.websocket("/subscribe")
def subscribe() = cask.WsHandler { connection =>
  connection.send(cask.Ws.Text(messageList().render))
  openConnections += connection
  cask.WsActor { case cask.Ws.Close(_, _) => openConnections -= connection }
}

initialize()
}
```

</> 14.35.scala

14.6 Conclusion

In this chapter, we have seen how to use Scala to implement a real-time chat website and API server. We started off with a static mock of a website, added form-based interactions, dynamic page updates with Ajax against a JSON API, and finally push notifications using websockets. We have done this using the Cask web framework, Scalatags HTML library, and uJson serialization library, in about 70 lines of straightforward code. Hopefully this has given you an intuition for how to make simple websites and API servers using Scala, which you can build upon for larger and more ambitious applications.

For learning more about the Cask web framework, the online documentation is a good reference:

- http://www.lihaoyi.com/cask/

While this book uses the Cask web framework for its examples, you may encounter other Scala web frameworks in the wild:

- Play Framework: https://www.playframework.com/
- Akka HTTP: https://github.com/akka/akka-http
- HTTP4S: https://github.com/http4s/http4s

The chat website presented here is deliberately simplified, with many limitations. One limitation is that the mutable variables `messages` and `openConnections` are not thread safe: we need to wrap their reads and updates in `synchronized{...}` blocks for them to be used safely in the presence of multiple incoming HTTP requests. Another limitation is the fact that the `messages` list is stored within a single webserver process: it cannot be shared between multiple server processes, nor does it persist if the process restarts.

In the next chapter, we will learn how to use Scala to read and write data from a database, and wire it up into our real-time chat website to make our chat history shareable and persistent across server restarts.

> **Exercise:** Add a HTML input to the chat website to let the user filter the chat history and only show messages by a specified user name.
>
> **See example 14.5 - WebsocketsFilter**

> **Exercise:** The HTML server we have so far relies on two in-memory variables that are shared between all HTTP requests: var `messages` and var `openConnections`. Synchronize all access to these variables using `synchronized{...}` blocks so that usage is safe even when there are multiple HTTP requests happening concurrently.
>
> **See example 14.6 - WebsocketsSynchronized**

Exercise: The online examples so far provide a simple test suite, that uses `String.contains` to perform basic validation on the web pages being generated. Use the Jsoup library we saw *Chapter 11: Scraping Websites* to make this validation more specific, ensuring that the `Scala Chat` title is rendered within the `<h1>` tag, and that the chat messages are being correctly rendered within the `<div id="messageList">` tag.

See example 14.7 - WebsocketsJsoup

Exercise: Write a simple website which will crawl with Wikipedia article graph using the web crawling techniques we saw in *Chapter 13: Fork-Join Parallelism with Futures*. It should take the title of the starting Wikipedia article and the depth to crawl to as HTML inputs, and display the crawled Wikipedia titles on the page each one hyper-linked to their respective URLs:

You may use any of the different crawlers we wrote in that chapter: sequential, parallel, recursive, or asynchronous. You may also implement the browser-server interaction via any of the techniques we learned in this chapter: HTML Forms (*14.3*), Dynamic Page Updates via Javascript (*14.4*), or in a streaming fashion via Websockets (*14.5*).

See example 14.8 - CrawlerWebsite

Discuss Chapter 14 online at https://www.handsonscala.com/discuss/14

15

Querying SQL Databases

15.1 Setting up Quill and PostgreSQL   288

15.2 Mapping Tables to Case Classes   290

15.3 Querying and Updating Data   293

15.4 Transactions   299

15.5 A Database-Backed Chat Website   300

```
@ ctx.run(query[City].filter(_.population > 5000000).filter(_.countryCode == "CHN"))
res16: List[City] = List(
  City(1890, "Shanghai", "CHN", "Shanghai", 9696300),
  City(1891, "Peking", "CHN", "Peking", 7472000),
  City(1892, "Chongqing", "CHN", "Chongqing", 6351600),
  City(1893, "Tianjin", "CHN", "Tianjin", 5286800)
)
                                                                </> 15.1.scala
```

Snippet 15.1: using the Quill database query library from the Scala REPL

Most modern systems are backed by relational databases. This chapter will walk you through the basics of using a relational database from Scala, using the Quill query library. We will work through small self-contained examples of how to store and query data within a Postgres database, and then convert the interactive chat website we implemented in *Chapter 14: Simple Web and API Servers* to use a Postgres database for data storage.

15.1 Setting up Quill and PostgreSQL

15.1.1 Library Setup

For the first part of this chapter, we will use the Ammonite Scala REPL. On top of Ammonite, we also need the Quill database query library, the Postgres Java library, and the OpenTable Embedded Postgres database library:

```
@ import $ivy.{
    `io.getquill::quill-jdbc:3.5.2`,
    `org.postgresql:postgresql:42.2.8`,
    `com.opentable.components:otj-pg-embedded:0.13.1`
}                                                            </> 15.2.scala
```

OpenTable's Embedded Postgres library will make it convenient to spin up a small Postgres database for us to work with, so we do not need to install a Postgres database globally. For production use, you will likely be using a separately managed database server, perhaps hosted on Heroku Postgres or Amazon RDS.

To begin with we will start our test database and set up a Quill database context connected to it:

```
@ import com.opentable.db.postgres.embedded.EmbeddedPostgres

@ val server = EmbeddedPostgres.builder().setPort(5432).start()
server: EmbeddedPostgres = EmbeddedPG-dee4bbc5-7e4e-4559-afb8-10155ecff124

@ {
  import io.getquill._
  import com.zaxxer.hikari.{HikariConfig, HikariDataSource}
  val pgDataSource = new org.postgresql.ds.PGSimpleDataSource()
  pgDataSource.setUser("postgres")
  val hikariConfig = new HikariConfig()
  hikariConfig.setDataSource(pgDataSource)
  val ctx = new PostgresJdbcContext(LowerCase, new HikariDataSource(hikariConfig))
  import ctx._
}                                                            </> 15.3.scala
```

ctx will be our primary interface to the Postgres database through Quill. The HikariConfig and PGSimpleDataSource classes expose most of the things you can configure when connecting to the Postgres database, e.g. setUser above, but for now we will mostly stick with the defaults. In addition to the Postgres PGSimpleDataSource, we also set up a HikariDataSource which improves performance by allowing database connections to be re-used.

15.1.2 Sample Data

As sample data for this chapter, we will be using a Postgres version of the popular `world.sql` dataset:

```
CREATE TABLE IF NOT EXISTS city (
    id integer NOT NULL,
    name varchar NOT NULL,
    countrycode character(3) NOT NULL,
    district varchar NOT NULL,
    population integer NOT NULL
);

CREATE TABLE IF NOT EXISTS country (
...
```
</> 15.4.sql

This can be downloaded from:

- world.sql *(https://github.com/handsonscala/handsonscala/tree/v1/resources/15)*

This file defines a simple database including all the cities in the world, all the countries in the world, and the languages each country speaks. We will be using this dataset to exercise our database queries and actions.

15.1.3 PG-CLI

In a separate terminal, we will be using the open source PG-CLI tool to directly connect to our test Postgres database:

- https://www.pgcli.com/install

After installation, you can connect PG-CLI to the local test database via `pgcli`:

```
$ pgcli -U postgres -p 5432 -h localhost
Server: PostgreSQL 10.6
Version: 2.1.0
Chat: https://gitter.im/dbcli/pgcli
Mail: https://groups.google.com/forum/#!forum/pgcli
Home: http://pgcli.com
postgres@/tmp:postgres>
```
</> 15.5.bash

We can import out sample data into our postgres database using PG-CLI:

```
pg> \i world.sql;
```

PG-CLI uses the standard Postgres `\d` command to list tables and columns:

```
pg> \d
+-----------+------------------+----------+-----------+
| Schema    | Name             | Type     | Owner     |
|-----------+------------------+----------+-----------|
| public    | city             | table    | postgres  |
| public    | country          | table    | postgres  |
| public    | countrylanguage  | table    | postgres  |
+-----------+------------------+----------+-----------+
```
</> 15.6.sql

15.2 Mapping Tables to Case Classes

Quill expects tables to be represented by Scala `case class`es, with individual columns within each table mapping to primitive data types. As a first approximation, the mapping is as follows:

Postgres	Scala
real	Float, Double
boolean	Boolean
integer, smallint, bigint	Int, Long
character(n), character varying	String
numeric(n,m)	java.math.BigDecimal

This particular Postgres database uses a `lowercase` variable name convention, which doesn't quite match Scala's `PascalCase` for class names and `camelCase` for field names. To map between these two conventions, we had earlier defined our Quill `ctx` to use a `LowerCase` name mapper. There are also `SnakeCase`, `UpperCase`, or `CamelCase` name mappers you can use if your database uses those respective naming conventions.

Defining the `case class`es representing each table is straightforward. Here is the mapping from table schema to `case class` for each of the tables in this `world.sql`:

```
pg> \d city                              postgres        // case class                         City.sc
| Column       | Type           | Modifiers |           // mapping `city` table
|--------------+----------------+-----------|           case class City(
| id           | integer        | not null  |             id: Int,
| name         | character vary | not null  |             name: String,
| countrycode  | character(3)   | not null  |             countryCode: String,
| district     | character vary | not null  |             district: String,
| population   | integer        | not null  |             population: Int
                              </> 15.7.sql           )                         </> 15.8.scala
```

```
pg> \d country                           postgres        // case class                      Country.sc
| Column         | Type         | Modifiers |           // mapping `country` table
|----------------+--------------+-----------|           case class Country(
| code           | character(3) | not null  |             code: String,
| name           | character vary | not null |            name: String,
| continent      | character vary | not null |            continent: String,
| region         | character vary | not null |            region: String,
| surfacearea    | real         | not null  |             surfaceArea: Double,
| indepyear      | smallint     |           |             indepYear: Option[Int],
| population     | integer      | not null  |             population: Int,
| lifeexpectancy | real         |           |             lifeExpectancy: Option[Double],
| gnp            | numeric(10,2)|           |             gnp: Option[math.BigDecimal],
| gnpold         | numeric(10,2)|           |             gnpold: Option[math.BigDecimal],
| localname      | character vary | not null |            localName: String,
| governmentform | character vary | not null |            governmentForm: String,
| headofstate    | character vary |         |             headOfState: Option[String],
| capital        | integer      |           |             capital: Option[Int],
| code2          | character(2) | not null  |             code2: String
                              </> 15.9.sql           )                         </> 15.10.scala
```

```
pg> \d countrylanguage                   postgres        // case class                CountryLanguage.sc
| Column       | Type           | Modifiers |           // mapping `countrylanguage` table
|--------------+----------------+-----------|           case class CountryLanguage(
| countrycode  | character(3)   | not null  |             countrycode: String,
| language     | character vary | not null  |             language: String,
| isofficial   | boolean        | not null  |             isOfficial: Boolean,
| percentage   | real           | not null  |             percentage: Double
                              </> 15.11.sql          )                         </> 15.12.scala
```

Optional values which do not have a Postgres not `null` flag set are modeled using Scala `Option[T]`s.

You can then try out basic queries to fetch the various tables and map them to the Scala `case class`es, using the `query` method we imported from Quill:

```
@ ctx.run(query[City])
cmd7.sc:1: SELECT x.id, x.name, x.countrycode, x.district, x.population FROM city x
res7: List[City] = List(
  City(1, "Kabul", "AFG", "Kabol", 1780000),
  City(2, "Qandahar", "AFG", "Qandahar", 237500),
  City(3, "Herat", "AFG", "Herat", 186800),
  City(4, "Mazar-e-Sharif", "AFG", "Balkh", 127800),
...                                                                    </> 15.13.scala
```

```
@ ctx.run(query[Country])
cmd8.sc:1: SELECT x.code, x.name, x.continent, x.region, x.surfacearea, x.indepyear, ...
res8: List[Country] = List(
  Country(
    "AFG",
    "Afghanistan",
    "Asia",
    "Southern and Central Asia",
    652090.0,
    Some(1919),
...                                                                    </> 15.14.scala
```

```
@ ctx.run(query[CountryLanguage])
cmd9.sc:1: SELECT x.countrycode, x.language, x.isofficial, x.percentage FROM ...
res9: List[CountryLanguage] = List(
  CountryLanguage("AFG", "Pashto", true, 52.4000015),
  CountryLanguage("NLD", "Dutch", true, 95.5999985),
  CountryLanguage("ANT", "Papiamento", true, 86.1999969),
  CountryLanguage("ALB", "Albaniana", true, 97.9000015),
...                                                                    </> 15.15.scala
```

Note that dumping the entire database table to in-memory `case class` objects is probably not something you want to do on a large production database, but on this small sample database it's unlikely to cause issues. You can use `.take(n)` inside the `ctx.run(...)` if you want to limit the number of entries fetched from the database.

When compiling your code for each command above, Quill prints out the exact SQL query that is being prepared and will be executed at runtime. This can be useful if your Quill query is misbehaving and you are trying to figure out what exactly it is trying to do. You can always go to your PG-CLI console and enter that same SQL directly into the console:

```
pg> SELECT x.id, x.name, x.countrycode, x.district, x.population FROM city x
+------+----------------+--------------+-----------------------+---------------+
| id   | name           | countrycode  | district              | population    |
|------+----------------+--------------+-----------------------+---------------|
| 1    | Kabul          | AFG          | Kabol                 | 1780000       |
| 2    | Qandahar       | AFG          | Qandahar              | 237500        |
| 3    | Herat          | AFG          | Herat                 | 186800        |
| 4    | Mazar-e-Sharif | AFG          | Balkh                 | 127800        |
| 5    | Amsterdam      | NLD          | Noord-Holland         | 731200        |
...                                                               </> 15.16.sql
```

Throughout this chapter, the various Quill `query`, `.map`, `.filter`, etc. method calls you write in the `ctx.run(...)` call do not execute within your Scala application: instead, they are compiled to SQL code and executed directly in the database. Compared to just fetching everything and doing the `.maps` and `.filters` in your application, Quill's approach reduces the load on the application servers by moving the logic to the database, and also reduces the load on the database by greatly reducing the amount of data that the application server needs to fetch.

While you can also perform database operations by sending raw SQL strings to the database to execute, doing so is much more fragile than Quill's compiler-checked query expressions, and far more prone to security vulnerabilities.

15.3 Querying and Updating Data

Now that we have set up a simple sample database, and have configured Quill to work with it, we can start performing more interesting queries.

15.3.1 Filtering

A Scala `.filter` translates into a SQL `WHERE` clause. You can use that to find individual entries by `name` or by `id`:

```
@ ctx.run(query[City].filter(_.name == "Singapore"))
cmd10.sc:1: SELECT x1.id, x1.name, x1.countrycode, x1.district, x1.population
            FROM city x1 WHERE x1.name = 'Singapore'
res10: List[City] = List(City(3208, "Singapore", "SGP", "\u0096", 4017733))


@ ctx.run(query[City].filter(_.id == 3208))
cmd11.sc:1: SELECT x1.id, x1.name, x1.countrycode, x1.district, x1.population
            FROM city x1 WHERE x1.id = 3208
res11: List[City] = List(City(3208, "Singapore", "SGP", "\u0096", 4017733))</> 15.17.scala
```

You can also find all entries that match arbitrary predicates, e.g. based on `population` below:

```
@ ctx.run(query[City].filter(_.population > 9000000))
cmd12.sc:1: SELECT x1.id, x1.name, x1.countrycode, x1.district, x1.population
        FROM city x1 WHERE x1.population > 9000000
res12: List[City] = List(
  City(206, "S\u00e3o Paulo", "BRA", "S\u00e3o Paulo", 9968485),
  City(939, "Jakarta", "IDN", "Jakarta Raya", 9604900),
  City(1024, "Mumbai (Bombay)", "IND", "Maharashtra", 10500000),
  City(1890, "Shanghai", "CHN", "Shanghai", 9696300),
  City(2331, "Seoul", "KOR", "Seoul", 9981619),
  City(2822, "Karachi", "PAK", "Sindh", 9269265)
)                                                                  </> 15.18.scala
```

Predicates can have more than one clause, e.g. here we filter on both population and countryCode:

```
@ ctx.run(query[City].filter(c => c.population > 5000000 && c.countryCode == "CHN"))
cmd13.sc:1: SELECT c.id, c.name, c.countrycode, c.district, c.population
        FROM city c WHERE c.population > 5000000 AND c.countrycode = 'CHN'
res13: List[City] = List(
  City(1890, "Shanghai", "CHN", "Shanghai", 9696300),
  City(1891, "Peking", "CHN", "Peking", 7472000),
  City(1892, "Chongqing", "CHN", "Chongqing", 6351600),
  City(1893, "Tianjin", "CHN", "Tianjin", 5286800)
)                                                                  </> 15.19.scala
```

If there are relevant table indices present, the WHERE clause generated by filters will make use of them to speed up the lookup, otherwise it may end up doing a slow full table scan. A detailed discussion of database index performance is beyond the scope of this book.

15.3.2 Lifting

If you want to include dynamic values in your queries, e.g. filtering by a value that isn't a constant, you have to use the lift syntax:

```
@ def find(cityId: Int) = ctx.run(query[City].filter(_.id == lift(cityId)))
cmd14.sc:1: SELECT x1.id, x1.name, x1.countrycode, x1.district, x1.population
        FROM city x1 WHERE x1.id = ?


@ find(3208)
res15: List[City] = List(City(3208, "Singapore", "SGP", "\u0096", 4017733))


@ find(3209)
res16: List[City] = List(City(3209, "Bratislava", "SVK", "Bratislava", 448292))
                                                                  </> 15.20.scala
```

Notice how this query, with a variable `lift(cityId)` interpolated into it, is converted into a parameterized SQL query with a `WHERE x1.id = ?` clause. This avoids SQL injection vulnerabilities and makes it easier for the database to optimize your queries.

In general, anything within a `ctx.run(...)` clause is converted to SQL to run within your database, with the exception of the contents of `lift(...)` calls which run locally in your Scala program before being spliced into the query. That means that only a subset of operations are allowed on the code that Quill converts to SQL. Invalid operations outside that subset are a compilation error:

```
@ ctx.run(query[City].filter(_.name.length == 1))
cmd17.sc:1: Tree 'x$1.name.length()' can't be parsed to 'Ast'
val res17 = ctx.run(query[City].filter(_.name.length == 1))
                          ^
Compilation Failed                                                    </> 15.21.scala
```

15.3.3 Mapping

Often you do not need all the values in a particular table. For example, the `country` table has 15 different values per row, and if you are only interested in 2-3 of them, fetching them all is a waste of CPU time, memory, and network bandwidth. You can thus use `.map` to pick the columns that you are interested in:

```
@ ctx.run(query[Country].map(c => (c.name, c.continent)))
cmd17.sc:1: SELECT c.name, c.continent FROM country c
res17: List[(String, String)] = List(
  ("Afghanistan", "Asia"),
  ("Netherlands", "Europe"),
  ("Netherlands Antilles", "North America"),
...


@ ctx.run(query[Country].map(c => (c.name, c.continent, c.population)))
cmd18.sc:1: SELECT c.name, c.continent, c.population FROM country c
res18: List[(String, String, Int)] = List(
  ("Afghanistan", "Asia", 22720000),
  ("Netherlands", "Europe", 15864000),
  ("Netherlands Antilles", "North America", 217000),
...                                                                   </> 15.22.scala
```

You can combine the various operations in any order, e.g. here is a parameterized query that combines a `filter` and `lift` with a `map` to fetch the name of the city with a particular ID:

```
@ def findName(cityId: Int) = ctx.run(
    query[City].filter(_.id == lift(cityId)).map(_.name)
  )
cmd19.sc:1: SELECT x1.name FROM city x1 WHERE x1.id = ?


@ findName(3208)
res20: List[String] = List("Singapore")


@ findName(3209)
res21: List[String] = List("Bratislava")                              </> 15.23.scala
```

15.3.4 Joins

Joins allow you to make use of data split across multiple tables. For example, if we want to query "the name of every city in the continent of Asia", the city names are in the `city` table, but the continent name is in the country table. You can use `joins` to perform a query that uses data from both tables:

```
@ ctx.run(
    query[City]
      .join(query[Country])
      .on(_.countryCode == _.code)
      .filter{case (city, country) => country.continent == "Asia"}
      .map{case (city, country) => city.name}
  )
cmd22.sc:1: SELECT x01.name FROM city x01 INNER JOIN country x11
            ON x01.countrycode = x11.code WHERE x11.continent = 'Asia'
res22: List[String] = List(
  "Kabul",
  "Qandahar",
  "Herat",
  "Mazar-e-Sharif",
  "Dubai",
  "Abu Dhabi",
...                                                                  </> 15.24.scala
```

You can also join more than two tables, as long as there is some sort of key you can use to match the relevant rows in each table, similar to how above we are matching the countryCode in the City table with the code in the Country table.

15.3.5 Inserts

You can use the `.insert` method to insert data into a database table:

```
@ ctx.run(query[City].insert(City(10000, "test", "TST", "Test County", 0)))
cmd23.sc:1: INSERT INTO city (id, name, countrycode, district, population)
         VALUES (10000, 'test', 'TST', 'Test County', 0)
res23: Long = 1L

@ ctx.run(query[City].filter(_.population == 0))
res24: List[City] = List(City(10000, "test", "TST", "Test County", 0))    </> 15.25.scala
```

There is also a batch insertion syntax, using `liftQuery` and `foreach`:

```
@ val cities = List(
    City(10001, "testville", "TSV", "Test County", 0)  ,
    City(10002, "testopolis", "TSO", "Test County", 0),
    City(10003, "testberg", "TSB", "Test County", 0)
  )

@ ctx.run(liftQuery(cities).foreach(e => query[City].insert(e)))
cmd26.sc:1: INSERT INTO city (id, name, countrycode, district, population)
         VALUES (?, ?, ?, ?, ?)
res26: List[Long] = List(1L, 1L, 1L)

@ ctx.run(query[City].filter(_.population == 0))
res27: List[City] = List(
  City(10000, "test", "TST", "Test County", 0),
  City(10001, "testville", "TSV", "Test County", 0),
  City(10002, "testopolis", "TSO", "Test County", 0),
  City(10003, "testberg", "TSB", "Test County", 0)
)                                                                         </> 15.26.scala
```

15.3.6 Updates

You can use `.update` to replace an entire row with a new one:

```
@ ctx.run(
    query[City]
      .filter(_.id == 10000)
      .update(City(10000, "testham", "TST", "Test County", 0))
  )
cmd28.sc:1: UPDATE city SET id = 10000, name = 'testham', countrycode = 'TST',
          district = 'Test County', population = 0 WHERE id = 10000
res28: Long = 1L


@ ctx.run(query[City].filter(_.id == 10000))
res29: List[City] = List(City(10000, "testham", "TST", "Test County", 0)) </> 15.27.scala
```

You can update individual values within the row:

```
@ ctx.run(query[City].filter(_.id == 10000).update(_.name -> "testford"))
cmd30.sc:1: UPDATE city SET name = 'testford' WHERE id = 10000
res30: Long = 1L


@ ctx.run(query[City].filter(_.id == 10000))
res31: List[City] = List(City(10000, "testford", "TST", "Test County", 0))</> 15.28.scala
```

Or you can update multiple rows at once:

```
@ ctx.run(
    query[City].filter(_.district == "Test County").update(_.district -> "Test Borough")
  )
cmd32.sc:1: UPDATE city SET district = 'Test Borough' WHERE district = 'Test County'
res32: Long = 4L


@ ctx.run(query[City].filter(_.population == 0))
res33: List[City] = List(
  City(10001, "testville", "TSV", "Test Borough", 0),
  City(10002, "testopolis", "TSO", "Test Borough", 0),
  City(10003, "testberg", "TSB", "Test Borough", 0),
  City(10000, "testford", "TST", "Test Borough", 0)
)                                               </> 15.29.scala
```

15.4 Transactions

One of the primary features of a database is transactionality: the ability to start a transaction, perform some queries and updates isolated from changes others may be making, and then either committing your changes atomically or rolling them back at the end of the transaction. This helps ensure that if something crashes half way, you don't end up with a database full of corrupted data in a half-updated state.

Quill supports this via the `ctx.transaction{...}` syntax. Any updates within the transaction are only committed when the transaction completes: any other processes querying the database will not see any half-baked changes. Furthermore, if the transaction fails with an exception, the changes are never committed:

```scala
@ ctx.transaction{
    ctx.run(
      query[City].filter(_.district == "Test Borough").update(_.district -> "Test County")
    )
    throw new Exception()
  }
cmd34.sc:2: UPDATE city SET district = 'Test County' WHERE district = 'Test Borough'
java.lang.Exception
  ammonite.$sess.cmd46$.$anonfun$res34$1(cmd34.sc:3)
  io.getquill.context.jdbc.JdbcContext.$anonfun$transaction$2(JdbcContext.scala:81)
...


@ ctx.run(query[City].filter(_.population == 0)) // none of the districts have updated
res35: List[City] = List(
  City(10001, "testville", "TSV", "Test Borough", 0),
  City(10002, "testopolis", "TSO", "Test Borough", 0),
  City(10003, "testberg", "TSB", "Test Borough", 0),
  City(10000, "testford", "TST", "Test Borough", 0)
)
```
</> 15.30.scala

As you can see, even though the `update` call completed, the exception caused the transaction to abort, and thus the "Test Borough" column in the `City` table was never updated. This applies to both exceptions that happen accidentally in the process of executing your code, and also to exceptions you throw yourself e.g. to intentionally abort a transaction and discard the changes.

15.4.1 Why Transactions?

Transactions are a very useful tool to maintain the data integrity of your database.

- Transactions help ensure that an poorly-timed crash or failure doesn't leave your database in a half-baked state due to a series of updates that only partially completed.

- When multiple clients are reading and writing to a database concurrently, it ensures each client doesn't see another client's updates until the transaction completes, again ensuring the database is never in a half-updated state.

Note that it is also possible for a transaction to fail due to a conflict: e.g. if two concurrent transactions are reading and writing the same row at the same time. In such a case, the first transaction to complete wins, and the later transaction aborts and discards its changes. For more details on how Postgres transactions work and how they can be configured, check out the Postgres documentation on Transaction Isolation:

- https://www.postgresql.org/docs/9.5/transaction-iso.html

See example 15.1 - Queries

15.5 A Database-Backed Chat Website

In *Chapter 14: Simple Web and API Servers*, we built a simple chat website: users could enter messages in a chat room, where they were made available for other users to see. We will build on top of that code in this chapter, modifying it to turn the in-memory implementation into a database-backed website using Quill and Postgres.

The main limitation of that implementation was the way we stored the messages in-memory:

```
                                                          app/src/MinimalApplication.scala
var messages = Vector(("alice", "Hello World!"), ("bob", "I am cow, hear me moo"))
```

```
                                                          app/src/MinimalApplication.scala
messages = messages :+ (name -> msg)
```

As implemented above, this webserver stores the `messages` as an in-memory `Vector[Message]`. While this is convenient, the weakness of such a setup is that if the chat server goes down - whether due to failure or updates - all messages are lost. Furthermore, the `messages` cannot be shared between multiple webserver processes. The obvious solution would be to store the chat messages in a database that would persist the data, and can be queried by as many webservers as we have running.

15.5.1 Build Config & Database Setup

To use Quill and Postgres in our website, we first need to add the same libraries we used above to the build.sc file's `def ivyDeps`:

```
def ivyDeps = Agg(                                                    build.sc
+    ivy"io.getquill::quill-jdbc:3.5.2",
+    ivy"org.postgresql:postgresql:42.2.8",
+    ivy"com.opentable.components:otj-pg-embedded:0.13.1",
     ivy"com.lihaoyi::scalatags:0.9.1",
     ivy"com.lihaoyi::cask:0.7.4"
)                                                              </> 15.31.scala
```

Next, we need to replace the in-memory `messages` store with a database connection:

```
object MinimalApplication extends cask.MainRoutes {    app/src/MinimalApplication.scala
-    var messages = Vector(("alice", "Hello World!"), ("bob", "I am cow, hear me moo"))
+    case class Message(name: String, msg: String)
+    import com.opentable.db.postgres.embedded.EmbeddedPostgres
+    val server = EmbeddedPostgres.builder()
+      .setDataDirectory(System.getProperty("user.home") + "/data")
+      .setCleanDataDirectory(false).setPort(5432)
+      .start()
+    import io.getquill._
+    import com.zaxxer.hikari.{HikariConfig, HikariDataSource}
+    val pgDataSource = new org.postgresql.ds.PGSimpleDataSource()
+    pgDataSource.setUser("postgres")
+    val hikariConfig = new HikariConfig()
+    hikariConfig.setDataSource(pgDataSource)
+    val ctx = new PostgresJdbcContext(LowerCase, new HikariDataSource(hikariConfig))
+    ctx.executeAction("CREATE TABLE IF NOT EXISTS message (name text, msg text);")
+    import ctx._

     var openConnections = Set.empty[cask.WsChannelActor]          </> 15.32.scala
```

This replaces the `messages` in-memory data structure with a database connection, and calls `ctx.executeAction` to initialize the database with the `message (name text, msg text)` schema. This ensures that not only do messages persist if the web server goes down, it means other servers will be able to read and write the same data, allowing you to deploy multiple servers to spread the load if necessary.

For now, we are just running the Postgres database process locally on your computer, using `com.opentable.db.postgres.embedded.EmbeddedPostgres`. For a real deployment you usually want a database deployed and managed separately from your application code. Note that although we are still using a local database, `setCleanDataDirectory(false)` ensures that the actual data being stored in the database persists between process and database restarts.

15.5.2 Storing Messages in the Database

Now that we have the database configured, we need to update the places where we read and write messages to point them at the database.

First, we should make reads fetch data from the database, rather than to the in-memory `Vector`. This can be done by defining a `def` `messages` method that reads from the database, saving us from needing to modify the rest of the application:

```
                                                    app/src/MinimalApplication.scala
    import ctx._
+   def messages = ctx.run(query[Message].map(m => (m.name, m.msg)))


    var openConnections = Set.empty[cask.WsChannelActor]          </> 15.33.scala
```

Next, we need to store submitted messages in the database. This involves replacing the `messages` `=` `message :+ (name -> msg)` call with the Quill insert syntax we saw earlier (*15.3.5*):

```
                                                    app/src/MinimalApplication.scala
    else {
-       messages = messages :+ (name -> msg)
+       ctx.run(query[Message].insert(lift(Message(name, msg))))
        for (conn <- openConnections) conn.send(cask.Ws.Text(messageList().render))
                                                                 </> 15.34.scala
```

Now, every call to `messages` will run a query on the Postgres database rather than read from the in-memory `Vector`, and submitted messages will get stored in the database where other processes can access them. That's all we need to turn our in-memory chat website into a simple database-backed web service!

15.5.3 Testing our Database-backed Website

You can test it out by starting the app via:

```
$ ./mill app.runBackground
```

Once the app is running, you can submit a few messages in the browser to see them show up on the website. When you are done, you can stop the app via:

```
$ ./mill clean app.runBackground
```

If you then restart your app, you will see the messages are still present.

15.5.4 Complete Webserver

The complete code for `MinimalApplication.scala` now looks like this:

app/src/MinimalApplication.scala

```scala
package app
import scalatags.Text.all._
object MinimalApplication extends cask.MainRoutes {
  case class Message(name: String, msg: String)
  import com.opentable.db.postgres.embedded.EmbeddedPostgres
  val server = EmbeddedPostgres.builder()
    .setDataDirectory(System.getProperty("user.home") + "/data")
    .setCleanDataDirectory(false).setPort(5432)
    .start()
  import io.getquill._
  import com.zaxxer.hikari.{HikariConfig, HikariDataSource}
  val pgDataSource = new org.postgresql.ds.PGSimpleDataSource()
  pgDataSource.setUser("postgres")
  val hikariConfig = new HikariConfig()
  hikariConfig.setDataSource(pgDataSource)
  val ctx = new PostgresJdbcContext(LowerCase, new HikariDataSource(hikariConfig))
  ctx.executeAction("CREATE TABLE IF NOT EXISTS message (name text, msg text);")
  import ctx._

  def messages = ctx.run(query[Message].map(m => (m.name, m.msg)))

  var openConnections = Set.empty[cask.WsChannelActor]
  val bootstrap = "https://stackpath.bootstrapcdn.com/bootstrap/4.5.0/css/bootstrap.css"

  @cask.staticResources("/static")
  def staticResourceRoutes() = "static"

  @cask.get("/")
  def hello() = doctype("html")(
    html(
      head(
        link(rel := "stylesheet", href := bootstrap),
        script(src := "/static/app.js")
      ),
      body(
        div(cls := "container")(
          h1("Scala Chat!"),
```

```scala
          div(id := "messageList")(messageList()),
          div(id := "errorDiv", color.red),
          form(onsubmit := "submitForm(); return false")(
            input(`type` := "text", id := "nameInput", placeholder := "User name"),
            input(`type` := "text", id := "msgInput", placeholder := "Write a message!"),
            input(`type` := "submit")
          )
        )
      )
    )
  )
)

def messageList() = frag(for ((name, msg) <- messages) yield p(b(name), " ", msg))


@cask.postJson("/")
def postChatMsg(name: String, msg: String) = {
  if (name == "") ujson.Obj("success" -> false, "err" -> "Name cannot be empty")
  else if (msg == "") ujson.Obj("success" -> false, "err" -> "Message cannot be empty")
  else {
    ctx.run(query[Message].insert(lift(Message(name, msg))))
    for (conn <- openConnections) conn.send(cask.Ws.Text(messageList().render))
    ujson.Obj("success" -> true, "err" -> "")
  }
}


@cask.websocket("/subscribe")
def subscribe() = cask.WsHandler { connection =>
  connection.send(cask.Ws.Text(messageList().render))
  openConnections += connection
  cask.WsActor { case cask.Ws.Close(_, _) => openConnections -= connection }
}


  initialize()
}
```
</> 15.35.scala

The online version of this code also comes with a simple test suite, which tests that we can restart the server without losing the chat messages that have been posted:

See example 15.2 - Website

15.6 Conclusion

In this chapter, we have walked through how to work with a simple PostgreSQL database from Scala, using the Quill query library. Starting in the REPL, we seeded our database with a simple `world.sql` set of sample data, defined the mapping `case class`es, and explored using Quill to run queries which filtered, mapped, joined, inserted, and updated the data in our postgres database. We then wired up Quill into our simple chat website, giving our website the ability to persist data across process restarts.

This is a simple chat website with a simple local database, but you can build upon it to turn it into a more production-ready system if you wish to do so. This may involve wrapping the endpoints in `transaction` blocks, `synchronize`ing references to `openConnections`, or making the database setup configurable to point towards your production database once the code is deployed.

The Quill database library has online documentation, if you wish to dig deeper into it:

- https://github.com/getquill/quill

You may encounter other libraries in the wild. These work somewhat differently from Quill, but follow roughly the same principles:

- **Scala SLICK:** http://scala-slick.org/
- **ScalikeJDBC:** http://scalikejdbc.org/

This chapter rounds off the third section of our book, `Part III Web Services`. In this section we have broadened our horizons beyond a single process or computer, working with code querying databases or serving the role of clients and servers in a broader system. This should give you a solid foundation for using Scala in the distributed environments that are common in modern software engineering.

Exercise: In addition to `map`, `filter`, and `take`, Quill also supports `groupBy` (which must always be followed by a `map`) and `sortBy` in its queries. Use these operators to write a Quill query on the `world.sql` dataset to find:

- The 10 languages spoken in the largest number of cities
- The 10 languages spoken by the largest population

See example 15.3 - FancyQueries

Exercise: Modify our chat website to keep track each message's send time and date in the database, and display it in the user interface.

See example 15.4 - WebsiteTimestamps

Exercise: Add the ability to reply directly to existing chat messages, by giving each message a unique id and adding another optional input field for user to specify which message they are replying to. Replies should be indented under the message they are replying to, nested arbitrarily deeply to form a tree-shaped "threaded" discussion.

As a convenience, you can define your id column in the database as the Postgres serial type, making it a 32-bit value that's automatically incremented by the database when a row is inserted with the other columns specified explicitly but with serial column elided:

```
query[Message]
  .insert(_.parent -> lift(p), _.name -> lift(n), _.msg -> lift(m)) </> 15.36.scala
```

See example 15.5 - ThreadedChat

Exercise: One limitation of the current push-update mechanism is that it can only updates to browsers connected to the same webserver. Make use of Postgres's LISTEN/NOTIFY feature to push updates to all servers connected to the same database, allowing the servers to be horizontally scalable and easily replaceable. You can use the "Asynchronous Notifications" functionality in the com.impossibl.pgjdbc-ng:pgjdbc-ng:0.8.4 package to register callbacks on these events.

- LISTEN/NOTIFY: https://www.postgresql.org/docs/current/sql-notify.html
- pgjdbc-ng: http://impossibl.github.io/pgjdbc-ng/docs/current/user-guide

See example 15.6 - ListenNotify

Discuss Chapter 15 online at https://www.handsonscala.com/discuss/15

Part IV: Program Design

16 Message-based Parallelism with Actors   309

17 Multi-Process Applications   329

18 Building a Real-time File Synchronizer   347

19 Parsing Structured Text   365

20 Implementing a Programming Language   387

The fourth and last part of this book explores different ways of structuring your Scala application to tackle real-world problems. This chapter builds towards another two capstone projects: building a real-time file synchronizer and building a programming-language interpreter. These projects will give you a glimpse of the very different ways the Scala language can be used to implement challenging applications in an elegant and intuitive manner.

16

Message-based Parallelism with Actors

16.1 Castor Actors   310

16.2 Actor-based Background Uploads   311

16.3 Concurrent Logging Pipelines   317

16.4 Debugging Actors   324

```scala
class SimpleUploadActor()(implicit cc: castor.Context) extends castor.SimpleActor[String]{
  def run(msg: String) = {
    val res = requests.post("https://httpbin.org/post", data = msg)
    println("response " + res.statusCode)
  }
}
                                                                      </> 16.1.scala
```

Snippet 16.1: a simple actor implemented in Scala using the Castor library

Message-based parallelism is a technique that involves splitting your application logic into multiple "actors", each of which can run concurrently, and only interacts with other actors by exchanging asynchronous messages. This style of programming was popularized by the Erlang programming language and the Akka Scala actor library, but the approach is broadly useful and not limited to any particular language or library.

This chapter will introduce the fundamental concepts of message-based parallelism with actors, and how to use them to achieve parallelism in scenarios where the techniques we covered in *Chapter 13: Fork-Join Parallelism with Futures* cannot be applied. We will first discuss the basic actor APIs, see how they can be used in a standalone use case, and then see how they can be used in more involved multi-actor pipelines. The techniques in this chapter will come in useful later in *Chapter 18: Building a Real-time File Synchronizer*.

For this chapter, we will be using the Castor library, which provides lightweight, typed actors for Scala:

```
import $ivy.`com.lihaoyi::castor:0.1.7`
```

We will be writing most of our code in Scala Scripts, which we will either load into the Ammonite Scala REPL for manual testing or test using a separate testing script. First, let us go into the core APIs that the Castor actor library exposes to users.

16.1 Castor Actors

At their core, actors are objects who receive messages via a `send` method, and asynchronously process those messages one after the other:

```
trait Actor[T]{
  def send(t: T): Unit


  def sendAsync(f: scala.concurrent.Future[T]): Unit
}                                                          </> 16.2.scala
```

This processing happens in the background, and can take place without blocking. After a message is sent, the thread or actor that called `.send()` can immediately go on to do other things, even if the message hasn't been processed yet. Messages sent to an actor that is already busy will be queued up until the actor is free.

Note that `Actor` is parameterized on the type `T`, which specifies what messages a particular `Actor` is expected to receive. This is checked at compile time to make sure any message you send to an `Actor` is of the correct type.

16.1.1 Actor Classes

Castor provides three primary classes you can inherit from to define actors:

16.1.1.1 SimpleActor

```
abstract class SimpleActor[T]()(implicit cc: Context) extends Actor[T]{
  def run(msg: T): Unit
}                                                          </> 16.3.scala
```

`SimpleActor` works by providing a run function that will be run on each message.

16.1.1.2 BatchActor

```
abstract class BatchActor[T]()(implicit cc: Context) extends Actor[T]{
  def runBatch(msgs: Seq[T]): Unit
}                                                          </> 16.4.scala
```

`BatchActor` allows you to provide a `runBatch` function that works on groups of messages at a time: this is useful when message processing can be batched together for better efficiency, e.g. making batched database queries or batched filesystem operations instead of many individual actions.

16.1.1.3 StateMachineActor

```scala
abstract class StateMachineActor[T]()(implicit cc: Context) extends Actor[T] {
  class State(val run: T => State)
  protected[this] def initialState: State
}                                                                   </> 16.5.scala
```

`StateMachineActor` allows you to define actors via a set of distinct states, each of which has a separate `run` callback that performs actions and returns the next state that we want the actor to transition to.

While all actors can maintain state in private fields and variables that are read and modified in the `run` or `runBatch` methods, `StateMachineActor` makes the state and state transitions explicit. This can make it easier to specify exactly which states are valid and how the actor transitions between them.

16.1.2 Contexts, Exceptions, and State

All Castor actors require an implicit `castor.Context` parameter, which is an extended `ExecutionContext` that is used to schedule and manage execution of your actors. Thus having an implicit `castor.Context` also allows you to perform `Future` operations that require an implicit `ExecutionContext` present.

Any uncaught exception that is thrown while an actor is processing a message (or batch of messages, in the case of `BatchActor`) is reported to the `castor.Context`'s `reportFailure` method: the default just prints to the console using `.printStackTrace()`, but you can hook in to pass the exceptions elsewhere e.g. if you have a remote error aggregating service.

After an exception is thrown, the actor continues processing messages as before. The internal state of the actor is unchanged from the point where the exception was thrown. In the case of `StateMachineActor`, state transitions only happen after the `run` method completes successfully, and so messages that result in exceptions do not end up changing the state.

Castor actors are meant to manage mutable state internal to the actor. Note that it is up to you to mark the state `private` to avoid accidental external access. Each actor may run on a different thread, and the same actor may run on different threads at different times, so you should ensure you do not share mutable variables between actors. Otherwise, you risk race conditions.

16.2 Actor-based Background Uploads

We will now look at three simple examples that exercise the three `Actor` base classes in a standalone fashion.

As a use case, imagine that we want to upload data to a server in the background, and we are using an actor because we do not want the upload to block the main program's execution. Furthermore, we may want batch uploads for performance, or to limit the frequency at which this actor performs uploads to avoid overloading the server.

16.2.1 Simple Upload Actor

A simple actor that receives messages and uploads them could be written as follows:

```scala
import $ivy.`com.lihaoyi::castor:0.1.7`                                    Simple.sc


class SimpleUploadActor()(implicit cc: castor.Context)
extends castor.SimpleActor[String]{
  var count = 0
  def run(msg: String) = {
    println(s"Uploading $msg")
    val res = requests.post("https://httpbin.org/post", data=msg)
    count += 1
    println(s"response $count ${res.statusCode} " + ujson.read(res)("data"))
  }
}


implicit val cc = new castor.Context.Test()
val uploader = new SimpleUploadActor()                              </> 16.6.scala
```

This snippet defines an `SimpleUploadActor` class that uploads all the messages it receives to the `https://httpbin.org/post` endpoint. Note that we need the `SimpleUploadActor` class to take an implicit parameter `cc: castor.Context`. We instantiate it as `uploader`, and external code can send messages to `uploader` via the `.send` method. `send` returns immediately while the actor processes the incoming messages one after the other in the background.

We can test this script by loading it into the Ammonite Scala REPL for interactive use via `amm --predef Simple.sc`, and using `{}`s to send three messages to the actor in quick succession:

```scala
@ {                                          sending hello
  println("sending hello")                   sending world
  uploader.send("hello")                     sending !

  println("sending world")                   Uploading hello
  uploader.send("world")                     response 1 200 "hello"
                                             Uploading world
  println("sending !")                       response 2 200 "world"
  uploader.send("!")                         Uploading !
}                           </> 16.7.scala   response 3 200 "!"          </> 16.8.output
```

Note how all three `sending` messages got printed before any of the HTTP requests were performed: calls to `.send` are asynchronous, and queue up a message for the actor to process later. Only later do the three `Uploading` and `response` messages get printed, indicating that the three requests to the `httpbin.org` server were performed.

16.2.2 Actors vs Futures

While actors and futures are both concurrency constructs, they have very different use cases.

16.2.2.1 Streaming vs Request-Response

Using actors is ideal for pipeline parallelism scenarios where the dataflow is *one way*. Taking logging as an example, an application writes logs but does not need to wait for them to be processed. In contrast, the futures we learned about in **Chapter 13: Fork-Join Parallelism with Futures** support a more request-response usage pattern, where an asynchronous computation takes a set of input parameters and produces a single result that the application needs to wait for before it can perform further work.

For most use cases, the choice of either streaming or request-response styles is made for you. Log processing tends to be a streaming process, HTTP handling tend to be request-response. Metrics and monitoring systems tend to fit streaming, whereas database queries tend to fit request-response. Actors and futures are complementary techniques, and which one you use to parallelize your code depends on whether a scenario fits better into a streaming or request-response style. Hybrid approaches that use both actors and futures together are also possible.

16.2.2.2 Preserving Ordering

Messages sent to an actor are always processed in the order in which the messages are sent. In contrast, computations running on futures may be scheduled and executed in arbitrary order, which may be different from the order in which the futures were created.

When processing application logs, the order of log messages needs to be preserved. In contrast, when hashing files, the order in which you hash the files probably does not matter. If the order of processing is important, using actors is the way to go.

16.2.2.3 Private Mutable State

Even in a concurrent environment with many messages being sent from different threads, each actor only processes messages in a single-threaded fashion one after the other. This means an actor can freely make use of private mutable fields without worrying about locks or thread-safety. In contrast, futures always have the possibility of running in parallel, and cannot safely access shared mutable variables without risking race conditions.

For example, the `SimpleUploadActor` earlier keeps track of a `count` of how many uploads have occurred. The actor's single-threaded execution means that `count` will always be incremented correctly, without race conditions or lost updates. If we want to use futures to perform our background uploads, we would need to make sure our `count` variable and any other mutable state can be safely accessed from multiple futures running at the same time: not impossible, but definitely tricky and easy to get wrong for anything more complicated than a single counter.

> See example 16.1 - Simple

Note that the `castor.Context.Test` has extra instrumentation to support a `.waitForInactivity()` method, useful for waiting for the actors to complete their work in testing scenarios. This instrumentation has overhead, and you can use a `castor.Context.Simple` in your production code if you wish to avoid that overhead.

16.2.3 Batch Upload Actor

The fact that `SimpleActor` uploads messages one at a time can be inefficient: we may instead want to upload as many messages as we can in each HTTP request to minimize the per-request overhead. To do so, we can use a `BatchActor`:

```scala
import $ivy.`com.lihaoyi::castor:0.1.7`                                          Batch.sc

class BatchUploadActor()(implicit cc: castor.Context)
extends castor.BatchActor[String]{
  var responseCount = 0
  def runBatch(msgs: Seq[String]) = {
    val res = requests.post("https://httpbin.org/post", data = msgs.mkString)
    responseCount += 1
    println(s"response ${res.statusCode} " + ujson.read(res)("data"))
  }
}


implicit val cc = new castor.Context.Test()
val batchUploader = new BatchUploadActor()                            </> 16.9.scala
```

Now, if we send multiple messages in quick succession, the `BatchUploadActor` calls `.mkString` to concatenate them together and only performs one HTTP POST:

```scala
@ {
  println("sending hello")
  batchUploader.send("hello")

  println("sending world")
  batchUploader.send("world")

  println("sending !")
  batchUploader.send("!")
}                            </> 16.10.scala
```

```
sending hello
sending world
sending !

Uploading helloworld!
response 200
```
</> 16.11.output

If further messages get sent to the `BatchActor` while the initial batch upload is taking place, they too are batched together and ready for the next batch upload. Essentially, every message that is received while a previous `runBatch` invocation is executing is batched together for the next invocation: this can be non-deterministic, and depends on thread scheduling, CPU load, networking, and many other factors.

Note that when extending `BatchActor`, it is up to the implementer to ensure that the `BatchActor`'s `runBatch` method has the same visible effect as if they had run a single `run` method on each message individually. Violating that assumption may lead to confusing bugs where the actor behaves non-deterministically depending on how the messages are batched.

> See example 16.2 - Batch

16.2.4 State Machine Upload Actor

Let us consider one more requirement: rather than sending batches of HTTP requests back to back, we would instead like to send a request at most once every N seconds. This is often called *throttling*, and is a common requirement to avoid overloading the remote server.

The easiest way to implement this is to define a state machine as follows:

- The uploader starts off `Idle`, and when a message is received it uploads the message and transitions into `Buffering`

- If messages are received when `Buffering`, it buffers the messages without sending them

- After N seconds in `Buffering`, it checks if there are buffered messages. If there are, it uploads them in one batch and remains `Buffering` for another N seconds. If there are not, it transitions to `Idle`

The following snippet defines an `StateMachineUploadActor` that implements this protocol:

```
import $ivy.`com.lihaoyi::castor:0.1.7`                          StateMachine.sc


sealed trait Msg
case class Text(s: String) extends Msg
case class Flush() extends Msg


class StateMachineUploadActor(n: Int)(implicit cc: castor.Context)
extends castor.StateMachineActor[Msg]{
  var responseCount = 0
  def initialState = Idle()
  case class Idle() extends State({
    case Text(msg) => upload(msg)
  })
  case class Buffering(msgs: Vector[String]) extends State({
    case Text(s) => Buffering(msgs :+ s)
    case Flush() =>
      if (msgs.isEmpty) Idle()
      else upload(msgs.mkString)
  })
```

```
  def upload(data: String) = {
    println("Uploading " + data)
    val res = requests.post("https://httpbin.org/post", data=data)
    responseCount += 1
    println(s"response ${res.statusCode} " + ujson.read(res)("data"))
    cc.scheduleMsg(this, Flush(), java.time.Duration.ofSeconds(n))
    Buffering(Vector.empty)
  }
}

implicit val cc = new castor.Context.Test()
val stateMachineUploader = new StateMachineUploadActor(n = 5)          </> 16.12.scala
```

This code snippet is somewhat more complex than what we saw earlier: rather than just receiving raw Strings, StateMachineUploadActor instead receives Msgs which are either Text objects or Flushs. The actor also has two states, Idle, or Buffering, each of which pattern matches on incoming messages to decide what action to perform as well as what next state to transition into.

The implementation of this actor matches almost exactly the state machine we described above. The only subtlety is the *"after N seconds of buffering"* logic is implemented via cc.scheduleMsg: this means the actor will receive the Flush() message N seconds after uploading a batch of messages and transitioning to Buffering, giving it a chance to either upload any buffered messages or transition back to Idle

We can test this logic by sending messages to StateMachineUploadActor in the REPL. The first message we send gets uploaded immediately, while subsequent messages are buffered according to our N second rule:

```
@ stateMachineUploader.send(Text("I am Cow"))

Uploading I am Cow
response 200 "I am Cow"

@ stateMachineUploader.send(Text("Hear me moo"))

@ stateMachineUploader.send(Text("I weigh twice as much as you"))

Uploading Hear me mooI weigh twice as much as you
response 200 "Hear me mooI weigh twice as much as you"

@ stateMachineUploader.send(Text("And I look good on the barbecue"))

Uploading And I look good on the barbecue
response 200 "And I look good on the barbecue"                        </> 16.13.scala
```

In general, `StateMachineActor` is very useful in cases where there are multiple distinct states which an actor can be in. It forces you to explicitly define:

- What the states are
- The data stored in each state
- The state transitions that occur when each message is processed

When the number of distinct states and messages is large, `StateMachineActor` can be easier to manage than a `SimpleActor` with many mutable `var`s inside of it.

Note that while multiple threads can send messages to `Logger` at once, and the `Flush` message can also be sent at an arbitrary time in the future, the actor will only ever process one message at a time. This ensures that it will transition between the two states `Idle` and `Buffering` in a straightforward manner, without needing to worry about race conditions when trying to update the internal state of the actor.

See example 16.3 - StateMachine

16.3 Concurrent Logging Pipelines

We will now work through a slightly more advanced example: using actors to build a concurrent logging pipeline. This logging pipeline will receive logs from an application and process them in the background without needing the application to stop and wait for it.

We will start with a single actor logging to disk, and extend it to form a multi-stage concurrent logging pipeline logging its messages to multiple destinations.

Unlike the simple HTTP upload actor we saw earlier, our logging actors will have to deal with concerns such as serializing writes to a log file, log rotation, and pipelining to run different parts of the logging logic in parallel. We will also see how to test your actors programmatically in a simple and deterministic way, using `castor.Context.Test`. We will be using Ammonite Scala Scripts to implement and test the rest of the examples in this chapter.

16.3.1 A Logging SimpleActor

Here is a small demonstration of using a `castor.SimpleActor` to perform asynchronous logging to disk:

```scala
import $ivy.`com.lihaoyi::castor:0.1.7`                          Classes.sc
class DiskActor(logPath: os.Path, rotateSize: Int = 50)
              (implicit cc: castor.Context) extends castor.SimpleActor[String]{
  val oldPath = logPath / os.up / (logPath.last + "-old")
  def run(s: String) = {
    val newLogSize = logSize + s.length + 1
    if (newLogSize <= rotateSize) logSize = newLogSize
    else { // rotate log file by moving it to old path and starting again from empty
      logSize = s.length + 1
      os.move(logPath, oldPath, replaceExisting = true)
    }
    os.write.append(logPath, s + "\n", createFolders = true)
  }
  private var logSize = 0
}
```
</> 16.14.scala

```scala
import $file.Classes, Classes._                        LoggingPipeline.sc

implicit val cc = new castor.Context.Test()

val diskActor = new DiskActor(os.pwd / "log.txt")

val logger = diskActor
```
</> 16.15.scala

We alias `diskActor` under the name `logger` for use by application code; this will simplify subsequent examples. To test this `DiskActor`, we will use a separate `TestLoggingPipeline.sc` script that imports the earlier `LoggingPipeline.sc` to interact with and assert on.

`DiskActor` doesn't just write to a log file: the actor also monitors the size of the file, and when it crosses a threshold archives it and starts from a new empty log file. This is called "log rotation", and is a common requirement when handling logs to avoid log files growing indefinitely and filling up your disk.

We can test this using the following script, which we can run via `amm TestLoggingPipeline.sc`.

```
import $file.LoggingPipeline, LoggingPipeline.{logger, cc}    TestLoggingPipeline.sc

logger.send("I am cow")
logger.send("hear me moo")
logger.send("I weight twice as much as you")
logger.send("And I look good on the barbecue")
logger.send("Yoghurt curds cream cheese and butter")
logger.send("Comes from liquids from my udder")
logger.send("I am cow, I am cow")
logger.send("Hear me moo, moooo")

// Logger hasn't finished yet, running in the background
cc.waitForInactivity()
// Now logger has finished

assert(os.read.lines(os.pwd / "log.txt-old") == Seq("Comes from liquids from my udder"))
assert(
  os.read.lines(os.pwd / "log.txt") ==
  Seq("I am cow, I am cow", "Hear me moo, moooo")
)
```
</> 16.16.scala

Note that `logger.send` is thread-safe: multiple threads can be sending messages to the `logger` at once, and the messages will be queued up and executed one at a time. Even if `logger` is in the middle of writing to disk, or is currently performing a log-rotation, the fact that it's in a separate actor means the processing happens in the background without slowing down the main logic of your program.

See example 16.4 - LoggingSimple

16.3.2 Multi-stage Actor Pipelines

Actors give you pipelined parallelism when processing data: the ability to feed your messages through multiple stages of processing, with each stage's processing occurring in parallel. In the following example, we add a `base64Actor` to form a two-stage pipeline:

`diskActor` handles the same writing-strings-to-disk-and-rotating-log-files logic we saw earlier, while `base64Actor` adds another step of encoding the data before it gets written to disk:

```
import $ivy.`com.lihaoyi::castor:0.1.7`                                    Classes.sc
class DiskActor...

+class Base64Actor(dest: castor.Actor[String])
+                    (implicit cc: castor.Context) extends castor.SimpleActor[String]{
+  def run(msg: String) = {
+    dest.send(java.util.Base64.getEncoder.encodeToString(msg.getBytes))
+  }
+}
                                                                      </> 16.17.scala
```

```
implicit val cc = new castor.Context.Test()                        LoggingPipeline.sc

val diskActor = new DiskActor(os.pwd / "log.txt", rotateSize = 50)
+val base64Actor = new Base64Actor(diskActor)
-val logger = diskActor
+val logger = base64Actor
                                                                      </> 16.18.scala
```

Although we have added another Base64 encoding step to the logging process, this new step lives in a separate actor from the original write-to-disk step, and both of these can run in parallel with each other as well as in parallel with the main application code.

We can modify TestLoggingPipeline.sc to verify that it writes lines to the log file base64-encoded, and that when decoded the contents are what we expect:

```
cc.waitForInactivity()                                          TestLoggingPipeline.sc

-assert(os.read.lines(os.pwd / "log.txt-old") == Seq("Comes from liquids from my udder"))
-assert(
-  os.read.lines(os.pwd / "log.txt") ==
-  Seq("I am cow, I am cow", "Hear me moo, moooo")
-)
+def decodeFile(p: os.Path) = {
+  os.read.lines(p).map(s => new String(java.util.Base64.getDecoder.decode(s)))
+}
+assert(decodeFile(os.pwd / "log.txt-old") == Seq("Comes from liquids from my udder"))
+assert(decodeFile(os.pwd / "log.txt") == Seq("I am cow, I am cow", "Hear me moo, moooo"))
                                                                      </> 16.19.scala
```

See example 16.5 - LoggingPipeline

16.3.3 Non-Linear Pipelines

Actor pipelines are not limited to two stages, nor are they limited to a single linear sequence. For the last example in this chapter, let us now consider the following 4 actors arranged in a T-shaped pipeline:

- `diskActor`, which writes to disk with log rotation
- `uploadActor`, uploading the log messages to a HTTP endpoint
- `base64Actor`, which does the base64 encoding of the log messages
- `sanitizeActor`, which masks credit card numbers with a regex

To implement this pipeline, we can modify `LoggingPipeline.sc` as follows::

```
                                                                    Classes.sc
class DiskActor...
class Base64Actor...
+class UploadActor(url: String)
+                  (implicit cc: castor.Context) extends castor.SimpleActor[String]{
+  def run(msg: String) = {
+    val res = requests.post(url, data = msg)
+    println(s"response ${res.statusCode} " + ujson.read(res)("data"))
+  }
+}
+class SanitizeActor(dest: castor.Actor[String])
+                   (implicit cc: castor.Context) extends castor.SimpleActor[String]{
+  def run(msg: String) = {
+    dest.send(msg.replaceAll("([0-9]{4})[0-9]{8}([0-9]{4})", "<redacted>"))
+  }
+}
                                                                   </> 16.20.scala
```

```
implicit val cc = new castor.Context.Test()                    LoggingPipeline.sc

 val diskActor = new DiskActor(os.pwd / "log.txt")
+val uploadActor = new UploadActor("https://httpbin.org/post")
-val base64Actor = new Base64Actor(diskActor)
+val base64Actor = new Base64Actor(new castor.SplitActor(diskActor, uploadActor))
+val sanitizeActor = new SanitizeActor(base64Actor)
-val logger = base64Actor
+val logger = sanitizeActor
                                                                   </> 16.21.scala
```

Apart from the new additions of uploadActor and sanitizeActor, we also use a castor.SplitActor to take the output of base64Actor and send it to two downstream destinations. SplitActor can be used to dispatch messages to any number of downstream actors.

Now, if we modify our TestLoggingPipeline.sc script to also send a 16-digit credit-card-like number as part of the logging message, we can see that it gets replaced by ‹redacted› in the base64 logged output:

```scala
logger.send("Comes from liquids from my udder")                    TestLoggingPipeline.sc
-logger.send("I am cow, I am cow")
+logger.send("I am cow1234567887654321")
logger.send("Hear me moo, moooo")

cc.waitForInactivity()

def decodeFile(p: os.Path) = {
  os.read.lines(p).map(s => new String(java.util.Base64.getDecoder.decode(s)))
}
assert(decodeFile(os.pwd / "log.txt-old") == Seq("Comes from liquids from my udder"))
-assert(decodeFile(os.pwd / "log.txt") == Seq("I am cow, I am cow", "Hear me moo, moooo"))
+assert(decodeFile(os.pwd / "log.txt") == Seq("I am cow<redacted>", "Hear me moo, moooo"))
                                                                          </> 16.22.scala
```

You will also see it print out the response 200 ... messages as the log messages are uploaded to the https://httpbin.org/post HTTP endpoint.

The messages we send to logger are processed with pipeline parallelism on the four actors: we can have one message being sanitized, another being base64 encoded, a third being uploaded, and a fourth being written to disk, all happening simultaneously. We gain this parallelism while preserving the order in which messages are processed, ensuring that our HTTP endpoint and log files receive the messages in the exact same order that they were originally sent in.

Any of the SimpleActors in this pipeline could also be replaced by BatchActors or StateMachineActors to improve performance or to implement additional functionality: e.g. batching writes to disk, batching HTTP uploads, or adding throttling. Doing so is left as an exercise to the reader.

See example 16.6 - LoggingLongPipeline

16.3.4 Re-arranging Actor Pipelines

The four actors in our last pipeline are defined as `class`es, with each class constructor taking a `cask.Actor[...]` reference. Defining our actors in this way gives us flexibility in how we want to arrange our pipeline: each actor doesn't need to know about the details of the other actors it is interacting with. It only needs to know what message type it expects to receive and the message type of the downstream actors it needs to send messages to.

For example, if we wanted to re-configure our 4-node pipeline to run without sanitizing credit card numbers, it is easy to remove `sanitizeActor` from the pipeline:

```scala
import $file.Classes, Classes._                                    LoggingPipeline.sc

implicit val cc = new castor.Context.Test()

val diskActor = new DiskActor(os.pwd / "log.txt")
val uploadActor = new UploadActor("https://httpbin.org/post")
val base64Actor = new Base64Actor(new castor.SplitActor(diskActor, uploadActor))

val logger = base64Actor                                           </> 16.23.scala
```

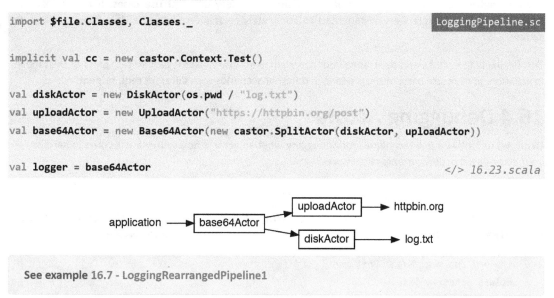

> See example 16.7 - LoggingRearrangedPipeline1

What if we wanted only the file logging to be base64 encoded, and only the HTTP logging to be sanitized? Again, it is straightforward to re-configure our actor pipeline to do this:

```scala
import $file.Classes, Classes._                                    LoggingPipeline.sc

implicit val cc = new castor.Context.Test()

val diskActor = new DiskActor(os.pwd / "log.txt")
val uploadActor = new UploadActor("https://httpbin.org/post")

val base64Actor = new Base64Actor(diskActor)
val sanitizeActor = new SanitizeActor(uploadActor)

val logger = new castor.SplitActor(base64Actor, sanitizeActor)     </> 16.24.scala
```

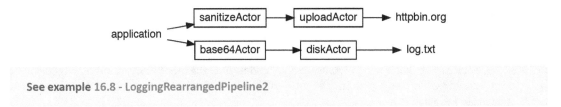

See example 16.8 - LoggingRearrangedPipeline2

As you can see, using actors to model your data processing pipelines allows a great deal of flexibility in how your pipelines will be laid out. Without any change to the implementation of individual actors, we have reconfigured our concurrent logging pipeline to support 4 very different use cases. It only took a tiny change in how the actors were instantiated to completely re-architect how the data flows through our system.

This flexibility to arrange and re-arrange your actor pipelines also makes it easy to test parts of the pipeline in isolation, or to re-use parts of the pipeline in different scenarios with different requirements.

16.4 Debugging Actors

Lastly, let us look at a few techniques for debugging what an actor is doing. These will come in handy when your actor-based code inevitably misbehaves!

16.4.1 Debug Logging State Machines

When using `StateMachineActor`, all your actor's internal state should be in the single `state` variable. You can thus easily override `def run` to print the state before and after each message is received:

```scala
override def run(msg: Msg): Unit = {
  println(s"$state + $msg -> ")
  super.run(msg)
  println(state)
}                                                              </> 16.25.scala
```

If your `StateMachineActor` is misbehaving, this should hopefully make it easier to trace what it is doing in response to each message, so you can figure out exactly why it is misbehaving. Here is the logging of the StateMachineUploadActor (*16.2.4*), where the logging prints out how the actor handles messages and transitions between states:

```scala
stateMachineUploader.send(Text("I am cow"))
// Idle() + Text(I am cow) ->
// Buffering(Vector(I am cow))
stateMachineUploader.send(Text("hear me moo"))
// Buffering(Vector(I am cow)) + Text(hear me moo) ->
// Buffering(Vector(I am cow, hear me moo))
Thread.sleep(100)
// Buffering(Vector(I am cow, hear me moo)) + Flush() ->
// Idle()                                                   </> 16.26.scala
```

Logging every message received and processed by one or more actors may get very verbose in a large system. You can use a conditional `if (...)` in your `override def` `run` to specify exactly which state transitions on which actors you care about (e.g. only actors handling a certain user ID) to cut down the noise:

```scala
override def run(msg: Msg): Unit = {
  if (...) println(s"$state + $msg -> ")
  super.run(msg)
  if (...) println(state)
}                                                           </> 16.27.scala
```

Note that if you have multiple actors sending messages to each other, by default they run on a thread pool and so the `println` messages above may become interleaved and hard to read. To resolve that, you can try running actors single threaded.

16.4.2 Running Actors Single Threaded

Another debugging strategy is to replace the `cask.Context` executor with a single-threaded executor. This can help our actor pipeline behave more deterministically:

```scala
implicit val cc = new castor.Context.TestThreadPool(1)
```

Any actor pipeline should be able to run on a single threaded executor. This makes it easier to track down logical bugs without multithreaded parallelism getting in the way.

16.4.3 Debugging using Context Logging

Apart from logging individual actors, you can also insert logging into the `castor.Context` to log state transitions or actions across *every* actor. For example, you can log every time a message is run on an actor by overriding the `reportRun` callback:

```scala
implicit val cc = new castor.Context.Test() {
  override def reportRun(a: castor.Actor[_],
                         msg: Any,
                         token: castor.Context.Token): Unit = {
    println(s"$a <- $msg")
    super.reportRun(a, msg, token)
  }
}
```
</> 16.28.scala

Running this on the four-actor pipeline example (*16.3.3*) from earlier, we can see the logging messages get interleaved as the different actors all run in parallel.

```
SanitizeActor@5ad26966 <- I am cow
SanitizeActor@5ad26966 <- hear me moo
Base64Actor@5578b956 <- I am cow
SanitizeActor@5ad26966 <- I weigh twice as much as you
SanitizeActor@5ad26966 <- And I look good on the barbecue
Base64Actor@5578b956 <- hear me moo
SanitizeActor@5ad26966 <- Yoghurt curds cream cheese and butter
castor.SplitActor@7cdcd738 <- SSBhbSBjb3c=
DiskActor@7aada8fd <- SSBhbSBjb3c=
SanitizeActor@5ad26966 <- Comes from liquids from my udder
UploadActor@775713fd <- SSBhbSBjb3c=
```
</> 16.29.output

By instrumenting the `castor.Context`, we can see the messages that are being sent and state transitions that are happening to all actors within our program. That can help greatly when you are not sure exactly which actor is the one that is misbehaving, and helps us visualize what our group of actors is doing. We can simplify the logging even further by also Running Actors Single-Threaded (*16.4.2*).

16.5 Conclusion

In this chapter, we have seen how to structure our code using actors. They allow us to process data concurrently, similar to what we did in *Chapter 13: Fork-Join Parallelism with Futures*, but with the following tradeoffs:

- Actors are a better fit for streaming computations, while futures are a better fit for request-response computations

- Actors always process data in the same order, whereas futures may run in an arbitrary order

- Actors ensure single-threaded access to mutable state, e.g. a log file on disk or an in-memory state machine, whereas futures work best without any mutable state

- Actors provide pipelined parallelism between *dependent* computations, whereas futures provide fork-join parallelism between *independent* computations

We have seen how we can easily construct actor pipelines of varying shape, where each stage of the pipeline processes the incoming messages in parallel, all without needing to deal with threads and locks ourselves.

Actors are a fundamental model of parallel computation, that together with the fork-join style provided by futures, is a valuable addition to your toolbox. Both models have their strengths and weaknesses, and Scala makes it very easy to pick the one that best fits the problem at hand.

This chapter makes use of the Castor actor library, which has its documentation online:

- https://github.com/lihaoyi/castor

In the wild you may encounter other projects using the Akka actor framework. This is a much larger and more complex framework than Castor, with much more to learn, but all the same concepts still apply:

- https://akka.io/

We will be making heavy use of actors and actor piplines later in *Chapter 18: Building a Real-time File Synchronizer*.

> **Exercise:** Use a single actor to implement an asynchronous web crawler using the same `fetchLinksAsync` method we saw in *Chapter 13: Fork-Join Parallelism with Futures*, but without the batch-by-batch limitation. The result of each HTTP request should be processed immediately once that requests completes, without waiting for all other requests in the same "batch", so that a single long-running request does not hold up the entire crawler. You will likely need to use the asynchronous Future operations together with the `sendAsync` method to integrate your actors with `fetchLinksAsync`'s futures.
>
> **See example** 16.9 - WebCrawler

Exercise: Combine the actor-based web crawler you wrote in the above exercise with the `DiskActor` we saw earlier in the chapter, to stream the crawled results to a file on disk in a simple pipeline.

See example 16.10 - WebCrawlerPipeline

Exercise: Add throttling to the actor-based web crawler above, to ensure it does not make more than a configurable `maxConcurrent: Int` open HTTP requests at a time.

See example 16.11 - WebCrawlerThrottled

Discuss Chapter 16 online at https://www.handsonscala.com/discuss/16

17

Multi-Process Applications

17.1 Two-Process Build Setup   330

17.2 Remote Procedure Calls   333

17.3 The Agent Process   336

17.4 The Sync Process   337

17.5 Pipelined Syncing   341

```scala
def send[T: Writer](out: DataOutputStream, msg: T): Unit = {
  val bytes = upickle.default.writeBinary(msg)
  out.writeInt(bytes.length)
  out.write(bytes)
  out.flush()
}
def receive[T: Reader](in: DataInputStream) = {
  val buf = new Array[Byte](in.readInt())
  in.readFully(buf)
  upickle.default.readBinary[T](buf)
}
```
</> 17.1.scala

Snippet 17.1: RPC send and receive methods for sending data over an operating system pipe or network

While all our programs so far have run within a single process, in real world scenarios you will be working as part of a larger system, and the application itself may need to be split into multiple processes. This chapter will walk you through how to do so: configuring your build tool to support multiple Scala processes, sharing code and exchanging serialized messages. These are the building blocks that form the foundation of any distributed system.

As this chapter's project, we will be building a simple multi-process file synchronizer that can work over a network. This chapter builds upon the simple single-process file synchronizer in *Chapter 7: Files and Subprocesses*, and will form the basis for *Chapter 18: Building a Real-time File Synchronizer*.

In *Chapter 7: Files and Subprocesses*, we learned how to work with the filesystem using Scala, and wrote a simple function that synchronizes the contents of two folders by comparing the files on each side and copying files as necessary from one to the other. However, there was one big limitation of the def sync function we wrote: it can only work if both src and dest folders are on the same computer! This is because it relies on having direct access to read and write to the files in both src and dest:

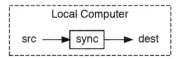

This of course rules out possibly the most common use case of file syncing: synchronizing the contents of a folder between two computers across a network. To allow for remote file syncing, we will need a slightly different approach:

- A sync process with direct access to the src/ folder will spawn an agent process with direct access to the dest folder

- When sync needs to query or perform some action on the dest/ folder, it will send a message to agent via the agent's standard input stream, and the agent will reply via its standard output stream

For the purposes of this exercise we will be running both sync and agent on the same computer, with the two processes connected by an operating system pipe:

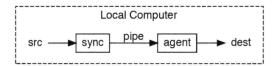

While the snippets in this chapter run both processes on the same computer, it is trivial to extend this to a remote scenario by e.g. spawning the child process over an SSH connection:

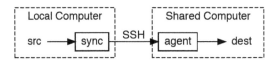

17.1 Two-Process Build Setup

We will set up this project using the Mill build tool. You can install Mill in your current project as follows:

```bash
$ curl -L https://github.com/lihaoyi/mill/releases/download/0.8.0/0.8.0 -o mill
$ chmod +x mill                                                    </> 17.2.bash
```

We will start with the following build.sc file:

```scala
import mill._, scalalib._                                                build.sc
trait SyncModule extends ScalaModule {
  def scalaVersion = "2.13.2"
  def ivyDeps = Agg(
    ivy"com.lihaoyi::upickle:1.2.0",
    ivy"com.lihaoyi::os-lib:0.7.1"
  )
}
object shared extends SyncModule
object sync extends SyncModule{
  def moduleDeps = Seq(shared)
}
object agent extends SyncModule{
  def moduleDeps = Seq(shared)
}
```
</> 17.3.scala

This build file defines two modules - `sync` and `agent` - each with their respective `sync/src/` and `agent/src/` folders. Both modules share the same Scala version and dependencies on the uPickle and OS-Lib libraries, as well as a dependency on a `shared` module with its corresponding `shared/src/` folder. You will need to manually create the `sync/src/`, `agent/src/` and `shared/src/` folders.

```
$ mkdir -p agent/src sync/src shared/src
```

You can then run `./mill mill.scalalib.GenIdea/idea` to load the project into your IDE:

17.1.1 Integrating our Simple File Syncer into Mill

First let us take the Ammonite REPL snippet we wrote in **Chapter 7: Files and Subprocesses** and integrate it into our Mill project. That involves taking the original def sync function and converting it into a proper def main(args: Array[String]) program entrypoint that takes its arguments from the command line:

```scala
-def sync(src: os.Path, dest: os.Path) = {                          sync/src/Sync.scala
+package sync
+object Sync {
+  def main(args: Array[String]): Unit = {
+    val src = os.Path(args(0), os.pwd)
+    val dest = os.Path(args(1), os.pwd)
    for (srcSubPath <- os.walk(src)) {
      val subPath = srcSubPath.subRelativeTo(src)
      val destSubPath = dest / subPath
      (os.isDir(srcSubPath), os.isDir(destSubPath)) match {
        case (false, true) | (true, false) => os.copy.over(srcSubPath, destSubPath)
        case (false, false)
          if !os.exists(destSubPath)
          || !os.read.bytes(srcSubPath).sameElements(os.read.bytes(destSubPath)) =>

          os.copy.over(srcSubPath, destSubPath, createFolders = true)

        case _ => // do nothing
      }
    }
  }
+}
```
</> 17.4.scala

17.1.2 Testing our File Syncer

We can then run the following script to package the compiled code into a self-contained executable, often called an `assembly`. Once packaged, we can run the executable manually to sync the files:

```
$ ./mill show sync.assembly
"ref:d5e08f13:/Users/lihaoyi/test/out/sync/assembly/dest/out.jar"

$ find sync -type f
sync/src/Sync.scala

$ mkdir test

$ out/sync/assembly/dest/out.jar sync test

$ find test -type f
test/src/Sync.scala
```
</> 17.5.bash

See example 17.1 - Main

17.2 Remote Procedure Calls

The next step is to take our various `os.*` calls in the `sync` process on the `dest` folder, and convert them into remote procedure calls (RPCs) that communicate with an `agent` process that can respond with the results. The calls we need to care about are:

- os.isDir(destSubPath)
- os.exists(destSubPath)
- os.read.bytes(destSubPath)
- os.copy.over(srcSubPath, destSubPath, createFolders = true)

To convert these into remote procedure calls, we need to define the messages that our two processes will exchange, and the protocol which the two processes will use to exchange them.

17.2.1 Defining our RPC Messages

We will put these messages in shared/src/Rpc.scala, since they will be used by both sync and agent processes:

```scala
package sync                                              shared/src/Rpc.scala
import upickle.default.{readwriter, ReadWriter, macroRW}
sealed trait Rpc
object Rpc{
  implicit val subPathRw = readwriter[String].bimap[os.SubPath](_.toString, os.SubPath(_))

  case class IsDir(path: os.SubPath) extends Rpc
  implicit val isDirRw: ReadWriter[IsDir] = macroRW

  case class Exists(path: os.SubPath) extends Rpc
  implicit val existsRw: ReadWriter[Exists] = macroRW

  case class ReadBytes(path: os.SubPath) extends Rpc
  implicit val readBytesRw: ReadWriter[ReadBytes] = macroRW

  case class WriteOver(src: Array[Byte], path: os.SubPath) extends Rpc
  implicit val writeOverRw: ReadWriter[WriteOver] = macroRW

  implicit val RpcRw: ReadWriter[Rpc] = macroRW
}                                                           </> 17.6.scala
```

Here we are defining Rpc as a sealed trait, because we know upfront that there are only a fixed number of messages we will want to pass between the sync and agent processes. For each case class, we define an implicit ReadWriter to allow serialization to JSON or messagepack binaries, as we saw earlier in ***Chapter 8: JSON and Binary Data Serialization***. We will need this in order to send them from one process to the other.

Note we also need to define a subPathRw, in order to handle the os.SubPaths that are part of the case classes we are serializing. Since os.SubPath can be easily converted to and from strings, we make use of bimap in order to convert our ReadWriter[String] into a ReadWriter[os.SubPath] for us to use.

17.2.2 Bytes over the Wire

Apart from the messages themselves, we need a standard way of sending and receiving `Rpc` messages between the two processes. Operating system processes communicate via "pipes", which are exposed to a Scala application as a `java.io.InputStream` you can read from and a `java.io.OutputStream` you can write to. These are streams of bytes, on top of which we'll need to define a protocol for sending our `case class` messages.

As our protocol for sending messages over these byte streams, we will send each message in a length-prefixed fashion: every message will be preceded by a single 4-byte `Int` that tells the `agent` how long that message is, allowing it to read the correct number of bytes to pass into `upickle.default.readBinary` to deserialize into an `Rpc` object:

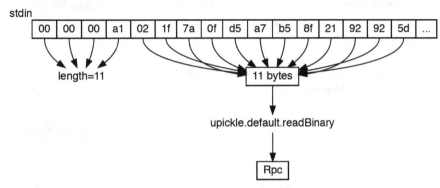

We assume that anyone receiving data over a stream of bytes will receive a constant stream of these messages, each one preceded by a 4-byte header telling it how many bytes that message contains. This can be implemented as follows:

```scala
package sync                                            shared/src/Shared.scala
import upickle.default.{Reader, Writer}
object Shared{
  def send[T: Writer](out: java.io.DataOutputStream, msg: T): Unit = {
    val bytes = upickle.default.writeBinary(msg)
    out.writeInt(bytes.length)
    out.write(bytes)
    out.flush()
  }
  def receive[T: Reader](in: java.io.DataInputStream) = {
    val buf = new Array[Byte](in.readInt())
    in.readFully(buf)
    upickle.default.readBinary[T](buf)
  }
}                                                              </> 17.7.scala
```

This protocol for sending messages via DataOutputStreams and receiving messages via DataInputStreams is implemented by the send and receive methods above. We use DataInputStreams and DataOutputStreams as they provide some conveniences e.g. for reading/writing 4-byte integers. We put this logic in shared/ because both the sync and agent processes will need to send messages to one another.

17.3 The Agent Process

Now that we've defined the case classes that will represent our RPCs, we can now implement our agent process. At a high level, the agent process does the following steps:

1. Read an Rpc from the sync process
2. Perform whatever action the Rpc wants it to do: read some bytes, over-write a file, etc.
3. Return any result to the sync process
4. Read the next message

We need some way to exchange data. The sync process that spawns agent will have access to agent's System.in and System.out streams, so we can use those two streams to exchange data between the two processes:

```scala
package sync                                            agent/src/Agent.scala
object Agent {
  def main(args: Array[String]): Unit = {
    val input = new java.io.DataInputStream(System.in)
    val output = new java.io.DataOutputStream(System.out)
    while (true) try {
      val rpc = Shared.receive[Rpc](input)
    } catch {case e: java.io.EOFException => System.exit(0)}
  }
}
                                                        </> 17.8.scala
```

Above, we wrap System.in and System.out in a DataInputStream and DataOutputStream respectively, to be compatible with the send/receive methods we defined earlier. Inside a loop, we call receive to read a single Rpc worth of bytes from sync and deserialize it into an Rpc object.

Lastly, we match on the rpc, and do what it tells us to do, and write the result back to sync using Shared.send:

```
    while (true) try {                                              agent/src/Agent.scala
      val rpc = Shared.receive[Rpc](input)
+     rpc match {
+       case Rpc.IsDir(path) => Shared.send(output, os.isDir(os.pwd / path))
+       case Rpc.Exists(path) => Shared.send(output, os.exists(os.pwd / path))
+       case Rpc.ReadBytes(path) => Shared.send(output, os.read.bytes(os.pwd / path))
+       case Rpc.WriteOver(bytes, path) =>
+         os.remove.all(os.pwd / path)
+         Shared.send(output, os.write.over(os.pwd / path, bytes, createFolders = true))
+     }
    } catch {case e: java.io.EOFException => System.exit(0)}
  }
}                                                                        </> 17.9.scala
```

For now, we assume that the agent process is spawned with its `os.pwd` set to the destination folder we want to sync files to.

The `try-catch` block around the body of the `while` loop makes sure that when the `sync` process terminates, the `agent` process exits cleanly without a stack trace. Our two-process file synchronizer can still work without the `try-catch`, but will print an ugly stack trace to the console when syncing is complete and the Agent shuts down.

The `agent` process is intentionally kept simple, running operations on behalf of the `sync` process that it is not able to run itself. The agent only knows how to handle one operation at a time, report the result, and nothing else: the complexity will live in the `sync` process, which we will cover next.

17.4 The Sync Process

17.4.1 Spawning the Agent

First, we need to give `sync` access to the `agent` executable. We can do this by adding `agent.assembly` to `sync`'s resources in `build.sc`:

```
object sync extends SyncModule{                                            build.sc
  def moduleDeps = Seq(shared)
+ def resources = T.sources{
+   os.copy(agent.assembly().path, T.dest / "agent.jar")
+   super.resources() ++ Seq(PathRef(T.dest))
+ }
}                                                                       </> 17.10.scala
```

This ensures that whenever the `sync` module is packaged and run, the `agent`'s `assembly` executable is prepared and ready to be loaded for use as `agent.jar`. We can then use `os.read.bytes` in `sync`'s Scala code to load the binary contents of `agent.jar`, write it to a file, and execute it via `os.proc.spawn` to create a child process we can communicate with:

```
    val src = os.Path(args(0), os.pwd)                          sync/src/Sync.scala
    val dest = os.Path(args(1), os.pwd)
+   val agentExecutable = os.temp(os.read.bytes(os.resource / "agent.jar"))
+   os.perms.set(agentExecutable, "rwx------")
+   val agent = os.proc(agentExecutable).spawn(cwd = dest)
    for (srcSubPath <- os.walk(src)) {
      val subPath = srcSubPath.subRelativeTo(src)
      val destSubPath = dest / subPath                          </> 17.11.scala
```

This gives us a `val` `agent` that represents the running `agent` subprocess, which is a `os.SubProcess` object like those in ***Chapter 7: Files and Subprocesses***. Note that we need to write the `agent.jar` to a temporary file before executing it, as on the JVM packaged resource files are zipped into the enclosing `sync` executable and cannot be executed directly.

To make it more convenient to exchange messages with `agent`, we define a `callAgent` function that writes a message to `agent` using `send`, and reads the agent's response using `receive`:

```
    val agent = os.proc(agentExecutable).spawn(cwd = dest)      sync/src/Sync.scala
+   def callAgent[T: upickle.default.Reader](rpc: Rpc): T = {
+     Shared.send(agent.stdin.data, rpc)
+     Shared.receive[T](agent.stdout.data)
+   }
    for (srcSubPath <- os.walk(src)) {                          </> 17.12.scala
```

`callAgent` is parameterized on the type `T` that we expect in response to the `Rpc` we send, and `T` must be a type with a pre-defined `upickle.default.Reader`.

17.4.2 Delegating File Operations

Next, we need to update the filesystem walk-compare-copy logic to change all `os.*` calls that operate on the `dest` path to instead use `callAgent` to ask the `agent` process to do the work for us:

```scala
                                                                    sync/src/Sync.scala
      val subPath = srcSubPath.subRelativeTo(src)
      val destSubPath = dest / subPath
-     (os.isDir(srcSubPath), os.isDir(destSubPath)) match {
+     (os.isDir(srcSubPath), callAgent[Boolean](Rpc.IsDir(subPath))) match {
-       case (false, true) | (true, false) => os.copy.over(srcSubPath, destSubPath)
+       case (false, true) =>
+         callAgent[Unit](Rpc.WriteOver(os.read.bytes(srcSubPath), subPath))
+       case (true, false) =>
+         for (p <- os.walk(srcSubPath) if os.isFile(p)) {
+           callAgent[Unit](Rpc.WriteOver(os.read.bytes(p), p.subRelativeTo(src)))
+         }
        case (false, false)
-         if !os.exists(destSubPath)
-         || !os.read.bytes(srcSubPath).sameElements(os.read.bytes(destSubPath)) =>
+         if !callAgent[Boolean](Rpc.Exists(subPath))
+         || !os.read.bytes(srcSubPath).sameElements(
+             callAgent[Array[Byte]](Rpc.ReadBytes(subPath))
+         ) =>

-         os.copy.over(srcSubPath, destSubPath, createFolders = true)
+         callAgent[Unit](Rpc.WriteOver(os.read.bytes(srcSubPath), subPath))

        case _ => // do nothing
      }
                                                                         </> 17.13.scala
```

This is a relatively mechanical change, except for the `(true, false)` case: this is the case where a local path is a folder but the remote path is not. Previously we were relying on `os.copy.over` to recursively copy the source folder over the destination, but now we have to manually send individual `WriteOver` commands, one for each file in the source folder, to make sure they all get copied to the destination.

17.4.3 Working Syncer

The working Sync.scala code we have written now looks like this:

```scala
package sync
object Sync {
  def main(args: Array[String]): Unit = {
    val src = os.Path(args(0), os.pwd)
    val dest = os.Path(args(1), os.pwd)
    val agentExecutable = os.temp(os.read.bytes(os.resource / "agent.jar"))
    os.perms.set(agentExecutable, "rwx------")
    val agent = os.proc(agentExecutable).spawn(cwd = dest)
    def callAgent[T: upickle.default.Reader](rpc: Rpc): T = {
      Shared.send(agent.stdin.data, rpc)
      Shared.receive[T](agent.stdout.data)
    }
    for (srcSubPath <- os.walk(src)) {
      val subPath = srcSubPath.subRelativeTo(src)
      val destSubPath = dest / subPath
      (os.isDir(srcSubPath), callAgent[Boolean](Rpc.IsDir(subPath))) match {
        case (false, true) =>
          callAgent[Unit](Rpc.WriteOver(os.read.bytes(srcSubPath), subPath))
        case (true, false) =>
          for (p <- os.walk(srcSubPath) if os.isFile(p)) {
            callAgent[Unit](Rpc.WriteOver(os.read.bytes(p), p.subRelativeTo(src)))
          }
        case (false, false)
          if !callAgent[Boolean](Rpc.Exists(subPath))
            || !os.read.bytes(srcSubPath).sameElements(
            callAgent[Array[Byte]](Rpc.ReadBytes(subPath))
          ) =>

          callAgent[Unit](Rpc.WriteOver(os.read.bytes(srcSubPath), subPath))

        case _ => // do nothing
      }
    }
  }
}
```

We can test this new multi-process application with both `agent` and `sync`, as we saw earlier in Testing our File Syncer (*17.1.2*), to verify that it works similarly to the earlier one-process version. The big difference is that now the only point of contact between `agent` and `sync` is the `agent`'s `stdin` and `stdout`.

This split makes it possible to take the two processes and have them run on different computers: e.g. `sync` may run on your laptop, and `agent` may run on a cloud server you are trying to sync files to. As long as you can provide a `stdin`/`stdout` interface (e.g. by running the `agent` over SSH) you would now be able to sync files across the network.

> **See example 17.2 - FileSyncer**

17.5 Pipelined Syncing

While we now have a simple two-process network-compatible file synchronizer, it behaves roughly the same way as our original one-process file synchronizer: for each file in the source folder, it reads the file on the destination folder, compares the two, and copies the source file over the destination if necessary. While this works, it is an exceedingly "chatty" protocol: the syncer needs to make multiple network round trips in order to sync each file:

- 2 round trips if the local file corresponds to a remote directory
- 2 round trips for each file in a local folder that doesn't exist remotely
- 3 round trips for a file that exists locally but not remotely
- 4 round trips for a file that exists both locally and remotely, but differs in contents

The round trips of the "file exists locally but not remotely" case can be visualized as follows:

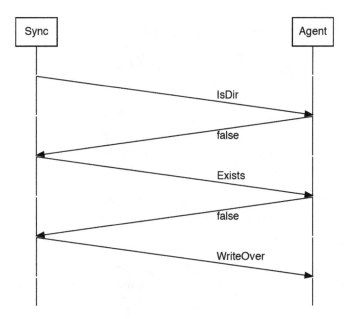

This is repeated over and over for every file in the source folder.

Network round trips are slow, and a fast file syncer must aim to minimize the number of trips we require. The technique we need is *Pipelining*: rather than waiting for every RPC to complete before proceeding with further work, we instead send our RPCs en-masse without waiting, and then aggregate all the responses as they are streamed back. This can allow $O(n)$ RPCs to be made at the cost of only a single round trip's worth of network latency.

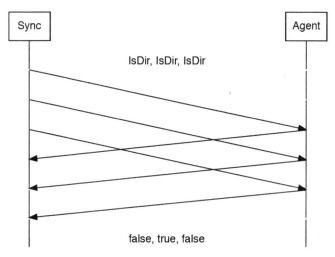

17.5.1 Pipelining RPCs

The first major change is to tweak the definition of `callAgent`:

```
- def callAgent[T: upickle.default.Reader](rpc: Rpc): T = {          sync/src/Sync.scala
+ def callAgent[T: upickle.default.Reader](rpc: Rpc): () => T = {
    Shared.send(agent.stdin.data, rpc)
-   Shared.receive[T](agent.stdout.data)
+   () => Shared.receive[T](agent.stdout.data)
  }                                                                  </> 17.15.scala
```

Instead of immediately reading a response to deserialize and return as T, we now delay reading and instead return a zero-argument function of type `() => T` that you can call to read and deserialize the response later. This lets the caller of `callAgent` decide when they want to call it:

- They could wait for a response immediately by calling the function
- Or they could send a number of `Rpc`s over to the agent, store the functions in a `Buffer`, and only later call every function to wait for all the responses to complete and aggregate their results

Next, we need a way to batch our usage of `callAgent`, since we want all our RPCs (whether `Rpc.Exists`, `Rpc.IsDir`, `Rpc.ReadBytes`, or `Rpc.WriteOver`) to be pipelined. We can do this with a `pipelineCalls` function:

```
   def main(args: Array[String]): Unit = {

   ...

   def callAgent[T: upickle.default.Reader](rpc: Rpc): () => T = ...
+  val subPaths = os.walk(src).map(_.subRelativeTo(src))
+  def pipelineCalls[T: upickle.default.Reader](rpcFor: os.SubPath => Option[Rpc]) = {
+    val buffer = collection.mutable.Buffer.empty[(os.RelPath, () => T)]
+    for (p <- subPaths; rpc <- rpcFor(p)) buffer.append((p, callAgent[T](rpc)))
+    buffer.map{case (k, v) => (k, v())}.toMap
+  }
-  for (srcSubPath <- os.walk(src)) { ... }
   }                                                                        </> 17.16.scala
```

This function walks over the subPaths, and for each path it calls rpcFor to create an Rpc that it sends to the agent (rpcFor can return None indicating no message should be sent for a particular path). After all messages have been sent, it then calls the buffered () => T functions to wait for all of the responses, and collects them into a Map for convenience.

Note that once we send over a batch of Rpcs to the agent, it immediately starts performing the specified actions one after the other, and sending responses back to the host process as each action completes. Calling the returned () => T function is for the *host process* to wait until a particular Rpc has been processed and its response received, but the actual processing has already started happening asynchronously in the agent.

17.5.2 Batching Pipelined Filesystem Operations

We can now write our syncing logic in terms of pipelineCalls:

```
   def main(args: Array[String]): Unit = {                         sync/src/Sync.scala

   ...

   def pipelineCalls[T: upickle.default.Reader](rpcFor: os.SubPath => Option[Rpc]) = ...
+  val existsMap = pipelineCalls[Boolean](p => Some(Rpc.Exists(p)))
+  val isDirMap = pipelineCalls[Boolean](p => Some(Rpc.IsDir(p)))
+  val readMap = pipelineCalls[Array[Byte]]{p =>
+    if (existsMap(p) && !isDirMap(p)) Some(Rpc.ReadBytes(p))
+    else None
+  }
+  pipelineCalls[Unit]{ p =>
+    if (os.isDir(src / p)) None
+    else {
+      val localBytes = os.read.bytes(src / p)
+      if (readMap.get(p).exists(java.util.Arrays.equals(_, localBytes))) None
+      else Some(Rpc.WriteOver(localBytes, p))
+    }
+  }
   }                                                                        </> 17.17.scala
```

Essentially, `pipelineCalls` lets us turn our individual path-by-path RPCs into batch streaming RPCs that operate on the entire folder tree, while only paying for a single network round trip. Rather than interleaving the calls to `Exists`, `IsDir`, `ReadBytes` and `WriteOver`, we now perform them all en-masse: first make all the `Exists` calls, then all the `IsDir` calls, `ReadBytes` calls, `WriteOver` calls.

The final pipelined version of `Sync.scala` is now as follows:

```scala
package sync                                                    sync/src/Sync.scala
object Sync {
  def main(args: Array[String]): Unit = {
    val src = os.Path(args(0), os.pwd)
    val dest = os.Path(args(1), os.pwd)
    val agentExecutable = os.temp(os.read.bytes(os.resource / "agent.jar"))
    os.perms.set(agentExecutable, "rwx------")
    val agent = os.proc(agentExecutable).spawn(cwd = dest)
    def callAgent[T: upickle.default.Reader](rpc: Rpc): () => T = {
      Shared.send(agent.stdin.data, rpc)
      () => Shared.receive[T](agent.stdout.data)
    }
    val subPaths = os.walk(src).map(_.subRelativeTo(src))
    def pipelineCalls[T: upickle.default.Reader](rpcFor: os.SubPath => Option[Rpc]) = {
      val buffer = collection.mutable.Buffer.empty[(os.RelPath, () => T)]
      for (p <- subPaths; rpc <- rpcFor (p)) buffer.append((p, callAgent[T](rpc)))
      buffer.map{case (k, v) => (k, v())}.toMap
    }
    val existsMap = pipelineCalls[Boolean](p => Some(Rpc.Exists(p)))
    val isDirMap = pipelineCalls[Boolean](p => Some(Rpc.IsDir(p)))
    val readMap = pipelineCalls[Array[Byte]]{p =>
      if (existsMap(p) && !isDirMap(p)) Some(Rpc.ReadBytes(p))
      else None
    }
    pipelineCalls[Unit]{ p =>
      if (os.isDir(src / p)) None
      else {
        val localBytes = os.read.bytes(src / p)
        if (readMap.get(p).exists(java.util.Arrays.equals(_, localBytes))) None
        else Some(Rpc.WriteOver(localBytes, p))
      }
    }
  }
}                                                                  </> 17.18.scala
```

While pipelining may incur additional overhead (e.g. CPU time to construct these `Maps` and memory to store them) it reduces our previously *O(number-of-files)* network round trips to just *O(4)*. Perhaps not a big deal when syncing files locally, but much more significant if you're syncing files over a network and each round trip is 100s of milliseconds!

You can test this pipelined implementation the same way we tested the naive two-process implementation earlier. The final code for `Sync.scala` is as follows:

See example 17.3 - Pipelined

17.6 Conclusion

In this chapter, we have walked through how to build a simple multi-process Scala application, by taking the simple local file synchronizer we built earlier and turning it into a pipelined multi-process file synchronizer. To do so, we replaced direct calls to `os.*` functions with RPCs that send `case class` instances of type `Rpc` over to a remote agent process, serialized as length-prefixed MessagePack binaries, and the agent process handles each message and returns a response.

Finally, we re-architected the synchronization logic to pipeline it: rather than interleaving many calls to local and remote operations and waiting for each one to complete, we perform our remote filesystem operations en-masse in a streaming fashion. This involved sending multiple RPCs over to the agent without waiting for a response, and then only after all RPCs have been sent do we wait for them all and aggregate the responses.

This chapter should have given you a good intuition for how serialization of messages and remote procedure calls can be used to coordinate work in a multi-process Scala application. Data serialization, message passing, and RPCs of some kind are the foundation on which all distributed systems are built. While you may bump into a range of other libraries or frameworks in the wild, the general principles would be the same.

This file synchronizer is still relatively simple, with many limitations. One such limitation is that it is a batch program: we run it once, it processes and syncs all the files, and then terminates. Often, what a user wants is a real-time file synchronizer, that constantly keeps the local and remote filesystems in sync even as the local files keep changing. This is something we will re-visit in *Chapter 18: Building a Real-time File Synchronizer*.

> **Exercise:** Modify the multi-process file synchronizer from this chapter to support deletions: any file or folder that is present in the destination folder and not present in the source folder should be deleted from the destination when the synchronizer is run.
>
> **See example** 17.4 - Deletes

Exercise: In distributed multi-process applications the greatest bottleneck is often the latency and bandwidth of the network. Add Gzip compression to the data we are exchanging between `Sync` and `Agent` by wrapping the subprocess' input and output streams in `java.util.zip.GZIPInputStream` and `GZIPOutputStream`.

Make sure construct the `GZIPOutputStream` with `syncFlush = true` to avoid unwanted buffering, and that the `GZIPInputStreams` are only constructed once some data has been written to the other end of the stream. You may find Scala's `lazy val` syntax useful, as a convenient way to define `val`s whose evaluation is deferred until they are referenced.

See example 17.5 - Gzip

Exercise: Use `ssh` to run the `Agent` process on a separate computer, allowing the program to synchronize files over to a remote computer over the network.

You can use `ssh` ‹host› ‹cmd› to run a command on a remote host, and invoke that via `os.proc().call()` or `os.proc().spawn()` to do so from your Scala codebase. Note that you will need to install java on the remote host, copy the `agent.jar` over e.g. via `scp`, and any local commands like `mkdir` or `os.perms.set` will need to be run on the remote computer via `ssh`.

See example 17.6 - Ssh

Discuss Chapter 17 online at https://www.handsonscala.com/discuss/17

18

Building a Real-time File Synchronizer

18.1 Watching for Changes   348

18.2 Real-time Syncing with Actors   349

18.3 Testing the Syncer   357

18.4 Pipelined Real-time Syncing   358

18.5 Testing the Pipelined Syncer   361

```scala
object SyncActor extends castor.SimpleActor[Msg]{
  def run(msg: Msg): Unit = msg match {
    case ChangedPath(value) => Shared.send(agent.stdin.data, Rpc.StatPath(value))
    case AgentResponse(Rpc.StatInfo(p, remoteHash)) =>
      val localHash = Shared.hashPath(src / p)
      if (localHash != remoteHash && localHash.isDefined) {
        Shared.send(agent.stdin.data, Rpc.WriteOver(os.read.bytes(src / p), p))
      }
  }
}
                                                                  </> 18.1.scala
```

Snippet 18.1: an actor used as part of our real-time file synchronizer

In this chapter, we will write a file synchronizer that can keep the destination folder up to date even as the source folder changes over time. This chapter serves as a capstone project, tying together concepts from *Chapter 17: Multi-Process Applications* and *Chapter 16: Message-based Parallelism with Actors*.

The techniques in this chapter form the basis for "event driven" architectures, which are common in many distributed systems. Real-time file synchronization is a difficult problem, and we will see how we can use the Scala language and libraries to approach it in an elegant and understandable way.

The file synchronizers we have seen in previous chapters were fundamentally *batch* processes. They assume all the files on disk are static, read all files in the source and destination folders, compare them, and decide which files they need to sync over. Both the single-process and multi-process versions of our file synchronizer worked the same way, except in the multi-process version we had to make RPCs to the `agent` process to perform actions such as querying or writing files to the destination folder.

This batch syncing works well for some usage patterns - such as one off or nightly filesystem backups - but less well for folders with many small changes you want to sync over quickly. In such a scenario, our batch syncer would repeatedly walk the entire folder and scan large numbers of unchanged files only to perform a small number of useful changes. This can greatly slow down the process of syncing one small change from the source folder to the destination.

18.1 Watching for Changes

The key to converting our batch file syncer into an efficient real-time version is the os.watch API:

```
os.watch.watch(roots: Seq[os.Path], onEvent: Set[os.Path] => Unit): Unit
```

- https://github.com/lihaoyi/os-lib#oswatchwatch

`os.watch` allows you to register an `onEvent` listener on one or more root folders: every time a file or folder is changed within one of those folders, `onEvent` is called with the path to the changed file. This allows you to efficiently detect changes within a folder, without needing to repeatedly scan the contents of files and folders to see if anything changed.

`os.watch` uses FSEvents on OS-X, and relies on the JVM's builtin support for inotify on Linux or WSL2. At time of writing, it does not support watching for file changes on Windows.

You can import this API in the Ammonite REPL to try it out, registering a watch and then performing filesystem actions to see the watch get triggered.

```
@ import $ivy.`com.lihaoyi::os-lib-watch:0.7.1`

@ os.makeDir(os.pwd / "out")

@ os.watch.watch(
    Seq(os.pwd / "out"),
    paths => println("paths changed: " + paths.mkString(", "))
  )

@ os.write(os.pwd / "out" / "i am", "cow")
paths changed: /Users/lihaoyi/test/out/i am

@ os.move(os.pwd / "out"/ "i am", os.pwd / "out" / "hear me")
paths changed: /Users/lihaoyi/test/out/i am,/Users/lihaoyi/test/out/hear me</> 18.2.scala
```

Note that `os.watch` spawns a separate thread to watch the filesystem and call the `onEvent` callback. Thus you need to make sure the `onEvent` callback is safe to run in a multi-threaded environment.

18.2 Real-time Syncing with Actors

18.2.1 Architecture

At a high level, our real-time file synchronizer will be architected as follows:

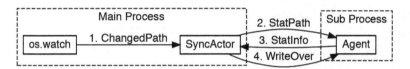

1. First, we feed the results of `os.watch`'s `onEvent` callback into `SyncActor`. This is an actor that processes incoming messages one at a time

2. Next, `SyncActor` will send a `StatPath` message to the `Agent` to ask for the hash for the file at a particular path

3. `Agent` will query the destination folder for the hash of that path, and return it as a `StatInfo` message to `SyncActor`

4. `SyncActor` compares the source and destination hashes. If they differ, `SyncActor` sends `WriteOver` messages to `Agent`, containing the contents of files we wish to copy over

Rather than treating the file synchronizer as a one-off program that reads data, performs some action, and then exits, we are treating it as a pipeline: for every file change in the source folder, it will go through these steps. Thus it doesn't matter if the files continue changing while our sync is in progress, or if more files change after the sync is complete: we can feed those file changes through the same pipeline and bring the destination folder up to date.

The insight here is that the various files we are syncing are *mostly* independent, but steps like sending messages to the `Agent` need to happen in a single-threaded fashion, and updates to any particular file need to have their order preserved. This makes it a good problem to model using Actors.

Note that the fact that `SyncActor` is an actor handling messages one after another is important. `SyncActor` is receiving messages from two different sources concurrently - both `os.watch` and `Agent` - while also executing its own logic. Making it an actor ensures that these messages are processed sequentially, letting us avoid thinking about race conditions, memory models and other multi-threading-related issues.

18.2.2 Build Configuration

First, let's define our `build.sc` file:

```scala
import mill._, scalalib._                                                      build.sc
trait SyncModule extends ScalaModule {
  def scalaVersion = "2.13.2"
  def ivyDeps = Agg(
    ivy"com.lihaoyi::upickle:1.2.0",
    ivy"com.lihaoyi::os-lib:0.7.1",
    ivy"com.lihaoyi::os-lib-watch:0.7.1",
    ivy"com.lihaoyi::castor:0.1.7"
  )
}
object sync extends SyncModule{
  def moduleDeps = Seq(shared)
  def resources = T.sources{
    os.copy(agent.assembly().path, T.dest / "agent.jar")
    super.resources() ++ Seq(PathRef(T.dest))
  }
}
object agent extends SyncModule{
  def moduleDeps = Seq(shared)
}
object shared extends SyncModule
```
</> 18.3.scala

This is the configuration used by the Mill build tool to compile our code. It defines three modules: `sync`, `agent`, and `shared`. The configuration is mostly similar to that used in **Chapter 17: Multi-Process Applications**, except for the addition of two external dependencies:

- `com.lihaoyi::os-lib-watch:0.7.1`: this provides the filesystem-watching functionality we will use to detect changes in the source folder we need to sync to the destination

- `com.lihaoyi::castor:0.1.7`: this is a small actor library, introduced in **Chapter 16: Message-based Parallelism with Actors**, that we will use to set up our actor pipelines

Next, we need to download the Mill launcher:

```bash
$ curl -L https://github.com/lihaoyi/mill/releases/download/0.8.0/0.8.0 -o mill

$ chmod +x mill
```
</> 18.4.bash

You can then use `./mill mill.scalalib.GenIdea/idea` to generate an IntelliJ config, `echo "0.8.0" > .mill-version` to import it into VSCode, `./mill __.compile` to compile everything, or `./mill show sync.assembly` to create an executable that you can run. This is similar to what we saw in ***Chapter 17: Multi-Process Applications***.

18.2.3 Shared Code

Next, let us define the shared code and messages that will be passed between the `Agent` and the `SyncActor` over the wire:

```scala
package sync                                                    shared/src/Rpc.scala
import upickle.default.{ReadWriter, macroRW, readwriter}


sealed trait Rpc
object Rpc{
  implicit val subPathRw = readwriter[String].bimap[os.SubPath](_.toString, os.SubPath(_))

  case class StatPath(path: os.SubPath) extends Rpc
  implicit val statPathRw: ReadWriter[StatPath] = macroRW

  case class WriteOver(src: Array[Byte], path: os.SubPath) extends Rpc
  implicit val writeOverRw: ReadWriter[WriteOver] = macroRW

  case class StatInfo(p: os.SubPath, fileHash: Option[Int])
  implicit val statInfoRw: ReadWriter[StatInfo] = macroRW

  implicit val msgRw: ReadWriter[Rpc] = macroRW
}                                                                </> 18.5.scala
```

The main things to note are:

- `sealed trait Rpc`, which represents all messages that can be sent from `SyncActor` to `Agent`. There are two: `case class StatPath` asking for the metadata of a path in the destination folder, and `case class WriteOver` telling it to place a file's contents at a particular path

- `case class StatInfo`, which represents the metadata about a particular path that the `Agent` will return to the `SyncActor` in response to the `StatPath` command. For now, it just contains the hash of the file contents at that path (if any) and the path itself

- `implicit val subPathRw`, which we use to make `os.SubPath`s serializable. This is similar to what we did in ***Chapter 17: Multi-Process Applications***

We re-use the same wire protocol, and `send` and `receive` methods, that we used earlier in ***Chapter 17: Multi-Process Applications***:

```scala
package sync
import upickle.default.{Reader, Writer}
object Shared{
  def send[T: Writer](out: java.io.DataOutputStream, msg: T): Unit = {
    val bytes = upickle.default.writeBinary(msg)
    out.writeInt(bytes.length)
    out.write(bytes)
    out.flush()
  }
  def receive[T: Reader](in: java.io.DataInputStream) = {
    val buf = new Array[Byte](in.readInt())
    in.readFully(buf)
    upickle.default.readBinary[T](buf)
  }
  def hashPath(p: os.Path) = {
    if (!os.isFile(p)) None
    else Some(java.util.Arrays.hashCode(os.read.bytes(p)))
  }
}
```

</> 18.6.scala

This implements the same wire protocol we saw earlier: we send messages by first sending the length of
the message as a 4-byte integer, followed by the messagepack-serialized binary blob that uPickle converts
the message classes into. We also define a shared `hashPath` method, which hashes the contents of a file at
a particular path, if one exists. This is used in both `Agent` and `SyncActor`, since we need to compare the
hash of the file in source and destination folders to decide if it needs to be copied.

18.2.4 Agent

Next, we will define our `Agent`. This will run on the destination side of our file synchronizer (possibly across the network), receive commands from the `sync` process and respond with results:

```scala
package sync                                                    agent/src/Agent.scala
object Agent {
  def main(args: Array[String]): Unit = {
    val input = new java.io.DataInputStream(System.in)
    val output = new java.io.DataOutputStream(System.out)
    while (true) try {
      val rpc = Shared.receive[Rpc](input)
      System.err.println("Agent handling: " + rpc)
      rpc match {
        case Rpc.StatPath(path) =>
          Shared.send(output, Rpc.StatInfo(path, Shared.hashPath(os.pwd / path)))

        case Rpc.WriteOver(bytes, path) =>
          os.remove.all(os.pwd / path)
          os.write.over(os.pwd / path, bytes, createFolders = true)
      }
    } catch { case e: java.io.EOFException => System.exit(0) }
  }
}
                                                                  </> 18.7.scala
```

Our `Agent` is somewhat simpler than that in **Chapter 17**, due to the smaller set of `Rpc` messages it needs to handle. Our `Rpc.StatPath` message is enough to replace the trio of `Rpc.IsDir`, `Rpc.Exists` and `Rpc.ReadBytes` that we were using before

We use `System.err.println` to add some logging of what the Agent is doing. The Agent subprocess inherits the `stderr` of the host process by default, making it an ideal channel to send debug logging or other diagnostics without interfering with the main data exchange happening over `System.in` and `System.out`.

18.2.5 Sync

Lastly, we will define the main entry-point of our program, `Sync.scala`.

18.2.5.1 Initializing the Agent

```
package sync                                              sync/src/Sync.scala
object Sync {
  def main(args: Array[String]): Unit = {
    val (src, dest) = (os.Path(args(0), os.pwd), os.Path(args(1), os.pwd))
    val agentExecutable = os.temp(os.read.bytes(os.resource / "agent.jar"))
    os.perms.set(agentExecutable, "rwx------")
    val agent = os.proc(agentExecutable).spawn(cwd = dest)
  }
}
                                                              </> 18.8.scala
```

We define a simple `main` method, parse the first two command-line args into `src` and `dest` paths, and spawn the agent. This is again similar to what we did in ***Chapter 17: Multi-Process Applications***. Note that by default `.spawn` forwards the standard error stream of the subprocess directly to the host process' standard error, so the `System.err.println` logging output in `Agent.scala` will show up in the console when `Sync.scala` is run.

18.2.5.2 SyncActor Messages

Before we define the implementation of `SyncActor`, let us consider the messages the actor will send and receive. As stated earlier, it will receive `ChangedPath` messages from the `os.watch` thread, and `Rpc.StatInfo` responses from the Agent.

```
    def main(args: Array[String]): Unit = {                sync/src/Sync.scala
      ...
+     sealed trait Msg
+     case class ChangedPath(value: os.SubPath) extends Msg
+     case class AgentResponse(value: Rpc.StatInfo) extends Msg
    }
                                                              </> 18.9.scala
```

We wrap the `Rpc.StatInfos` in an `AgentResponse` class to make it part of our `Msg` hierarchy.

18.2.5.3 SyncActor

`SyncActor` is a `castor.SimpleActor[Msg]`. For now, we only have one `SyncActor`, so we make it a singleton `object` for simplicity. `SyncActor` is the only thing writing to `agent.stdin`, which is important because its single-threaded nature ensures messages are written to `agent.stdin` one after another and not all jumbled together.

```scala
import castor.Context.Simple.global                         sync/src/Sync.scala
object SyncActor extends castor.SimpleActor[Msg]{
  def run(msg: Msg): Unit = {
    println("SyncActor handling: " + msg)
    msg match {
      case ChangedPath(value) => Shared.send(agent.stdin.data, Rpc.StatPath(value))
      case AgentResponse(Rpc.StatInfo(p, remoteHash)) =>
        val localHash = Shared.hashPath(src / p)
        if (localHash != remoteHash && localHash.isDefined) {
          Shared.send(agent.stdin.data, Rpc.WriteOver(os.read.bytes(src / p), p))
        }
    }
  }
}
```
                                                                    </> 18.10.scala

ChangedPath messages are forwarded directly to the agent as StatPath commands, while the
Rpc.StatInfo responses are then used to decide whether or not a file needs to be synced. If the hashes of
the source and destination files differ, and the file exists locally, we sync it using an Rpc.WriteOver message
containing the bytes of the file.

18.2.5.4 agentReader and os.watch

The last section of Sync.scala involves two threads we are spinning up:

```scala
val agentReader = new Thread(() => {                        sync/src/Sync.scala
  while (agent.isAlive()) {
    SyncActor.send(AgentResponse(Shared.receive[Rpc.StatInfo](agent.stdout.data)))
  }
})
agentReader.start()
val watcher = os.watch.watch(
  Seq(src),
  onEvent = _.foreach(p => SyncActor.send(ChangedPath(p.subRelativeTo(src))))
)
Thread.sleep(Long.MaxValue)
```
                                                                    </> 18.11.scala

- agentReader reads StatInfo responses from agent.stdout, and sends them to SyncActor
- watcher reads file changes from the filesystem, and sends the ChangedPaths to SyncActor

Both of these threads are running concurrently. However, because each thread's input is only read by that
thread, and each thread sends its output to an actor, we can be confident that we won't have any
multithreading issues here. After starting the two threads, we make the main method Thread.sleep while
the syncer runs in the background so the program does not terminate prematurely.

The complete implementation of Sync.scala is as follows:

```scala
package sync
object Sync {
  def main(args: Array[String]): Unit = {
    val (src, dest) = (os.Path(args(0), os.pwd), os.Path(args(1), os.pwd))
    val agentExecutable = os.temp(os.read.bytes(os.resource / "agent.jar"))
    os.perms.set(agentExecutable, "rwx------")
    val agent = os.proc(agentExecutable).spawn(cwd = dest)
    sealed trait Msg
    case class ChangedPath(value: os.SubPath) extends Msg
    case class AgentResponse(value: Rpc.StatInfo) extends Msg
    import castor.Context.Simple.global
    object SyncActor extends castor.SimpleActor[Msg]{
      def run(msg: Msg): Unit = {
        println("SyncActor handling: " + msg)
        msg match {
          case ChangedPath(value) => Shared.send(agent.stdin.data, Rpc.StatPath(value))
          case AgentResponse(Rpc.StatInfo(p, remoteHash)) =>
            val localHash = Shared.hashPath(src / p)
            if (localHash != remoteHash && localHash.isDefined) {
              Shared.send(agent.stdin.data, Rpc.WriteOver(os.read.bytes(src / p), p))
            }
        }
      }
    }
    val agentReader = new Thread(() => {
      while (agent.isAlive()) {
        SyncActor.send(AgentResponse(Shared.receive[Rpc.StatInfo](agent.stdout.data)))
      }
    })
    agentReader.start()
    val watcher = os.watch.watch(
      Seq(src),
      onEvent = _.foreach(p => SyncActor.send(ChangedPath(p.subRelativeTo(src))))
    )
    Thread.sleep(Long.MaxValue)
  }
}
```

</> 18.12.scala

18.3 Testing the Syncer

We can test out the syncer we have written so far by making two folders, running the `sync.assembly` executable on them, and then in another terminal creating a bunch of files and folders in the `src/` folder to verify that they appear in `dest/`:

First Terminal	Second Terminal

`$ ./mill show sync.assembly`
`...`
`"ref:out/sync/assembly/dest/out.jar"`
 	
`$ mkdir src dest`
 	
`$ out/sync/assembly/dest/out.jar src dest`
	`$ mkdir src/hello`
	
	`$ echo "Hello World" > src/hello/world.txt`
	
	`$ echo "I am Cow" > src/moo`
	
	`$ find src -type f`
	`src/moo`
	`src/hello/world.txt`
	
	`$ find dest -type f`
	`dest/moo`
	`dest/hello/world.txt`
	
	`$ cat dest/hello/world.txt`
	`Hello World`
	
	`$ cat dest/moo`
	`I am Cow`

</> 18.13.bash	*</> 18.14.bash*

As you can see, we can create files and folders while the syncer is running, and they are immediately synced over. The one-file-at-a-time implementation means that we only need to sync the files that have changed, and do not need to waste time on files that have not: this is a big advantage for interactive use cases where you are syncing lots of small changes. In our original terminal where the syncer is running, we can see the logging output from `SyncActor` as it processes each file and folder we created:

```
SyncActor handling: ChangedPath(hello)
Agent handling: StatPath(hello)
SyncActor handling: AgentResponse(StatInfo(hello,None))

SyncActor handling: ChangedPath(hello/world.txt)
Agent handling: StatPath(hello/world.txt)
SyncActor handling: AgentResponse(StatInfo(hello/world.txt,None))
Agent handling: WriteOver([B@7995092a,hello/world.txt)

SyncActor handling: ChangedPath(moo)
Agent handling: StatPath(moo)
SyncActor handling: AgentResponse(StatInfo(moo,None))
Agent handling: WriteOver([B@76908cc0,moo)
```
</> 18.15.output

See example 18.1 - Simple

If we continue making changes in the source folder, our program will pick them up via os.watch and synchronize them over to the destination. Note that we do not need to handle the case where a file changes in the middle of being synced over: such a file change would result in another event being sent to os.watch, which would be processed after the current message processing is complete. Even if the SyncActor logic misbehaves if a file changes underneath it, we can expect a future ChangedPath message to arrive and give SyncActor a chance to sync the file over correctly.

18.4 Pipelined Real-time Syncing

We now have a simple real-time file synchronizer which can continuously sync changes from the source folder to the destination. We use the single-threaded nature of our SyncActor to help manage our concurrent system with data coming in from both filesystem events as well as agent responses.

However, the fact that SyncActor processes messages one at a time in a single-threaded fashion is both a blessing and a curse: this means that the actions of SyncActor cannot happen in parallel. We will now look at breaking up SyncActor into two smaller actors, in order to get some pipeline parallelism in between different stages in the file sync pipeline.

18.4.1 Pipelined Architecture

SyncActor has two main tasks that are taking up all of its time:

1. The two Shared.send calls, which send commands and data over to the agent process

2. The Shared.hashPath call, which hashes the bytes of a local file, compares it to the destination hash we received from agent, and decides whether to copy the file contents over

While these two operations are currently running in the same `SyncActor`, they could be pipelined: sending commands over the network shouldn't get in the way of hashing and comparing local files, and vice versa. Luckily this sort of pipelining is exactly what Actors are good at!

Thus, we will introduce another actor in the pipeline, `HashActor`:

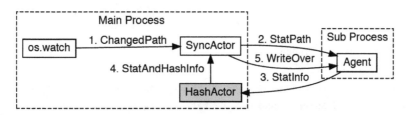

`HashActor` will hash and compare local files with the remote file hash, so that `SyncActor` only needs to send messages over the network. The two actors can then run concurrently.

18.4.2 Pipelined Implementation

We can do this by modifying the `SyncActor` and `agentReader` we defined earlier as follows:

```scala                                                    sync/src/Sync.scala
  sealed trait Msg
  case class ChangedPath(value: os.SubPath) extends Msg
- case class AgentResponse(value: Rpc.StatInfo) extends Msg
+ case class HashStatInfo(localHash: Option[Int], value: Rpc.StatInfo) extends Msg
  import castor.Context.Simple.global
  object SyncActor extends castor.SimpleActor[Msg]{
    def run(msg: Msg): Unit = {
      println("SyncActor handling: " + msg)
      msg match {
        case ChangedPath(value) => Shared.send(agent.stdin.data, Rpc.StatPath(value))
-       case AgentResponse(Rpc.StatInfo(p, remoteHash)) =>
-         val localHash = Shared.hashPath(src / p)
+       case HashStatInfo(localHash, Rpc.StatInfo(p, remoteHash)) =>
          if (localHash != remoteHash && localHash.isDefined) {
            Shared.send(agent.stdin.data, Rpc.WriteOver(os.read.bytes(src / p), p))
          }
      }
    }
  }
                                                              </> 18.16.scala
```

```
+    object HashActor extends castor.SimpleActor[Rpc.StatInfo]{        sync/src/Sync.scala
+      def run(msg: Rpc.StatInfo): Unit = {
+        println("HashActor handling: " + msg)
+        val localHash = Shared.hashPath(src / msg.p)
+        SyncActor.send(HashStatInfo(localHash, msg))
+      }
+    }
```
</> 18.17.scala

```
    val agentReader = new Thread(() => {                               sync/src/Sync.scala
      while (agent.isAlive()) {
-       SyncActor.send(AgentResponse(Shared.receive[Rpc.StatInfo](agent.stdout.data)))
+       HashActor.send(Shared.receive[Rpc.StatInfo](agent.stdout.data))
      }
    })
```
</> 18.18.scala

Here, we rename AgentResponse as HashStatInfo, and give it a localHash: Option[Int] field. In agentReader, instead of sending the StatInfo directly to SyncActor, we send it to our new HashActor. HashActor computes the localHash before bundling that together with the original StatInfo in a HashStatInfo to send to SyncActor.

Thus, we now have the slow hashPath call being run in a separate castor.SimpleActor from the slow Shared.send calls. That ensures that they can run in parallel, giving us a nice pipeline parallelism while the use of castor.SimpleActor helps us avoid needing to think about race conditions or other multi-threading related issues.

We can test this by clearing out the src/ and dest/ folders we populated earlier and repeating the manual test (18.3). We should again see that any files we create in src/ are quickly synced over to dest/. The complete implementation of the pipelined version of Sync.scala is presented below. The other files build.sc, Agent.scala, Shared.scala, and Rpc.scala are unchanged from the non-pipelined implementation we saw earlier:

```
package sync                                                          sync/src/Sync.scala
object Sync {
  def main(args: Array[String]): Unit = {
    val (src, dest) = (os.Path(args(0), os.pwd), os.Path(args(1), os.pwd))
    val agentExecutable = os.temp(os.read.bytes(os.resource / "agent.jar"))
    os.perms.set(agentExecutable, "rwx------")
    val agent = os.proc(agentExecutable).spawn(cwd = dest)
    sealed trait Msg
    case class ChangedPath(value: os.SubPath) extends Msg
    case class HashStatInfo(localHash: Option[Int], value: Rpc.StatInfo) extends Msg
    import castor.Context.Simple.global
    object SyncActor extends castor.SimpleActor[Msg]{
      def run(msg: Msg): Unit = {
```

```scala
        println("SyncActor handling: " + msg)
        msg match {
          case ChangedPath(value) => Shared.send(agent.stdin.data, Rpc.StatPath(value))
          case HashStatInfo(localHash, Rpc.StatInfo(p, remoteHash)) =>
            if (localHash != remoteHash && localHash.isDefined) {
              Shared.send(agent.stdin.data, Rpc.WriteOver(os.read.bytes(src / p), p))
            }
        }
      }
    }
  }
  object HashActor extends castor.SimpleActor[Rpc.StatInfo]{
    def run(msg: Rpc.StatInfo): Unit = {
      println("HashActor handling: " + msg)
      val localHash = Shared.hashPath(src / msg.p)
      SyncActor.send(HashStatInfo(localHash, msg))
    }
  }
  val agentReader = new Thread(() => {
    while (agent.isAlive()) {
      HashActor.send(Shared.receive[Rpc.StatInfo](agent.stdout.data))
    }
  })
  agentReader.start()
  val watcher = os.watch.watch(
    Seq(src),
    onEvent = _.foreach(p => SyncActor.send(ChangedPath(p.subRelativeTo(src))))
  )
  Thread.sleep(Long.MaxValue)
}
}
```
</> 18.19.scala

See example 18.2 - Pipelined

18.5 Testing the Pipelined Syncer

We can test this pipelined implementation the same way we tested our first actor-based file synchronizer:
creating an `assembly`, creating two empty folders `src` and `dest`, and starting the sync. If we create files
and folders in `src/` in quick succession, e.g. in the same shell command, we will see that the the logging
from `SyncActor`, `Agent`, and `HashActor` become interleaved as they all run in parallel:

```
$ mkdir src/hello; echo "Hello World" > src/hello/world.txt; echo "I am Cow" > src/moo
```

```
SyncActor handling: ChangedPath(hello)
SyncActor handling: ChangedPath(hello/world.txt)
SyncActor handling: ChangedPath(moo)
Agent handling: StatPath(hello)
Agent handling: StatPath(hello/world.txt)
Agent handling: StatPath(moo)
HashActor handling: StatInfo(hello,None)
SyncActor handling: HashStatInfo(None,StatInfo(hello,None))
HashActor handling: StatInfo(hello/world.txt,None)
HashActor handling: StatInfo(moo,None)
SyncActor handling: HashStatInfo(Some(-1262502777),StatInfo(hello/world.txt,None))
SyncActor handling: HashStatInfo(Some(-15566917),StatInfo(moo,None))
Agent handling: WriteOver([B@70be0a2b,hello/world.txt)
Agent handling: WriteOver([B@49b0b76,moo)                      </> 18.20.output
```

While these small tests do not really benefit from the pipeline parallelism our two actors give us, if you create a large number of files quickly we would see that the pipelined file syncer runs significantly faster than our earlier single-actor implementation.

As a convenient way of creating a large number of files quickly, try going into the `src/` folder and cloning a small Git repository such as `https://github.com/lihaoyi/fansi`. This will create dozens of files as the repository is downloaded. Our file synchronizer will begin working immediately as the first file is created, and once complete we should be able to run `git show` or `git log dest/fansi/` folder and have it print the same output as if we ran them in `src/fansi/`:

```
$ cd src

$ git clone https://github.com/lihaoyi/fansi
Cloning into 'fansi'...

$ cd ../dest/fansi

$ git show
commit 21a91b22366aa2761eb0b284049aa2a0eec8e565 (HEAD -> master, origin/master)
Merge: ad7aa6b a723c95
Author: Li Haoyi <haoyi.sg@gmail.com>
Date:   Mon Mar 2 06:49:15 2020 +0800

    Merge pull request #23 from lolgab/add-scala-native

    Add support for Scala Native 0.3 and 0.4.0-M2            </> 18.21.bash
```

This demonstrates that even though we are creating files on disk while the file synchronizer is in progress, it is able to keep up with the ongoing changes and eventually bring the destination folder up to date with the contents of the source folder.

18.6 Conclusion

In this chapter, we took the batch-style file synchronizer we wrote in *Chapter 17: Multi-Process Applications* and turned it into a real-time file synchronizer that can incrementally synchronize two folders. We are now processing only the files that have changed, and do not need to redundantly scan files that have not.

In order to manage the constant stream of messages we are getting from both `os.watch` and our `agent` subprocess, we used a `castor.SimpleActor` to ensure that the messages are processed in a single-threaded fashion. We then split our monolithic `SyncActor` into two: `SyncActor` and `HashActor`, allowing the process of hashing local files and sending commands to the `agent` to happen in parallel.

This file syncing program is still relatively simple: we do not handle deletions, we buffer file contents entirely in-memory, and we do not perform any sub-file-level syncing of large files. In addition, the code as-written only performs incremental syncing, and does not synchronize files that were present when the application starts. Adding these additional features is left as an exercise to the reader.

Hopefully this concise example has given you a feel for how an actor's single-threaded nature and the ability to chain them together into parallel pipelines are useful in solving real-world problems in an elegant way. In larger event-driven systems, your messages may be stored in some kind of shared queue service, and instead of actors you may have entire servers, but the same principles apply. This event-driven approach can be used in all sorts of scenarios where we have multiple processes we need to coordinate in a highly concurrent environment.

> **Exercise:** Modify the pipelined file synchronizer to make it support synchronizing folders which start off with files and subfolders that need to be copied over.
>
> **See example 18.3 - InitialFiles**

> **Exercise:** Modify the pipelined file synchronizer to make it hash local files in parallel, using `Futures`. Note that although different files can be hashed and processed independently, we need to ensure that events related to each individual file are processed in order.
>
> **See example 18.4 - ForkJoinHashing**

> **Exercise:** Modify the pipelined file synchronizer to support deletes: if a user deletes a file from the source folder, the syncer should delete the corresponding file from the destination folder.
>
> **See example 18.5 - Deletes**

Exercise: Assuming the file synchronizer is the only process writing to the destination folder, we should not need to ask agent what's on disk: the only files in the destination are the files that `SyncActor` put there. Modify the pipelined file synchronizer to keep track of the hashes of synchronized files locally, so we can avoid exchanging `StatPath` and `StatInfo` messages for files the syncer sent over itself.

See example 18.6 - VirtualFileSystem

Discuss Chapter 18 online at https://www.handsonscala.com/discuss/18

19

Parsing Structured Text

19.1 Simple Parsers   366

19.2 Parsing Structured Values   371

19.3 Implementing a Calculator   376

19.4 Parser Debugging and Error Reporting   381

```
@ def parser[_: P] =
    P( ("hello" | "goodbye").! ~ " ".rep(1) ~ ("world" | "seattle").! ~ End )

@ fastparse.parse("hello seattle", parser(_))
res41: Parsed[(String, String)] = Success(("hello", "seattle"), 13)

@ fastparse.parse("hello     world", parser(_))
res42: Parsed[(String, String)] = Success(("hello", "world"), 15)          </> 19.1.scala
```

Snippet 19.1: parsing simple text formats using the FastParse library

One common programming task is parsing structured text. This chapter will introduce how to parse text in Scala using the FastParse library, before diving into an example where we write a simple arithmetic parser in Scala. This will allow you to work competently with unusual data formats, query languages, or source code for which you do not already have an existing parser at hand.

We will build upon the parsing techniques learned in this chapter as part of ***Chapter 20: Implementing a Programming Language***.

19.1 Simple Parsers

For this chapter, we will rely on FastParse being bundled with the Ammonite Scala REPL. The simplest FastParse parser is shown below:

```
@ import fastparse._, NoWhitespace._


@ def parser[_: P] = P( "hello" )                                    </> 19.2.scala
```

Here, we import the `fastparse` library and define a parser with the P(...) function and `[_: P]` context bound. Every FastParse parser must be defined with these, and in this case our `def` parser parses a single string, `"hello"`, and nothing else. You can use this parser by calling `fastparse.parse` on it:

```
@ fastparse.parse("hello", parser(_))
res2: Parsed[Unit] = Success((), 5)


@ fastparse.parse("goodbye", parser(_))
res3: Parsed[Unit] = Parsed.Failure(Position 1:1, found "goodbye")    </> 19.3.scala
```

We can see that parsing `"hello"` succeeded, returning () (which is Unit, meaning "no value" in Scala) and parsing until index 5. On the other hand, trying to parse `"goodbye"` failed at row 1 character 1: the first character. We can make it print out what it expected by asking for the `trace`.

```
@ val Parsed.Failure(expected, index, extra) = fastparse.parse("goodbye", parser(_))


@ println(extra.trace().longMsg)
Expected parser:1:1 / "hello":1:1, found "goodbye"                    </> 19.4.scala
```

The `.trace().longMsg` tells us that it expected `"hello"` but instead found `"goodbye"`. Asking for the `.trace().msg` or `.trace().longMsg` gives a more detailed error message, but at a cost: FastParse needs to re-parse the entire input with additional instrumentation. This takes additional time, and so is not done by default unless you ask for it.

While in the above example we pattern-matched using `val Parsed.Failure(...) =` since we know the parse failed, in production code you would handle the result of a parse using a `match` block as below:

```
fastparse.parse("goodbye", parser(_)) match {
  case Parsed.Success(value, index) => ...
  case Parsed.Failure(expected, index, extra) => ...
}                                                                     </> 19.5.scala
```

You can then handle the error however you like: logging it, showing it to the user, etc.

19.1.1 Partial & Incomplete Parses

`fastparse.parse` also fails if there's not enough input to parse:

```
@ fastparse.parse("hel", parser(_))
res4: Parsed[Unit] = Parsed.Failure(Position 1:1, found "hel")                    </> 19.6.scala
```

On the other hand, if there's *too much* input, `fastparse.parse` succeeds but with the index showing how much it actually parsed:

```
@ fastparse.parse("hellogoodbye", parser(_))
res5: Parsed[Unit] = Success((), 5)                                               </> 19.7.scala
```

If we want to catch the case where we didn't completely parse the input, it's straightforward to compare the success index (5) against the length of the input string (12) to see whether or not the input was fully consumed. We can also use the `End` operator, which we'll discuss later in Sequence Parsers (*19.1.3*).

19.1.2 Alternative Parsers

`a | b` can parse anything `a` or `b` can parse, tried left-to-right (i.e. `a` gets priority, and `b` is only tried if `a` fails):

```
@ def parser[_: P] = P( "hello" | "goodbye" )

@ fastparse.parse("hello", parser(_))
res7: Parsed[Unit] = Success((), 5)

@ fastparse.parse("goodbye", parser(_))
res8: Parsed[Unit] = Success((), 7)

@ fastparse.parse("dunno", parser(_))
res9: Parsed[Unit] = Parsed.Failure(Position 1:1, found "dunno")                  </> 19.8.scala
```

As you can see, parsing either `"hello"` or `"goodbye"` works, but parsing `"dunno"` makes it fail. Again, you can call `.trace().longMsg` for info:

```
@ val Parsed.Failure(expected, index, extra) = fastparse.parse("dunno", parser(_))

@ println(extra.trace().longMsg)
Expected parser:1:1 / ("hello" | "goodbye"):1:1, found "dunno"                    </> 19.9.scala
```

Above, we can see that it expected `"hello" | "goodbye"` at row 1 character 1 but instead found a `"dunno"`. You can chain more alternatives together with `|`, and FastParse will try all of them left-to-right.

19.1.3 Sequence Parsers

a ~ b parses a *followed by* b:

```
@ def parser[_: P] = P( "hello" ~ "goodbye" )

@ fastparse.parse("hellogoodbye", parser(_))
res11: Parsed[Unit] = Success((), 12)

@ fastparse.parse("hello", parser(_))
res12: Parsed[Unit] = Parsed.Failure(Position 1:6, found "")

@ fastparse.parse("goodbye", parser(_))
res13: Parsed[Unit] = Parsed.Failure(Position 1:1, found "goodbye")       </> 19.10.scala
```

The parser above parses "hellogoodbye" all at once.

- If you give it just "hello", it fails since it's looking for "goodbye" at row 1 character 6, but found no input since it had reached the end of the string

- If you try to parse just "goodbye", it fails since it's looking for "hello" at row 1 character 1, but instead found "goodbye"

Like |, ~ is chainable: you can ~ together as many parsers as you want in sequence and they'll each run one after the other. If you want to ensure your parser is able to consume all the given input, you can end with a ~ End parser. This will fail the parse if there is input left over:

```
@ def parser[_: P] = P( "hello" ~ "goodbye" ~ End )

@ fastparse.parse("hellogoodbye", parser(_))
res15: Parsed[Unit] = Success((), 12)

@ fastparse.parse("hellogoodbyeworld", parser(_))
res16: Parsed[Unit] = Parsed.Failure(Position 1:13, found "world")

@ val Parsed.Failure(msg, idx, extra) = fastparse.parse("hellogoodbyeworld", parser(_))

@ extra.traced.longMsg
res17: String = "Expected parser:1:1 / end-of-input:1:13, found \"world\""</> 19.11.scala
```

Here, parsing "hellogoodbyeworld" failed because it was expecting to have parsed until the End of the input string, but instead it found more characters left over. This is something you usually only want to do at the "end" of the parser when you know nothing should be left over, and saves you from always needing to check if the success-index and input-length line up.

19.1.4 Combining Alternatives with Sequences

You can combine | and ~, which is when things start getting interesting:

```
@ def parser[_: P] = P( ("hello" | "goodbye") ~ " " ~ ("world" | "seattle") ~ End )
```

This passes on the following inputs:

```
@ fastparse.parse("hello world", parser(_))
res19: Parsed[Unit] = Success((), 11)

@ fastparse.parse("hello seattle", parser(_))
res20: Parsed[Unit] = Success((), 13)

@ fastparse.parse("goodbye world", parser(_))
res21: Parsed[Unit] = Success((), 13)                              </> 19.12.scala
```

And fails on the following:

```
@ fastparse.parse("hello universe", parser(_)) // Not "world" or "seattle"
res22: Parsed[Unit] = Parsed.Failure(Position 1:7, found "universe")

@ fastparse.parse("helloworld", parser(_)) // Missing the single " " blank space
res23: Parsed[Unit] = Parsed.Failure(Position 1:6, found "world")

@ fastparse.parse("hello  world", parser(_)) // Too many blank spaces
res24: Parsed[Unit] = Parsed.Failure(Position 1:7, found " world")

@ fastparse.parse("i love seattle", parser(_)) // Not a hello or goodbye
res25: Parsed[Unit] = Parsed.Failure(Position 1:1, found "i love sea")

@ fastparse.parse("hello seattle moo", parser(_)) // Did not consume entire string
res26: Parsed[Unit] = Parsed.Failure(Position 1:14, found " moo")     </> 19.13.scala
```

If you want more verbose error logging for why the parse failed, you can ask for the .traced.longMsg as we did earlier.

We now have a FastParse parser which is about as powerful as the regex (hello|goodbye) (world|seattle), though with more informative errors when the parse fails.

19.1.5 Repeated Parsers

You can call `.rep(n)` on any parser to repeat it:

```
@ def parser[_: P] = P( ("hello" | "goodbye") ~ " ".rep(1) ~ ("world" | "seattle") ~ End )

@ fastparse.parse("hello world", parser(_))
res28: Parsed[Unit] = Success((), 11)

@ fastparse.parse("hello      world", parser(_))
res29: Parsed[Unit] = Success((), 15)

@ fastparse.parse("helloworld", parser(_))
res30: Parsed[Unit] = Parsed.Failure(Position 1:6, found "world")           </> 19.14.scala
```

Here, `.rep(1)` means it repeats the `" "` parser at least once.

- If we have one or more spaces between the `"hello"` and `"world"`, the parser consumes all of them

- If we have no spaces at all, it fails with a message that it was looking for a `" "` but instead found a `"world"` at character 6

You can also pass in explicit `min=...`, `max=...` arguments if you want to bound it to a particular range, or `exactly=...` if you want it to repeat exactly N times.

19.1.6 Optional Parsers

Marking a parser as optional is done using `.?`:

```
@ def parser[_: P] =
    P( ("hello" | "goodbye") ~ (" ".rep(1) ~ ("world" | "seattle")).? ~ End )/>  19.15.scala
```

Here, you can see that the `" ".rep(1)` parser as well as the `("world" | "seattle")` parser are all optional. That means that the parser lets you include or omit the entire `" world"` suffix:

```
@ fastparse.parse("hello      world", parser(_))
res31: Parsed[Unit] = Success((), 15)

@ fastparse.parse("hello", parser(_))
res32: Parsed[Unit] = Success((), 5)                                        </> 19.16.scala
```

If a blank space `" "` is present, the parser expects `"world"` or `"seattle"` to follow:

```
@ fastparse.parse("hello ", parser(_))
res33: Parsed[Unit] = Parsed.Failure(Position 1:6, found " ")               </> 19.17.scala
```

This is because when we try to parse `"hello "` with a trailing space:

- `" ".rep(1)` succeeds in parsing the space

- `("world" | "seattle")` then fails since there's no more input after the space.

- Since the whole trailing-space-world is optional, the parse backtracks to character `6` just after `"hello"`

- FastParse then tries to continue the parse without the optional portion, now expecting to see the `End` of input

- Since it isn't the end, with one more `" "` at index `6`, the parse fails

This last parser is similar to the regex `(hello|goodbye)( +(world|seattle))?` The next few sections of this chapter will cover features of the FastParse library that go beyond what a regex is capable of.

19.2 Parsing Structured Values

So far, all our parsers have been of type `Parser[Unit]`, returning `()` in the `Success` result. `Unit` in Scala means "no value": i.e. these parsers parse the input, check that it matches what the parser expects, but doesn't return any concrete value representing the parsed input. This is the default because most parsers don't care about most of the things they're parsing. For example, If you are parsing Java you don't care about all the whitespace, all the `{` or `}`s, `(`s or `)`s, `,`s or `;`s, `//` comments or `/**/` comments. FastParse thus avoids building data structures that will ultimately be ignored or discarded.

19.2.1 Capturing Strings

In the cases where we care about the text we're parsing, we must capture it using the `.!` operator:

```
@ def parser[_: P] =
  P( ("hello" | "goodbye").! ~ " ".rep(1) ~ ("world" | "seattle").! ~ End )

@ fastparse.parse("hello seattle", parser(_))
res34: Parsed[(String, String)] = Success(("hello", "seattle"), 13)

@ fastparse.parse("hello     world", parser(_))
res35: Parsed[(String, String)] = Success(("hello", "world"), 15)          </> 19.18.scala
```

As you can see, we added `.!` to capture both the `("hello" | "goodbye")` as well as the `("world" | "seattle")`, and we successfully parsed it to get the results as a tuple containing the two strings. We did *not* `.!` capture the one-or-more-spaces parser in the middle, so the spaces it parsed did not appear in the output.

19.2.2 Parsing Case Classes

Often we don't want tuples of strings, and would prefer some kind of object with named fields that contains the data we want, such as an instance of a case class. Below we define such a case class Phrase to represent our phrases, and use .map to transform the parsed tuple of (String, String) into a Phrase:

```scala
@ case class Phrase(isHello: Boolean, place: String)

@ def parser[_: P]: P[Phrase] =
    P( ("hello" | "goodbye").! ~ " ".rep(1) ~ ("world" | "seattle").! ~ End ).map{
      case ("hello", place) => Phrase(true, place)
      case ("goodbye", place) => Phrase(false, place)
    }

@ val Parsed.Success(result, index) = fastparse.parse("goodbye   seattle", parser(_))
result: Phrase = Phrase(false, "seattle")
index: Int = 17

@ result.isHello
res39: Boolean = false

@ result.place
res40: String = "seattle"                                               </> 19.19.scala
```

On successful parses, we thus get a Phrase object we can work with. We can then conveniently refer to parts of the parsed data via .isHello or .place, rather than the ._1 and ._2s we would need if we were working directly with tuples. This is much less error-prone than using a regex with capturing groups to retrieve portions of parsed string by index (result.group(0), result.group(1), ...).

19.2.3 Modularizing and Typing our Parsers

The above example is getting a bit long, but it is easy to break it up. We define smaller parsers using the same `def foo[_: P] = P(...)` syntax, and make use of them in the "main" parser:

```scala
@ def prefix[_: P]: P[String] = P( "hello" | "goodbye" ).!

@ def suffix[_: P]: P[String] = P( "world" | "seattle" ).!

@ def ws[_: P]: P[Unit] = P( " ".rep(1) ) // white-space

@ def parser[_: P] = P( prefix ~ ws ~ suffix ).map{
    case ("hello", place) => new Phrase(true, place)
    case ("goodbye", place) => new Phrase(false, place)
  }


@ val Parsed.Success(result, index) = fastparse.parse("goodbye    world", parser(_))
result: Phrase = Phrase(false, "world")
index: Int = 15
```
</> 19.20.scala

Here we can see that the individual `prefix` and `suffix` parsers are `P[String]` rather than `P[Unit]`. This means they will return a `String` if their parse succeeds. `ws` is still `P[Unit]` since it did not capture anything, `prefix ~ ws ~ suffix` is still `P[(String, String)]`, which we `.map` into a `P[Phrase]`.

FastParse parsers generally parse typed values - `case class`es, tuples, `Seq`s, primitives, and so on. That makes working with their results very convenient: the compiler can make sure your parsers are producing results that your downstream code can use, and mistakes are compile errors rather than runtime exceptions. This makes it very easy to safely combine simpler parsers to form complex ones, something that is difficult or error-prone when working with untyped regexes.

For example, if we made a mistake and in the `.map` call assumed that the `prefix ~ " ".rep(1) ~ suffix` produced a 3-tuple `(String, String, String)`, the compiler will catch it right away, before any code is run:

```scala
@ def parser[_: P] = P( prefix ~ ws ~ suffix ).map{
    case ("hello", spaces, place) => new Phrase(true, place)
    case ("goodbye", spaces, place) => new Phrase(false, place)
  }
cmd3.sc:2: constructor cannot be instantiated to expected type;
 found    : (T1, T2, T3)
 required: (String, String)
  case ("hello", spaces, place) => new Phrase(true, place)
       ^
Compilation Failed
```
</> 19.21.scala

19.2.4 Using Sub-Parsers Independently

A `prefix` or `suffix` are themselves `P[String]` parsers, we can use them on their own to parse input:

```
@ fastparse.parse("hello", prefix(_))
res46: Parsed[String] = Success("hello", 5)


@ fastparse.parse("goodbye", prefix(_))
res47: Parsed[String] = Success("goodbye", 7)


@ fastparse.parse("moo", prefix(_))
res48: Parsed[String] = Parsed.Failure(Position 1:1, found "moo")          </> 19.22.scala
```

With FastParse, every `P[T]` can have its components easily broken out into separate parts, each of which is statically typed as `P[String]`, `P[Unit]`, `P[(String, String)]`, `P[Phrase]`, etc.. The compiler can help ensure that the combinations and transformations are valid, and every sub-parser can be used and tested independently.

In the end, all these `def prefix`, `def suffix`, `def parser` definitions are just methods returning a `ParsingRun[T]` type, abbreviated as `P[T]`. They can be defined anywhere, as part of objects or classes or within method bodies. You can refactor parts of a large parser into smaller parsers, assign them meaningful names, and in general manage them as you would any other piece of code.

19.2.5 Recursive Parsers

This ability to reference parsers by name inside another parser means parsers can be recursive! For example here we change `Phrase` into a tree-like object: it's either a `Word` containing a string, or a `Pair` containing two other phrases. This can be modeled as a `sealed trait Phrase` with two subclasses:

```
@ {
  sealed trait Phrase
  case class Word(s: String) extends Phrase
  case class Pair(lhs: Phrase, rhs: Phrase) extends Phrase
}                                                                          </> 19.23.scala
```

Here, we wrap everything in `{}`s, so the REPL will execute the three statements as one "block" rather than separate commands. This is necessary here and for the subsequent definitions, which are recursive and thus only make sense when defined together. We can now parse these `Phrase`s as follows, again using `{}`s to define the parser as a single block:

```
@ {
  def prefix[_: P] = P( "hello" | "goodbye" ).!.map(Word)
  def suffix[_: P] = P( "world" | "seattle" ).!.map(Word)
  def ws[_: P] = P( " ".rep(1) )
  def parened[_: P] = P( "(" ~ parser ~ ")" )
  def parser[_: P]: P[Phrase] = P( (parened | prefix) ~ ws ~ (parened | suffix) ).map{
    case (lhs, rhs) => Pair(lhs, rhs)
  }
}
```
</> 19.24.scala

Compared to our earlier non-recursive `Phrase` parser, this has the following major changes:

- We introduce a new `parened` parser, which wraps `parser` with a `"("` before it and `")"` after

- Inside `parser`, prefix is now `(parened | prefix)` and suffix is now `(parened | suffix)`

- `prefix` and `suffix` have their result transformed using `.map(Word)` to turn them from `P[String]`s into `P[Word]`s, which is a subtype of `P[Phrase]`

- `parser` has its result transformed using `.map` to become a `P[Pair]`, also a subtype of `P[Phrase]`

Thus, `parser` and `parened` are now mutually recursive: each one can call the other as part of their parse. The definitions of `prefix`, `suffix` and `ws` themselves are unchanged from what we saw earlier. We can pass in various combinations of phrases and parentheses to see it in action:

```
@ fastparse.parse("(hello world)   ((goodbye seattle) world)", parser(_))
res51: Parsed[Phrase] = Success(
  Pair(
    Pair(Word("hello"), Word("world")),
    Pair(
      Pair(Word("goodbye"), Word("seattle")),
      Word("world")
    )
  ),
  42
)
```
</> 19.25.scala

We now have a working parser that can parse a given tree-shaped input string into a tree-shaped data-structure. We just needed to write 7 short lines of code to define the shape of the input we want to parse, and the FastParse library did the rest of the work of parsing the string and transforming it into the data structure we need.

See example 19.1 - Phrases

19.3 Implementing a Calculator

As a capstone project for this chapter, we will implement a small arithmetic evaluator. This is a common programming interview challenge, but we will add a twist: it must work on the English representations of numbers! For example, while a traditional arithmetic evaluator may evaluate the following to return 18:

```
(1 + 2) * (9 - 3)
```

For this exercise, we will instead parse input such as:

```
(one plus two) times (nine minus three)
```

To simplify things, we will limit the numbers to the range `zero` to `nine`, avoiding all the complexities around parsing English numbers like `fifteen` or `twelve` or `one hundred twenty eight`.

19.3.1 Defining our Syntax Tree

The first thing we need to do is define exactly what structure we want to parse our arithmetic expressions into. Since we only care about binary operations on numbers, with the numbers being integers, we could model that structure as follows:

```scala
@ {
  sealed trait Expr
  case class BinOp(left: Expr, op: String, right: Expr) extends Expr
  case class Number(Value: Int) extends Expr
}
                                                                </> 19.26.scala
```

It is always a judgement call how much information you want to model in your syntax tree. Here we ignore whitespace, line numbers, or parentheses, since they are not necessary for evaluation. Exactly how much detail about the input text you want to model in your syntax tree depends on what you need to do with it.

19.3.2 Parsing Literals

To begin let's implement a parser for simple numbers:

```scala
@ def number[_: P]: P[Expr] = P(
    "zero" | "one" | "two" | "three" | "four" |
    "five" | "six" | "seven" | "eight" | "nine"
).!.map{
  case "zero"  => Number(0); case "one"   => Number(1)
  case "two"   => Number(2); case "three" => Number(3)
  case "four"  => Number(4); case "five"  => Number(5)
  case "six"   => Number(6); case "seven" => Number(7)
  case "eight" => Number(8); case "nine"  => Number(9)
}
                                                                </> 19.27.scala
```

Here, we manually list out all the possible numbers, and inside the `map` we pattern-match on the value and assign each string to the integer value it represents. You can see that due to our `map` call, `number` is now a `P[Int]`: on success, the parse returns an `Int`. This can be tested as follows:

```
@ fastparse.parse("seven", number(_))
res54: Parsed[Int] = Success(Number(7), 5)


@ fastparse.parse("zero", number(_))
res55: Parsed[Int] = Success(Number(0), 4)


@ fastparse.parse("lol", number(_))
res56: Parsed[Int] = Parsed.Failure(Position 1:1, found "lol")        </> 19.28.scala
```

Next, we need to define how to parse operators: let's restrict it to the four basic arithmetic operators for now, and use `.!` on the `operator` parser so we can capture which operator was parsed:

```
@ def operator[_: P]: P[String] = P( "plus" | "minus" | "times" | "divide" ).!
```

The last terminal parser we will need is to parse whitespace; for now we will use the same `def ws` parser we used earlier:

```
@ def ws[_: P] = P( " ".rep(1) )
```

19.3.3 Parsing Arithmetic

Next, we have to parse the recursive tree-like structure, so we can handle inputs like:

```
(one plus two) times (nine minus three)
```

The syntax we want to be able to parse is a left-hand-side expression, followed by an operator, followed by a right-hand-side expression. Each side's expression is either a `number`, or the `parser` itself surrounded by parentheses. Let's call this `def expr`:

```
def expr[_: P]: P[Expr] = P( "(" ~ parser ~ ")" | number )
def parser[_: P]: P[Expr] = P( expr ~ ws ~ operator ~ ws ~ expr )        </> 19.29.scala
```

Now, we're almost done. But if you try to run this, you get a compile error:

```
@ {
  def expr[_: P] = P( "(" ~ parser ~ ")" | number )
  def parser[_: P]: P[Expr] = P( expr ~ ws ~ operator ~ ws ~ expr )
}
cmd80.sc:2: type mismatch;
 found    : fastparse.core.Parser[(Expr, String, Expr)]
 required: fastparse.all.Parser[Expr]
    (which expands to)  fastparse.core.Parser[Expr]
val parser: Parser[Int] = P( expr ~ ws ~ operator ~ ws ~ expr )
                                                                ^
Compilation Failed
```
</> *19.30.scala*

As you can see, it's failing because the right hand side of def parser is a P[(Expr, String, Expr)], whereas we annotated it as a P[Expr]. This is because it is made of three sub-parsers which return values:

(expr: P[Expr]) ~ ws ~ (operator: P[String]) ~ ws ~ (expr: P[Expr])

To convert the P[(Int, String, Int)] to a P[Expr], we need to map it. In this case, let's make the map function combine the lhs and rhs results, depending on what the operator was:

```
@ {
  def expr[_: P] = P( "(" ~ parser ~ ")" | number )
  def parser[_: P]: P[Expr] = P( expr ~ ws ~ operator ~ ws ~ expr ).map{
    case (lhs, op, rhs) => BinOp(lhs, op, rhs)
  }
}
```
</> *19.31.scala*

Now our parser is able to parse the recursive syntax of our arithmetic expressions:

```
@ val t = fastparse.parse("(one plus two) times (three plus four)", parser(_)).get.value
t: Parsed[Expr] = Success(
  BinOp(
    BinOp(Number(1), "plus", Number(2)),
    "times",
    BinOp(Number(3), "plus", Number(4))
  ),
  38
)
```
</> *19.32.scala*

19.3.4 Manipulating the Syntax Tree

Now that we have our input string parsed into an `Expr` tree, we can use pattern matching to traverse and manipulate. For example, we can pretty-print it back into a `String`, or evaluate it into a `Int` value:

```scala
@ def stringify(e: Expr): String = e match {
    case BinOp(left, op, right) => s"(${stringify(left)} $op ${stringify(right)})"
    case Number(0) => "zero";   case Number(1) => "one"
    case Number(2) => "two";    case Number(3) => "three"
    case Number(4) => "four";   case Number(5) => "five"
    case Number(6) => "six";    case Number(7) => "seven"
    case Number(8) => "eight";  case Number(9) => "seven"
  }

@ stringify(t)
res59: String = "((one plus two) times (three plus four))"

@ def evaluate(e: Expr): Int = e match {
    case BinOp(left, "plus", right) => evaluate(left) + evaluate(right)
    case BinOp(left, "minus", right) => evaluate(left) - evaluate(right)
    case BinOp(left, "times", right) => evaluate(left) * evaluate(right)
    case BinOp(left, "divide", right) => evaluate(left) / evaluate(right)
    case Number(n) => n
  }

@ evaluate(t)
res61: Int = 10
```
</> 19.33.scala

In general, once we have the input parsed into a syntax tree structure, it is easy to recursively traverse the tree using pattern matching to do useful things: evaluating it, pretty-printing it, validating it, and so on.

We have now written a simple FastParse parser for "English-like" arithmetic expressions, letting us evaluate the arithmetic expression to an integer or pretty-print it back as a string. The entire program is 40 short lines of code, as follows:

```
import fastparse._, NoWhitespace._                              Arithmetic.sc

sealed trait Expr
case class BinOp(left: Expr, op: String, right: Expr) extends Expr
case class Number(Value: Int) extends Expr
def number[_: P] = P(
  "zero" | "one" | "two" | "three" | "four" |
  "five" | "six" | "seven" | "eight" | "nine"
).!.map{
  case "zero"  => Number(0); case "one"   => Number(1)
  case "two"   => Number(2); case "three" => Number(3)
  case "four"  => Number(4); case "five"  => Number(5)
  case "six"   => Number(6); case "seven" => Number(7)
  case "eight" => Number(8); case "nine"  => Number(9)
}
def ws[_: P] = P( " ".rep(1) )
def operator[_: P] = P( "plus" | "minus" | "times" | "divide" ).!
def expr[_: P] = P( "(" ~ parser ~ ")" | number )
def parser[_: P]: P[Expr] = P( expr ~ ws ~ operator ~ ws ~ expr ).map{
  case (lhs, op, rhs) => BinOp(lhs, op, rhs)
}
                                                              </> 19.34.scala
```

```
import $file.Arithmetic, Arithmetic._                          Traversals.sc

def stringify(e: Expr): String = e match {
  case BinOp(left, op, right) => s"(${stringify(left)} $op ${stringify(right)})"
  case Number(0) => "zero"; case Number(1) => "one"
  case Number(2) => "two"; case Number(3) => "three"
  case Number(4) => "four"; case Number(5) => "five"
  case Number(6) => "six"; case Number(7) => "seven"
  case Number(8) => "eight"; case Number(9) => "seven"
}
def evaluate(e: Expr): Int = e match {
  case BinOp(left, "plus", right) => evaluate(left) + evaluate(right)
  case BinOp(left, "minus", right) => evaluate(left) - evaluate(right)
  case BinOp(left, "times", right) => evaluate(left) * evaluate(right)
  case BinOp(left, "divide", right) => evaluate(left) / evaluate(right)
  case Number(n) => n
}
                                                              </> 19.35.scala
```

19.4 Parser Debugging and Error Reporting

The happy path of correctly parsing input is only half of your experience working with parsers. The other half is when things go wrong: your parsers are not parsing what you want them to, or your users are submitting invalid input and causing the parse to fail. In both cases, we need to figure out *why* a parser is misbehaving. This section will go through two techniques: Debugging Parsers via .log (*19.4.1*), and Error Reporting with Cuts (*19.4.2*).

19.4.1 Debugging Parsers via .log

Consider the arithmetic parser we implemented earlier. This works great when the input is correct, but less great when the input is erroneous:

```scala
@ fastparse.parse("(two plus ten) times seven", parser(_))
res62: Parsed[Int] = Parsed.Failure(Position 1:1, found "(two plus ")         </> 19.36.scala
```

In the parse above, our parser fails with the message `Position 1:1, found "(two plus "`. Our input was wrong starting from the first character. That tells us nothing about what is wrong with the input!

19.4.1.1 Adding Logs

In order to find out more, we can use the `.log` method to insert logging on the various parser methods:

```scala
def number[_: P] = P(
  "zero" | "one" | "two" | "three" | "four" |
  "five" | "six" | "seven" | "eight" | "nine"
).!.map{
  case "zero" => Number(0); case "one"  => Number(1)
  ...
-}
+}.log


def ws[_: P] = P( " ".rep(1) )

-def operator[_: P] = P( "plus" | "minus" | "times" | "divide" ).!
+def operator[_: P] = P( "plus" | "minus" | "times" | "divide" ).!.log     </> 19.37.scala
```

Arithmetic.sc

```
-def expr[_: P] = P( "(" ~ parser ~ ")" | number )                        Arithmetic.sc
+def expr[_: P] = P( "(" ~ parser ~ ")" | number ).log

 def parser[_: P]: P[Expr] = P( expr ~ ws ~ operator ~ ws ~ expr ).map{
   case (lhs, op, rhs) => BinOp(lhs, op, rhs)
-}
+}.log                                                                    </> 19.38.scala
```

19.4.1.2 Logging a Successful Parse

By appending .log onto a parser, we are telling FastParse to print out exactly what it is doing. For example, here is the log of successfully parsing a small input:

```
@ fastparse.parse("one plus two", parser(_))
+parser:1:1, cut
  +expr:1:1, cut
    +number:1:1
    -number:1:1:Success(1:4)
  -expr:1:1:Success(1:4, cut)
  +operator:1:5, cut
  -operator:1:5:Success(1:9, cut)
  +expr:1:10, cut
    +number:1:10
    -number:1:10:Success(1:13)
  -expr:1:10:Success(1:13, cut)
-parser:1:1:Success(1:13, cut)
res77: Parsed[Int] = Success(BinOp(Number(1), "plus", Number(2)), 12)    </> 19.39.scala
```

Every line starting with a + indicates at which line and column in the input text a parser began, and every line starting with - indicates where a parser completed either with a Success or Failure.

Above, we can see parser beginning 1:1 (row 1 column 1), expr at 1:1, number at 1:1, number succeeding at 1:4, and so on. Eventually, we see parser succeed at 1:13, producing our final result.

19.4.1.3 Logging a Failed Parse

If we feed our earlier incorrect input to our logged parser, we can see the following logs:

```
@ fastparse.parse("(two plus ten) times seven", parser(_))
+parser:1:1, cut
  +expr:1:1, cut
    +parser:1:2
      +expr:1:2
        +number:1:2
        -number:1:2:Success(1:5)
      -expr:1:2:Success(1:5)
      +operator:1:6
      -operator:1:6:Success(1:10)
      +expr:1:11
        +number:1:11
        -number:1:11:Failure(number:1:11 / ("zero" | "one" ...):1:11 ..."ten) times")
      -expr:1:11:Failure(expr:1:11 / ("(" | number):1:11 ..."ten) times")
    -parser:1:2:Failure(parser:1:2 / expr:1:11 / ("(" | number):1:11 ..."two plus t")
    +number:1:1
    -number:1:1:Failure(number:1:1 / ("zero" | "one" | "two" ...):1:1 ..."(two plus ")
  -expr:1:1:Failure(expr:1:1 / ("(" ~ parser | number):1:1 ..."(two plus ", cut)
-parser:1:1:Failure(parser:1:1 / expr:1:1 / ("(" ~ parser | number):1:1 ..."(two plus ")
                                                                    </> 19.40.scala
```

Here, we can see it successfully parsing all the way until row `1:11` (row 1 column 11), at which the `number` parser fails: it expected a number of the form `"zero" | "one" ...`, but instead saw a `ten`. We can then see it backtrack out of the parse, eventually failing at `1:1`. Now the problem is obvious: `ten` is not a valid number in our parser.

In this small parser, we can add `logs` throughout the code. In a larger parser we may have to be a bit more selective in what we `log` to avoid drowning in logging output. In either case, by adding `logs` to the part of the parser that might be misbehaving, we can get visibility in what the parser is doing. This will help us narrow down exactly which part of the parser or which part of the input is incorrect.

Instrumenting our parser with `.logs` works fine for the developer trying to investigate a misbehavior in the parser. But if the mistake was in user input, that user likely would not have the freedom to sprinkle `.logs` throughout our code. What then?

19.4.2 Error Reporting with Cuts

The reason the erroneous input above gives a poor error message is as follows:

- The parser fails at `1:11` because `ten` is not a `"("` nor is it a valid `number`
- It backtracks to `1:2` where it was trying to parse `parser`, finds no other alternatives, and fails
- It backtracks out to `1:1` where it earlier tried to parse `"("`, tries to parse `number`, and fails
- Only when *that* fails does the parse fail since there is nowhere left to backtrack to

When a parse fails, FastParse backtracks to try the other alternatives defined by |s, in an attempt to find one that can successfully parse. When all of alternatives fail, FastParse does not know which one was "meant" to succeed. Thus can only provide the vague error saying "something is wrong at 1:1".

To produce a better error message, we need to limit how much backtracking FastParse will do.

19.4.2.1 Minimal Example: No Cuts

The basic idea of a *cut* is a point in which the parser cannot backtrack. For example, let us consider the following standalone parser nocut:

```
def alpha[_: P] = P( CharIn("a-z") )
def nocut[_: P] = P( "val " ~ alpha.rep(1).! | "def " ~ alpha.rep(1).!)


val Parsed.Success("abcd", _) = parse("val abcd", nocut(_))
val failure = parse("val 1234", nocut(_)).asInstanceOf[Parsed.Failure]
val trace = failure.trace().longAggregateMsg
failure.index // 0
trace //  Expected nocut:1:1 / ("val " ~ alpha.rep(1) | "def "):1:1, found "val 1234"
                                                            </> 19.41.scala
```

Above we have a simple parser: it either parses a val or def, a space, and its (lower-case only) name. On success this works as expected. On failure, it backtracks all the way to the start of the input. This is a minimized example of the backtracking behavior we saw earlier.

The reason it needs to backtrack is that FastParse does not know that after successfully parsing "val ", only the left branch of the alternative is viable regardless of what input text is being parsed. Thus it has no choice but to offer both alternatives in the error message. *We* might know that after seeing val , only "val " ~ alpha.rep(1).! could possibly succeed, but FastParse does not know that.

19.4.2.2 Minimal Example: Cuts

To solve this issue, we can add cuts using the ~/ operator:

```
def alpha[_: P] = P( CharIn("a-z") )
def hascuts[_: P] = P( "val " ~/ alpha.rep(1).! | "def " ~/ alpha.rep(1).!)


val Parsed.Success("abcd", _) = parse("val abcd", hascuts(_))
val failure = parse("val 1234", hascuts(_)).asInstanceOf[Parsed.Failure]
val trace = failure.trace().longAggregateMsg
failure.index // 4
trace // Expected hascuts:1:1 / alpha:1:5 / [a-z]:1:5, found "1234"        </> 19.42.scala
```

~/ is similar to the Sequence operator ~. The difference is that once the parse has crossed a cut, it can no longer backtrack past that point. This basically makes FastParse "commit" to the current branch of the alternative, so it knows that if the parse fails the error must be within the current branch and not in any of the other branches.

Once we have added the cut `~/`, FastParse no longer backtracks to index `0` on failure. Instead, it shows a much more precise error: at index `4`, expecting one of the small set of alphanumeric characters.

19.4.2.3 Arithmetic Parser Cuts

Going back to our Arithmetic parser above, we know that once we see an open `(`, there is no point backtracking: an open `(` *must* be followed by a `parser`, then a closing `)`. FastParse doesn't know this, but we can tell it via a cut after the open `(`:

```
-def expr[_: P] = P( "(" ~ parser ~ ")" | number )                          Arithmetic.sc
+def expr[_: P] = P( "(" ~/ parser ~ ")" | number )                         </> 19.43.scala
```

After we add the cut `~/`, our error message is improved greatly:

```
@ val result = fastparse.parse("(two plus ten) times seven", parser(_))
result: Parsed[Int] = Parsed.Failure(Position 1:11, found "ten) times")

@ val Parsed.Failure(msg, idx, extra) = result

@ println(extra.trace().msg)
Expected ("(" | number):1:11, found "ten) times"                            </> 19.44.scala
```

We now get a precise error telling us that the `ten` in our string is problematic. Using `.trace().msg` to get more information, we can see that the parser expected either a `"("` or a `number` column `11`, but instead found `"ten"`. This tells us precisely where the problematic input is and what the parser was expecting!

In general, adding cuts greatly helps improve the error reporting when your parser is given invalid input. Whenever you have a parser that can backtrack:

- Alternative `a | b | c` parsers
- Repeated `a.rep` parsers
- Optional `a.?` parsers

It is worth considering if there is a point in the parse past which backtracking is futile. If there is, adding a cut `~/` would greatly improve the error messages the parser produces.

Logging and Cuts are two complementary techniques that help figure out why the parser is not doing what you expect. In the inevitable situation where something is going wrong, it is good to have both in your toolbox.

19.5 Conclusion

We have now walked through the basics of parsing structured text into useful values: parsing arithmetic expressions into a syntax tree that we can traverse and evaluate in various ways. Note this is a minimal example of what you can do with the FastParse library. The actual FastParse documentation has a lot more details in how to write parsers, and is available online at:

- http://www.lihaoyi.com/fastparse/

FastParse can be used in any Scala project, using the following dependency:

```
ivy"com.lihaoyi::fastparse:2.3.0"
```
`Mill`

FastParse parsers are flexible and performant enough to build production parsers for complex, real-world languages like CSS, JSON, Scala, or Python. While in this chapter we parsed a strawman arithmetic syntax, there are many real-world use cases for writing your own parser: handling uncommon data formats, writing a simple query language, or parsing your existing source code for static analysis.

Next, in **Chapter 20: Implementing a Programming Language** we will use FastParse as the basis for writing a simple programming language interpreter.

Exercise: Extend our arithmetic parser to allow parsing chained operators like `one plus two plus three plus four` which should evaluate to `10`. For now, ignore operator precedence, such that `one plus two times three plus four` evaluates to `13` rather than `11`.

See example 19.3 - ArithmeticChained

Exercise: Extend our arithmetic parser to support operator precedence with chained operators, such that `one plus two times three plus four` evaluates to `11` instead of `13`. One possible approach is using precedence climbing.

See example 19.4 - ArithmeticPrecedence

Exercise: Modify the arithmetic parser to evaluate the arithmetic expression during the parse and return a single `Int` once the parse completes, rather than first parsing into an `Expr` structure that we need to recursively traverse and evaluate later. What exact type out parser methods return is up to us, depending on what we do in the `.map` calls.

See example 19.5 - ArithmeticDirect

Discuss Chapter 19 online at https://www.handsonscala.com/discuss/19

20

Implementing a Programming Language

20.1 Interpreting Jsonnet   388

20.2 Jsonnet Language Features   389

20.3 Parsing Jsonnet   390

20.4 Evaluating the Syntax Tree   399

20.5 Serializing to JSON   406

```scala
def evaluate(expr: Expr, scope: Map[String, Value]): Value = expr match {
  case Expr.Str(s) => Value.Str(s)
  case Expr.Dict(kvs) => Value.Dict(kvs.map{case (k, v) => (k, evaluate(v, scope))})
  case Expr.Plus(left, right) =>
    val Value.Str(leftStr) = evaluate(left, scope)
    val Value.Str(rightStr) = evaluate(right, scope)
    Value.Str(leftStr + rightStr)
}
```
</> 20.1.scala

Snippet 20.1: evaluating a syntax tree using pattern matching

This chapter builds upon the simple parsers we learned in *Chapter 19: Parsing Structured Text*, and walks you through the process of implementing a simple programming language in Scala.

Working with programming language source code is a strength of Scala: parsing, analyzing, compiling, or interpreting it. This chapter should will you how easy it is to write a simple interpreter to parse and evaluate program source code in Scala. Even if your goal is not to implement an entirely new programming language, these techniques are still useful: for writing linters, program analyzers, query engines, and other such tools.

20.1 Interpreting Jsonnet

The goal of this chapter is to implement an interpreter for a subset of the Jsonnet programming language.

```jsonnet
local greeting = "Hello ";
local person = function(name) {
  "name": name,
  "welcome": greeting + name + "!"
};
{
  "person1": person("Alice"),
  "person2": person("Bob"),
  "person3": person("Charlie")
}
```
</> 20.2.jsonnet

```json
{
  "person1": {
    "name": "Alice",
    "welcome": "Hello Alice!"
  },
  "person2": {
    "name": "Bob",
    "welcome": "Hello Bob!"
  },
  "person3": {
    "name": "Charlie",
    "welcome": "Hello Charlie!"
  }
}
```
</> 20.3.json

Jsonnet is a simple language meant to construct JSON configuration files: the output of evaluating a .jsonnet file is a single JSON structure containing dictionaries, lists, strings, numbers, and booleans. The output JSON can then be used to configure Kubernetes, CloudFormation, Terraform, or other software systems.

While you can construct JSON structures in any programming language, Jsonnet makes it much more convenient than doing it in a general-purpose language like Java or Python. Jsonnet is used heavily in industry in order to manage large and complex system configurations.

Our interpreter will roughly follow the following steps:

- Parse a Jsonnet source code `string` into a syntax tree structure called `Expr`
- Evaluate the `Expr` into a Jsonnet value called `Value`
- Serialize the final Jsonnet `Value` into an output JSON `string`

We can visualize these steps as follows:

This chapter will walk you through all three phases of implementing our simple interpreter, giving you an intuition for the techniques, data structures and algorithms involved. While not a comprehensive or production-ready implementation, this chapter should give you enough foundation to get started with your own simple language-related projects.

20.2 Jsonnet Language Features

Jsonnet is similar to JSON, but introduces the constructs that help you tidy up verbose or repetitive portions of your JSON config: local variables, function definitions, and basic operations like concatenating strings with +. You can learn more about the syntax and experiment with the language interactively on the official website:

- https://jsonnet.org/

For the purpose of this exercise, we will stop at implementing these three simple features. Further features and improvements can be implemented the same way, and we will leave the task of exhaustively implementing the entire Jsonnet language to production intepreters like google/jsonnet.

20.2.1 Primitives

Jsonnet has a similar set of primitives as JSON. For this chapter, we will consider just a subset of them:

```
"hello world" // strings
{"key": "value", "thing": "123"} // dictionaries                    </> 20.4.jsonnet
```

We will assume that strings do not contain escape sequences like \n or \", and leave out additional data types like numbers, booleans, arrays, or null. We will also assume that strings only support a single operation: concatenation via +.

```
"hello" + "world"        jsonnet     "helloworld"        json
```

20.2.2 Locals and Functions

You can define locals using the `local` keyword, and define local functions by combining the `local` keyword with a `function` expression. As in most programming languages, functions are called using parentheses containing the arguments you wish to pass:

```
local greeting = "Hello ";        jsonnet     "Hello Hello "        json
greeting + greeting       </> 20.5.jsonnet
```

```
local hello =        jsonnet     "Hello Bob"        json
  function(name) "Hello " + name;
hello("Bob")       </> 20.6.jsonnet
```

Local variables and functions can also return structured data in dictionaries:

```jsonnet
local person = function(name) {        jsonnet
  "name": name,
  "welcome": "Hello " + name + "!",
};
person("Bob")                    </> 20.7.jsonnet
```

```json
{                                       json
  "name": "Bob",
  "welcome": "Hello Bob!",
};
                                  </> 20.8.json
```

20.2.3 Composition

The language features described here can be combined in arbitrary ways, e.g. a function can be called inside a dictionary value. And that function may itself return a dictionary, that gets nested within:

```jsonnet
local f = function(x) "Hello " + x;    jsonnet
{"key": "value", "thing": f("World")}

                                  </> 20.9.jsonnet
```

```json
{                                       json
  "key": "value",
  "thing": "Hello World"

}                                 </> 20.10.json
```

```jsonnet
local f = function(x) {                jsonnet
  "nested key": "Hello " + x
};
{"key": "value", "thing": f("World")}

                                 </> 20.11.jsonnet
```

```json
{                                       json
  "key": "value",
  "thing": {
    "nested key": "Hello World"
  }
}                                 </> 20.12.json
```

This quick tour is only a small subset of the full Jsonnet language, but will be enough for this chapter.

20.3 Parsing Jsonnet

First, let us look at parsing:

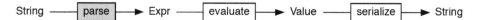

String ⟶ parse ⟶ Expr ⟶ evaluate ⟶ Value ⟶ serialize ⟶ String

To parse Jsonnet, we will be using the FastParse library introduced in *Chapter 19: Parsing Structured Text*.

20.3.1 Defining the Syntax Tree

We will do all our work inside the Ammonite Scala REPL. Let's start by defining a syntax tree of what our minimal Jsonnet syntax looks like: strings, dictionaries, functions, and local definitions. We will use a Scala `sealed trait` and `case class`es:

```scala
sealed trait Expr                                                Exprs.sc
object Expr{
  case class Str(s: String) extends Expr
  case class Ident(name: String) extends Expr
  case class Plus(left: Expr, right: Expr) extends Expr
  case class Dict(pairs: Map[String, Expr]) extends Expr
  case class Local(name: String, assigned: Expr, body: Expr) extends Expr
  case class Func(argNames: Seq[String], body: Expr) extends Expr
  case class Call(expr: Expr, args: Seq[Expr]) extends Expr
}                                                            </> 20.13.scala
```

Here, the `Expr` data structure (short for "expression") represents the meaningful parts of the Jsonnet syntax. As stated earlier, we want to be able to support strings with `+`, dictionaries, local identifiers, and function definitions and calls. Each of these language constructs maps straightforwardly to one of the `case class`es in the `Expr` AST.

The `Expr` type is recursive: a `Plus` is an `Expr`, but also contains `left: Expr, right: Expr` within it. `Dict` is an `Expr` that contains a `pairs: Map[String, Expr]`.

20.3.2 Example Parses

Here are some example snippets and what we expect them to parse to.

20.3.2.1 Strings

```
"hello"                  jsonnet    Expr.Str("hello")                parsed
```

20.3.2.2 Dictionaries

```
{"hello": "world", "123": "456"}    jsonnet    Expr.Dict(Map(       parsed
                                        "hello" -> Expr.Str("world"),
                                        "123" -> Expr.Str("456")
                                    ))                    </> 20.14.scala
```

20.3.2.3 Functions

```
function(a, b) a + " " + b                    jsonnet
```

```                                                parsed
Expr.Func(
  List("a", "b"),
  Expr.Plus(
    Expr.Plus(
      Expr.Ident("a"),
      Expr.Str(" ")
    ),
    Expr.Ident("b")
  )
)                                           </> 20.15.scala
```

20.3.2.4 Locals

```
local f = function(a) a + "1";                jsonnet
f("123")
```

```                                                parsed
Expr.Local(
  "f",
  Expr.Func(
    List("a"),
    Expr.Plus(
      Expr.Ident("a"),
      Expr.Str("1")
    )
  ),
  Expr.Call(
    Expr.Ident("f"),
    List(Expr.Str("123"))
  )
```

```
                        </> 20.16.jsonnet  )                    </> 20.17.scala
```

As Jsonnet syntax is recursive, we expect to be able to parse any combination of these language features combined together.

20.3.3 Parsing Terminals

To begin using FastParse, we will use the following imports:

```
@ import fastparse._, MultiLineWhitespace._
import fastparse._, MultiLineWhitespace._                      </> 20.18.scala
```

For this exercise, we will be using FastParse's support for automatic whitespace skipping, using MultiLineWhitespace. That lets us skip all spaces, tabs, and newlines automatically when parsing so we can write our grammar without needing an explicit ws parser like we did in **Chapter 19: Parsing Structured Text**.

It is simplest to parse the non-recursive parts of our Jsonnet syntax, often called "terminals". Of the `case` `class`es defined above, only two of them are terminals: `Str` and `Ident`.

20.3.3.1 Parsing Strings

First, let's write the parser for `Str`. We will ignore escape characters for simplicity, meaning a string is simply a ", followed by zero-or-more non-" characters, closed by another ":

```
@ def str[_: P] = P( "\"" ~~/ CharsWhile(_ != '"', 0).! ~~ "\"" ).map(Expr.Str)

@ fastparse.parse("\"hello\"", str(_))
res3: Parsed[Expr.Str] = Success(Str("hello"), 7)

@ fastparse.parse("\"hello world\"", str(_))
res4: Parsed[Expr.Str] = Success(Str("hello world"), 13)

@ fastparse.parse("\"\"", str(_))
res5: Parsed[Expr.Str] = Success(Str(""), 2)

@ fastparse.parse("123", str(_))
res6: Parsed[Expr.Str] = Parsed.Failure(Position 1:1, found "123")          </> 20.19.scala
```

Note how we use the `~~/` operator after the `"\""` open quote. The `~~` means we do not want to consume whitespace here (since we are inside a string) and the `/` is a FastParse Cut meaning we want to avoid backtracking if the parse fails. This is because only string literals can start with a double quote character ", so the parser does not need to backtrack and try other alternatives if the parse fails after seeing a ". That helps the parser report more informative error messages when the parse fails.

20.3.3.2 Parsing Identifiers

Identifiers are similar: an alphabet or underscore, followed by zero or more alphanumeric characters.

```
@ def ident[_: P] =
    P( CharIn("a-zA-Z_") ~~ CharsWhileIn("a-zA-Z0-9_", 0) ).!.map(Expr.Ident)

@ fastparse.parse("hello", ident(_))
res8: Parsed[Expr.Ident] = Success(Ident("hello"), 5)

@ fastparse.parse("123", ident(_)) // Identifiers cannot start with a number
res9: Parsed[Expr.Ident] = Parsed.Failure(Position 1:1, found "123")          </> 20.20.scala
```

20.3.4 Parsing Plus

Now that we have the ability to parse the terminal non-recursive syntax tree nodes, Strs and Idents, we need to move on to the recursive parts of the syntax tree. The simplest recursive syntax tree node is Expr.Plus, used to model the a + b syntax.

The Expr.Plus nodes representing + and all other case classes in our syntax tree have a recursive definition. Plus contains left and right Exprs, but an Expr could be a Plus node. This can be solved by making our parsers recursive, as follows:

```scala
@ {
  def expr[_: P]: P[Expr] = P( prefixExpr ~ plus.rep ).map{
    case (left, rights) => rights.foldLeft(left)(Expr.Plus(_, _))
  }
  def plus[_: P] = P( "+" ~ prefixExpr )
  def prefixExpr[_: P] = P( str | ident )
  def str[_: P] = P( "\"" ~~/ CharsWhile(_ != '"', 0).! ~~ "\"" ).map(Expr.Str)
  def ident[_: P] =
    P( CharIn("a-zA-Z_") ~~ CharsWhileIn("a-zA-Z0-9_", 0) ).!.map(Expr.Ident)
}
                                                                </> 20.21.scala
```

In the above snippet, we define an expr parser that contains a prefixExpr, followed by zero or more plus parsers, each of which parses a + followed by another prefixExpr. The expr parser is recursive, so to satisfy the compiler we need to annotate its type as : P[Expr] representing a parser that produces an Expr value on success.

That lets us parse the following:

```
"hello" + "world"                    jsonnet    Expr.Plus(              parsed
                                                  Expr.Str("hello"),
                                                  Expr.Str("world")
                                                )
                                                                </> 20.22.scala
```

```
hello + " " + world                  jsonnet    Expr.Plus(              parsed
                                                  Expr.Plus(
                                                    Expr.Ident("hello"),
                                                    Expr.Str(" ")
                                                  ),
                                                  Expr.Ident("world")
                                                )
                                                                </> 20.23.scala
```

Note that prefixExpr can be either a str or ident, but cannot be an expr node with its own plus nodes within. That is because any plus nodes will already get parsed by the existing plus.rep parser. We also cannot simply define plus as expr ~ "+" ~ expr: this is because the plus parser would then be *Left Recursive*, causing an infinite recursion at parse time. For more details, see the following article:

Chapter 20 Implementing a Programming Language   *394*

- https://en.wikipedia.org/wiki/Left_recursion

20.3.4.1 Constructing Parse Nodes with Fold Left

Since `prefixExpr` is a `P[Expr]`, and plus is a `P[Expr]`, the combined `prefixExpr ~ plus.rep` would by default be a `P[(Expr, Seq[Expr])]`: a parser that produces a tuple of `(Expr, Seq[Expr])`. The first item in the tuple represents the `Expr` parsed by the first `prefixExpr`, and the second item represents the `Seq[Expr]` parsed by the `plus.rep`, each repetition of which produces an `Expr`. To allow our `def expr` parser to produce a single `Expr`, we need to transform the produced `(Expr, Seq[Expr])` using `.map`. The `foldLeft` expression:

```
rights.foldLeft(left)(Expr.Plus(_, _))
```

This can also be written out more verbosely as follows:

```
rights.foldLeft(left)((lhs, rhs) => Expr.Plus(lhs, rhs))
```

`foldLeft` starts off with the value `left`, and for every item in the `rights` list, it wraps both of them in a `Plus` node. This builds a tree of `Plus` nodes from the flat list of `rights`. In a more sophisticated parser the shape of the tree may depend on the precedence of the operators, but for this exercise we end up building a simple left-associative binary tree.

a + b + c + d

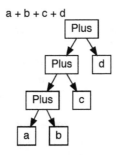

We can test this out as follows:

```
@ fastparse.parse("a + b", expr(_))
res12: Parsed[Expr] = Success(Plus(Ident("a"), Ident("b")), 5)

@ fastparse.parse("""a + " " + c""", expr(_))
res13: Parsed[Expr] = Success(Plus(Plus(Ident("a"), Str(" ")), Ident("c")), 11)
```
                                                                    </> 20.24.scala

20.3.5 Parsing Dictionaries

Expr.Dict nodes are also recursive, with each comma-separated key-value pair containing an string key and an Expr value. We can extend our parser to handle those via:

```scala
  def expr[_: P]: P[Expr] = P( prefixExpr ~ plus.rep ).map{
    case (left, items) => items.foldLeft(left)(Expr.Plus(_, _))
  }
  def plus[_: P] = P( "+" ~ prefixExpr )
- def prefixExpr[_: P] = P( str | ident )
+ def prefixExpr[_: P] = P( str | ident | dict )
+ def dict[_: P] =
+   P( "{" ~/ (str0 ~ ":" ~/ expr).rep(0, ",") ~ "}" ).map(kvs => Expr.Dict(kvs.toMap))
- def str[_: P] = P( "\"" ~~/ CharsWhile(_ != '"', 0).! ~~ "\"" ).map(Expr.Str)
+ def str[_: P] = P( str0 ).map(Expr.Str)
+ def str0[_: P] = P( "\"" ~~/ CharsWhile(_ != '"', 0).! ~~ "\"" )
  def ident[_: P] =
    P( CharIn("a-zA-Z_") ~~ CharsWhileIn("a-zA-Z0-9_", 0) ).!.map(Expr.Ident)    20.25.scala
```

The three main changes we have here are:

- Adding dict as one of the alternatives in def prefixExpr

- Extracting the str0 parser from str, where str0 returns the raw String that was parsed, while str wraps it in an Expr.Str syntax tree node. We do this because Expr.Dict keys have the same syntax as Expr.Strs, but do not need to be wrapped in Expr.Str nodes.

- Parsing dictionary literals as a {, followed by zero-or-more key-value pairs separated by ,s. Each key-value pair is a str0, followed by :, followed by any expr. This repetition of key-value pairs would by default give us a Seq[(String, Expr)], which we need to .map on to transform into an Expr.Dict node.

We can test these changes as follows:

```scala
@ fastparse.parse("""{"a": "b", "cde": id, "nested": {}}""", expr(_))
res15: Parsed[Expr] = Success(
  Dict(Map("a" -> Str("b"), "cde" -> Ident("id"), "nested" -> Dict(Map()))),
  35
)
                                                                    </> 20.26.scala
```

20.3.6 Parsing Functions, Locals, and Function Calls

Adding the parsers for `func`, `local` and `call` to this code requires the following changes:

```scala
  def expr[_: P]: P[Expr] = P( prefixExpr ~ plus.rep).map{
    case (left, items) => items.foldLeft(left)(Expr.Plus(_, _))
  }
  def plus[_: P] = P( "+" ~ prefixExpr )
- def prefixExpr[_: P] = P( str | ident | dict )
+ def prefixExpr[_: P]: P[Expr] = P( callExpr ~ call.rep ).map{
+   case (left, items) => items.foldLeft(left)(Expr.Call(_, _))
+ }
+ def callExpr[_: P] = P( str | dict | local | func | ident )
  def dict[_: P] =
    P( "{" ~/ (str0 ~ ":" ~/ expr).rep(0, ",") ~ "}" ).map(kvs => Expr.Dict(kvs.toMap))
+ def call[_: P] = P( "(" ~/ expr.rep(0, ",") ~ ")" )
+ def local[_: P] =
+   P( "local" ~/ ident0 ~ "=" ~ expr ~ ";" ~ expr ).map(Expr.Local.tupled)
+ def func[_: P] =
+   P( "function" ~/ "(" ~ ident0.rep(0, ",") ~ ")" ~ expr ).map(Expr.Func.tupled)
  def str[_: P] = P( str0 ).map(Expr.Str)
  def str0[_: P] = P( "\"" ~~/ CharsWhile(_ != '"', 0).! ~~ "\"" )

- def ident[_: P] =
-   P( CharIn("a-zA-Z_") ~~ CharsWhileIn("a-zA-Z0-9_", 0) ).!.map(Expr.Ident)
+ def ident[_: P] = P( ident0 ).map(Expr.Ident)
+ def ident0[_: P] = P( CharIn("a-zA-Z_") ~~ CharsWhileIn("a-zA-Z0-9_", 0) ).!
```
</> 20.27.scala

The main changes here are:

- Turning `prefixExpr` into a `callExpr` followed by one or more function `call`s suffix

- Splitting out `ident0` from `ident`, since `func` uses the same syntax as `ident` for parsing its parameter list but does not need the identifiers to be boxed into `Expr.Ident` nodes

- Defining a function `call` suffix as an open `(`, a comma-separated list of `expr`s, and a closing `)`

- Defining `function` and `local`: each starting with a keyword, followed by their respective syntaxes

Like we saw earlier when parsing `Plus` nodes, we use `foldLeft` to convert the `(Expr, Seq[Expr])` tuple that the `callExpr ~ call.rep` parser gives us into nested `Call` nodes.

Wrapping all of this up into an `object` `Parser` for tidyness gives us:

```
import $file.Exprs, Exprs._                                                    Parse.sc
object Parser {
  import fastparse._, MultiLineWhitespace._
  def expr[_: P]: P[Expr] = P( prefixExpr ~ plus.rep ).map{
    case (e, items) => items.foldLeft(e)(Expr.Plus(_, _))
  }
  def prefixExpr[_: P]: P[Expr] = P( callExpr ~ call.rep ).map{
    case (e, items) => items.foldLeft(e)(Expr.Call(_, _))
  }
  def callExpr[_: P] = P( str | dict | local | func | ident )

  def str[_: P] = P( str0 ).map(Expr.Str)
  def str0[_: P] = P( "\"" ~~/ CharsWhile(_ != '"', 0).! ~~ "\"" )
  def ident[_: P] = P( ident0 ).map(Expr.Ident)
  def ident0[_: P] = P( CharIn("a-zA-Z_") ~~ CharsWhileIn("a-zA-Z0-9_", 0) ).!

  def dict[_: P] = P( "{" ~/ (str0 ~ ":" ~/ expr).rep(0, ",") ~ "}" )
    .map(kvs => Expr.Dict(kvs.toMap))
  def local[_: P] = P( "local" ~/ ident0 ~ "=" ~ expr ~ ";" ~ expr )
    .map(Expr.Local.tupled)
  def func[_: P] = P( "function" ~/ "(" ~ ident0.rep(0, ",") ~ ")" ~ expr )
    .map(Expr.Func.tupled)

  def plus[_: P] = P( "+" ~ prefixExpr )
  def call[_: P] = P( "(" ~/ expr.rep(0, ",") ~ ")" )
}
                                                                   </> 20.28.scala
```

20.3.7 Testing the Parser

We can test the parser manually and see that it does what we want:

```
@ fastparse.parse("""{"a": "A", "b": "bee"}""", Parser.expr(_))
res17: Parsed[Expr] = Success(Dict(Map("a" -> Str("A"), "b" -> Str("bee"))), 22)

@ fastparse.parse("""f()(a) + g(b, c)""", Parser.expr(_))
res18: Parsed[Expr] = Success(
  Plus(
    Call(Call(Ident("f"), List()), List(Ident("a"))),
    Call(Ident("g"), List(Ident("b"), Ident("c")))
  ),
  16
)
                                                                   </> 20.29.scala
```

The syntax of our programming language is recursive: `local`, `function`, `plus`, and `dict` expressions can contain other expressions, nested arbitrarily deeply. We can test this out by feeding such nested examples into the `expr` parser:

```scala
@ val input = """local thing = "kay"; {"f": function(a) a + a, "nested": {"k": v}}"""

@ fastparse.parse(input, Parser.expr(_))
res21: Parsed[Expr] = Success(
  Local(
    "thing",
    Str("kay"),
    Dict(
      Map(
        "f" -> Func(List("a"), Plus(Ident("a"), Ident("a"))),
        "nested" -> Dict(Map("k" -> Ident("v")))
      )
    )
  ),
  65
)
```
</> 20.30.scala

See example 20.1 - Parse

20.4 Evaluating the Syntax Tree

Now that we have a syntax tree of `Expr` nodes, the next step is to evaluate the syntax tree to produce a runtime data structure of `Value`s.

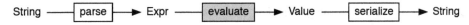

We will define `Value` as follows:

```scala
sealed trait Value                                          Values.sc
object Value{
  case class Str(s: String) extends Value
  case class Dict(pairs: Map[String, Value]) extends Value
  case class Func(call: Seq[Value] => Value) extends Value
}
```
</> 20.31.scala

20.4.1 Expr vs Value

Note that while the `Expr` syntax tree contains nodes that represent identifiers, locals, function applications, and so on, a `Value` can only be a `Str`, a `Dict`, or a `Func`. This is similar to the `ujson.Value` we saw in **Chapter 8: JSON and Binary Data Serialization**, but simplified and with the addition of the `Func` class.

The key thing to know about `Value` is that it doesn't matter where a `Value` came from. For example, a `Value.Str` could have been:

- A literal `Expr.Str` in the source code
- Passed in as a function parameter to an `Expr.Func`
- Bound to a local variable via `Expr.Local`
- Constructed via `Expr.Plus` node

Regardless of where the `Value.Str` was produced syntactically, it is still the same `Value.Str`. The final `Value` for the entire Jsonnet program will later be converted to a JSON string as the output.

The contents of `Value.Str` and `Value.Dict` should be self explanatory. `Value.Func` is a bit less obvious: by defining it as `Func(call: Seq[Value] => Value)`, we are saying "a function is something you can pass a list of argument values to and returns a value". We will see how to instantiate these `Value.Func` nodes later.

20.4.2 Defining Evaluate

The basic task here is to write a function that converts an `Expr` into a `Value`. Naively, such a function would look something like this:

```
def evaluate(expr: Expr): Value
```

However, the `Value` returned by evaluating an `Expr` isn't only dependent on the contents of that `Expr`: it also depends on the enclosing scope. Consider a loose identifier:

```
foo
```

The value of this `Expr.Ident` doesn't just depend on the name of the identifier (`"foo"`), but also on what value was bound to that name. For example. this binding may be done via a `local` declaration:

```
local foo = "I am Cow";
foo
```
</> 20.32.jsonnet

This mapping of names to `Value`s is often known as the "lexical scope" within your program. Thus we might instead define `evaluate` as:

```
def evaluate(expr: Expr, scope: Map[String, Value]): Value
```

From here we can start fleshing it out.

20.4.3 Evaluating Literals

The simplest case is literal `Expr.Str`, which are evaluated to the identical `Value.Str`:

```scala
def evaluate(expr: Expr, scope: Map[String, Value]): Value = expr match {
  case Expr.Str(s) => Value.Str(s)
}
```
</> 20.33.scala

Literal dictionaries are also straightforward: `Expr.Dicts` become `Value.Dicts`, with the same keys, except we need to evaluate each value into its corresponding expression:

```scala
  def evaluate(expr: Expr, scope: Map[String, Value]): Value = expr match {
    case Expr.Str(s) => Value.Str(s)
+   case Expr.Dict(kvs) => Value.Dict(kvs.map{case (k, v) => (k, evaluate(v, scope))})
  }
```
</> 20.34.scala

Dictionary literals do not add or remove anything from the lexical scope, so the `scope` parameter is passed through unchanged. We can test these two cases as follows:

```scala
@ evaluate(fastparse.parse("\"hello\"", Parser.expr(_)).get.value, Map.empty)
res24: Value = Str("hello")

@ val input = """{"hello": "world", "key": "value"}"""

@ evaluate(fastparse.parse(input, Parser.expr(_)).get.value, Map.empty)
res25: Value = Dict(Map("hello" -> Str("world"), "key" -> Str("value")))
```
</> 20.35.scala

For now, we are passing in `Map.empty` as the `scope`, since evaluating literal strings and dictionaries always results in the same thing regardless of what values are in scope.

20.4.4 Evaluating Plus

Next, we will look at the `Expr.Plus` nodes. We have only defined their behavior to work on string values (`Value.Str`), so evaluating them involves:

- Evaluating each child expression into a `Value.Str`
- Extracting the contents of each string
- Concatenating them
- Wrapping the concatenated string back into a `Value.Str`

```
def evaluate(expr: Expr, scope: Map[String, Value]): Value = expr match {
  ...
  case Expr.Dict(kvs) => ...
+ case Expr.Plus(left, right) =>
+   val Value.Str(leftStr) = evaluate(left, scope)
+   val Value.Str(rightStr) = evaluate(right, scope)
+   Value.Str(leftStr + rightStr)
}                                                            </> 20.36.scala
```

```
@ evaluate(fastparse.parse("\"hello\" + \"world\"", Parser.expr(_)).get.value, Map.empty)
res28: Value = Str("helloworld")                             </> 20.37.scala
```

If one of the children of Expr.Plus is not a Value.Str, the val assignments in the above code fails with a MatchError. Providing a nicer error message is left as an exercise to the reader.

So far, nothing we have evaluated so far depends on what values are in the scope of the evaluation. This will change when we start handling local declarations, which add values to the scope, and identifiers like foo which use those values.

20.4.5 Evaluating Locals and Identifiers

Let's consider the following local syntax:

```
@ val input = """local greeting = "Hello "; greeting + greeting"""
```

```
@ fastparse.parse(input, Parser.expr(_))
res30: Parsed[Expr] = Success(
  Local("greeting", Str("Hello "), Plus(Ident("greeting"), Ident("greeting"))),
  45
)                                                            </> 20.38.scala
```

20.4.5.1 Evaluating Locals

The point of local is to evaluate the assigned expression to a value, assign that value to the name, and then evaluate the body expression with that value bound to that name in the scope. We can write that in code as follows:

```
def evaluate(expr: Expr, scope: Map[String, Value]): Value = expr match {
  ...
  case Expr.Plus(left, right) => ...
+ case Expr.Local(name, assigned, body) =>
+   val assignedValue = evaluate(assigned, scope)
+   evaluate(body, scope + (name -> assignedValue))
}                                                            </> 20.39.scala
```

Note that because `scope` is a Scala immutable `Map`, `+ (name -> assignedValue)` doesn't modify the existing `Map`, but instead creates a new `Map` with the additional key-value pair included. This is a relatively efficient $O(log\ n)$ operation due to how immutable `Map`s are implemented.

20.4.5.2 Evaluating Identifiers

Once a `local` has put a name into `scope`, evaluating `Ident` nodes is straightforward: we just fetch the value of that name in the `scope`:

```scala
  def evaluate(expr: Expr, scope: Map[String, Value]): Value = expr match {
    ...
    case Expr.Local(name, assigned, body) => ...
+   case Expr.Ident(name) => scope(name)
  }
```
</> 20.40.scala

We can test it to see that it works when the identifiers and declarations line up, even when multiple `local`s are chained together:

```scala
@ val input = """local greeting = "Hello "; greeting + greeting"""

@ evaluate(fastparse.parse(input, Parser.expr(_)).get.value, Map.empty)
res33: Value = Str("Hello Hello ")

@ val input = """local x = "Hello "; local y = "world"; x + y"""

@ evaluate(fastparse.parse(input, Parser.expr(_)).get.value, Map.empty)
res35: Value = Str("Hello world")
```
</> 20.41.scala

Lastly, we can verify that it fails when an identifier is not found:

```scala
@ val input = """local greeting = "Hello "; nope + nope"""

@ evaluate(fastparse.parse(input, Parser.expr(_)).get.value, Map.empty)
java.util.NoSuchElementException: key not found: nope
  scala.collection.immutable.Map$Map1.apply(Map.scala:242)
  ammonite.$sess.cmd93$.evaluate(cmd93.sc:10)
  ammonite.$sess.cmd93$.evaluate(cmd93.sc:5)
  ammonite.$sess.cmd95$.<clinit>(cmd95.sc:3)
```
</> 20.42.scala

20.4.6 Evaluating Functions

The last thing we have left to evaluate are the `Expr.Func` function literals and `Expr.Call` function applications:

```scala
case class Func(params: Seq[String], body: Expr) extends Expr
case class Call(expr: Expr, args: Seq[Expr]) extends Expr                    </> 20.43.scala
```

Evaluating an `Expr.Func` should give us a `Value.Func`, and evaluating an `Expr.Call` on a `Value.Func` should give us the result of evaluating that function. The result could be a `Value.Str`, a `Value.Dict`, or even another `Value.Func`.

20.4.6.1 Evaluating Function Calls

Evaluating a `Expr.Call` can be thought of as the following steps:

- Evaluate the expr: `Expr` into a `Value.Func`
- Evaluate the args: `Seq[Expr]` into a `Seq[Value]` of argument values
- Call the `Value.Func#call` function on the evaluated argument values to produce the result

```scala
  def evaluate(expr: Expr, scope: Map[String, Value]): Value = expr match {
    ...
    case Expr.Ident(name) => ...
+   case Expr.Call(expr, args) =>
+     val Value.Func(call) = evaluate(expr, scope)
+     val evaluatedArgs = args.map(evaluate(_, scope))
+     call(evaluatedArgs)
  }
                                                                            </> 20.44.scala
```

The tricky thing here is: how do we evaluate the `Expr.Func` to produce a `Value.Func` whose `call` attribute does what we want?

20.4.6.2 Evaluating Function Definitions

When you think about what `calling` a function really means, it boils down to four steps:

- Store the original scope of the function at the definition-site
- Take the values of the arguments passed to the function at call-site
- Create a modified copy of the original scope at definition-site with the values of the arguments passed at call-site bound to the names of the arguments specified at definition-site
- Evaluate the body of the function with the modified copy of the scope

```scala
def evaluate(expr: Expr, scope: Map[String, Value]): Value = expr match {
    ...
  case Expr.Call(expr, args) => ...
+ case Expr.Func(argNames, body) =>
+   Value.Func(args => evaluate(body, scope ++ argNames.zip(args)))
}
```
</> 20.45.scala

Again, `scope ++ argNames.zip(args)` is an efficient $O(log\ n)$ operation on the scope `Map`. We can then test this with some of the functions we saw earlier:

```scala
@ val input = """local f = function(a) a + "1";  f("123")"""

@ evaluate(fastparse.parse(input, Parser.expr(_)).get.value, Map.empty)
res40: Value = Str("1231")

@ val input = """local f = function(a, b) a + " " + b; f("hello", "world")"""

@ evaluate(fastparse.parse(input, Parser.expr(_)).get.value, Map.empty)
res42: Value = Str("hello world")
```
</> 20.46.scala

The `evaluate` function now looks like:

```scala
import $file.Exprs, Exprs._                              Evaluate.sc
import $file.Values, Values._
def evaluate(expr: Expr, scope: Map[String, Value]): Value = expr match {
  case Expr.Str(s) => Value.Str(s)
  case Expr.Dict(kvs) => Value.Dict(kvs.map{case (k, v) => (k, evaluate(v, scope))})
  case Expr.Plus(left, right) =>
    val Value.Str(leftStr) = evaluate(left, scope)
    val Value.Str(rightStr) = evaluate(right, scope)
    Value.Str(leftStr + rightStr)
  case Expr.Local(name, assigned, body) =>
    val assignedValue = evaluate(assigned, scope)
    evaluate(body, scope + (name -> assignedValue))
  case Expr.Ident(name) => scope(name)
  case Expr.Call(expr, args) =>
    val Value.Func(call) = evaluate(expr, scope)
    val evaluatedArgs = args.map(evaluate(_, scope))
    call(evaluatedArgs)
  case Expr.Func(argNames, body) =>
    Value.Func(args => evaluate(body, scope ++ argNames.zip(args)))
}
```
</> 20.47.scala

20.5 Serializing to JSON

In the last two sections, we saw how to parse an input `string` of Jsonnet source code into an `Expr` syntax tree structure, and then evaluate the `Expr` into a `Value` data structure that represents a JSON value. In this last section of the chapter, we will see how to serialize the `Value` data structure to an output JSON `string`:

The signature of our `serialize` function looks like this:

```scala
def serialize(v: Value): String = v match {
  case Value.Str(s) => ...
  case Value.Dict(kvs) => ...
}
```
</> 20.48.scala

A `Value` can only be a `Value.Str`, `Value.Dict`, or `Value.Func`. For now, we will assume there are no longer any `Value.Func` nodes in the final data structure, as functions cannot be serialized to JSON. Production implementations of Jsonnet like google/jsonnet simply raise an error if an un-called function is present in the output, and the above snippet would fail with a `MatchError`. Since earlier we assumed there are no escape sequences in our strings, we can serialize `Value.Str` nodes by adding double quotes `"`s around them:

```scala
  def serialize(v: Value): String = v match {
+   case Value.Str(s) => "\"" + s + "\""
  }
```
</> 20.49.scala

As for `Value.Dict`s, we should serialize each key-value pair as `"foo": "bar"`, separated by commas, and wrap the whole thing in curly brackets:

```scala
  def serialize(v: Value): String = v match {
    case Value.Str(s) => "\"" + s + "\""
+   case Value.Dict(kvs) =>
+     kvs.map{case (k, v) => "\"" + k + "\": " + serialize(v)}.mkString("{", ", ", "}")
  }
```
</> 20.50.scala

Now all we need to do is wrap the entire `parse` -> `evaluate` -> `serialize` pipeline in a nice helper function, and it is ready for use!

```scala
@ def jsonnet(input: String): String = {
    serialize(evaluate(fastparse.parse(input, Parser.expr(_)).get.value, Map.empty))
  }
```
</> 20.51.scala

```scala
@ println(jsonnet(
"""local greeting = "Hello ";
  local person = function (name) {
    "name": name,
    "welcome": greeting + name + "!"
  };
  {
    "person1": person("Alice"),
    "person2": person("Bob"),
    "person3": person("Charlie")
  }"""
))                                    </> 20.52.scala
```

```json
{"person1": {
  "name": "Alice",
  "welcome": "Hello Alice!"},
 "person2": {
  "name": "Bob",
  "welcome": "Hello Bob!"},
 "person3": {
  "name": "Charlie",
  "welcome": "Hello Charlie!"}}
                              </> 20.53.output-json
```

See example 20.3 - Serialize

20.5.1 Complete Jsonnet Interpreter

The complete code of the Jsonnet interpreter is given below, combined into a single self-contained file:

```scala
sealed trait Expr
object Expr{
  case class Str(s: String) extends Expr
  case class Ident(name: String) extends Expr
  case class Plus(left: Expr, right: Expr) extends Expr
  case class Dict(pairs: Map[String, Expr]) extends Expr
  case class Local(name: String, assigned: Expr, body: Expr) extends Expr
  case class Func(argNames: Seq[String], body: Expr) extends Expr
  case class Call(expr: Expr, args: Seq[Expr]) extends Expr
}
object Parser {
  import fastparse._, MultiLineWhitespace._
  def expr[_: P]: P[Expr] = P( prefixExpr ~ plus.rep ).map{
    case (e, items) => items.foldLeft(e)(Expr.Plus(_, _))
  }
  def prefixExpr[_: P]: P[Expr] = P( callExpr ~ call.rep ).map{
    case (e, items) => items.foldLeft(e)(Expr.Call(_, _))
  }
  def callExpr[_: P] = P( str | dict | local | func | ident )

  def str[_: P] = P( str0 ).map(Expr.Str)
  def str0[_: P] = P( "\"" ~~/ CharsWhile(_ != '"', 0).! ~~ "\"" )
  def ident[_: P] = P( ident0 ).map(Expr.Ident)
  def ident0[_: P] = P( CharIn("a-zA-Z_") ~~ CharsWhileIn("a-zA-Z0-9_", 0) ).!

  def dict[_: P] = P( "{" ~/ (str0 ~ ":" ~/ expr).rep(0, ",") ~ "}" )
    .map(kvs => Expr.Dict(kvs.toMap))
  def local[_: P] = P( "local" ~/ ident0 ~ "=" ~ expr ~ ";" ~ expr )
    .map(Expr.Local.tupled)
  def func[_: P] = P( "function" ~/ "(" ~ ident0.rep(0, ",") ~ ")" ~ expr )
    .map(Expr.Func.tupled)

  def plus[_: P] = P( "+" ~ prefixExpr )
  def call[_: P] = P( "(" ~/ expr.rep(0, ",") ~ ")" )
}
sealed trait Value
object Value{
```

```scala
    case class Str(s: String) extends Value
    case class Dict(pairs: Map[String, Value]) extends Value
    case class Func(call: Seq[Value] => Value) extends Value
}
def evaluate(expr: Expr, scope: Map[String, Value]): Value = expr match {
  case Expr.Str(s) => Value.Str(s)
  case Expr.Dict(kvs) => Value.Dict(kvs.map{case (k, v) => (k, evaluate(v, scope))})
  case Expr.Plus(left, right) =>
    val Value.Str(leftStr) = evaluate(left, scope)
    val Value.Str(rightStr) = evaluate(right, scope)
    Value.Str(leftStr + rightStr)
  case Expr.Local(name, assigned, body) =>
    val assignedValue = evaluate(assigned, scope)
    evaluate(body, scope + (name -> assignedValue))
  case Expr.Ident(name) => scope(name)
  case Expr.Call(expr, args) =>
    val Value.Func(call) = evaluate(expr, scope)
    val evaluatedArgs = args.map(evaluate(_, scope))
    call(evaluatedArgs)
  case Expr.Func(argNames, body) =>
    Value.Func(args => evaluate(body, scope ++ argNames.zip(args)))
}
def serialize(v: Value): String = v match {
  case Value.Str(s) => "\"" + s + "\""
  case Value.Dict(kvs) =>
    kvs.map{case (k, v) => "\"" + k + "\": " + serialize(v)}.mkString("{", ", ", "}")
}
def jsonnet(input: String): String = {
  serialize(evaluate(fastparse.parse(input, Parser.expr(_)).get.value, Map.empty))
}
```
</> 20.54.scala

See example 20.4 - Jsonnet

20.6 Conclusion

In this chapter, we have walked through how to use Scala to implement an interpreter for a simple programming language: a subset of Jsonnet. We used FastParse to parse the source code string into an `Expr` syntax tree, recursively evaluated the `Expr` syntax tree into a `Value` data structure, and serialized the `Value` data structure to a JSON `string`.

Parsing and evaluating programming language source code is a very different use case than the distributed real-time file synchronizer we wrote in **Chapter 18: Building a Real-time File Synchronizer**. The style of Scala we have written is correspondingly different, utilizing recursive parsing and tree traversals rather than concurrent actor-based event pipelines. Nevertheless, the Scala language and libraries makes this easy, and in 70 lines of code we have a working implementation of a simple interpreted programming language.

While the interpreter we implemented in this chapter is relatively simple, the same techniques apply to implementing most interpreted programming languages, including production-ready implementations like google/jsonnet. Hopefully this chapter has given you an intuition for how a simple programming language is implemented. Even if you never need to implement your own programming language, these techniques may still be useful if you find yourself writing linters, program analyzers, query engines, and other such tools.

Exercise: Modify our Jsonnet interpreter to be able to handle basic numbers as well. For simplicity assume numbers can only be positive integers, and the only operation they support is addition via a + b.

```jsonnet
local bonus = 15000;
local person = function (name,
baseSalary) {
  "name": name,
  "totalSalary": baseSalary + bonus
};
{"person1": person("Alice", 50000)}
```
</> 20.55.jsonnet

```json
{
  "person1": {
    "name": "Alice",
    "totalSalary": 65000
  }
}
```
</> 20.56.json

See example 20.5 - JsonnetNumbers

Exercise: Modify `def serialize` to generate the `ujson.Value`s we used in **Chapter 8: JSON and Binary Data Serialization**, and make it use `ujson.write(..., indent = 2)` to pretty-print the output JSON rather than having it all generated on a single line

See example 20.6 - JsonnetPrettyPrinting

Exercise: Modify our Jsonnet interpreter to provide simple Jsonnet stack traces when the interpretation fails for whatever reason. You can use the Index parser from FastParse to capture the character-index of each Expr node we are parsing, and combine that with the input string to find the line and column number for any Expr node whose evaluation failed with an exception.

```
local f = function(x) y;
f("abc")
```

```jsonnet
Jsonnet error at line 1 column 23
    at line 2 column 2
    at line 1 column 1
```

`</> 20.57.jsonnet`   `</> 20.58.error`

See example 20.7 - JsonnetStackTraces

Discuss Chapter 20 online at https://www.handsonscala.com/discuss/20

Conclusion

This is not the end. It is not even the beginning of the end. But it is, perhaps, the end of the beginning.

Winston Churchill

If you have made it this far through *Hands-on Scala*, you should by now be comfortable using the Scala programming language in a wide range of scenarios. You've implemented algorithms, API clients, web servers, file synchronizers, and programming languages. You've dealt with concurrency and parallelism. You've worked with the filesystem, databases, data serialization, and many other cross-cutting concerns that you would find in any real-world software system.

This book only walks you through a narrow slice of the Scala ecosystem: there is a wealth of libraries and frameworks that people use writing Scala in production, and it is impossible to cover them all in one book. Nevertheless, the core concepts you learned here apply regardless of which specific toolset you end up using. Breadth-first search is breadth-first search, and a HTTP request is a HTTP request, regardless of how the exact method calls are spelled.

Scala is a flexible, broadly useful programming language. By now you have seen how Scala can be used to tackle even difficult, complex problems in an elegant and straightforward manner. While this book is not the final word in learning Scala, it should be enough for you to take off on your own, and get started solving real problems and delivering real value using the Scala language.

CPSIA information can be obtained
at www.ICGtesting.com
Printed in the USA
LVHW061409250322
714080LV00019B/24